The Airline Profit Cycle

T0331422

The air transport industry has high economic impact; it supports more than 60 million jobs worldwide. Since the early years of commercial air travel, passenger numbers have grown tremendously. However, for decades airlines' financial results have been swinging between profits and losses. The airline industry's aggregate net average profit between 1970 and 2010 was close to zero, which implies bankruptcies and layoffs in downturns. The profit cycle's amplitude has been rising over time, which means that problems have become increasingly severe and also shows that the industry may not have learned from the past. More stable financial results could not only facilitate airline management decisions and improve investors' confidence but also preserve employment. This book offers a thorough understanding of the airline profit cycle's causes and drivers, and it presents measures to achieve a higher and more stable profitability level.

This is the first in-depth examination of the airline profit cycle. The airline industry is modelled as a complex dynamic system, which is used for quantitative simulations of 'what if' scenarios. These experiments reveal that the general economic environment, such as GDP or fuel price developments, influence the airline industry's profitability pattern as well as certain regulations or aircraft manufactures' policies. Yet despite all circumstances, simulations show that airlines' own management decisions are sufficient to generate higher and more stable profits in the industry.

This book is useful for aviation industry decision makers, investors, policy makers, and researchers because it explains why the airline industry earns or loses money. This knowledge will advance forecasting and market intelligence. Furthermore, the book offers practitioners different suggestions to sustainably improve the airline industry's profitability. The book is also recommended as a case study for system analysis as well as industry cyclicality at graduate or postgraduate level for courses such as engineering, economics, or management.

Eva-Maria Cronrath is Executive Assistant to the Executive Board Member for Aeronautics, German Aerospace Center (DLR), Germany.

Routledge Studies in Transport Analysis

For a complete list of titles in this series, please visit www.routledge.com/
Routledge-Studies-in-Transport-Analysis/book-series/RSTA

The Airline Profit Cycle

A System Analysis of Airline
Industry Dynamics

Eva-Maria Cronrath

LONDON AND NEW YORK

First published 2018 by Routledge

2 Park Square, Milton Park, Abingdon, Oxfordshire OX14 4RN

52 Vanderbilt Avenue, New York, NY 10017

Routledge is an imprint of the Taylor & Francis Group, an informa business

First issued in paperback 2020

British Library Cataloguing-in-Publication Data
A catalogue record for this book is available from the British Library

Library of Congress Cataloging-in-Publication Data
A catalog record for this book has been requested

ISBN: 978-1-138-73196-7 (hbk)
ISBN: 978-0-367-59491-6 (pbk)

Typeset in Bembo
by Swales & Willis Ltd, Exeter, Devon, UK

Contents

Figures

Tables

Foreword

The Airline Profit Cycle: A System Analysis of Airline Industry Dynamics deals with highly important aspects of this particular branch of the economy. Since the early beginnings in the 1950s, commercial air travel showed a strong and persistent general growth trend, with passenger numbers doubling approximately every 18 years, thus growing more than the global economy. The financial situation of the airline industry – the term 'airline industry' comprises all airlines providing scheduled or non-scheduled air transportation – is nowhere near as healthy as the growth numbers might lead one to expect. Over this time span the world airlines profit average is virtually zero but it shows significant fluctuations; fluctuation with both a strong and growing amplitude and a declining cycle's period. This overall behaviour pattern is very similar for all major carriers. Some airlines manage to achieve financial results much above the world's average, but even those superior performers generate only a meagre return on invested capital.

The consequences of this behaviour are obvious. Especially in the down cycle periods, bankruptcies occur rather frequently; on the supplier side, aircraft manufacturers face a highly fluctuating order income. Over the past three or four decades, this performance made the airline industry rather unattractive for investors. On this basis, three questions guide the author's research process:

1 Why are the airline profits cyclical?
2 What are the causes and dynamics that determine the profit cycle's shape?
3 How can the situation be improved?

Because of its importance, Cronrath starts with a thorough analysis of business cycles in general, their drivers and their common characteristics. She then opens the perspective to oscillations as a fundamental mode of behaviour and introduces the concept of (negative) feedback. Time delays between the actual state of the system, the perceived state, the discrepancy between perceived and (explicit or implicit) desired state – the goal – and corrective action, have an impact on the state of the system. An effective 'controller' can curb such an oscillating system. A key example of oscillating systems in the business world is the supply chain, which frequently shows increasing amplitudes of fluctuations for each successive stage upstream.

Industry practitioners' views on airline profit cyclicality revealed that even though the airline profit cycle is highly relevant to business in the industry, only two-thirds of those interviewed reported knowledge about it. The cycle was largely seen as something exogenous, something 'happening to them', to which they can only react. Overcapacity is seen as a cycle's driver, and cost cutting the appropriate remedy.

The chapter with the System Dynamics model of airline industry profit development is the 'core theory' of the publication. Here the findings from the previously investigated different sources come together, are integrated and transformed into a concise model, which in turn is the basis for the experiments and mitigation policies in the subsequent chapter. The author emphasises the complexity of the research questions by statistical examination of three popular cycle driver hypotheses. These hypotheses are that airlines' profit cycles are caused either by the general economic development (H1) or by external shocks like oil crises, the gulf war, financial crises, etc. (H2) or finally by fluctuating fuel prices (H3). Empirical evidence shows that all three factor sets do have influence on airline profits; however, none of them alone can explain the actually observed behaviour. Their interrelationships are interdependent, non-linear, and time delays play an important role. The methodology suitable to address such a conundrum of problems is System Dynamics. And the subsequently developed model is used to answer the author's above-mentioned research questions.

The airlines' behavior as driver of cyclicality focuses on the impact of internal mechanisms, on the airlines' own influence on the profit cycle. Capacity planning, ordering policies, utilisation strategies, aircraft retirement practice and aircraft leasing, and finally price setting and cost adjustment, are all investigated. And they show that, indeed, airlines' own behaviour can cause profit cycles. Flexible cost structures and a rather steady aircraft order policy are successful remedies. The strife for ancillary yields can help but also distracts from genuine tasks. A multitude of highly interesting and important findings for practical airline management are compiled here. They underline the potential of the model and the power of having such a device at hand.

Eva-Maria Cronrath's book – it is the outgrow of a PhD Manuscript submitted to the Fakultät für Betriebswirtschaftslehre der Universität Mannheim, Germany – deals with an important topic of corporate management and business administration. It presents the findings in a competent and convincing way; the research questions are clearly formulated; the investigation proceeds in a logical manner. Eva-Maria Cronrath's results are remarkable, both from the scientific or academic point of view and from the importance of her findings for airline management.

Professor em. Dr Dr h. c. Peter-M. Milling

Foreword

For the past 50 years the airline industry has generally experienced cyclic profitability at approximately ten-year periods. This type of cyclic behaviour is not unique to airlines but this industry represents one of the most consistent examples of this behaviour and it is important to understand the dynamics. This book starts with an empirical analysis of available airline profit data and potential exogenous factors, including a statistical analysis of simple mechanisms which have been hypothesised to drive this cyclic behavior. The conclusion of the empirical analyses is that the general economy, external demand shocks, and the fuel price have influence on airline profits. However, each of them alone cannot explain the airline profit cycle.

A number of researchers have investigated this cyclicality using simple system dynamics models which can be shown to capture general oscillatory behaviour, but this work takes the system dynamics analysis of the airline industry to a significantly higher level of detail and fidelity than any of the prior studies. The analysis includes well reasoned, supported and calibrated sub-models for processes such as Pricing, Cost and Supply which really capture the actual practice in the airline industry.

For example, in the Supply sub-model Cronrath models the flows of available aircraft assets considering retirement of older aircraft and modeling airline purchasing decisions. What is impressive is the next level of modeling where she captures the productivity of the aircraft asset (e.g. how many seats are sold), the utilisation of the aircraft (e.g. how many hours a day is the asset utilised). In these second-level models she is able to capture subtle but important effects. For example, the productivity of aircraft has changed over the past 20 years due to the development of yield-management approaches by airlines.

By capturing these effects Cronrath is more accurately able to calibrate the model with historical data from the United States and other worldwide data sources. The calibrated model is then used to conduct a series of simulation experiments to investigate how changes in market factors and airline behaviour impact the airline industry profit cycles.

One interesting and important finding explores the impact of yield management on the profit cycle. The model indicated that the extensive use of revenue management was found to be a major cycle amplifier. If airlines refrained entirely from revenue management as a technique for short-term demand stimulation by price, they would eliminate the profit cycle after a demand shock. The model was also able to observe the cycle driving impact of aircraft ordering behaviour due to delay in aircraft delivery which had been hypothesised by a number of previous researchers. However, Cronrath was uniquely able to investigate how aircraft utilisation can be used to manage and dampen the cycle. Experiments show that if aircraft utilisation adjustments after a demand shock were completely prevented, the profit cycle's amplitude would double compared to the reference.

The book concludes with a discussion on what can be done to manage cyclicality in the airline industry and gives practical advice for airline executives and decision makers which is insightful and useful.

This book provides an excellent and comprehensive analysis of the factors that drive the system dynamics of the global airline industry.

Professor R. John Hansman
Director, MIT International Center
for Air Transportation

Preface

Why do airlines altogether suffer deep losses only a few years after they earned record high profits? Why does this pattern repeat itself over and over again? How can that happen in an industry that is as advanced and popular as aviation? The repeated loss periods cost several thousand people their jobs. Yet, in my time as a consultant in the aviation industry I learnt that the airlines' profitability cycle is not understood, and even the awareness for the phenomenon is low. This is why I decided to focus my PhD research on the airline profit cycle in order to explain why the airline industry exhibits this very particular profitability pattern and to conclude how the situation could be improved.

The methodology I chose to approach the problem is System Dynamics. This way to address complex and dynamic problems has fascinated me since I first heard about it in my Master studies at the University of Mannheim. Even though the modelling process proved to be challenging in many ways, the results of my model simulation experiments show how useful and powerful System Dynamics can be.

This book is based on my doctoral dissertation at the University of Mannheim and the Massachusetts Institute of Technology. Writing this PhD thesis would not have been possible without invaluable help.

First of all, I would like to thank Prof e.m. Dr Dr h.c. Peter Milling for supervising my thesis, for his constant support and academic guidance. Likewise, I would like to express my gratitude towards my second supervisor, Prof Dr R. John Hansman, for challenging ideas to help me find the best solutions, and for giving me the opportunity of working with him in the inspiring environment of MIT. Furthermore, I thank Prof Dr Andreas Größler who would always make time to help me with precious advice and motivating comments. Thank you to Alexander Zock, PhD for providing the idea to research the airline profit cycle and for giving me faith in the feasibility of this project. In addition, I am grateful to Prof Dr Jürgen Strohhecker for helping me with my modelling issues, and to Prof Dr Raik Stolletz for reviewing my work.

This research was generously funded by the Erich-Becker-Stiftung (foundation of the Fraport AG) and the DAAD Deutscher Akademischer Austauschdienst (German Academic Exchange Service), and supported by the

European Center for Aviation Development. Thank you to Prof Dr Uwe Klingauf, Michael Stumpf, and Prof Dr Martin Harsche for helping me to organise the financing for this PhD project.

Many thanks for giving me expert interviews go to employees/members of Boeing, Deutsche Lufthansa, Deutsche Flugsicherung (German ATC), Fraport, MIT Aeronautics Department, Star Alliance, and the System Dynamics Society.

Thank you to my former fellow PhD students at the University of Mannheim's Industrieseminar who have accompanied me during my years of doctoral studies. Also, I would like to thank my former colleagues at the European Center for Aviation Development and at the MIT International Center for Air Transportation for their support. Discussions with Dr Mark Azzam were especially enjoyable as they were productive.

This book has benefited from intense feedback on the last versions. Thank you to Ulrich Cronrath, Friederike Flory, Jens Hemmerich, and Nike Trost who invested their free time in improving my manuscript.

I am more than grateful to my family and friends for their patience and persistent support. In particular, my husband's good humour and his constant encouragement carried this project to its conclusion. THANK YOU.

Eva Cronrath
Frankfurt, October 2015

1 The airline profit cycle as a persistent phenomenon

1.1 The development of airline traffic and cyclic financial results

Ever since the early years of commercial air travel in the 1950s the air transport industry has followed a general growth trend. Since 1997 worldwide passenger air traffic has more than doubled (see Figure 1.1).[1] In 1987 the threshold of 1 billion air passengers per annum worldwide was crossed.[2] Only 18 years later, in 2005, over 2 billion passengers were counted. Despite past economic crises and demand shocks, the airline industry returned to the growth track and passenger numbers increased.

In terms of output the airline industry grew more than the global economy. The 'airline industry' comprises all airlines around the world providing scheduled or non-scheduled air transportation.[3] The industry's output, measured in passengers, is compared to the world economy's output, expressed as gross domestic product (GDP).[4] While the world economy's real (= inflation adjusted) GDP grew by 3.1% per year on average from 1970 to 2010, airline passenger numbers expanded at 5.0% average annual

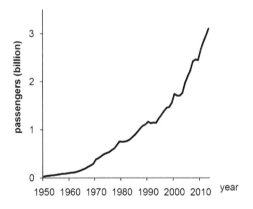

Figure 1.1 Worldwide passenger air travel 1950–2013

Figure 1.2 Aggregate airline revenues worldwide

growth.[5] Especially in recent years the airline industry exhibited almost twice as much growth as the general economy.[6] In 2010, the world had 1,568 commercial airlines which operated 26.7 million commercial aircraft movements.[7] The world's 3,846 airports provided sufficient infrastructure for this traffic load.[8]

Given the overall positive air traffic growth trend it may be expected that the industry is highly prosperous. In line with passenger traffic, airlines' revenues have grown progressively (see Figure 1.2).[9] Between 1970 and 2010 the compound annual growth rate of worldwide airline revenues amounted to 9.0%, and 4.3% in real values, respectively.

However, the airline industry's financial situation is not as healthy as one might expect. Figure 1.3 illustrates aggregate world airline operating and net profits since 1970,[10] and Figure 1.4 depicts profitability relative to revenues.[11] Operating profits are earnings before interest and taxes (EBIT); net profits are earnings after deduction of interest and tax payments, and consideration of non-operating items.[12] It can be observed that the profit development does not mirror the traffic volume and revenue increases. Over time aggregate airline profits do not seem to develop randomly either. On the contrary, the profit history looks surprisingly systematic. It seems to follow a cycle which has the shape of an expanding sine wave (see Figure 1.3).

The world airlines' profit average is zero. To be precise, the average net annual profit from 1978 to 2010 amounts to -0.04 billion USD, and 0.10 billion USD for real net profit. For the period operating profit has a positive annual average of 5.6 billion USD, the real operating profit's mean is 6.5 billion USD.

The amplitude of the worldwide aggregate airline profit cycle is growing. Between 1970 and 2013 every profit peak is higher than the previous one. On the downside, every profit trough was followed by even greater losses in the next downcycle phase. The highest peak so far was reached in 2010 with net profits of 17.3 billion USD and operating profits of 27.6 billion USD. The biggest net loss was reported in 2008, after the breakout of the financial crisis, amounting to -26.1 billion USD. The largest operating losses of -11.8 billion USD occurred in 2001, after the 9/11 terror attacks in the United States.

The world airlines' profit cycle's period was found to be 10 years between 1978 and 2002,[13] and seems to have become shorter after 2007. So far, the

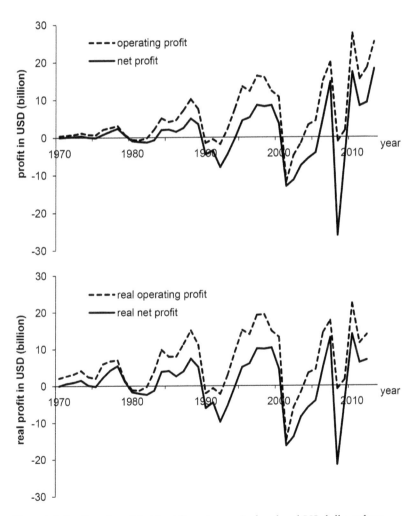

Figure 1.3 Profits of worldwide airlines in nominal and real US dollar values

airline industry has experienced four profit cycles. Cycles from peak to peak were: 1978–1988, 1988–1997, 1997–2007, and 2007–2010.

Cyclicality in airline profitability can be observed throughout world regions. Figure 1.5 shows the operating profitability development in North America, Europe, and Asia, which are the world regions with most air traffic.[14] North America exhibits more cyclicality than other world regions, and than the world airlines' aggregate. Profitability in Europe is in line with the world's development. Airlines in Asia-Pacific are generally more profitable. However, their profits are also cyclic.

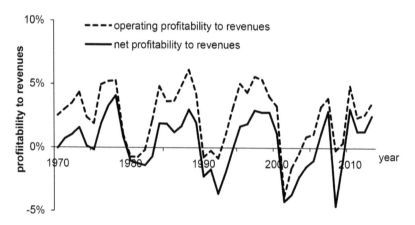

Figure 1.4 Operating and net profitability to revenues of worldwide airlines

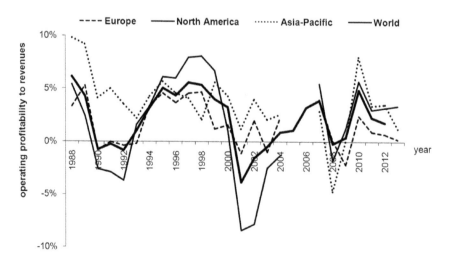

Figure 1.5 Airline profitability throughout world regions

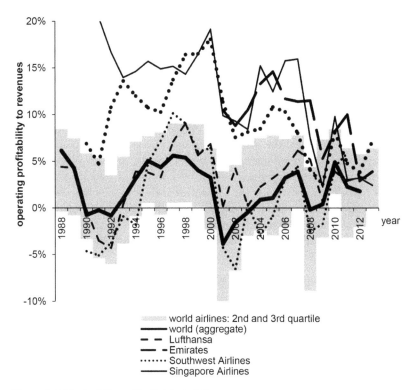

Figure 1.6 Profitability of individual airlines

Profitability does not only differ by geographic region but also among individual airlines. Some airlines manage to achieve financial results significantly above the world's average, for example Singapore Airlines, Emirates, or Southwest Airlines (see Figure 1.6).[15] These financially successful airlines cannot easily be categorised.[16] They have different business models, different sizes, and operate in different world regions. Regardless of their financial success over time, all airlines appear to experience a cyclic profitability pattern (see Figure 1.6). Examples of airlines with a rather average profitability performance are Lufthansa or Continental Airlines. Their average operating profitability over three cycles from 1988–2010 of 3.1% for Lufthansa and 1.0% for Continental Airlines is in line with the world's operating profitability average of 2.1%. The net profitability average of global airlines between 1988 and 2010 is -0.1%.

The International Air Transport Association (IATA) investigated the financial performance of airlines around the world and concludes:

> The evidence of the last cycle suggests that poor airline profitability is certainly not fully explained by business model nor geography. It is true that LCCs [= low cost carriers] as a group tend to have a higher return on

capital than network airlines in their region. It is also the case that network airline profitability has been lowest on the more mature N. American and European regions. However, none have managed to generate a ROIC [= return on invested capital] sufficient to meet the minimum expected by investors. [. . .] The ubiquity of this under-performance points to **system wide issues** affecting all airlines.[17]

The research presented here aims to identify the 'system wide issues'[18] which negatively impact the airline industry's profitability. Hence, this study takes a system approach to reveal the airline profit cycle's causes, to explain its particular shape, and to derive measures which mitigate or even eliminate the profit cycle. Simulation experiments will be conducted based on a System Dynamics model[19] calibrated for the US airline industry, which is the world's most cyclic one and has already been deregulated in 1978, and offers exceptional data availability.[20] To underline the importance of this research, the airline profit cycle's consequences will be described in the subsequent section.

1.2 Consequences of the airline profit cycle

The airline profit cycle, and especially the fact that net profits are zero on average, has several negative implications. Downcycle periods involve bankruptcies. Some recent examples of airlines in the United States going out of business or filing for bankruptcy protection are: Continental Airlines in 1990; Pan American Airways in 1991; United Airlines in 2002; US Airways in 2002 and 2004; Northwest Airlines and Delta Air Lines in 2005; and American Airlines in 2011.[21] Gritta and Lippman find in 2010 that since 1978 'over 155 air carriers [in the US market] have declared bankruptcy and reorganized or ceased operations, and this rate has increased in recent years. Just since the year 2000, more than 50 airlines have declared bankruptcy'.[22] Outside the United States the profit cycle's downswings have also involved several financial breakdowns, for example: Swissair,[23] Sabena,[24] and Aerolineas Argentinas[25] in 2001, Air Canada[26] in 2003, Olympic in 2003[27] and 2009,[28] Sterling,[29] and Alitalia[30] in 2008.

Though bankrupt airlines do not necessarily cease operations, their financial struggle nonetheless entails major restructuring and workforce reductions. American Airlines, for example, announced in 2012 that 'it has notified more than 11,000 workers they could lose their jobs as part of its bankruptcy reorganization'.[31] Furthermore, as part of the restructuring process, airlines are likely to cut unprofitable connections and hence reduce their traffic supply.

Consequently, other industries, which rely on air transportation, also suffer from airline bankruptcies and restructuring processes. Globally the air transport industry supports 58.1 million jobs, 52% of international tourists travel by air, and in 2013 aviation carried 35% of interregional exports of goods by value.[32] Airline bankruptcies and traffic reductions thus have negative employment, social, and economic consequences outside the airline industry. More stable positive

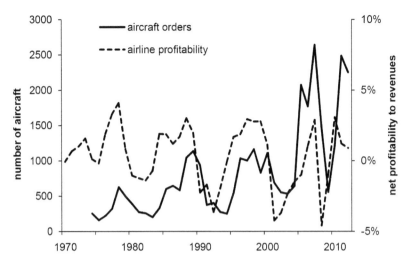

Figure 1.7 Worldwide airline profitability and aircraft orders of Boeing and Airbus

airline profits could create a more reliable business environment for air transport dependent industries, ensure tourism and trade, and preserve employment.

Being a direct supplier for the airline industry, aircraft manufacturers strongly experience the airline profit cycle's negative effects. Airlines tend to buy aircraft when they have money and refrain from ordering new capacity when they struggle financially. Figure 1.7 illustrates the almost parallel evolution of the world aggregate airline profitability and aircraft orders placed with Boeing and Airbus.[33]

In the past, the aircraft manufacturer Boeing reacted strongly to the cyclic behaviour by trying to match production capacity to incoming orders.[34] As a consequence, in upcycle periods many employees are hired to increase production. For example, Boeing's number of employees increased by approximately 85% from 1983 to 1989, by 40% from 1995 to 1997, and by 35% from 2004 to 2007. However, airlines' downcycle periods entailed sharp workforce reductions at the aircraft manufacturer. From 1981–1983 approximately 30% of Boeing's employees were made redundant, 35% between 1989 and 1995, and 45% between 1997 and 2004. Presumably, more stable airline profits would positively impact aircraft manufacturers' business through smoother aircraft order patterns, which ensure steady production capacity utilisation and enable manufacturers to retain their workforce.

Another consequence of the airline industry's financial performance is its comparable unattractiveness for investors. To judge the attractiveness of an investment the return on invested capital (ROIC) is compared to the weighted average cost of capital (WACC).[35] The main difference between ROIC and operating profitability to revenues is that the costs of operating leases are deduced to compute the return on invested capital, because only owned aircraft form part of airlines' invested capital. Hence, the ROIC is significantly higher than airlines' profitability. The WACC indicates what investors could earn if they invested their capital elsewhere (in an asset of similar risk in the same country). For the airline industry Figure 1.8 shows that the ROIC is constantly below the WACC.[36] Broadly speaking this means investors lose money on every dollar invested in the airline industry. They could have earned more if they had invested their capital in alternatives.

If the airline industry was more profitable, the ROIC would be higher, and investments would be more attractive. The industry's persistent financial under-performance may be expected to encourage investors to withdraw their money and invest elsewhere. Nonetheless, the airline industry has attracted large investments in the past. These must have thus been made for reasons other than mere returns on investment. To ensure future growth the IATA estimates the immense investment of 4–5 trillion USD in new aircraft will be needed, especially in emerging economies.[37] Given this great financial need the IATA concludes that '[w]ithout an improvement in the return on capital invested in the airline industry it may well be difficult to attract such investment capital'.[38]

The airlines' financial struggle is not mirrored in other aviation industries. Along the aviation value chain, airlines achieve the lowest returns on invested capital. Figure 1.9 shows how returns on capital vary throughout the value chain between 2004 and 2011.[39] In contrast to airlines, many other aviation businesses earned more or close to their WACC. Among airlines' suppliers, service providers earned returns higher than their cost of capital. Manufacturers, lessors, and airports did not reach their WACC. Airline distributers generated the highest return in the aviation value chain. Computer reservation system (CRS) services, travel agents, and freight forwards produce returns more than twice their cost of capital.

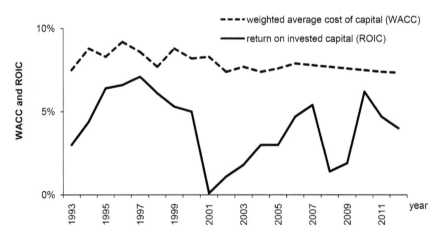

Figure 1.8 Evaluation of investments in the global airline industry

Source: IATA

Comparing the airline industry to 28 other industries, such as chemicals, IT services, or department stores, the IATA finds even more evidence for the airline industry's striking profit problem: 'Over the past 30–40 years the airline industry has generated one of the lowest returns on invested capital among all industries.'[40]

During the last decades the airline industry made considerable efforts to improve its financial situation. Between 1990 and 2010 real costs per unit of output have been reduced by almost a third (see Figure 1.10).[41] This implies

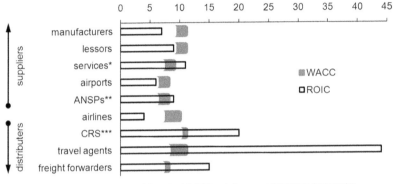

* services: maintenance/ repair/ overhaul (MRO), catering, ground handling, fuel supply)
** ANSPs: air navigation service providers
*** CRS = computer reservation systems

Figure 1.9 Profitability along the aviation value chain – return of invested capital (ROIC) versus costs of capital (WACC)

Source: IATA

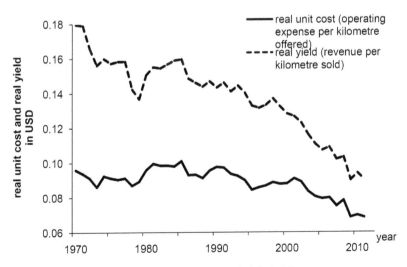

Figure 1.10 Unit cost and yield development of global airlines

airlines achieved substantial efficiency gains. However, airlines' revenue per unit sold, which is called 'yield' in the airline industry, has also declined. Figure 1.10 illustrates how yields have fallen over the past four decades.

In summary, it is evident that the airlines' cyclic profitability with repeated loss periods has negative consequences for many stakeholders. Not only the airline industry itself but also its supply chain partners, dependent businesses, and investors suffer as a consequence of the airlines' poor financial performance. More stable positive financial results could not only facilitate airline management decisions and improve investors' confidence but also preserve employment.

1.3 Research objective and approach

The question is how the airline industry can achieve more stable positive profits to prevent the airline profit cycle's negative consequences. To be able to answer this question it is necessary to understand the airline profit cycle's causes, and the drivers behind its particular shape (zero average profit, rising amplitude, regular and recently shorter cycle period). A literature analysis will reveal that research on the airline profit cycle's causes and drivers is scarce, and previous studies contradict each other in several aspects. The purpose of this study is to address these aspects in order to achieve a detailed understanding of the airline profit cycle, and to suggest cycle mitigating measures. Accordingly, three questions are formulated to guide the research process:

1   Why are airline profits cyclical?
2   What are the causes and dynamics that determine the profit cycle's shape?
3   How can the situation be improved?

The research process to answer these questions is presented in five chapters, as outlined in Table 1.1. Chapter 1 has introduced the phenomenon 'airline profit cycle' and motivated the research questions. In Chapter 2 previous airline profit cycle research is examined, as well as related literature on cyclicality. Potential causes and drivers of the airline profit cycle are derived from literature and expert interviews. In addition, potential cycle mitigation measures are compiled. In Chapter 3 an empirical investigation of the most popular cycle drivers reveals the need for further analysis with a systemic approach. Hence, a System Dynamics model of the airline industry's profit development is constructed and calibrated for the US airline industry. Once confidence in the model's behaviour has been gained, the potential airline profit cycle causes, drivers, and mitigation measures gathered in Chapter 2 are examined in model simulation experiments in Chapter 4. Their impact on the airline profit cycle will be assessed to reveal the cycle's causes and drivers as well as dampers. Chapter 5 concludes how the airline industry's profit situation could be improved.

Table 1.1 Outline of this airline profit cycle study

Outline of content			
Ch.	*Stage*	*Summary*	*Main results*
1	Problem definition	The airline profit cycle: What is the problem? Why is it a problem? Research questions: 1 Why are airline profits cyclical? 2 What determines the cycle's shape? 3 How can the situation be improved?	Relevant research questions
2	Inventory	What is known about the airline profit cycle's causes and drivers? What can be learned from cyclicality in other contexts? (Sources: literature and experts)	Potential cycle causes, drivers, and mitigation policies
3	Model formulation, calibration, and validation	• Empirical analysis of selected potential cycle causes (→ need for a system approach) • Formulation of a System Dynamics model of the airline industry • Calibration for the US airline industry • Tests to build confidence in model structure and behaviour	First insights about cycle causes and System Dynamics model of the airline industry
4	Model experiments	Potential cycle causes, drivers, and mitigation measures (from Chapter 2) are tested for their impact on airline profitability	Actual airline profit cycle causes, drivers, and mitigation policies
5	Conclusion	• Discussion and summary of results • Counter-factual illustration of promising cycle mitigation measures • Suggestions for further research	Compilation and illustration of key results

Notes

1 Data source: A4A Airlines for America, 'World airlines: Annual results. Traffic and operations 1929 – present', web page, accessed: 21 Nov 2014.
2 Note for clarification: A 'billion' equals 10^9.
3 Definition corresponds to Standard Industrial Classification (SIC) codes 451* and 452*. This includes airlines' passenger and cargo transportation as well as ancillary businesses.
4 Data source: Passenger numbers: A4A Airlines for America, 'World airlines: Annual results. Traffic and operations 1929–present', accessed: 21 Nov 2014. – Real GDP data: 'UN Statistics, World. GDP, at constant 2005 prices' – US Dollars, web page, accessed: 14 Nov 2013.
5 Own calculation of Compound Annual Growth Rates = (end value / start value) ^ (1/years) −1.

6 In 2000–2010 annual growth rate of real GDP 2.6%, of airline passengers 4.3%.
7 See International Air Transport Association (IATA), *Fact sheet: Economic and social benefits of air transport* (2012).
8 Globally, 94% of all flights in 2008 operated in unconstrained airport capacity conditions. See Gelhausen, Marc, Peter Berster and Dieter Wilken, 'Do airport capacity constraints have a serious impact on the future development of air traffic?', *Journal of Air Transport Management* 28 (2013): p. 9. – Data source of airport number: International Air Transport Association (IATA), *Fact sheet: Economic and social benefits of air transport.*
9 Revenue data source: A4A Airlines for America, 'World airlines annual results: Financial results 1947–present', web page, accessed: 21 Nov 2014. – Inflation adjusted by Implicit Price Deflator in 2005 US dollar values, data source: UN Statistics, 'World. GDP, Implicit Price Deflators – US Dollars. Implicit Price Deflator (2005 = 100)', web page, accessed: 21 Nov 2014.
10 Profit data source: A4A Airlines for America, 'World airlines annual results: Financial results 1947–present', accessed: 21 Nov 2014. Inflation adjusted by Implicit Price Deflator in 2005 US dollar values, data source: UN Statistics, 'World. GDP, Implicit Price Deflators – US Dollars. Implicit Price Deflator (2005 = 100)', accessed: 21 Nov 2014.
11 Own calculation. Data source: A4A Airlines for America, 'World airlines annual results: Financial results 1947–present', accessed: 21 Nov 2014.
12 See International Civil Aviation Organisation (ICAO), *Air transport reporting form: Financial data – Commercial air carriers (FORM EF)* (2013).
13 See Jiang, Helen and R. John Hansman, 'An analysis of profit cycles in the airline industry', *6th AIAA Aviation Technology, Integration and Operations Conference (ATIO)*, (Wichita, Kansas: 2006), p. 9.
14 Data sources: North America, Europe, and Asia-Pacific: For 1988–2004: ICAO via Morrell, Peter S., *Airline finance*, 3rd ed. (Aldershot, UK; Burlington, VT: Ashgate, 2007) p. 5, Figure 1.4. – For 2007–2009: International Air Transport Association (IATA), *Fact sheet: Industry statistics, December 2010* (2010). For 2010–2012: International Air Transport Association (IATA), *Fact sheet: Industry statistics, September 2013* (2013). For 2013: International Air Transport Association (IATA), *Fact sheet: Industry statistics, December 2014* (2014). – World profitability: Own calculation, data source: A4A Airlines for America, 'World airlines: Annual results. Financial results 1947–present', web page, accessed: 15 Nov 2013.
15 Own calculation. Data sources: financial results from BTS (US airlines only), Compustat, A4A, and financial statements on company websites. See US Bureau of Transportation Statistics (BTS), 'Schedule P-1.2 Air carrier financial', web page, accessed: 28 Jan 2014. And Compustat, 'Fundamentals Annual Data', web page, accessed: 28 Jan 2015. And A4A Airlines for America, 'World airlines: Annual results. Financial results 1947–present', accessed: 15 Nov 2013. And Lufthansa, 'Financial statements 1988–2013', web page, accessed: 28 Jan 2015. And Emirates, 'Financial statements 2004–2014', web page, accessed: 28 Jan 2015.
16 See International Air Transport Association (IATA), *Vision 2050* (Singapore 2011), p. 14. – The recipe for an individual airline's success remains to be discovered. To date (2014) the only one large-scale empirical study on airlines' critical success factors; also published in International Air Transport Association (IATA), *Profitability and the air transport value chain* (2013).
17 International Air Transport Association (IATA), *Profitability and the air transport value chain* (2013), p. 16. – Emphasis not in original.
18 Ibid.

19 A brief introduction to System Dynamics will be given in section 3.1.2 before the airline industry model is presented in sections 3.2–3.3.
20 The model calibration choice is explained in section 3.5.1.
21 See The Associated Press, 'American joins long list of airline bankruptcies', 2011, web page, accessed: 15 Nov 2013.
22 Gritta, Richard and Ellen Lippman, 'Aircraft leasing and its effect on air carriers debt burdens: A comparison over the past several decades', *Journal of the Transportation Research Forum* 49, no. 3 (2010): p. 101.
23 See SWISS, 'Swissair: Switzerland's former national airline ceased operations in 2002, 2013', web page, accessed: 15 Nov 2013.
24 See Sabena, 'A historic airline is gone', 2013, web page, accessed: 15 Nov 2013.
25 See Jayanti, Rama K. and S.V. Jayanti, 'Effects of airline bankruptcies: An event study', *Journal of Service Marketing* 25, no. 6 (2011): p. 401.
26 See Simon, Bernhard, 'Air Canada is granted bankruptcy court protection', *New York Times*, 2 April 2003, web page, accessed: 15 Nov 2013.
27 See The Agence-France Presse, 'Olympic Airways changes name, strategy but keeps rings', *USA Today*, 2003, web page, accessed: 15 Nov 2013.
28 See Freshfields, Bruckhaus and Deringer, 'Olympic Airlines: Judgement clarifies definition of "establishment" in secondary insolvency proceedings', 2013, web page, accessed: 15 Nov 2013.
29 See CAPA Centre for Aviation, 'Bankruptcy of Denmark's Cimber Sterling will leave no long-lasting network gaps', 2012, web page, accessed: 15 Nov 2013.
30 See BBC News, 'Alitalia seeks bankruptcy measure', 2008, 29 August, web page, accessed: 15 Nov 2013.
31 Reuters, 'American Airlines issues layoff notices, cuts flight schedule', 2012, web page, accessed: 15 Nov 2013.
32 See International Air Transport Association (IATA), *Fact sheet: Economic and social benefits of air transport* (2014).
33 Own calculation. Aircraft orders are the sum of received commercial aircraft order published by Boeing and Airbus. – Data source for Boeing orders: 'Boeing, Orders and deliveries', 2013, web page, accessed: 20 Nov 2013. – Data sources for Airbus orders: For 1975–2009: 'Airbus, Historical orders and deliveries 1974–2009', 2010, web page, accessed: 8 Sept 2010. For 2010–2012: Airbus, 'Airbus summary results 1989–2012', updated Jan 2013, 2013, web page, accessed: 21 Nov 2013. – Data source for world aggregate airline profits: A4A Airlines for America, 'World airlines: Annual results. Financial results 1947–present', accessed: 15 Nov 2013.
34 Data source employee numbers on Boeing's prime production site in Washington state: For 1997–2012: Boeing, 'About us: Boeing employment numbers', 2013, web page, accessed: 21 Nov 2013. Values for 1971, 1980, 1983, 1989, and 1995 in: Sgouridis, Sgouris P., 'Symbiotic strategies in enterprise ecology: Modeling commercial aviation as an Enterprise of Enterprises', PhD thesis, Massachusetts Institute of Technology, 2007, p. 123. – Data source aircraft orders: Boeing, 'Orders and deliveries', accessed: 20 Nov 2013.
35 Definitions of ROIC and WACC (used in Figure 1.8): The ROIC is the payment investors receive for providing capital and bearing risk. It is the after-tax operating profit (adjusted for operating leases) expressed as a percentage of invested capital. The ROIC differs from operating profitability to revenues mainly because it is a return on the capital invested, not on revenues. – The WACC indicates the opportunity costs for investors, i.e. what the investor would earn if their capital was invested elsewhere in an asset of similar risk in the same country. Source: International Air Transport Association (IATA), *Profitability and the air transport value chain*, p. 15.

36 Ibid., chart 5, p. 11.
37 See ibid., p. 13.
38 Ibid.
39 Ibid., chart 12, p. 19. Illustrated is ROIC excluding goodwill of sample, period 2004–2011, in per cent. Only limited sample for travel agents.
40 Ibid., p. 12.
41 Own calculations. Data sources: A4A Airlines for America, 'World airlines: Annual results. Financial results 1947–present', accessed: 15 Nov 2013. A4A Airlines for America, 'World airlines: Annual results. Traffic and operations 1929–present', accessed: 21 Nov 2014. Inflation adjustment by Implicit Price Deflator, in 2005 values, data source: UN Statistics, 'World. GDP, Implicit Price Deflators – US Dollars. Implicit Price Deflator (2005 = 100)', accessed: 14 Nov 2013.

2 Potential causes of the airline profit cycle

This chapter examines the existing body of knowledge regarding cyclicality, with the aim of identifying potential airline profit cycle causes, drivers, and mitigation measures. These will be analysed for their actual impact on the cycle in subsequent chapters. Insights will be gained from:

- theories about the business cycle in the general economy and factors that make some industries more cyclical than others (in section 2.1).
- a theoretical examination of why systems oscillate, and of the supply chain as an example of an oscillating system (in section 2.2).
- a review of the airline profit cycle in aviation business literature and the few studies that focus explicitly on the phenomenon (in section 2.3).
- the insiders' view, i.e. opinions of people working in and closely with the airline industry, derived in expert interviews and from secondary data (in section 2.4).

As the conclusion in section 2.5 a set of factors that potentially cause, drive, or mitigate the airline profit cycle will be presented.

2.1 Literature review on business cycle drivers

2.1.1 Business cycles in the general economy

Cyclical fluctuations of economic output, usually measured by real GDP, have long been discussed in economic research. There is general agreement that these economic fluctuations exist in all economies and throughout history.[1]

The business cycle with a length of 9–10 years was first documented by Juglar in the 1860s.[2] Schumpeter classifies additional economic cycles: Kondratieff's 40–70 years long wave[3] and Kitchin's '40-months' short wave of 2–4 years[4]. A typical business cycle is displayed in Figure 2.1.[5] It is defined as fluctuation around the economy's long-term growth trend and character-ised by four phases: peak, recession, trough, and recovery.[6] At the peak, real GDP, production capacity utilisation, and business profits are at the high-est level compared to recent years. When the economy slows down after a

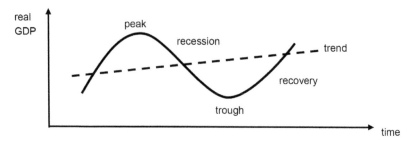

Figure 2.1 Phases of the business cycle

peak, this setback is called recession or contraction. Real GDP and profits decline, production capacity becomes underutilised. The trough is reached when the economy is at its worst. However, a trough marks not only the bottom but also the turning point of economic developments. The following upswing is called recovery or expansion. During that period real GDP and profits generally improve until the peak is reached, and the cycle repeats itself. Throughout the cycle business profits show much greater amplitudes than other economic indicators.[7]

Having described what happens in the economy throughout the business cycle, the next step is to explain the economy's development. The business cycle's causes and its possible damping are still a contentious issue among economists. The debate was kindled during the Great Depression in the United States in the 1930s and reignited in the 1970s. Early business cycle theories were compiled by Habeler in 1937.[8] The first mathematical business cycle model was developed by Frisch in 1933 who compared the business cycle to swings of a pendulum.[9] Today economists still have not found a common answer to the question about causes and mitigation levers of economic fluctuations.[10] Their main ideas will be presented in the following brief non-exhaustive overview.[11]

In classical business cycle theories the economy has a long-term equilibrium around which economic output oscillates due to medium-term mismatches of demand and supply. The economy's self-correcting mechanism, which moves it back to equilibrium, is price flexibility. Adam Smith's 'invisible hand' is frequently interpreted as the price mechanism that preserves general equilibrium.[12] According to classical theories firms producing under their production capacity lower prices to stimulate demand. When their production capacity is exhausted, they raise prices to gain more profit. High prices discourage demand and the cycle repeats itself. Any artificial price adjustment, such as taxes or governmental price control, would distort decisions of buyers and suppliers and will thus prevent the optimal allocation of resources.[13] Haberler divided the classical theories into several categories depending on the main cycle driving force: psychology, over-investment, and under-consumption.[14]

Psychological theories:[15] Profits earned in upswings lead to positive expectations about future incomes. In consequence the profitability of investments is overestimated. When reality disappoints expectations, the overestimation converts into exaggerated pessimism. Investments are disproportionately reduced which accelerates the downturn. Hence, expectations act as cycle amplifiers.

Theories of over-investment:[16] Over-investment occurs in expectation of an upswing but actually leads to a downswing because consumption saturates, prices decrease, and firms lack savings for new investments. There are different explanations as to how the following upswing is induced:

- Monetary over-investment theories:[17] Banks trigger the upswing by offering cheap credit and thus stimulating investment in production capital.
- Non-monetary over-investment theory:[18] Investments in new markets and new production technology trigger upswings. The production of investment goods increases, facilitated but not induced by low credit rates. Income rises and hence the demand for consumption goods. This again initiates investments in production capacity and amplifies the initial impulse ('accelerator principle').
- Schumpeter's theory:[19] Profound technological inventions trigger economic development. They are a structural change which leads to an upswing of the economic long wave (Kondratieff). Jular and Kitchin cycles occur as a consequence of different innovation projects around the invention which progressively discover its potential. The cycle length is a result of the projects' periods.

Under-consumption theories:[20] The problem in recessions is the lack of consumer demand created by excessive saving. (In contrast, in over-investment theories a downturn is the result of a lack of savings.)

Sharp critique of the classical theories and their self-correcting mechanisms was presented by Keynes.[21] In his view, markets are inherently instable. He states that prices and wages are rigid, i.e. fixed in the short run. In consequence, markets cannot be cleared. Wages adjust slowly because long-term contracts are desirable for firms and workers since they avoid frequent negotiation costs. Likewise, prices on input markets are rigid due to firms desiring long-term agreements. Since firms are assumed to apply mark-up pricing, rigid input factor prices result in price rigidity on output markets as well. Monopolistic market structures and credit restrictions are further rigidities in the economy. Given the economy's instability, it is the government's task to intervene actively and provide stabilisation. In recessions a lack of demand is the main problem. The suggested response is demand stimulation by counter-cyclical investments. If necessary, a state should borrow money and invest it (deficit spending). In recovery and boom phases state savings can be replenished.

Friedman proclaimed an alternative to the Keynesian theory, the neo-classical theory.[22] His explanation for the business cycle is a market-clearing model. If expectations were accurate, the economy would be in equilibrium.

Though consumers and producers form their expectations rationally, they will in reality never have perfect information and their assumptions will thus not be accurate.[23] Hence, imperfect information causes economic fluctuations. Consequently, policies to mitigate the business cycle are bound to be ineffective because price level expectations would adjust accordingly and might even aggravate an economic downturn. Only an action which the public cannot anticipate may achieve stabilisation. A state's only market intervention should be to regulate the economy's money supply in a way that counteracts inflation or deflation because both would distort the price level and hence prevent proper market–clearing.

In the closely related Real Business Cycle theory, supply shocks cause the business cycle.[24] That means the economy does not move away from its equilibrium but the equilibrium level of output shifts due to an exogenous shock. Such a shock could appear in technology, oil price, or by unpredictable fiscal policy. Thus, business cycles are households' and firms' reactions to exogenous shocks. Government intervention would only disturb their actions.

Besides these traditional theories on economic fluctuations there are many other approaches. While some are similar, others explain the business cycle differently. Mauβer, Jacobs, or Zarnowitz, among others, give overviews of controversial aspects among business cycle explanations.[25] These are primarily:

- *Systematic behaviour vs. coincidence*: Some understand the business cycle as regular cyclic movements comparable to the swings of a pendulum. The focus is thus on forecasting turning points. Meanwhile others assume economic developments coincidentally result in a cyclic pattern.
- *Cycle seeks equilibrium vs. disequilibrium*: Neo-classical equilibrium theories claim that a deregulated economy will return to stability, whereas Keynesian concepts imply market imperfections or even disequilibrium.
- *Exogenous vs. endogenous cycle drivers*: Some theories explain the business cycle with exogenous influences. They shift the economy temporarily away from its otherwise stable equilibrium, to which it automatically returns. Permanent fluctuations can only arise from on-going exogenous penetration. In contrast, other theories explain the business cycle with the economy's mechanisms. An exogenous event may be needed to start economic oscillations but afterwards the cycle develops without further interference, as in Frisch's pendulum analogy. [26] The economy's internal mechanisms are the cycle-driving forces.
- *Supply vs. demand side*: In some theories reasons for the business cycle, and especially for downturns, lie on the supply side, in others on the demand side. The former complain of too little consumption, the latter claim that the economy suffers from too much investment.
- *Role of psychology and politics*: It is argued whether individuals build their expectations purely rationally or whether optimism and pessimism interfere. Furthermore, political business cycles theory see governments' self-interest to be re-elected as an essential cycle generating force.

2.1.2 Common characteristics of cyclical industries

While business cycle studies look at a country's economy, industry cycle research examines output fluctuations of individual industries. Per definition 'cyclical industries [are] industries in which sales tend to magnify cyclical changes in gross national product and national income'.[27] It is found that some industries exhibit much more cyclicality than others. Largely cyclical industries are, for example, telecommunication, semi-conductors, personal computers, chemicals, and air transportation.[28] The literature on reasons why some industries are more cyclical than others is rather limited.[29] A non-exhaustive review will be given in this chapter.

The first observed industry cycles were the 'hog cycle' and the 'shipbuilding cycle'.[30] Several attempts to explain the hog cycle are formalised into a more general industry cycle theory called the cobweb theorem by Ezekiel in 1938.[31] At some point in time, the supply of pork is smaller than the demand for it. Hence, prices rise which makes it more attractive for farmers to grow more pigs. There may even be additional farmers endeavouring into pork production. By the time the pigs are slaughtered there will be more supply than demand in the market which deteriorates prices. Consequently, the pork supply will be cut back and the cycle continues. Tinbergen explains shipbuilding cycles in a similar way.[32] According to him, cyclicality is determined by the time it takes suppliers to react on prices and the intensity of reactions. Furthermore he finds there is a difference between durable goods and consumption goods cycles. In 1917 this was already established by Clark who discovered that durable goods industries exhibit more fluctuation than non-durable ones.[33]

The cobweb theorem is systemically analysed by Meadows.[34] He builds a System Dynamics model of commodity markets, which have exhibited strong fluctuations in price, production, and income, to test the impact of different behavioural policies on market performance and stability. His main results are as follows:

- The commodity market becomes more cyclical with factors that make production react more strongly on price changes. The market is stabilised by factors which make demand more responsive to price changes. Altogether, alterations in the consumption sector have more impact on the system's stability than alterations in the production sector.[35]
- Adding flexibility in certain areas of the system has much smaller impacts on cyclicality than the factors stated above. To stabilise the market it is more effective to vary the use of a commodity becoming just available for distribution than to vary the utilisation of existing production capacities. For example, it is more stabilising to be flexible with harvesting mature crops than with planting them.[36]
- The commodity markets' stability is found to depend strongly on pricing decisions of processors and distributors. Their decisions to cut desired inventory levels that act as a buffer to stabilise price levels, cause major fluctuations in the market.[37]

Also employing a systemic approach Weil finds that many technology-based industries exhibit recurring cycles in investment, capacity utilisation, prices, margins, and returns on capital.[38] His examples are, among others, semi-conductors, personal computers, telecommunication, chemicals, petroleum, metals, and air transportation. Weil develops a generic System Dynamics model of market dynamics that lead to the industries' cyclicalities. The industries are all characterised by 'commoditization' which Weil defines by them having 'a competitive environment in which product differentiation is difficult, customer loyalty and brand values are low, and sustainable advantage comes primarily from cost (and often quality) leadership'.[39] Cyclicality in those industries is, according to Weil, a result of overcapacities which are caused by forecasting errors, a deficit in financial constraints, and an increase in players due to the market's liberalisation.[40] Since it is 'much easier to expand capacity than to reduce it', Weil expects future boom and bust cycles to be increasingly irregular and severe.[41]

In a broad empirical study Petersen and Strongin explore the determinants of industries' relative cyclicality.[42] Based on a literature review they identify the following demand side, supply side, and market structure characteristics as potential cycle determinants:

- Durability of output: Durable goods industries, such as automobiles or electrical appliances, are generally more cyclical than non-durable goods industries.[43] There are several explanations for this finding. One explanation is that a comparatively small percentage change in desired capital goods can lead to large percentage changes in the current demand for durable goods by consumers and investors (see 'acceleration principle', section 2.1.1).[44] Another explanation, supported by empirical evidence, is that people prefer to make larger investments when they have more money. Hence, more expensive durable goods are more likely to be bought in economic upturns. A third explanation is that because purchasing a durable good is usually binding for a long time, there is an option value for waiting in order to obtain new information about economic developments. In downturns the option value rises and the purchase is often postponed.[45]
- Variability of inputs: A firm's ability to respond to demand or supply shocks depends strongly on how variable its inputs are in the short run. Petersen and Strongin's hypothesis is thus, the greater an industry's variable to total costs ratio, the more cyclical the industry. They regard production workers, non-energy materials, and energy intensity as variable inputs.[46]
- Labour hoarding: In times of temporary low demand firms in several US manufacturing industries are found to be reluctant to lay off workers due to high training and search costs. The incentive to hoard labour is thus larger than to cut output. Likewise, in boom periods these firms or industries are reluctant to hire workers. The hypothesis is thus that, other things being equal, the more labour hoarding an industry engages in, the less cyclical its output fluctuations.[47]

- Inventory usage: To what extent a manufacturer relies on inventories, if it produces to order or to stock, varies greatly across firms and industries. In case of a demand shock inventories enable firms to smooth production and thus dampen cyclicality. In contrast, given a shock in, for example, production costs, the firm's ability to store finished goods may amplify the output swing in case firms bunch production in low-cost periods. So Petersen and Strongin conclude that the impact of inventories for cyclicality is uncertain.[48]
- Market power: Petersen and Strongin pick up the New Keynesian argument that wage rigidities, mostly caused by labour unions' negotiated contracts, lead to greater output cyclicality (see section 2.1.1). Bils finds empirical evidence for this hypothesis.[49] Carlton finds that an industry's degree of concentration is strongly correlated with the rigidity of prices.[50] If a firm has considerable market power, i.e. if the concentration in that market is high, this will translate into inflexible prices. Petersen and Strongin conclude that an industry's degree of unionisation and concentration may aggravate its cyclicality.[51]
- Other variables to be tested for their impact on cyclicality are the market power on the buyer side and the average industry growth.[52]

Using panel data for 296 manufacturing industries in the time period 1958–1986, Petersen and Strongin measure each industry's cyclicality and test its correspondence with explanations listed above. The analysis confirms that durable goods industries are three times more cyclical than non-durables, which are, in turn, no more cyclical than the aggregate economy. The variables they tested to explain this great difference did, however, not provide any statistical evidence.[53] Only the variation in cyclicality among durable goods industries can be partially (41%) explained. How intensely a durable goods industry relies on production inputs, such as non-energy materials, energy material, and production workers, has the most explanatory power. This is in line with the finding that labour hoarding seems to dampen an industry's cyclicality. However, the New Keynesian argument, that wage rigidities drive the cycle, is refuted by Peterson and Strongin's statistical analysis. The existence of labour unions, which may cause the wage rigidity, was found to be not important for relative cyclicality.

In a later study Deleersnyder et al. focus on durable goods industries.[54] They conduct an empirical investigation of 24 US consumer durables to analyse the cyclical sensitivity in sales and its underlying drivers.[55] Durable goods on average are found to exhibit a four times higher cyclical volatility than the general economy.[56] That is more than the factor three Petersen and Strongin found in their broader sample. Durables sales show an amplification of general business cycle swings. There is no evidence for deepness asymmetries, so troughs in durables are not deeper than peaks are high. Steepness asymmetry, on the other hand, is significant, indicating that in contractions durables sales are postponed so that they fall faster than they increase during expansions. For these observations Deleersnyder et al. find the following explanations:[57]

- Counter-cyclical pricing: In economic downturns companies can either lower prices to be competitive or increase prices to offset a revenue loss. Deleersnyder et al. empirically find the latter, the counter-cyclical pricing, to be widespread. This price reaction deceases consumers' propensity to buy durables and thus amplify sales cyclicality.
- Price rigidities: Rigid prices, i.e. inflexible slow price adjustments, are found to amplify sales cyclicality. Industries with swift price adjustments exhibit lower sales cyclicalities.
- Nature of the durable good: Convenience goods, which save customers time and effort, are found to be less cyclical than leisure goods.
- Familiarity with the durable: There is partial evidence that replacement purchases are less cyclical. It is inferred that the fact that customers are familiar with a product makes their purchase more likely during contractions.
- No empirical evidence is found to support that cyclicality depends on the product's expensiveness, which might be off-putting during contractions, or the economy's state during product launch.

From these insights Deleersnyder et al. conclude that companies can limit the impact of business cycle fluctuation on their product sales by a pricing strategy that is both pro-cyclical and responsive.[58] For example, in contractions prices are to be decreased quickly to keep sales up.

Specifically for the US semi-conductors industry, Tan and Mathews derive that this industry's strong cyclicality is caused by pro-cyclical investments. They result from an ignorance of delays between market dynamics.[59] Accordingly, Tan and Mathews find that companies can benefit from counter-cyclical capacity investments.[60]

The service sector is, according to Cuadrao-Roura and V.-Abarca, less cyclical than manufacturing industries. Their finding is based on an empirical analysis of the Spanish market.[61] They hypothesise the following reasons for the more stable performance of the service sector:[62]

- Consumption is less likely to be postponed because consumers cannot store the service.
- Services are less capital intensive (and capital, i.e. durables, are known to be highly cyclical).
- Service industries are less competitive than manufacturing industries.
- Substitution for high-qualified service workers is difficult, which supports a stable workforce.

Cuadrao-Roura and V.-Abarca observe that the service sector is becoming increasingly pro-cyclical. They explain this by the growing integration of manufacturing and service industries, for example in transportation.[63]

Conclusion

The literature review revealed there are mainly four reasons why some industries are more cyclical than others. Table 2.1 summarises these key points.

The first factor is the durability of an industry's output. There is consensus in the literature that durable goods industries are more cyclical. This may have several causes. Some argue that an additional investment in, for example, production capacity is amplified because it generates additional income which increases consumption. Others state that durable goods, which usually involve a greater investment, are more easily financed in economically good times. So durable goods industries depend largely on the general economy's cycle. Another explanation is that durable goods purchases are often postponed because, especially in economic downturns, it makes sense to wait for more information about future economic developments. The fact that durable goods industries are more cyclical can also explain why manufacturing industries, which heavily depend on durable goods such as production equipment, are also found to be overly cyclical. Service industries are generally less cyclical because services are less capital intensive and because they cannot store services which makes purchases less likely to be postponed. To mitigate the cycle-driving effect of a product's durability on its industry, the product's lifetime would need to be shortened.[64]

Second, capacity adjustment policies are often used to explain an industry's cyclicality. Overcapacity is identified by Weil as a common problem of cyclical industries. It can be caused by forecasting errors, lacking financial constraints, or increased competition due to market liberalisation. Besides, overcapacity can be caused by pro-cyclical investments which Tan and Matthews see as the main cycle driver. The timing of capacity adjustments was already a key point in the first industry cycle theories by Ezekiel and Tinbergen. According to them the time it takes suppliers to adjust their capacities and thus their supply in reaction to a price change and the intensity of their action determine the cycle. Correspondingly, Meadows finds an industry's cyclicality to be pronounced when production capacity is rather responsive to market changes. He also states that small inventories destabilise an industry. Including big buffers in the production process to stabilise prices is thus a suggested cycle mitigation measure. Furthermore, several authors recommend counter-cyclical investment. Besides, they advise to adapt production capacity slowly to changes in the market.

The third factor influencing an industry's cyclicality is its price mechanism. Slow and inflexible price adjustments, i.e. rigid prices, are found to be responsible for cyclicality. In contrast Meadows finds that vivid demand reactions to price changes, i.e. a very price-sensitive consumer base, stabilise an industry. Deleersnyder et al. discover that durables' prices are usually increased in contractions to ensure revenues and then relaxed in expansions. They hold this counter-cyclical pricing responsible for cyclicality. To mitigate cyclicality, they suggest pro-cyclical pricing, which means to decrease prices in contractions. They also argue that price adjustments need be prompt to dampen cyclicality.

A fourth factor potentially influencing an industry's cyclicality according to Petersen and Strongin is the variability in production inputs, such as production labour or oil. Their impact will be further examined in section 2.2.2 on oscillations in the supply chain. Industries that exhibit labour hoarding, i.e. keeping employees during contractions due to high training and search costs, are found to be less cyclical. Stable labour input and costs are thus assumed to mitigate cyclicality.

Table 2.1 Cycle drivers and mitigation policies in cyclical industries

Cyclical industries	
Cycle driver	durability of output: • investment in durables creates income that creates additional demand (acceleration principle) • wait and postpone purchase in downturns • financing of durables (people invest when they have money, i.e. in upturns) → manufacturing more cyclical than service sector capacity adjustment policy: • forecasting errors (→ overcapacity) • lacking financial constraints (→ overcapacity) • increased competition after market liberalisation (→ overcapacity) • responsive to price changes • small buffers in production process • pro-cyclical investment price mechanism: • slow and inflexible price adjustment, i.e. rigid prices • very price-sensitive demand • counter-cyclical pricing (increase in contraction to ensure revenue) variability in production inputs (labour, oil, etc.)
Mitigation policy	durability of output: shorten product lifetime capacity adjustment policy: • slow production adaptation (less responsive to price changes) • big buffers in production process • counter-cyclical investment • steady production capacity utilisation, but flexible in last processing stage price mechanism: • prompt price adjustment • pro-cyclical pricing (decrease in contraction) labour hoarding (keeping employees during contractions)

2.2 Systems literature on cyclical dynamics

2.2.1 Oscillation as a fundamental mode of behaviour

In the systems literature industry cycles are understood as oscillations. Systemic analyses on industry cycles have already been presented in the previous section (i.e. Meadows 1969; Weil 1996). In the following paragraphs, several theoretical aspects of system oscillations will be provided.

In physics, oscillations have long been a field of research. Around 1602 Galileo Galilei already observed the swings of a pendulum.[65] When given an initial push the pendulum, i.e. the system, starts to swing back and forth, creating an oscillation. After some time, friction and air resistance cause the amplitude of the oscillation to decline. They dampen the system until the pendulum is back in its equilibrium position. Similarly, a spring that is once compressed or stretched and then let go starts to vibrate.[66]

In case it is not clear how a system will react on a certain input, a system identification test can be conducted.[67] It provides knowledge about the relationship between the system's input and output signals. This information may be used to simulate scenarios, to predict the system's output, or to design a suitable 'controller', i.e. a mechanism that manipulates system inputs to obtain the desired effect on output (for example, stabilisation). The system identification process builds on elaborate mathematical algorithms to find a suitable mathematical formulation for the system.[68] In the process the system is treated as a black box about which nothing is known. In case more information is available, a grey-box approach can be taken by incorporating the features which are known to characterise the system.

Instead of black-box and grey-box approaches, white-box (also called transparent-box) modelling can be employed to test how a system will react on certain inputs and how it can be stabilised. White-box models are not purely correlational but 'causal-descriptive'.[69] They can be understood as a 'theory' about the system's behaviour. Their advantage is thus that they cannot only calculate the system's output reaction to certain inputs but also explain why the system behaves the way it does. A white-box modelling method developed especially for business and social science is System Dynamics.[70] An introduction to the System Dynamics modelling procedure will be given in section 3.1.2.

Dynamic models, and the actual systems they represent, can be divided into stable and unstable ones.[71] Forrester defines: 'A **stable** system is one that tends to return to its initial conditions after being disturbed. It may overshoot and oscillate (like a simple pendulum that is set in motion), but the disturbances decline and die out. In an **unstable** system that starts at rest, an initial disturbance is amplified, leading to growth or to oscillations whose amplitude increases.'[72] For example, a ball on a hill-top, once pushed, starts rolling downhill with accelerating speed. The behaviour of stable and unstable systems after a disturbance is illustrated in Figure 2.2.

Not all systems fit precisely into the categories 'stable' and 'unstable'. If a disturbance is too big to be processed in the system, other dynamics may emerge (for example, when the pendulum is swung too hard, it breaks). Such a system is called locally stable.[73] Furthermore, in reality amplifying oscillations will eventually hit limits, which prevent them from growing infinitely. Such restricted oscillations are called limit cycles.[74] The heartbeat or respiration, for example, are limit cycles. According to Sterman many models suggest that the economic long wave is a self-perpetuating limit cycle,[75] while the short-term business cycle can be understood as a locally stable oscillation.[76] Yet, in reality the short-term business cycle does not seem to die out. It appears persistent and irregular because the system is continuously bombarded with various influences and shocks.

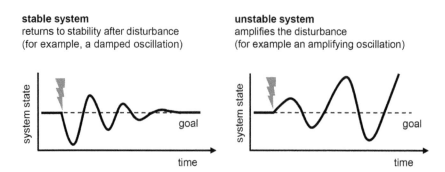

Figure 2.2 Reaction of stable and unstable systems to a disturbance

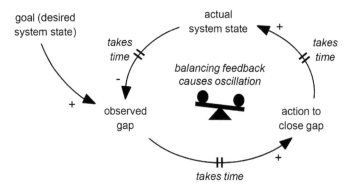

Figure 2.3 System structure causing cyclic behaviour/oscillations

Source: adapted from Sterman 2000, p.114

The system archetype, i.e. the building block of a system, which generates oscillations is a negative feedback loop with delays (see Figure 2.3).[77] A 'negative feedback loop' is the technical term for a circular causal structure that seeks to meet a goal.[78] The system goal is for example a profitability or growth target. The state of the system is compared to this goal, and in case a discrepancy is observed, corrective action is carried out to resolve it. This changes the state of the system. Its discrepancy from the goal is assessed again. In an oscillating system the state of the system will constantly overshoot, then undershoot the goal. This behaviour is caused by significant time delays in the system. They cause corrective action to continue even after the state of the system has reached the goal, so that the system is adjusted too much and over- or undershoots its goal. Delays can be in any part of the negative feedback loop. For example, discrepancy assessment may be delayed by measurement, reporting, and perception processing times. Administrative and decision-making delays can cause corrective action to be late.[79] According to Sterman, the second essential requirement for a system to oscillate, besides a negative feedback structure with delays, is that decision makers fail to account correctly for these delays.[80] Corrective actions which have already been taken but do not yet show effect need to be at least partially ignored or forgotten. Sterman presents evidence that this behaviour, though it may be foolish, is actually common.[81] He offers a hands-on example: someone intends to quickly cook dinner on an electric stove and thus turns the heat fully on. When the pan is hot enough, he turns the heat down. But the reaction will be too late because there is so much heat still in the supply line. The dinner gets burned.[82]

Conclusion

An oscillator system in equilibrium needs an initial disturbance to start swinging. The system structure generating swings is a negative feedback loop with delays. A negative feedback loop describes a system which seeks to achieve a goal. If delays in the system cause corrective actions or perceptions to be late, the system overshoots and undershoots its goal. This happens because people fail to account properly for the various time delays in the system.

A system can be classified as stable or unstable. A stable system, after being disturbed, may exhibit oscillations, but they will die out after some time and the system will return to equilibrium. An unstable system will, when disturbed, start to oscillate or grow and continue to amplify the initial disturbance until limited by other forces.

An oscillating system can be damped by adding a 'controller'. Its mechanisms ensure that corrective actions achieve their goal without over- or undershooting it. They can aim to reduce delays in the system or to more successfully account for them. Table 2.2 summarises the presented findings.

2.2.2 Amplification of oscillations along the supply chain

Supply chains are an illustrative example of oscillating systems. Many products' supply chains are found to be cyclical, for example those of apparels,

Table 2.2 Cycle drivers and mitigation policies for oscillating systems

System oscillations	
Cycle driver	initial disturbance (moves system away from equilibrium position)
	negative feedback loop with delays (goal seeking behaviour)
	failure to account for delays in the negative feedback loop
Mitigation policy	stable systems (damped oscillations) return to equilibrium if left undisturbed
	add a 'controller', i.e. mechanisms which ensures corrective actions do not over- or undershoot their goal (reduce delays, account for delays)

chemicals, and hardware.[83] Typically, the amplitude of fluctuations increases for each stage upstream the supply chain (see Figure 2.4). Lee et al. give the following example:

> Not long ago, logistics executives at Procter & Gamble (P&G) examined the order patterns for one of their best-selling products, Pampers. Its sales at retail stores were fluctuating, but the variabilities were certainly not excessive. However, as they examined the distributors' orders, the executives were surprised by the degree of variability. When they looked at P&G's orders of materials to their suppliers, such as 3M, they discovered that the swings were even greater. [. . .] While the consumers, in this case, the babies, consumed diapers at a steady rate, the demand order variabilities in the supply chain were amplified as they moved up the supply chain.[84]

The phenomenon of order variability amplification upstream the supply chain is called 'bullwhip effect'.[85] In practice it means that a factory may be unable to fulfill orders although at all times able to produce more goods than are being sold to consumers.[86] At other times the factory may produce excessive inventory. Lee et al. state that in many industries the total supply chain, from product manufacturing to arriving at retailers' shelves, hold more than 100 days' supply as inventory.[87] This is extremely costly and motivates firms to find measures to mitigate the bullwhip effect. Metters finds that without the bullwhip effect product profitability could be increased by 10%–30%.[88] Research on the bullwhip effect was initiated by Forrester in 1958 and has received much attention since.[89] A selection of studies will be presented below.

Forrester illustrates in several case studies that understanding the supply chain as an interrelated system is essential to mitigating the bullwhip effect. In order to be successful, managers are required to 'improve their understanding of the interrelationships between separate company functions, and between the company and its markets, its industry, and the national economy'.[90] In his case studies Forrester demonstrates the influence of management actions on the supply chain cyclicality. For example, if companies upstream the supply chain place their orders based directly on retail sales to consumers, the bullwhip effect can be

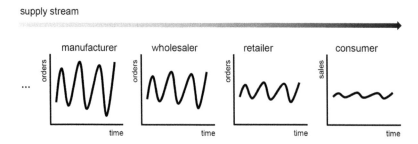

Figure 2.4 Illustration of supply chain oscillations (bullwhip effect)

significantly reduced. This implies information sharing between different stages of the supply chain or a cutback in the number of stages. Inventory adjustment policies are also found to be crucial for stability in the supply chain. It can be improved by adjusting inventories more gradually.[91]

While Forrester assumes the behavioural rules of industrial organisations, Sterman tests them empirically in a series of experiments with the Beer Distribution Game.[92] The game represents a manufacturing industry's supply chain with retailer, wholesaler, distributer, and factory. Managers (players) in all four independent stages have to meet incoming demand whilst minimising their costs of inventory.[93] Sterman's results confirm that a slight change in demand leads to amplified order variability upstream the supply chain. Besides, he observes a phase lag. The order rate tends to peak later moving upstream the supply chain.[94] Further analysis with a system model leads Sterman to the conclusion that the bullwhip effect is caused by misperceptions of feedback. Managers do not, or cannot, account properly for the supply line, i.e. the amount of orders already placed but not yet received.[95]

To mitigate supply chain oscillations Sterman suggests managers change their behaviour. '[T]he key to improved performance lies within the policy individuals use to manage the system and not in the external environment. Even a perfect forecast will not prevent a manager who ignores the supply line from overordering.'[96] Nonetheless, improved forecasting is supposed to be helpful.[97] Furthermore, Sterman derives in model simulations that the oscillations' amplification can be reduced by shortening the acquisition delay, i.e. the time between placing an order and receiving it. Lengthening the supply line adjustment time, i.e. the time it takes to place orders, shows the same damping effect.[98]

Steckel et al. experiment with different, more complex patterns of customer demand in the Beer Distribution Game. They research how changes in order and delivery cycles and the availability of shared point-of-sale (POS) information affect the bullwhip effect.[99] They find that shortening cycle times mitigates oscillations. However, sharing POS information only succeeds to mitigate the bullwhip effect if the demand pattern, i.e. the information about demand, that is being shared, is simply constant except for one step increase. If the demand pattern is S-shaped, which means that sales continually change, information sharing worsens the situation. The POS information distracts upstream members from the more immediately relevant information about received orders by their own customers which causes large costs for inventories or shortages.[100]

Chen et al. create the bullwhip effect in a modelling environment.[101] They test the impact of centralising customer demand information so each stage of the supply chain is completely informed about demand and all use the same forecasting technique. Their result is that centralised customer demand information can significantly reduce but not completely eliminate the increasing variability in demand.[102] Smaros et al. arrive at a similar conclusion.[103]

Lee et al. also argue that information distortions lie at the root of the bullwhip effect. They identify four areas where distorted information appears: demand signal processing, shortage gaming, order batching, and price variations.[104]

- The way demand signals are usually processed in supply chains is one cause of the bullwhip effect.[105] Consumers' end demand is not visible to upstream stages in the supply chain. Each stage uses its own forecasts to manage inventories, based on their past, already distorted information. Problems become more apparent the longer the supply chain, i.e. the product's lead-time, because information distortions increase with the number of intermediaries employed. Lee et al. thus recommend shortening the supply chain. In addition, they propose sales information be shared along the supply chain and forecasts be coordinated.
- Information distortion in the supply chain can also emerge when a retailer expects the manufacturer's supply to fall short.[106] To protect themselves against the shortage, retailers may place strategic orders. In consequence, the order information the manufacturer receives has little to do with actual demand. To prevent this from happening manufacturers could in a shortage situation allocate supply in proportion to the retailer's market share in previous periods. Retailers' unrestricted orders and free returns policy aggravate cyclicality and should thus be limited.
- Order batching amplifies oscillations up the supply chain.[107] It is encouraged by high order costs and a periodic review process, in which a retailer in each review cycle orders the amount for the previous review cycle's demand. The bullwhip effect can thus be alleviated by lowering transaction costs, and by sharing sell-thru and inventory data. Manufacturers could use this to produce to sales not to orders.
- Manufacturers' price variations, for example due to promotions and discounts, encourage forward-buying and diversion.[108] This should be limited to mitigate oscillations along the supply chain. Contracting sales for a future period that both retailer and manufacturer can care for in advance is advised. This is especially beneficial when manufacturers' desired delivery time does not meet retailers' requirements.

Even when operational causes of the bullwhip effect such as order batching, price fluctuations, and demand forecasting are eliminated, Corson and Donohue discover that variability along the supply chain still amplifies.[109] The reason is found to be that participants still underweight the supply line when making decisions.[110] In a second experiment Corson and Donohue show that sharing information about inventory levels along the supply chain does not remove the tendency to underweigh the supply line and thus does not eliminate the bullwhip effect. However, sharing inventory information mitigates oscillations, with upstream members benefiting most from the initiative.[111]

Conclusion

There is consensus in the literature that oscillations along the supply chain are created within the system by management behaviour and not by external influences. The bullwhip effect, i.e. the amplification of oscillations upstream the supply chain, is caused by managers' behaviour. Sterman and others argue that managers do not properly account for the supply line when placing orders. That may be due to psychological pitfalls or insufficient understanding of the system. Or the cause is distorted demand information, which many authors hold responsible.

Information distortion problems occur in different forms: the end-demand is not clearly visible to members upstream the supply chain. Each member produces its own forecast based on its limited information. The situation becomes worse the more companies are involved in the supply chain, or the longer cycle times or lead times are, respectively. Information can also actively be distorted by discount and promotion pricing, by protective action against other supply chain members' failures, or by unrestricted order sizes. Also, order batching blurs the actual demand information. It is encouraged by high order costs or only periodically conducted inventory reviews.

Table 2.3 Cycle drivers and mitigation policies for oscillation in supply chains

Supply chain oscillations	
Cycle driver	insufficient understanding of the system misperceptions of supply line demand information distortions along the supply chain • no visibility of end demand • multiple forecasts • length of the supply chain, length of cycle time/ lead-time/ acquisition delay • price variations (discount, promotion) • protective action against other supply chain members' inventory shortage (shortage gaming) • unrestricted orders, free return policy • order batching (likely when order cost high or periodic review process)
Mitigation policy	improve understanding of the system take supply line into account when ordering more gradual inventory adjustment (longer supply line adjustment time) information sharing among supply chain members prevent demand information distortions along the supply chain • high end-demand visibility (though if volatile it might be distracting for direct demand) • coordinated forecasting (more accurate forecasting) • shorten supply chain, cycle time/ lead-time/ acquisition delay • sales contracts (price stability and secured delivery timing) • avoid protective action (past orders as orientation) • implement order limits • produce to sales not to orders • lower transaction costs

To mitigate oscillations along the supply chain researchers suggest to improve managers' understanding of the system in order to change their behaviour. The bullwhip effect can be lessened by taking the supply line fully into account when placing orders. Also, it is regarded as helpful to improve information sharing among supply chain members. While most researchers favour this increased visibility of end-demand, Steckel et al. warn that it might be counterproductive because the end-demand information may distract companies from their direct demand, especially when the demand pattern is volatile.

More accurate forecasts as a result of information sharing are also named as oscillation damping action. Furthermore, shortening the supply chain or reducing lead times is often suggested. However, the time to actually place orders is advised to be lengthened so that inventories are adjusted more gradually.

Avoiding active information distortion mitigates supply chain oscillations. Sales contracts can generate more price stability and security about delivery timings. Protective action can be prevented by implementing order limits and comparing current to past orders for orientation. Order batching can be reduced by lower transaction costs and by a produce-to-sales policy. Table 2.3 summarises the potential cycle drivers and mitigation measures mentioned above.

2.3 Existing airline profit cycle research

2.3.1 Systemic analyses of the airline profit cycle

Only few studies so far focus particularly on cycles in the airline industry; and even fewer concentrate precisely on the airline profit cycle (see Table 2.4). Insights about the airline industry cycles' causes and drivers were first published by aviation business consultants:

- Lyneis and colleagues (Lyneis/Glucksmann 1989,[112] Lyneis 1998,[113] 1999,[114] 2000[115]); and
- Skinner and colleagues (Skinner/Stock 1998,[116] Skinner et al. 1999[117]).

The phenomenon was then further explored in three master's theses by

- Liehr at the University of Mannheim, Germany (Liehr et al. 2001[118]);
- Jiang at Massachusetts Institute of Technology, USA (Jiang/Hansman 2004,[119] Jiang/Hansman 2006[120]); and
- Segers at Cranfield University, UK (Segers 2005[121]).

In recent years, the airline profit cycle was explored as a case study in two PhD theses:

- Sgouridis at Massachusetts Institute of Technology, USA (Sgouridis et al. 2007[122], Sgouridis et al. 2008[123]); and
- Pierson at Massachusetts Institute of Technology, USA (Pierson 2009[124], Pierson 2011[125], Pierson/Sterman 2013[126]).

Table 2.4 In-depth studies of the airline profit cycle (literature review)

In-depth research on the airline industry cycle

Primary author	Type of research	Citation	Type of publication	Applied methodology
Lyneis	Consulting project: forecasting aircraft orders	Lyneis/ Gluckmann 1989	book chapter	System Dynamics • model described as being very detailed: consists of different aircraft manufacturers, domestic and international travel divided into major world regions, and airlines by regions
		Lyneis 1998 Lyneis 1999 Lyneis 2000	conference paper journal article journal article	• model equations and details not given • calibrated for worldwide airline industry, starting 1970
Skinner	Consulting project: competitive cycle management strategies for an airline	Skinner/Stock 1998	magazine article	System Dynamics (presumably because causal loop diagram given)
		Skinner et al. 1999	book chapter	System Dynamics • model only roughly outlined • market or airlines for which calibrated not mentioned
Liehr	Master thesis (University of Mannheim)	Liehr et al. 2001	journal article	System Dynamics • small model (one feedback loop) • calibrated for Lufthansa, starting 1970

(continued)

Table 2.4 Continued

In-depth research on the airline industry cycle

Primary author	Type of research	Citation	Type of publication	Applied methodology
Jiang	Master thesis (Massachusetts Institute of Technology)	Jiang/Hansman 2004 Jiang/Hansman 2006	thesis, not officially published conference paper	Control theory • undamped 2nd order system • calibrated for US and for worldwide air traffic
Segers	Master thesis (Cranfield University)	Segers 2005	thesis, not officially published	System Dynamics • unvalidated model • calibrated for US airlines, starting 1975
Sgouridis	PhD thesis (Massachusetts Institute of Technology): airline profit cycle as application example	Sgouridis 2007 Sgouridis et al. 2008	thesis, not officially published working paper not officially published	System Dynamics • model includes aircraft manufacturers • calibrated for US airline industry, starting 1984
Pierson	PhD thesis (Massachusetts Institute of Technology): airline profit cycle is one of three case studies	Pierson 2009 Pierson 2011 Pierson/ Sterman 2013	conference paper thesis, not officially published journal article	System Dynamics • model for airline industry only • calibrated for US airline industry, starting 1977

These studies vary widely concerning the degree of detail employed in the analyses and they examine different aspects of the problem. All authors use a system approach whereby all except one use System Dynamics as their method (Jiang/Hansman use control theory). A brief introduction to System Dynamics will be given in section 3.1. In the following sections, the existing systemic analyses of the airline profit cycle are summarised. Because of its introductory character Skinner et al.'s study is presented first, thereafter the remaining studies are presented in chronological order.

Skinner (Skinner and Stock 1998; Skinner et al. 1999)

Skinner and Stock regard the airline industry's cyclic profitability as a structural, endogenously generated problem. Its source is a mismatch between supply and demand which is caused by the feedback structure illustrated in Figure 2.5.[127] In order to achieve growth, airlines invest in new fleet capacity as soon as they perceive their profitability as sustained (perception delay). When the aircraft production is completed (delay for production), aircraft are delivered and enlarge the airlines' fleet capacity. Cyclicality arises as a consequence of the two delays. The capacity increase alters the supply demand ratio. Airlines lower prices to stimulate demand and fill the added capacity. As a result profitability suffers. Consequently, after the perception delay, capacity investments are reduced. Demand and supply become more and more balanced so prices can be raised. This makes airlines increasingly profitable, and the cycle continues.

Skinner and Stock suggest airlines make 'opportunistic moves' to successfully manage the profit cycle.[128] To outplay their competitors airlines need flexible capacity. Skinner and Stock advise them to keep 10% of their fleet flexible because they find that demand deviates within +/-5% or less from carriers' medium-term demand forecasts. In downturns, early aircraft retirements and lease returns are an option. All reasonable aircraft maintenance could be conducted. Additionally, orders should be placed and strategic acquisitions

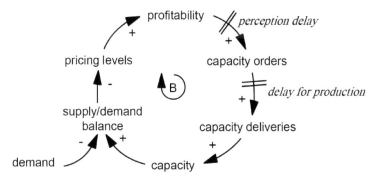

Figure 2.5 Airline industry dynamics according to Skinner/Stock

Source: adapted from Skinner/Stock 1998

conducted to take advantage of the low prices and to have capacity available in the upcycle. In an upturn, retirements should be deferred and flexible capacity should be added. Skinner and Stock suggest short-term (six months) wet-leases[129] but acknowledge that these are mostly not supported by labour groups. Ideally, in upturns capacity should be built up slowly, in small units over a longer ramp-up time. However, this entails the danger of losing market shares. In expectance of another downturn lease rights could be sold. Besides, an airline can take advantage of the upcycle by selling undesired route authorities and aircraft that do not fit well into the fleet. Throughout the cycle Skinner and Stock emphasise to aim for reductions in planning and capacity lead times. They also state the need for a proactive internal and external communication plan to gain support from investors, labour groups, and employees, which is crucial for the realisation of cycle management strategies. From an industry perspective Skinner and Stock assume that information sharing and collaborative behaviour, for example within airline alliances, would improve the unstable profitability situation and reduce the severity of downturns.[130]

None of the suggested opportunistic moves have been tested by Skinner and Stock in model simulations or real-life experiments. However, the existence of the two delays is corroborated empirically. Looking at worldwide airline profitability, aircraft orders, and deliveries from 1978 to 1997 Skinner and Stock find that orders lag one to two years behind profitability (perception delay) and that the time between aircraft orders and delivery is approximately two years (delay for production).[131]

In a later study Skinner et al. test the suggested strategies' success by simulating them with a System Dynamics model of the airline industry.[132] They do not mention for which market or airlines the model is calibrated, or how exactly it is constructed. Skinner et al. find that it is possible for airlines to improve their financial performance across the cycle:

> One strategy, [. . .] called the 'Retirement Adjuster', nearly doubled cumulative return on invested capital over our simulated period. By placing large long-term steady orders, keeping baseline retirements high, and ignoring industry forecasts, with our 'Retirement Adjuster' strategy our airline was able to maximize the peaks of the cycle, while minimizing the damage of the troughs.[133]

A strategy that dampens the cycle, though less effectively than the 'Retirement Adjuster', is the 'Order Adjuster' strategy. Aircraft orders are placed frequently to react short term to market conditions while retirements are steady, resulting in high-capacity growth.

As reasons for the airline profit cycle Skinner et al. endorse Skinner and Stock's explanation. The cycle is caused by a mismatch between supply and demand. Its structural source is the manufacturing lead time. A perception delay is not explicitly mentioned. In addition, Skinner et al. name the airline industry's high fixed costs as structural prerequisite for the cycle. Their model simulations reveal that the airline profit cycle is structurally driven and will not disappear on its own.[134] This conclusion is based on a scenario where demand grows steadily in 20 future years (exogenous input are stable), the result being that profits remain cyclic.[135]

Skinner and colleagues give advice on how an individual airline can improve its financial situation. They do not give recommendations for the industry as a whole. Altogether, their work leaves room for further research. Only a small part of the airline industry's complex feedback structure is captured in the Skinner/Stock model. For example, costs as an essential determinant of profit are not included. The apparently more elaborate Skinner et al. model is unfortunately not publicly available to form an opinion about its explanatory power.

Lyneis (Lyneis and Glucksman 1989; Lyneis 1998, 1999, 2000)

In their consulting work between 1987 and 1992 Lyneis and colleagues examined the global jet aircraft industry which is naturally interlinked with the airline industry and its financial performance.[136] Following their aim to understand and forecast the cyclicality in aircraft orders, they implicitly address the airline profit cycle. They find that internal dynamics of the airline industry are more important than external factors.[137] The industry produces capacity overexpansions in boom times which result in later busts.

Lyneis's results are based on System Dynamics model simulations. The constructed model is described as detailed and extensive; model equations are not given due to the model's proprietary nature. Demand is disaggregated into domestic and international travel, and into major world regions. Airlines are also disaggregated by region. All prime aircraft manufacturers are represented. The model calibration starts in 1970.

According to Lyneis et al. the basic model structure which causes the airline industry's cyclicality consists of one balancing and three reinforcing feedback loops (see Figure 2.6).[138] A balancing feedback is a process where corrective actions are balanced to achieve a goal; a reinforcing feedback reinforces an initial action further and further (for more information see the introduction to System Dynamics in section 3.1). Supposing that demand increases, two effects reinforce this growth. First, greater load factors reduce short-term unit costs and improve profit margins. While maintaining the same level of profitability, fares can be reduced to further stimulate demand growth. In contrast, in basic economic theory and in Skinner's model a demand increase would cause fares to be increased. The relationship that Lyneis proposes implies that there is a strong competitive pressure to reduce fares. However, if demand decreased, fares in Lyneis's model would be raised instead of lowered to stimulate demand. Reason is that fares would need to compensate the unit cost increase, which is a consequence of the industry's high fixed cost share. Second, an 'experience effect' drives demand growth, which means that 'if more people fly, the more they get used to flying, and so they fly more (or are reluctant to reduce flying in a recession)'.[139] Meanwhile the balancing feedback loop works as follows. Airlines forecast future travel demand and derive future capacity needs. If demand is expected to grow, airlines need additional aircraft and place orders. Given the manufacturing lead time airlines now enjoy years of high load factors and profitability. When the ordered aircraft enter the fleet, industry dynamics start to reverse direction. The fixed cost base rises, and as a result operating margins sink and fares need to be increased. This raise reduces demand growth, which may even become negative. Airlines then realise that they ordered too many aircraft, that revenues did not increase as fast as costs, and so they refrain from ordering aircraft. After some time, initiated by due aircraft retirements or demand growth, unit costs start to fall again and a new cycle starts. When aircraft are ordered, the third reinforcing feedback takes effect. Given that aircraft manufacturers' production capacities are limited and not short-term adaptable, manufacturing lead times increase. In consequence airlines order further ahead. The additional orders cause manufacturing lead times to rise even further, which aggravates the cycle.

Model experiments reveal that three features of the system aggravate the aircraft order cycle in addition to the reinforcing feedbacks described above.[140] First, the cycle is amplified by significant delays around the major balancing loop. Second, airlines in total fail to account for the number of aircraft orders in the supply chain. And third, airlines' forecasting methods, such as trend extrapolation, and airlines' competitive policies, e.g. gaining market shares, amplify the order cycle. External factors, such as GDP, population, fuel prices, and interest rates, can also influence the cycle but are found to be less important than the industry's internal dynamics.[141] To reduce an airline's or aircraft manufacturer's risks in the cyclic environment Lyneis and colleagues suggest improving forecasting capabilities to determine more appropriate buffers and contingencies for forecast inaccuracies.[142]

The fit between Lyneis's model simulations and historical data is extraordinary. Figure 2.7 depicts airlines' aggregate aircraft orders which are the

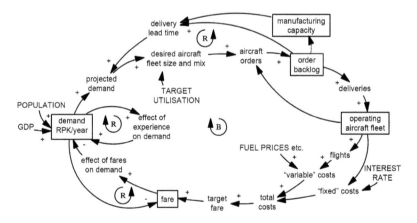

Figure 2.6 Basic dynamics generating the aircraft order cycle according to Lyneis
(1999, p. 64, arrow polarities added)

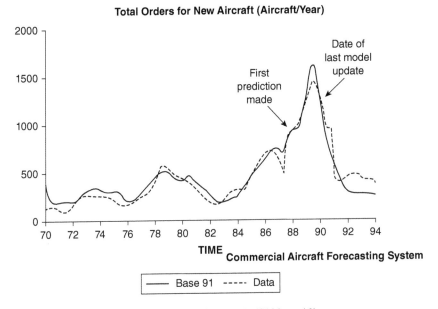

Figure 2.7 Model fit for aircraft orders by Lyneis (2000, p. 13)

focus of Lyneis's research. Unfortunately, due to the model's proprietary nature a deeper discussion of the industry mechanisms employed is not possible. Suggestions for mitigating the airline profit cycle are not explicitly given since the studies' focus is on forecasting aircraft orders and not on improving the airline industry's financial situation.

Liehr et al. 2001

According to Liehr et al. the cyclical behaviour in the airline industry is mostly endogenously generated.[143] Their findings are based on a 'structurally parsimonious'[144] System Dynamics model, built to advise Lufthansa's cycle management strategies. The model contains three modules: one for Lufthansa; the second representing the rest of the market; and the third to capture how Lufthansa and the market interact. The cycle generating structure is one balancing feedback loop with two delays (see Figure 2.8).[145] With growing passenger demand, the surplus of seats offered compared to demand becomes smaller. After a perception delay airlines realise the industry's capacity surplus. If there is still less seat capacity in the market then desired, aircraft are ordered. After another delay, the manufacturing lead time, the ordered aircraft join the airline's fleet and enlarge the seat capacity offered. At the end of their service lifetime aircraft are retired from the fleet.

Model simulations reveal that demand developments do not influence the existence of the cycle.[146] Hence, Liehr et al. conclude that the decision rules within the industry are the root of the system's cyclic behaviour. External factors can, however, alter the cycle's amplitude and period.[147]

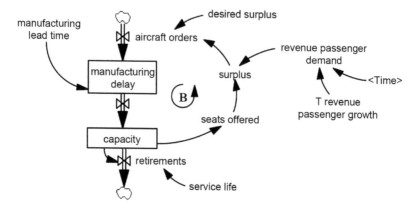

Figure 2.8 Airline profit cycle generating structure by Liehr et al. (2001, p. 315)

The original model does not include feedbacks such as the influence of price on demand, the influence of load factors on unit costs, or the influence of costs on price. An expanded version of the original model does include a basic price-setting mechanism and a price-demand function. It reveals that 'price management cannot dampen the long-term waves in the market. Different price strategies only affect the amplitude and period of the cycles but not their existence.'[148]

To stabilise the airline profitability's cyclic development, Liehr et al. suggest several policies and leverage points.[149] Damping can potentially be achieved by altering the aircraft order policy ('aircraft ordering'), by reorganising the seat capacity offered ('network planning'), and by managing aircraft capacity flexibly ('flexibility'). Aircraft ordering should be counter-cyclical to benefit from lower aircraft prices and shorter lead times. It may, however, be difficult to finance investments in downturns. Creating transparency about aircraft orders within alliances could be helpful and even lead to coordinated action. Network planning can stabilise the cycle in the short term. If for example an unforeseen demand shock occurs, overcapacities can be shifted to other regions with higher demand. The third suggestion, a flexible aircraft fleet, can be realised by aircraft leasing or late retirement. The older aircraft in the fleet can quickly be retired in downturns. However, Liehr at al. advise this fast relief only in combination with counter-cyclic ordering to ensure that sufficient aircraft capacity will be available in upswings. Leasing aircraft in and selling lease rights in upswings may also be an option to manage capacity flexibly. This option is shown to successfully dampen the demand supply balance in a model simulation. Its effect on profits is not shown, neither are the necessary lease contract conditions, i.e. lease periods and costs.

Liehr et al.'s model simulation exhibits a good fit to the actual historical development (see Figure 2.9). Since they hold the aircraft order cycle responsible for the airline profit cycle, not profits but orders are shown. However,

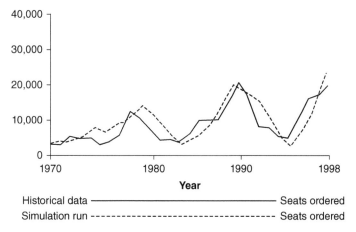

Figure 2.9 Model fit for aircraft orders by Liehr et al. (2001, p. 319)

focusing on the capacity cycle they neglect other potentially cycle-driving feedbacks in the system. For example, the influence of price on demand, or the impact of the financial results on cost-cutting efforts are not included. Besides, for the model simulation in Figure 2.9 prices are completely exogenous and do not result from interaction in the market.

Jiang and Hansman (2004, 2006)

Jiang and Hansman find that the fundamental periods of the airline profitability cycle in the world and the US industry are endogenous.[150] They discover a cycle length of 11.3 years for the US airline industry after deregulation and 10.5 years for the world industry.[151]

Drawing from control theory Jiang and Hansman model the airline industry profitability as an undamped second order system. They show that neither deregulation nor the 9/11 crisis significantly influenced the industry's cycle periods. However, both events are found to have strong effects on the cycle's amplitude.[152]

Jiang and Hansman identify the combined effect of two delays in the system as drivers of the cycle: the lag in capacity response and the lag in cost adjustment.[153] The capacity response lag consists primarily of the decision time in placing orders, the order processing time and the manufacturing lead time.[154] The cost adjustment lag includes for example labour contract negotiation times.[155] Using parametric models both time delays are first tested separately then jointly for their explanatory power for profit oscillations. The coupled model, which jointly simulates capacity and cost effects, explains the US airline industry dynamics better than each individual model. Figure 2.10 shows the fit between simulated and historical data series.

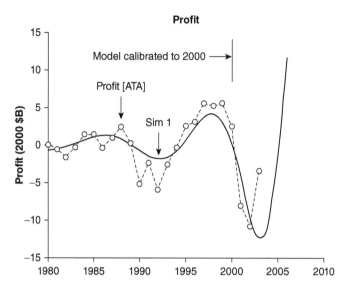

Figure 2.10 Model fit for profit by Jiang/Hansman (2006, p. 15)

The separate analysis of the capacity response lag suggests that a delay reduction would mitigate the cycle.[156] However, Jiang and Hansman emphasise that the empirical work only yields some insights into causalities and does not address the industry's entire complexity.[157] This is left for further research.

Segers (2005)

According to Segers the airline profit cycle is the result of industry internal behavioural mechanisms and not caused by external factors, such as demand shocks or fuel price fluctuations.[158] His findings are based on a System Dynamics model which is calibrated for the US airline industry starting 1975.[159]

The impacts of demand shocks, fuel price fluctuations, GDP fluctuations, and aircraft manufacturing lead time are tested in model simulations. Resulting airline profits are still cyclical, though the shape of the cycle changes significantly. Segers concludes that external factors do not lie at the root of the airline profit cycle but that the industry's internal mechanisms cause it.[160]

In model experiments the airline industry's internal mechanisms are examined and three cycle mitigating measures are identified. First, if productivity was not allowed to decrease after consecutive profitable years, profitability would still be cyclic but oscillate around values significantly above break even.[161] Second, the profit situation could be improved via yield control if airlines would no longer react to serious overcapacities by lowering fares.[162] Third, Segers assumes, but has not tested, that it would be beneficial to base aircraft order on demand forecasts, rather than on market shares targets, to avoid overcapacities.[163]

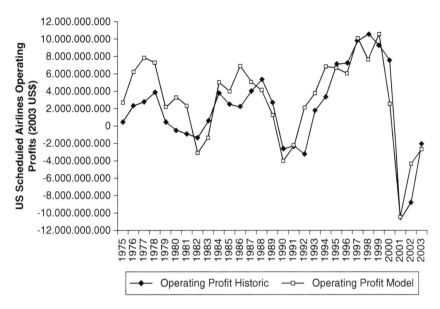

Figure 2.11 Model fit for operating profit by Segers (2005, p. 167)

Segers emphasises that his model is not yet satisfactorily validated and robust.[164] However, the model includes many feedbacks of the airline industry. Not included are, for example, the opportunity to lease instead of buy aircraft, a mechanism to actively manage aircraft retirements, and an influence of costs on price. Furthermore, the price- setting mechanism that brings demand and supply together, and potentially creates much of the industry's dynamic behaviour, is largely exogenous. As a result Figure 2.11 shows that Segers' model simulation fits historic operating profits in the US airline industry well.[165]

Sgouridis (2007, et al. 2008)

Sgouridis et al. find that in a competitive airline industry 'internal dynamics amplify external signals generating the status quo of a notoriously cyclical industry'.[166] Main external influences are the volatile fuel prices and the economic cycle.[167] Sgouridis' insights are based on System Dynamics model experiments. The model incorporates interactions between aircraft manufacturers, airlines, and passengers, and is calibrated for the US airline industry starting in 1984.[168]

The primary reason for the airline profit cycle is the repeated mismatch between capacity supply and demand.[169] In the past, airlines' race for market share led to capacity increases and price reductions to fill the additional capacity. The price-induced demand rise created the illusion that additional capacity was needed. Price wars and substantial losses were the consequence.

The situation was exacerbated by three factors determining the retention of capacity in the industry: (1) high medium-term fixed costs; (2) airlines' ability to generate revenues with elaborate price setting by revenue management systems; and (3) high market exit barriers such as subsidies, mergers, and bankruptcy protections.

Alternative strategies to mitigate the effects of the profit cycle are investigated in model experiments. Their effect is evaluated using a value function for each stakeholder.[170] Sgouridis et al. define that airlines look for high economic return, persistent stability of return and short downturn time, i.e. average time with negative returns. The strategic alternatives suggested require none or very limited political intervention or collaboration among actors. Between the evaluated strategic alternatives, creating more transparency in the supply chain is most beneficial from the airlines' point of view.[171] Only one pareto efficient solution for all stakeholders has proven to be both robust and feasible. The two large aircraft manufacturers, Airbus and Boeing, need to respond slowly rather than quickly to orders received from airlines, which means that Boeing is required to adopt the strategy that Airbus has pursued in the last decades.[172]

Sgouridis' model comprises many feedbacks within the airline industry, the aircraft manufacturing industry, and between the two. His model simulation reproduces historic profit developments less well than previous approaches (see Figure 2.12) which may be accredited to the model's higher complexity. However, the price determination mechanism employed in the model is mainly exogenously driven. The only endogenous influence on price is unit costs.[173] Endogenous feedback from, for example, profitability pressure or load factor expectations is not implemented. Neglecting these potentially cycle-driving dynamics limits the explanatory power of the model.

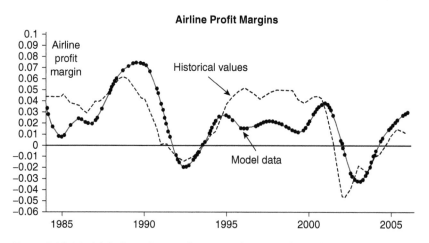

Figure 2.12 Model fit for airline profit margins by Sgouridis et al. (2008, p. 12)

Pierson (2009, 2011); Pierson and Sterman (2013)

Pierson and Sterman hold the airline industry's internal mechanisms responsible for the profit cycle. In his 2011 thesis Pierson concludes that 'misperception of the delay in adjusting capacity is central to the genesis of profit cycles exhibited by the airline industry'.[174] However, Pierson (2011) and Pierson and Sterman (2013) focus on airlines' price determination policies. In particular, the airlines' 'yield management' is found to have more influence on profit oscillations than changes in the capacity part of the model.[175] By yield management (also called revenue management) Pierson and Sterman mean the short-term price reaction to changes in the supply demand balance (load factor). Airlines lower prices when they perceive their planes as too empty and they raise prices when planes are nearly full. Specifically, the authors find that the elimination of yield management from the price-setting process would 'worsen every measure of system stability'.[176] Meanwhile, doubling the influence of yield management in price setting 'increases system stability substantially'.[177] It is however to note that though yield management creates damping it also increases the magnitude of profit change after a demand shock.[178] In consequence some airlines may go bankrupt. The US airlines' current degree of yield management usage is found to be undesirable because bankruptcy risk is high and stability given to the system is low.[179]

Pierson's and Sterman's findings are based on a System Dynamics model of the US airline industry since 1977. To calibrate the model, parameters are simultaneously estimated by minimising the statistical error between historic and simulated data series.[180] Model simulations reproduce historic profit developments well, they only fail to generate last profit peaks' height (see Figure 2.13).

Pierson and Sterman's model incorporates the majority of the airline industry's complex feedback structure. Among documented airline profit cycle models

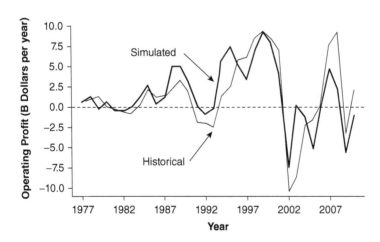

Figure 2.13 Model fit for operating profit by Pierson/Sterman (2013, p. 142)

it is, together with Sgouridis model (see above), the most elaborate one so far. An essential feedback which is missing is the influence of an airline's perfor-mance on their load factor targets. These are inserted externally.[181] Yet, load factor targets are likely a result of the competitive dynamics in the industry that force airlines to increase efficiency. Yield management, that Pierson and Sterman emphasise as important for stability, is modelled as price reaction on load factor compared to the load factor's target. The yield management mecha-nism is thus not fully endogenous which constrains the explanatory value of results. Furthermore, Pierson and Sterman assume aircraft orders depend only on demand forecasts.[182] However, the airlines' financial situation also has an influence on ordering. As show in the introductory section 1.2, empirically, aircraft orders follow the airline profit cycle.

Conclusion

The systemic analyses of the airline profit cycle conducted so far all arrive at the conclusion that the cycle is endogenously created within the airline indus-try. External factors, such as GDP fluctuations or fuel price developments, are found to only impact the profit cycle's shape.

In line with the system literature (see section 2.2) most studies see the origin of the profit cycle in the aircraft capacity adjustment process. The airlines' prof-itability dependent and thus cyclic aircraft ordering behaviour is highlighted. Besides, the airlines' process to determine their desired capacity level (with fore-casting and market share targets) is found to be driving cyclicality. Delays in the capacity process, e.g. the manufacturing lead time or the time to perceive profitability as sustained and place orders, are identified as cycle causes. Another relevant delay in the system concerns cost adjustments, e.g. the duration of labour negotiations.

Furthermore, characteristics of the airline industry are named to be cycle drivers: the industry's high fixed costs, high barriers to exit, and its capacity ser-vice lifetime which well exceeds the time horizon for reliable demand forecasts.

Some studies see price mechanisms as a driver of profit cyclicality. According to Lyneis price amplifies demand changes and Sgouridis finds that revenue management systems drive the cycle because their demand stimulation cre-ates the illusion of overcapacities. In contrast, Pierson and Sterman stress the importance of revenue management systems as profit cycle damper. The impact of price mechanisms on the airline profit cycle remains thus uncertain. Even more so because all models use price determination mechanisms which are at least partly driven by external data series that pre-dictate price changes.[183] Price needs to be modelled completely endogenously not to limit an airline industry model's explanatory power.

The suggested measures to mitigate the airline profit cycle depend on the origins identified. Many studies advise to use a profit-independent aircraft ordering policy: either counter-cyclical or steady ordering. Meanwhile, aircraft retirements should be either managed counter-cyclically or kept steady as well. Sgouridis shifts the responsibility for smoother aircraft orders from airlines to the manufacturers and advises them to adjust their production only slowly. To improve the airlines' desired capacity levels in a cycle damping way, information sharing along the supply chain, coordinated action within alliances, and improved forecasting are recommended. A general reduction of delay times, especially concerning capacity adjustments, is often suggested.

Those studies that find industry characteristics such as high fixed costs drive the cycle suggest to avoid them by leasing aircraft instead of buying aircraft. However, this option has so far only been discussed and has not yet been tested in model experiments.[184]

To dampen the cycle, Sgouridis implies to refrain from lowering fares when faced with excess capacity, i.e. to employ less revenue management. On the contrary, to stabilise the industry Pierson and Sterman advise to focus completely on revenue management systems in the price-setting process.

Table 2.5 summarises the potential cycle driver and mitigation measures identified in airline profit cycle research as presented above.

The airline profit cycle model which will be introduced in Chapter 3 will build on the studies outlined above. Shortcomings of existing models will be overcome to gain more reliable insights about the airline profit cycle's causes and suitable mitigation policies. Which model formulations are chosen and how they relate to previous work will be explained during the model-building process in Chapter 3.

Table 2.5 Cycle drivers and mitigation policies in systemic airline profit cycle analyses

Systemic airline profit cycle analyses	
Cycle driver	industry behaviour causes the cycle, external factors affect its shape
	• simulation: 20 years steady demand growth → profits still cyclic
	aircraft capacity adjustment:
	• cyclic ordering (order when profitable)
	• determination of desired capacity: market share targets and forecasting (trend extrapolation, forecasting horizon shorter than manufacturing lead time)
	• manufacturing lead time (longer than demand forecasting horizon)
	• order processing time, incl. profitability perception delays
	• misperception of delays in capacity adjustment
	labour cost adjustment: delays due to contract negotiations
	industry characteristics:
	• high fixed costs
	• high barriers to exit (subsidies, mergers, bankruptcy protection)

(continued)

Table 2.5 Continued

Systemic airline profit cycle analyses

| | external influences:
• economic development, GDP fluctuations
• demand changes amplified by experience effect
• deregulation
• demand shocks, e.g. 9/11
• fuel price fluctuations
price determination process: extensive vs. little use of revenue
   management systems (i.e. short-term demand stimulation by price) |
| Mitigation
policy | profit independent aircraft order policy:
• counter-cyclical ordering
• steady ordering (based on demand forecast not market share target)
slower production adjustment for aircraft manufacturers

aircraft retirement policy:
• counter-cyclical
• steady
• prevent productivity decrease after consecutive profitable years

improve determination of desired capacity:
• increase transparency in the aircraft supply chain
• coordinate action (aircraft ordering) in strategic alliances
• improve forecasting (→ appropriate buffers for forecast inaccuracy)

reduce processing times ('delays'), especially in capacity adjustment
lease aircraft: avoid high fixed costs and long aircraft service lifetime
price determination:
extensive vs. little use of revenue management systems (do/do not lower
   prices when facing excess capacity) |

2.3.2 Aviation management literature on the airline profit cycle

Since the airline profit cycle is highly relevant for airline management decisions, investment issues, and employment (see Chapter 1), it may be expected that the phenomenon enjoys much attention in aviation research. Yet, the number of studies concerned with the airline profit cycle is surprisingly limited in the aviation management literature.

A search in several popular airline business publications (academic journals and magazines) for the terms 'profit cycle', 'profitability cycle', or 'boom and bust' results in altogether four articles in the last 20 years. A search for aviation/airline management/economics books addressing the airline profit cycle is similarly unsuccessful, revealing only one airline management book specifically on the issue.[185] Several other authors merely describe the airline profit cycle as part of their introduction without giving a deeper analysis of causes and implications. In contrast, in industry briefings by the International Air Transport Association (IATA) the airline profit cycle enjoys much attention, with nine publications being available on the website. This search for airline profit cycle literature is by no means complete. There may be more publications outside the aviation management literature. (For example, only one of the airline profit cycle studies presented in the previous section was published in an aviation management publication.) However, the conducted search among popular

Table 2.6 Airline management literature on the airline profit cycle

Publication		Search result
Academic journal[186]	Journal of Air Transport Management (1994–2014)	3
	Journal of Air Transportation (2001–2007)	0
	Journal of Transport Economics and Policy (1967–2010)	0
	Transportation Research Part A: Policy and Practice (1979–1991, 1992–2014)	0
	Transportation Research Part B: Methodological (1979–2014)	0
	Transportation Research Part D: Transport and Environment (1996–2014)	0
	Transportation Research Part E: Logistics and Transportation (1997–2014)	0
	Transportation Science (1967–2013)	0
Magazine[187]	Airline Business (2002–2013)	1
Books[188]	Air Transport in the 21st Century: Key Strategic Developments[189]	1 full article
	Airline Finance[190]	in intro
	An Introduction to Airline Economics[191]	0
	Aviation Systems: Mgt. of the Integrated Aviation Value Chain[192]	in intro
	Business and Corporate Aviation Management[193]	0
	Designing and Executing Strategy in Aviation Management[194]	0
	Flying Off Course: Airline Economics and Marketing[195]	Subchapter
	Foundations of Airline Finance: Methodology and Practice[196]	in intro, and in risk chapter
	Management in the Airline Industry[197]	in intro
	Risk Management and Corporate Sustainability in Aviation[198]	0
	Stormy Skies: Airlines in Crisis[199]	in intro
	Straight and Level: Practical Airline Economics[200]	in intro
	Strategic Management in the Aviation Industry[201]	chapter part
	The Global Airline Industry[202]	in intro
	Why Can't We Make Money in Aviation?[203]	whole book
Industry briefings	International Air Transport Association (IATA): publications on industry profitability[204]	9

aviation management publications indicates that while the issue is pressing for practitioners, suggestions from the research side are still rather scarce. Table 2.6 provides an overview of the search results.

In this section insights about the airline profit cycle from the listed aviation management publications as well as additional aviation management studies derived in a wider search will be presented. The only book on the subject will be a starting point. Its author Pilarski answers the title question, 'Why can't we make money in aviation?' as an industry practitioner in an anecdotal non-scientific way.[205] According to him airlines' cyclic profitability is due to exogenous reasons, endogenous factors, and overregulation.

Exogenous reasons are firstly the airlines' easy access to capital, even in economic downturns,[206] and secondly the industry's popularity which attracts a disproportionate quantity of 'bad managers'.[207] Pilarski sees several management mistakes, i.e. endogenous factors, which cause the profit cycle. The prime mistake, he claims, is poor yield management. Pilarski does not object to yield management's essential idea to charge customers based on their ability and willingness to pay. Yet, he objects to 'the capricious, random, unpredictable, confrontational type of yield management.'[208] The quantity of different fares and their complex conditions have increased to a degree that leaves customers confused and even angry or frustrated. As a result they refrain from flying or hunt lowest fares.[209] Airlines have not yet realised, Pilarski argues, that business travellers are not willing to pay the extremely high fares airlines assume they would.[210] Lastly, Pilarski makes regulatory issues responsible for the airlines' poor profitability. The industry is heavily taxed.[211] Moreover, he argues that the US chapter 11 bankruptcy protection, which allows bankrupt airlines to continue operations and restructure, retains bad managers in the industry and depresses prices.[212]

The argument that public airline ownership is bad for the industry's financial position is objected to by Pilarski because 'public ownership does not exist today as a major force among the world's airlines but the weak financial profile of the industry is still with us'.[213] Neither does he support the argument that labour unions are to blame for their airline's weak financial performance, stating that salaries have been much higher at successful Southwest Airlines than at twice-bankrupt United Airlines.[214] However, Pilarski recognises that the timing of labour contract negotiations and their durations may be unfortunate with regard to the economic cycle.[215] Furthermore, he does not believe that the airline industry would benefit from capacity constraints[216] or consolidation. Since planes are not empty but record full, he does not see need for capacity reductions.[217] Also, though in theory a bigger company benefits from economies of scale and scope, in reality Pilarki finds there are diseconomies hindering efficiencies.

Pilarski's suggestions to improve airline industry profits remain rather vague:

> Airlines have to remember that they are in the service business. [. . .] A positive thing to do would be to eliminate the extreme versions of yield management which only aggravate customers. Another positive would be

to adjust the whole pricing system that many airlines use today. Improving labor relations would constitute another positive. A positive that might seem counter intuitive would be to accept the fact that if the airline industry is sexy it may be underperforming financially [due to bad management].[218]

Concretely, Pilarski advises airlines to minimise short-term profits because their maximisation leads to long-term consumer resentment.[219]

In contrast to Pilarski, the IATA postulates consolidation in the airline industry. The IATA sees the explanation of airlines' profitability fluctuations mainly in the industry's structure, more than in supply chain issues.[220] Competition among airlines is described as intense.[221] Airlines' price policies, especially their yield management systems, are assumed to contribute to the industry's poor financial performance because they focus more on generating volume than margins.[222] The commoditisation of the airline product, for which price is a major differentiation feature, the product's non-storable nature, and the very low marginal cost of flying an additional passenger pressure prices below full costs and create a difficult business environment. The underlying force is the industry's (in most regions) highly fragmented and unconsolidated structure which results in overcapacities. The IATA calls for consolidation, vertical integration, and improved information flows along the supply chains to mitigate the airlines' profit situation.[223] In addition, the IATA postulates further deregulation and lower market exit barriers.[224]

The IATA's call for consolidation suggests that the organisation believes the airline industry can, due to network and scope economies, only be efficiently supplied by a small number of firms. In the extreme, this would make the airline industry a natural monopoly. However, for the US industry Borenstein and Rose find no empirical evidence in the last 25 years that cost advantages are giving the largest airlines increasingly dominant positions.[225]

Another approach to explain airlines' cyclical financial performance by industry structure is the theory of destructive competition. It became popular in the early 1990s, after the Iraq crisis and an unprecedented downturn in the airline industry.[226] The fundamental idea is that unconstrained competition leads to prices too low for airlines to survive.[227] As a result of many bankruptcies a monopoly or oligopoly may emerge and earn high profits. This again attracts investments and competitors, which restarts the process.[228] To stabilise the industry, Tretheway and Waters argue that a price cap limiting price increases would not be beneficial. Instead they suggest to consider a minimum price regulation, similar to predatory pricing provisions in competition law.[229]

Closely related to the theory of destructive competition is the concept of the 'empty core'. Button suggests that the airline industry's profit instability is inherent and can be explained using Edgeworth's 'core' model from 1881.[230] 'An allocation of goods and services is said to be in the core when there is no group within the economy who could be better off by trading amongst itself.'[231] A trade outcome in the core is a version of the Nash cooperative solution.[232] If an industry does not have a core, i.e. if the core is 'empty', it means that an equilibrium cannot be found because for every possible allocation of goods at least one group would benefit from trading. Button finds indications that deregulated airline markets have an 'empty core'.[233] His conclusion is based on testing the presence of conditions which have been found to be typical of 'empty core' markets.[234] First, the airline industry is characterised by network effects because one airline, he argues, can benefit from another airline's route offers at a destination which gives passengers more travel choices. Second, the airline industry has large fixed costs (indivisible costs), e.g. for one scheduled flight, but faces finely divisible demand, e.g. for one seat on that flight. This frequently leads to short-run overcapacity. In order to fill the excess capacity suppliers have an incentive to lower prices until some suppliers go out of business. The result is excess demand and consequently higher prices, which attracts new entrants, which again entails excess capacity.[235] Button stresses that an industry with an empty core is not necessarily inefficient.[236] Accordingly, a suitable policy response cannot be immediately suggested.[237]

In their analysis of the US airline industry's economic development for the US National Bureau of Economic Research, Borenstein and Rose suggest two explanations for the airline industry's profit volatility: the industry's high level of business-model experimentation and the fundamental economics of the industry.[238] First, the airline industry has undergone many changes concerning pricing, logistics, competitive strategy, and organisational form. Borenstein and Rose regard it as part of this experimentation process that airlines make strategic errors and successes which result in negative and positive profits.[239] Second, several market fundamentals cause airlines' profits to change quickly and drastically.[240] Their demand is volatile which is particularly challenging as flights are not storable. Furthermore, fixed costs in the industry are high. The value of aircraft fluctuates with demand and is highly correlated across airlines which means there are, for example, hardly any sale options in an economic downturn. Adjusting capacity supply to demand is thus difficult and slow. So is the adjustment of labour costs, given the highly unionised industry. Unions are generally hesitant to reduce wages and benefits in downturns and likely to request increases in upturns which airline management may be hesitant to grant. Moreover, airlines have to deal with volatile fuel prices. Fuel costs are also difficult to adjust quickly because cancelling flights disturbs the airlines' complex network logistics. Accordingly, Borenstein and Rose find no supply response to fuel price shocks in US post-deregulation data. To examine whether volatile demand, slowly adjusting labour and capacity costs, and fluctuating fuel costs are sufficient to explain the magnitude of airline profit volatility, Borenstein and Rose compute a simple spreadsheet analysis. They conclude that 'demand and fuel cost fluctuations combined with sticky adjustment on the supply side can easily generate the observed magnitude of earnings volatility, without any appeal to "empty core" or destructive competition arguments'.[241]

From an empirical investigation of Asian airlines Chin and Tay conclude that airlines' profit cyclicality is caused by economic cycles.[242] Airlines amplify economic cycles through their aircraft capacity investments. Chin and Tay find that aircraft are usually ordered one year after airlines make good profits and then delivered two to three years later.[243] This delay causes aircraft to arrive in the market when economic conditions have already deteriorated. Chin and Tay assume airlines would benefit from improved forecasting to anticipate order delivery cycles, as well as from more flexible capacity, for example via aircraft leasing, and from more careful (slower) aircraft ordering.[244]

Wojahn also names cyclic investment and over-investment as reasons for the airline industry's overall poor financial performance.[245] He explores why capital is nonetheless flowing into the industry, and why the industry is willing to take it and expand the merely profitable or unprofitable business. The empirical investigations show that multiple factors contribute to over-investment. There is strong support for the following explanation:[246] over-investment is the result of profitable airlines rationally expanding capacity and unprofitable airlines not cutting capacity. Unprofitable airlines do not sell their aircraft to profitable ones because, first, they regard the aircraft investment as sunk costs and thus do not seek to refund them, and second, cutting capacity would cause additional costs which airlines refrain from, e.g. for lease contract violations, termination payments to workers, or the cost of abandoning valuable slots. Consequently, the emergence of growth-seeking profitable low-cost carriers aggravated over-capacity in the industry.[247]

Werner argues that the airlines' aircraft capacity is an important cause of the industry's profit variability.[248] From a financial perspective aircraft imply high leverage. Leverage means amplification and works through a force, i.e. the airline's revenue stream, and a magnifier, i.e. the airline's fixed costs.[249] The example in Table 2.7 illustrates how a 10% increase in revenues and corresponding variable costs results in an 80% operating profit surplus if fixed costs are high, compared to only 30% surplus if fixed costs are low.

Given the airline industry's high leverage, volatile revenues will lead to extremely volatile profits. To reduce leverage some fixed costs need to be made variable.[250] Werner states this will hardly be possible for airlines in the short run, but it is feasible as a long-run strategy. Measures are to employ mainly variable cost contracts, e.g. to pay personnel per flight or lease aircraft and crew on a per-flight basis. Outsourcing operations such as catering, or routine maintenance, or ground service activities may also be an option, as well as

Table 2.7 Example leverage effect

	high leverage (FC)			low leverage (FC)		
revenues	1000	1100	+10%	1000	1100	+10%
– variable operating costs	200	220	+10%	700	770	+10%
contribution	800	880		300	330	
– fixed operating costs (FC)	700	700		200	200	
operating profit (EBIT)	100	180	=> +80%	100	130	=> +30%

entering code-sharing agreements in which a route's fixed costs can be shared with another carrier. In profitable times, when high leverage is an advantage, Werner advises to stabilise revenues and thus ensure amplified high profits.[251] Stabilisation can be achieved by government regulation, for example, by competition limits or fixed prices.

In contrast to the above cited authors, Garvett and Hilton do not see airlines' costs as a cause of the profit cycle. They empirically investigated explanatory factors for airline profitability and find no correlation between worldwide airlines' unit costs and their profitability.[252] Neither do they see a significant correlation between productivity and profitability.[253] Airline size, aircraft size, aircraft age, fleet diversity, or flight stage length also cannot explain profitability.[254] Finally, a combination of three factors relates well to airline profitability: yield management effectiveness, revenue per unit (seat mile) offered, and airline ownership.[255] Yield management effectiveness is an index describing how well a yield management system is set up and used. Garvett and Hilton emphasise the importance of yield management:

> Experts usually agree that the revenue difference between effective and ineffective yield management is typically 4 to 8 per cent. Thus yield management can be responsible for the entire profit of an airline in this industry in which pre-tax profit margins are typically just 3 to 6 per cent of revenue.[256]

Concerning ownership Garvett and Hilton find that privately held airlines tend to be more profitable and thus postulate deregulation.[257] This is strongly supported by Kahn,[258] the 'father of US airline deregulation'.[259]

Neidl, in line with Garvett and Hilton, emphasises the benefits of elaborate yield management systems for airline profitability. In 1999 Neidl predicted earnings in the airline industry would remain strong due to the industry's managerial improvements and yield management.[260] He saw improvements in three areas.[261] First, capacity was reduced by slower aircraft ordering and fast retirement of old aircraft. Second, operational performance was increased by more efficient network planning, e.g. channelling traffic through hub airports, and by code sharing among airlines. Third, stricter cost controlling was implemented and especially labour costs lowered through outsourcing. The industry's primary success factor, however, is according to Neidl the heavy use of advanced yield management, i.e. the endeavour to allocate seats to passengers according to their willingness to pay.[262] In Neidl's view, future losses could only result from external influences, such as fuel prices or labour costs, or from economic downturns which negatively affect air traffic demand.[263]

In contrast, Adler and Gellman see the airlines' yield management systems as reason for the industry's overall poor financial results because they do not necessarily assure full cost coverage.[264] Consequently, airlines should focus more on long-term instead of short-term profit maximisation. To improve profitability Adler and Gellman furthermore suggest airlines reduce their costs via code sharing or specialisation on market segments.

Conclusion

Though the airline industry's persistently poor financial performance is a pressing issue, the number of in-depth analyses of profit cycle causes and potential mitigation measures in the aviation management literature is surprising limited. Profit cycle causes and mitigation measures named in the literature have a broad range. A summary is given in Table 2.8.

Some authors see structural problems in the industry, stating the industry has an 'empty core' or suffers from 'destructive competition'. Their fundamental idea is unconstrained competition will lead to prices too low for airlines to survive. Many exit the market and the remaining earn high profits. This again attracts market entries, which restarts the process. On the contrary, the IATA sees the problem that airlines do not exit the market and the industry is consequently fragmented. Hence, they call for consolidation to reduce overcapacities.

The aviation management literature gives reasons for the emergence of overcapacities. First, the airline product is non-storable which gives an incentive to produce too much in order not to offer too little. Second, airlines have (too) easy access to capital because of the industry's general attractiveness. Third, bankruptcy protection regulations such as the US chapter 11 keep failed airlines in the market. Fourth, unprofitable airlines do not divest because they regard aircraft as sunk costs. All these reasons for overcapacities would still apply if the industry was consolidated. Besides, some authors doubt that merged airlines really achieve lower costs because of the inefficiencies observed in very large enterprises and high merger costs. In order to avoid overcapacities it is argued that airlines should slow down their aircraft ordering but be responsive concerning the retirement of old aircraft.

There is wide agreement that airlines' high fixed costs are problematic. They imply high leverage, so volatile demand has severe effects on the profit situation. Fixed costs are mainly incurred by aircraft and labour. Reducing fixed costs is difficult because aircraft values develop with the airline profit cycle. Generally, flexible lease contracts should be preferred. Furthermore, labour unions prevent quick cost adjustments. Improving relations with unions and aiming for flexible contracts is thus advised. Additional measures to reduce costs are to outsource non-key functions such as catering or ground services, to enter code-shares to split costs for a route, to specialise on certain market segments, and to develop more efficient networks.

Some authors see management issues in the airline industry. They range from widespread managerial incompetence (see Pilarski 2007) to management by trial and error. Airlines' experiments with different business models entail strategic errors and successes that lead to cyclic profitability. Consequently, increased knowledge about the profit cycle is expected to improve management decisions.

Few authors attribute the airline profit cycle to external factors such as fuel price developments or the general economic cycle. The airline industry, they argue, only amplifies the economic cycle through their aircraft ordering behaviour.

Furthermore, regulations such as high taxes or government airline ownership are stated to deteriorate airlines' profitability. Hence, these authors desire a more competitive environment for airlines. Meanwhile others proclaim limits for competition such as a minimum price regulation or even fixed prices.

Most controversial in the aviation management literature is the role of airlines' price-setting mechanisms for the airline profit cycle. Some make advanced yield management systems responsible for it, arguing that extensive yield management is too short-term oriented and deteriorates customer satisfaction. They postulate a more long-term approach to profit maximisation. Others see elaborate yield management as the cure to poor airline profitability because it maximises revenues on every flight. There is, however, agreement that pressure on price is high in the airline industry because of its very low marginal costs and the increasing importance of price for product differentiation among airlines.

Table 2.8 Cycle drivers and mitigation policies in aviation management literature

Airline management literature

Cycle driver	exogenous factors:
	• economic development (business cycle) → volatile demand
	• volatile fuel price
	
	industry characteristics:
	• non-storable product
	• easy access to capital (even in economic downturns)
	• commoditisation of airline product: differentiation mainly by price
	• aircraft order delivery cycle amplifies economic developments
	
	industry structure:
	• fragmented → overcapacities
	• 'destructive competition' → destructively low prices
	• 'empty core', industry is inherently instable: network effects, plus large fixed costs but finely divisible demand
	  → short-term overcapacities → (destructively) low prices
	• very low marginal cost of flying an additional passenger
	  → prices below full costs
	• government airline ownership
	
	regulation:
	• taxes: high burden for airlines
	• bankruptcy protection → retains bad managers, depresses prices
	
	mismanagement:
	• business model experiments entail strategic errors and successes
	• management failures
	
	over-investment in capacity:
	• profitable airlines invest in capacity
	• unprofitable carriers do not divest (because aircraft investments are sunk costs and cutting capacity is costly)

high fixed costs, slow adjustment → high leverage

- aircraft: aircraft value is similar among airlines, i.e. sales in downturns hardly possible
- labour: labour unions prevent quick cost adjustments, contract durations, unfortunate negotiation timing
- fuel: cancelling routes disturbs complex network logistics

yield management

- not enough or too inefficient yield management
- versus: too much yield management (too short-term oriented)

Mitigation policy

industry structure:
- consolidation
- improved information flows along supply chain
- competition

regulation:
- minimum price regulation
- fixed prices
- restricted competition
- private airline ownership

management improvements:
- improve knowledge about the cycle
- avoid management failures

capacity reduction to prevent overcapacity
- slower aircraft ordering
- fast retirement of old aircraft

reduce costs (leverage), especially in unprofitable times:
- improve relation with labour unions
- variable cost contracts, flexible capacity and labour (e.g. leasing)
- outsourcing (e.g. catering, routine maintenance, ground services)
- code-sharing to share fixed costs for route
- specialisation on market segments
- more efficient network planning (e.g. hubbing)

more yield management (to maximise short-term profits)

versus: *less* yield management
- less extreme price discrimination to improve customer satisfaction
- short-term profit *mini*misation to maximise customer satisfaction
- long-term perspective on profit maximisation

2.4 Industry practitioners' views on airline profit cyclicality

2.4.1 Secondary data on airline managers' and stakeholders' explanations

In this section several statements by industry practitioners will be presented in which they explain their airline's or the industry's poor financial performance. The selection represents arguments popular with aviation managers but is not statistically representative.

- Tony Tyler, Director, International Air Transport Association (IATA), 2011:[265]
  After announcing that airlines' projected profit will be lower than in the last year, Tyler said: 'The high price of oil and an anemic economic outlook are the biggest issues.'
  → arguments: high oil price, slow growth of general economy
- Gordon Bethune, CEO, Continental Airlines, 2004:[266]
  'All-time-high oil prices and the ever-increasing burden of government taxes and fees are killing the industry.'
  → arguments: high oil prices, increasing government taxes and fees
- John Heimlich, Economist, Airlines for America (A4A), 2013:[267]
  Asked why the financial metrics were so poor for the industry, Heimlich responded: 'We've had compressed margins in the face of rising fuel prices (and) in the past year, we were not done with residual bankruptcy costs, which will be put behind us, (and) some one time integration costs from consolidation. (That) will lead to a structurally more healthy industry in the next few years.'
  → arguments: exceptional costs (restructuring, only temporary), high fuel prices
- Carolyn McCall, CEO, easyJet, 2011:[268]
  Across the Atlantic easyJet reported a pre-tax loss of GBP153 million in the first half amid 'tough' trading conditions. McCall named 'sharply rising fuel costs combined with cautious behaviour by consumers' and an adverse effect from taxes on passengers as defining factors.
  → arguments: rising fuel costs, cautious consumer behaviour, taxes
- Singapore Airlines (SIA), 2011:[269]
  SIA warns the 'twin challenges of near term weakness in load factors and high fuel prices will adversely affect operating performance of airlines'. As a result the SIA Group's outlook for FY2011/12 is unclear. SIA says its Japanese routes continue to be affected by the March 2011 earthquake with forward bookings remaining weak. It also points out that the global economic picture is uncertain and jet fuel prices 'are likely to remain high and volatile in the near term'.
  → arguments: high fuel prices, weak load factors due to weak demand, earthquake
- CAPA Centre for Aviation about Thai Airways, 2011:[270]
  Thai's profits drop in 1Q2011 as oil prices and external factors affect demand.
  → arguments: oil price, external influences on demand
- Leonardo Pereira, CFO, Gol, 2011:[271]
  CFO Leonardo Pereira explained to analysts that the carrier's operating margin would have been 14% to 15% if fuel costs remained at the levels Gol initially projected for 1Q2011. Gol's profitability excluding the impact of fuel has improved significantly as a result of strong demand and a reduction in non-fuel costs.
  → arguments: fuel costs

- Rakesh Gangwal, CEO, US Airways, April 2001:[272]
  'US Airways is experiencing the combined impact of a weak economic environment and expanding competition from low-cost competitors and network carriers.'
  → arguments: weak economy, increasing competition from other airlines
- Bruce Lakefield, CEO, US Airways, 2004:[273]
  'Since we still lack the new labor agreements that are needed for the transformation plan to succeed, we must preserve the company's cash resources that are required to implement the plan.'
  → arguments: sticky labour costs
- Airliners.net, internet discussion forum for aviation professionals, thread started 2004:[274]
  'As a frequent reader of this forum, I've observed that many people who post in here seem to blame the problems of the major carriers on labor costs and say that the high wages are what put the airlines in this mess. Very few point to poor management as the cause of airline failures or financial crises.'
  → arguments: high labour costs (usual argument; possibility of poor management to be discussed)
- Donald Carty, CEO, AMR Corp. (parent of American Airlines), April 2001:[275]
  AMR reported it lost $43 million, or 28 cents a share, in the quarter. 'Without a doubt, the weakening US economy caused a reduction in business travel that affected our performance in the first quarter,' said Don Carty. He also pointed out that bad weather and high fuel prices affected financial results.
  → arguments: weak economy, bad weather, high fuel prices
- Philippe Calavia, CFO, Air France–KLM, 2013:[276]
  The Franco-Dutch company said its net loss grew by 47% in 2012 to €1.19 billion ($1.57 billion), weighed by a sharply higher fuel bill and a hefty restructuring charge. Calavia said he is confident that the goal of returning to profitability by 2014 will be met, even though Europe's stagnant economy continues to hold back passenger and especially cargo traffic.
  → arguments: high fuel costs, restructuring costs, weak economy/demand

To return to profitability and sustain it, airlines typically propose various cost cuttings and efficiency improvements, possibly through mergers.[277] Some examples are provided as follows:

- IATA, press release, 2004:[278]
  'Airlines continue to be aggressive in cost cutting. In 2003 the industry achieved a 2.5% reduction in non-fuel unit costs and indications are for a further 3.0% reduction for 2004, which is above expectations.'
  → measures: continued aggressive cost-cutting
- Industry analyst, *New York Times*, 1994:[279]

'Cost-cutting measures have included layoffs – 36,000 jobs have been cut among IATA member carriers since 1991 – cancelled aircraft orders, refinancing, sales or leasing of aircraft, the scrapping or consolidating of routes, alliance agreements between carriers, the subcontracting of back-office activities and maintenance, and even franchising, whereby a small regional carrier takes over less lucrative operations under a major carrier's name and flight numbers.'

→ measures: layoffs, outsourcing (back-office, maintenance), cancelled aircraft orders, aircraft refinancing, aircraft sales or leasing, route network restructuring, alliances

- Alan Joyce, CEO, Qantas, June 2010:[280]

'During the past 18 months, our management headcount has been reduced by 20%. We are also working to improve the efficiency of the way in which we work with our suppliers. We have some 30,000 suppliers, and we want to streamline this. We want to use our purchasing power more efficiently, while also reducing administration costs.'

→ measures: reduce administration labour cost, improve supply chain efficiency

- Industry Analyst, *Forbes*, 2013:[281]

There is a consolidation trend in the US airline industry. 'In less than five years, 8 major US carriers have become 4: Delta + Northwest = Delta, Southwest + AirTran = Southwest, United + Continental = United, American + US Airways = American. [. . .] But is the merger of American and US Airways into "the world's largest airline" a match made in heaven?' 'Joining forces' is supposed to mean more efficiencies, market access, and price leverage.

→ measure: industry consolidation (efficiency gains, cost benefits, market access)

Conclusion

When industry practitioners are asked to explain their airline's or the airline industry's poor financial performance, they tend to give similar answers. Mostly, they name high fuel prices and the weak economy as reasons for financial distress. Tax burdens, high and slowly adjustable labour costs, and special event costs for restructuring etc. are also mentioned. Furthermore, tough competition among airlines and other external influences such as bad weather are stated. It is worth noting that the factors airlines hold responsible for financial losses are fully or at least largely outside the airlines' control sphere.

As measures to regain profitability and sustain it, airline analysts generally propose cost cuttings and efficiency improvements. These can be labour cost and aircraft capacity reductions as well as efficiency gains to be achieved through airline mergers. However, given the persistence of the airline profit cycle, these strategies have not yet paid off. Table 2.9 summarises the presented key points.

Table 2.9 Secondary data on aviation insiders' view

Airline managers' view	
Cycle driver	fuel price
	development of general economy and hence demand
	exceptional costs (for restructuring)
	labour costs (amount and slow adjustment)
	Taxes
	competition among airlines
	external influences, e.g. bad weather/earthquake
Mitigation policy	cost cutting
	efficiency gains through consolidation

2.4.2 Primary data from interviews with airline industry experts

First-hand information from airline industry practitioners will complete the search for potential airline profit cycle causes, drivers, and mitigation measures. Airline managers' and stakeholders' understanding of the phenomenon was the focus of a series of face-to-face interviews.

As interviewees revealed pieces of strategically relevant information, many have asked to stay anonymous. Assurance was given that only aggregated and impersonalised information will be presented. This does not compromise the interviews' purpose to gain an inside view on the airline profit cycle from industry practitioners.

Interviews were conducted between 2009 and 2013. To learn as much as possible about the interviewees' mental models, interviews were designed to be qualitative and semi-structured, with a length of one to two hours.[282] Altogether 19 interviews were conducted, mostly with one person at a time. Four interviews were scheduled as group discussions with up to eight people. Participants debated topics with each other while the process was structured by the interviewer. Interview partners were airline, air traffic control, airport, and aircraft manufacturer employees, as well as advisory board members and airline management consultants.[283] Interviewees held leading positions that involve budget responsibilities, decision making and management scope. It is thus assumed that they have experience with strategic issues such as the airline profit cycle.

Before the interviews, participants received information about the research purpose and a very brief introduction to the airline profit cycle phenomenon. Key questions in interviews are listed below, not necessarily in that order. Each question's purpose is indicated below.

- Are you familiar with the phenomenon 'airline profit cycle'?
    → warm-up, clarification of definitions etc.
    → perceived relevance of the problem

- Is the airline profit cycle a topic that is explicitly discussed in your team or elsewhere in your company?
  → relevance of the problem in daily business
- Why do you think the airline profit cycle exists? What drives it?
  → profit cycle causes and drivers
- Are there special measures you or others in your company take to mitigate the cycle or take advantage of it/manage it?
  → mitigation measures

Interview results

Relevance? – Not all interviewees were familiar with the airline profit cycle. Every third person either declared not to know the phenomenon, or reported faint memories of a worldwide airline profit graph but passed when asked to describe it. Among interviewed advisory board members and airline management consultants the awareness of the financial struggle in the airline industry and the problems it entails (see section 1.2) was 100%. Of those interviewees who did know about the cycle and work at an airline, two thirds stated to be much more focused on their own airline's performance and would consequently not care too much about the industry phenomenon.

Cycle causes and drivers? – Almost all interviewed airline employees saw the reasons for the airline profit cycle outside the airlines' control. The general economic development, crises such as wars, terror attacks, or diseases, and the fuel price were mentioned. Furthermore, airline interviewees named the industry's high fixed costs and the non-storable nature of the product. One airline interviewee hinted at the airlines' own potential responsibility for the industry's overall poor financial performance by saying that individually rational decisions may sometimes in aggregate be unfavourable for the industry as a whole. Asked for an example, he named the airlines' race for capacity expansion that in aggregate produces overcapacities in the industry which result in low prices. The leader of an airline's pricing department attributed the industry's financial distress to competitive pressures resulting from the increasing speed with which price changes are published. Among non-airline interviewees, opinions about reasons for the airline profit cycle were mixed. Several named cyclic overcapacities in line with the 'hog cycle theory' as reason for the profit cycle (see section 2.1.2), the aircraft manufacturers' production lead time being the cycle driving delay. Altogether, the following cycle causes and drivers were mentioned:

- Economy
- crises (terror attacks, wars, diseases, weather, etc.)
- fuel price
- high fixed costs and a non-storable product
- overcapacity
- aircraft production lead time

- inflexible capacity adjustment
- slow labour cost adjustment
- extremely fast price changes

Potential remedies? – A popular solution to achieve better profitability in the airline industry, emphasised in approximately 80% of the interviews, is to save costs. A lower cost base is intended to improve margins and to increase airlines' flexibility. Measures taken to save costs are consolidation, i.e. formation of alliances and mergers, massive restructuring, e.g. under US chapter 11 bankruptcy protection, and leasing aircraft. Counter-cyclic aircraft ordering was suggested by one airline interviewee but he dismissed it as unfeasible due to difficulties in explaining to shareholders why a loss-making company should venture into an immense investment. Two strategists suggested airlines improve their risk management by including crises and cyclicality into their plans. So far, they explained, many airlines use smooth trend extrapolations for their long-term planning processes though airlines are in reality much affected by the actual highs and lows which are 'smoothed away' in the planning process. An airline pricing department leader saw the solution to improve airline profitability in even more elaborate (detailed) price-setting mechanisms. Some non-airline employees focused on aircraft manufacturers to improve airlines' profitability. Suggested measures are intended to prevent overcapacities in the airline industry. Aircraft manufacturers are required to have more reliable (on time) aircraft deliveries and slower aircraft production capacity adjustment. Altogether, the following measures to improve the airline industry's profitability were suggested:

- cost saving

  - consolidation (mergers and alliances to save costs)
  - restructuring after bankruptcy
  - leasing to improve flexibility
  - counter-cyclic aircraft ordering

- improved risk management by including crisis and cyclicality in plans
- even more elaborate (detailed) price-setting mechanisms
- more reliable (on time) aircraft delivery
- slow production adjustment for aircraft manufacturers

Conclusion

Interviews with industry practitioners revealed that, even though the airline profit cycle is highly relevant to business in the industry, only two thirds of the interviewees reported knowledge about it. Table 2.10 summarises the interview results.

The interviews disclosed that airline managers tend to see the profit cycle as something that is happening to them. The majority thinks the cycle is caused

Table 2.10 Primary data on aviation insiders' view

Aviation managers' view	
Cycle driver	economic developments
	crises (terror attacks, wars, diseases, weather, etc.)
	fuel price
	high fixed costs and a non-storable product
	Overcapacity
	aircraft production lead time
	inflexible capacity adjustment
	slow labour cost adjustment
	price changes extremely fast
Mitigation policy	cost saving:
	• consolidation (mergers and alliances to save costs)
	• restructuring after bankruptcy
	• leasing to improve flexibility
	• counter-cyclic aircraft ordering
	improved risk management by including crisis and cyclicality in plans
	even more elaborate price-setting mechanisms
	aircraft manufacturers:
	• more reliable (on time) aircraft delivery
	• slow production adjustment for aircraft manufacturers

externally (by economic or fuel price developments) so they can only react to it (mainly with cost cuttings). Interviewees from other organisations see the cycle's causes at least partly within the airline industry. Their main suggested remedy however is the same, namely to save costs. Furthermore, interviewees recommended to include cyclicality in strategic planning as well as to develop even more detailed price-setting mechanisms. Aircraft manufacturers are said to be able to improve airlines' profitability by preventing overcapacities in the industry with more reliable aircraft deliveries or a slow production adaptation.

2.5 Categorisation of airline profit cycle drivers

To derive potential airline profit cycle causes, drivers, and mitigation measures several insights have been compiled. Sources were:

- business cycle and industry cycle theories (see section 2.1)
- literature on system oscillations and the supply chain as an example of an oscillating system (see section 2.2)
- aviation business literature on the airline profit cycle and previous studies focused on the phenomenon (see section 2.3)
- industry practitioners' opinions, gathered from secondary data and expert interviews (see section 2.4)

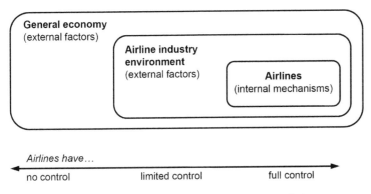

Figure 2.14 Categories for cycle drivers and mitigation policies

The framework to summarise the derived results consists of two main categories: factors that are external to the airline industry and the industry's internal factors or mechanisms. External factors can be divided into influences that an airline cannot control, such as the general economic development, the fuel price, or wars, and factors that airlines have at least limited control over. These are for example aviation specific regulations and taxes, or the actions of aircraft manufacturers and other supply chain partners. Altogether they form the airlines' business environment. By lobby work, skilful negotiating, and other activities airlines have distinctly more influence over these industry environment factors than over developments in the general economy. Naturally, airlines only have full control over their own actions and internal mechanisms. Figure 2.14 illustrates the introduced categorisation.

Literature and aviation industry practitioners have different opinions about the airline profit cycle's causes and drivers. Six general observations can be made:

1   **Airline managers see the profit cycle's causes outside the industry, researchers see them within.** Airline managers hold mainly external factors responsible for the airline profit cycle. Most mentioned are the general economic development, fuel prices, and crises such as terror attacks, wars, inclement weather, or epidemics. Researchers, on the other hand, tend to explain the cycle with the airlines' behaviour. Their focus is on airlines' capacity adjustment policies, especially the aircraft ordering behaviour. Some business cycle theories explain oscillations with a combination of external developments and the industry's internal mechanisms. While external factors initialise a cycle, the industry's internal mechanisms propagate it. There is a debate whether or not an industry can mitigate its cyclicality and stabilise itself.

2   **Overcapacity is commonly said to be a cycle driver.** Managers and researchers provide different explanations for periodic overcapacities in

the airline industry. First, the airline product is non-storable which gives an incentive to produce too much in order not to offer too less. Second, airlines have (too) easy access to capital because of the industry's general attractiveness. Third, bankruptcy protection regulations such as the US chapter 11 keep unprofitable airlines in the market. Fourth, airlines do not divest in unprofitable times because cutting capacity is costly and investments are regarded as sunk costs. Fifth, trend extrapolation in forecasting overrides the beginnings of upswings or downswings. Sixth, the industry's fragmentation is argued to cause overcapacities because many carriers seek to enlarge their market shares and invest accordingly. Finally, some authors blame aircraft manufacturers and their order delivery performance.

3   **The role of the price mechanism as cycle driver is highly controversial.** Some business cycle and industry cycle theories make price rigidities, i.e. slowly adapting prices, responsible for cyclicality. On the contrary, some aviation researchers and managers see the very responsive price mechanism (revenue management systems) as cycle driver. They argue it contributes to the considerable downward pressure on prices in the airline industry. This pressure is aggravated, first, by the very low marginal cost of flying an additional passenger which encourages price decreases to fill planes. Second, overcapacity in the industry is stated to depress prices. Third, the commoditisation of the airline product requires differentiation mainly by price.

4   **The aviation management literature emphasises industry environment factors as cycle drivers.** There is agreement that the airline industry's high fixed costs are problematic. They imply high leverage, so demand fluctuations have strong effects on the profit situation. Airlines' largest fixed cost components are the expenses for labour and aircraft. Besides high fixed costs, the airline industry's easy access to capital is often mentioned to drive the airline profit cycle. Though the industry persistently destroys shareholder value (return on capital invested below the weighted average costs of capital), financing seems always available to airlines, probably due to the industry's overall attractiveness. The third factor, which is argued to drive the profit cycle, is regulation. Regulation comprises taxes, bankruptcy legislation, ownership issues, and market liberalisation. Airline managers and a few aviation management researchers see the airlines' tax burden as a problem. Others criticise bankruptcy regulations that allow insolvent airlines to stay in the market to restructure because this protection, they argue, leads to overcapacity and depressed prices. Airline ownership regulation is identified as a cycle driver. Empirical investigations revealed that government owned airlines are less profitable than private ones. Finally, market regulation, or rather deregulation, is stated to cause structural problems in the airline industry, for example 'destructive competition' with prices too low for airlines to survive.

5   **The airline industry shares characteristics of other cyclical industries** (see Table 2.11). Cyclical industries typically have three characteristics (see section 2.1.2). The first and most important one is the durability

Table 2.11 Airline industry shares characteristics of other cyclical industries

Reasons for industry cyclicality	*Apply to airline industry?*
durability of output: durable goods	• NO, air transportation is a service industry BUT essential inputs (aircraft) are durable
capacity adjustment policy	
• pro-cyclical investment	• YES, aircraft orders depend on profits
• lacking financial constraints	• YES, hardly any financing constraints
• competition after liberalisation	• YES, competition, e.g. from low-cost
• forecasting errors (→ overcapacity)	carriers
• responsive to price changes	• YES, industry tends to smooth cyclicality
• production process buffers small	away and seems to believe in unlimited growth
	• NO, capacity cannot be adjusted quickly
	• YES, a service is delivered immediately
price mechanism	
• slow price adjustment	• NO, airline ticket prices change quickly
• counter-cyclical pricing (increase in contraction to ensure revenue)	• NO, prices fall in downturns
• very price sensitive demand	• YES, airline customers are price sensitive

of output. Durable goods industries are more cyclical than non-durable goods and service industries. Though air transportation is a service industry, its essential production factor, the aircraft, is a durable good. Second, capacity adjustment in the airline industry is similar to the one in other cyclical industries. For example pro-cyclical investment behaviour and a lack of financial constraints for capacity investments are common. Third, the airline industry faces a price sensitive demand.[284] However, the airline industry's price mechanism differs from that in other cyclical industries. Price adjustments are not slow but fast and prices are not counter-cyclical but decrease in economic downturns.

6   **Typical origins of supply chain and system oscillations do not apply to the airline industry.** Supply chain research and the system oscillation literature agree that deficient information processing causes oscillations. Misperceptions of the supply line, i.e. capacity already on order, are found to be common. Given the high costs of aircraft it is likely that each airline considers its supply line carefully. An airline will, however, not be perfectly informed about its competitors' investment decisions so that the industry's total supply line is uncertain. Yet, aircraft manufacturers publish their aircraft orders and deliveries, and airlines and airports publish their passenger numbers. Altogether, the airline industry can be described as comparatively transparent as far as capacity is concerned. Consequently, the cycle is not expected to be caused by information processing deficits.

Table 2.12 shows how the cycle drivers identified in sections 2.1–2.4 are sorted into the categorisation introduced in Figure 2.14 above.

Table 2.12 Compiled potential cycle drivers

Cycle drivers		
general economy	*airline industry environment*	*airlines (internal mechanisms)*
• general economic development • external shocks (terror attacks, wars, diseases, weather, etc.) • fuel price fluctuations	• investors' behaviour: easy access to capital, accurate forecasts • regulation: high taxes, bankruptcy law (high barriers to exit), government airline ownership, market liberalisation • high fixed costs (aircraft's long service lifetime, labour contract duration, unions) → slow adjustment → low marginal costs • aircraft manufacturers' behaviour: responsive production, production lead time • market structure: fragmented /empty core / destructive competition • non-changeable features: based on durable good (aircraft), non-storable product, imperfect information • demand features: price sensitive, herding behaviour amplifies demand changes, commoditisation (flying becomes normal)	• business model experimentation, management mistakes **capacity adjustment** • planning (limited forecasting horizon, forecast errors, trend extrapolation, market share targets) • aircraft ordering (pro-cyclical investment, long order processing time, misperception of delays) • capacity management (inflexible) • aircraft retirement (no divestment in unprofitable times due to sunk costs and cutting costs and aircraft value develops with airline industry profits) • misperception of delays **price setting** • rigid prices versus: • flexible, quickly adjusting prices (extensive yield management) • short-term demand stimulation by price **cost adjustment** • restructuring costs • slow labour cost adjustment due to contract negotiations

Researchers and managers suggest several measures to mitigate airlines' profit cyclicality. Proposed theories outlined in sections 2.1–2.4 are assigned to the previously introduced categories, as shown in Table 2.13. The following general observations about potential airline profit cycle mitigation measures can be made:

1   **Most proposed mitigation measures are within airlines' control, only few measures require regulation.** Some researchers expect a return to fixed price regulation or a minimum price would improve airlines' profitability. Others desire less regulation. They postulate lower market exit barriers, for example less bankruptcy protection. It is an open debate whether more or less competition in the airline market would be beneficial for airline profits.

2   **Airline managers, industry organisations, and management literature call for consolidation in the industry.** Systemic analyses of the airline profit cycle do not propagate this idea. The motivation behind the call for consolidation is that merged bigger airlines can benefit from economies of scale and scope, and thus have lower costs and higher profitability. However, some authors point out that there is no empirical evidence that large airlines have lower costs than smaller ones. Inefficiencies observed in very large enterprises and high merger costs may be a reason. On industry level, consolidation is intended to avoid overcapacities. This again is doubted by several researchers who argue that overcapacity does not depend on the number of competitors in the market (see above for factors causing overcapacity).

3   **Whether price setting should be short-term or long-term oriented is an open issue.** As discussed in the cycle driver section above, it is undecided which price-setting mechanism approach is most beneficial for airlines. Some authors advocate revenue management with its prompt responsive price adjustments. In contrast, others argue that less use of revenue management systems, and hence less elaborate price discrimination, would increase customer satisfaction. They postulate to focus on long-term rather than short-term profit maximisation.

4   **Airline managers bank on cutting costs.** To dampen losses and increase profits airline managers focus on cost savings. Suggested measures are organisational restructuring, outsourcing of e.g. catering or ground services, and code-sharing for flights to split route costs. Since labour costs is one of the largest cost items for airlines, more flexible contracts or lower rates would be an advantage. Moreover, network optimisations, such as channelling traffic more extensively through hub airports or specialising on certain market segments, can make airlines more cost efficient.

5   **There is a focus on airlines' fleet management, especially on slow aircraft capacity adjustment.** Some researchers shift the responsibility for capacity adjustment to aircraft manufacturers. To stabilise airlines' profitability they advise aircraft manufactures to adapt their production only slowly to airlines' orders, or even to implement order limits. Moreover, aircraft manufacturers are requested to insert big buffers in the production process and shorten their lead times. Suggestions for airlines to mitigate profit cyclicality are to order their aircraft steadily, not in quick response to market changes, and even independent of profits. In contrast, some researchers propose counter-cyclic ordering.

Table 2.13 Compiled potential cycle mitigation measures

Mitigation measures		
general economy	*airline industry environment*	*airlines (internal mechanisms)*

	aircraft manufacturers: • slow production adaptation, order limits, big buffers in production (longer supply line adjustment time), produce to sales not to orders • more reliable on time delivery • shorten lead times **regulation:** • minimum price, fixed price • airline ownership privatisation • allow consolidation, limit competition versus more competition • lower barriers to market exit (less bankruptcy protection)	• avoid management mistakes • improve knowledge about cycle **capacity adjustment:** • planning (improve risk management by including crisis and cyclicality in plans, buffers for forecast inaccuracy, coordinate forecasting in alliance and prevent protective action) • slow aircraft capacity adjustment • reduce processing times • capacity reduction • aircraft ordering (slow, steady, profit independent, counter-cyclical, take supply line into account, based on demand forecast not market share target) • leasing (to avoid high fixed costs and long aircraft service lifetime) • capacity utilisation (flexible) • aircraft retirement (responsive, steady, counter-cyclical) **price setting:** • prompt adjustment, more elaborate yield management versus: • less elaborate yield management (less extreme price discrimination for more customer satisfaction) • focus on long-term profit maximisation • no demand stimulation by price **cost adjustment (cost reductions):** • consolidation (efficiency gains, vertical integration, scale and scope economies) • restructuring (more efficient, lower cost) • outsourcing, code-sharing (spilt route costs) • network optimisation: more efficient network planning (e.g. hubbing), specialisation on market segments • prevent productivity decrease after consecutive profitable years • variable capacity and labour contracts (→ leasing) • no labour decrease in contractions

6 **Aircraft leasing is suggested to make airlines' capacity more flexible.** Airline managers, aviation management literature, and systemic airline profit cycle analyses emphasise the benefits of aircraft leasing. It is intended to reduce the industry's high fixed costs for aircraft. A lease contract artificially shortens the aircraft's service lifetime in the fleet and thus increases flexibility. Some authors suggest 'wet leases' (i.e. short-term aircraft leases including crew, maintenance, and insurance) to achieve an even more flexible cost base.

Which of the suggested factors actually cause or drive the airline profit cycle and what measures successfully mitigate it, will be assessed in the next chapters.

Notes

1 Mankiw, N. Gregory, *Principles of macroeconomics*, 6th ed. (Cengage Learning, 2012), p. 424.
2 See Schumpeter, Joseph A., 'The Analysis of Economic Change', *The Review of Economics and Statistics* 17.4 (1935): 2, 8. Other publications define Juglar wave by a period of 7 to 11 years.
3 Gabisch, Günter and Hans-Walter Lorenz, *Business cycle theory – A survey of methods and concepts*, 2nd ed. (Berlin and others: Springer, 1989), p. 8. In other publications the length of Kondratieff waves is stated as 40–60 years, see for example Schumpeter, Joseph A., *Business cycles: A theoretical, historical and statistical analysis of the capitalist process* (New York: McGraw-Hill, 1939), p. 173.
4 The '40-month-cycle' is a quote from: Gabisch and Lorenz, *Business cycle theory – A survey of methods and concepts*, p. 8. Other publications document Kitchin waves to be 2–4 years long, for example: Schumpeter, *Business cycles: A theoretical, historical and statistical analysis of the capitalist process*, p. 173.
5 Adapted from Tucker, Irvin B., *Macroeconomics for today*, 7th edn. (Australia; United Kingdom: South-Western/Cengage Learning, 2011), p. 161.
6 See ibid., pp. 159–162.
7 Gabisch and Lorenz, *Business cycle theory – A survey of methods and concepts*, p. 10.
8 Haberler, Gottfried von, *Prosperity and depression*, 3rd edn. (New York: United Nations, 1946 [1937]).
9 Frisch, Ragnar, 'Propagation problems and impulse problems in dynamics economics.' In *Reprinted from: Economic Essays in honour of Gustav Calles* (London: George Allen & Unwin Ltd, 1933). It is the first mathematical business cycle model according to Maußner, Alfred, *Konjunkturtheorie [Business cycle theory]* (Berlin et al.: Springer, 1994) p. 32.
10 Gabisch and Lorenz, *Business cycle theory – A survey of methods and concepts*, p. 10.
11 Comprehensive information on business cycle theories can for example be found in: Zarnowitz, Victor, *Business cycles: Theory, history, indicators, and forecasting*, NBER Studies in business cycles, Vol. 27 (Chicago, London: University of Chicago Press, 1992).
12 See Grampp, William D., 'What did Smith mean by the invisible hand?', *Journal of Political Economy* 108.3 (2000): 445. The article also discusses other interpretations of the 'invisible hand'.
13 Comment on Adam Smith's concept of economic development, in: See Maußner, *Konjunkturtheorie [Business cycle theory]*, pp. 28–31.

14 The selected theories offer insights transferable to the airline profit cycle. However, there are also purely monetary theories, harvest theories, trade cycle theories, and depression explanations by changes in cost, horizontal maladjustments, or over-indebtedness. See Haberler, *Prosperity and depression*, pp. 5–254.

15 See ibid., pp. 142–150. Psychological aspects play the greatest role in theories by Keynes, Lavingston, Pigou, and Taussig. See ibid., p. 143.

16 See ibid., pp. 29 et seq.

17 For example by Friedrich A. von Hayek or Wilhelm Röpke. See ibid., pp. 33–72.

18 For example by Gustav Cassel or Arthus Spiethoff. See ibid., pp. 72–85.

19 Schumpeter, Joseph A., *The theory of economic development: An inquiry into profits, capital, credit, interest and the business cycle* (Cambridge, MA: Harvard University Press, 1934 (German original 1911)). And: Schumpeter, *Business cycles: A theoretical, historical and statistical analysis of the capitalist process.*

20 For example by John A. Hobson or Emil Lederer. See Haberler, *Prosperity and depression*, pp. 118–141.

21 See Keynes, John Maynard, *The General Theory of Employment, Interest and Money* (London: Macmillan, 1936). See Michl, Thomas, *Macroeconomic theory: A short course* (Armonk, New York: M.E. Sharpe, 2002) pp. 29–48.

22 Explained in Friedman, Milton, *Studies in the quantity theory of money*, Phoenix books (Chicago: University of Chicago Press, 1956). Or: Friedman, Milton and Rose D. Friedman, *Capitalism and freedom* (Chicago/ London: University of Chicago Press, 1982).

23 Lucas added the assumption of rational expectations to Friedman's Monetarist model. See for example: Lucas, Jr, Robert E., *Models of business cycles* (Oxford: Basil Blackwell, 1987).

24 See Kydland, Finn E. and Edward C. Prescott, 'Time to build and aggregate fluctuations', *Econometrica* 50.6 (1982).

25 See Maußner, *Konjunkturtheorie [Business cycle theory]*, pp. 38–40. And see Jacobs, Jan, *Econometric business cycle research* (Boston, London: Kluwer Academic, 1998), pp. 1–3. And see Zarnowitz, *Business cycles: Theory, history, indicators, and forecasting.*

26 See Frisch, 'Propagation problems and impulse problems in dynamics economics', p. 1.

27 Mankiw, *Principles of macroeconomics*, p. 12.

28 See Weil, Henry B., 'Commoditization of technology-based products and services: A generic model of market dynamics', *Massachusetts Institute of Technology: Sloan Working Paper* 144–196 (1996): 5.

29 See Mankiw, *Principles of macroeconomics*, p. 11. And see Deleersnyder, Barbara et al., *Weathering tight economic times: The sales evolution of consumer durables over the business cycle* (Erasmus Research Institute of Management (ERIM), Rotterdam School of Management, 2003), pp. 1, 26.

30 See Haberler, *Prosperity and depression*, p. 136. And see: Harlow, Arthur A., 'The hog cycle and the cobweb theorem', *Journal of Farm Economics* 42.4 (1960).

31 See Ezekiel, Mordecai, 'The cobweb theorem' *The Quarterly Journal of Economics* 52, no. 2 (1938).

32 See Tinbergen, Jan, 'Ein Schiffbauzyklus? [A shipbuilding cycle?]', *Weltwirtschaftliches Archiv* 34 (1931).

33 See Clark, J. Maurice, 'Business acceleration and the law of demand: A technical factor in economic cycles', *Journal of Political Economy* 25.3 (1917): 235.

34 See Meadows, Dennis L., 'The dynamics of commodity production cycles: A dynamic cobweb theorem', Massachusetts Institute of Technology, 1969.

35 See ibid., pp. 119–121.

36 See ibid., pp. 123–127.

37 See ibid., p. 127.
38 Weil, 'Commoditization of technology-based products and services', p. 1.
39 Ibid.
40 See ibid., pp. 8–14.
41 Ibid., p. 14.
42 See Petersen, Bruce and Steven Strongin, 'Why are some industries more cyclical than others?', *Journal of Business & Economic Statistics* 14, no. 2 (1996).
43 See Lucas Jr, Robert E., 'Understanding business cycles', *Carnegie-Rochester Conference Series on Public Policy* 5 (1977): 9. And see Mitchell, Wesley C., *What happens during business cycles: A progress report* (Cambridge, MA: National Bureau of Economic Research, 1951), pp. 106, 117.
44 The 'acceleration principle' is a non-monetary over-investment business cycle theory: The investment in new production technology augments incomes and thus raises the demand for consumption goods. This triggers investments in production capacity and amplifies the initial impulse. The accelerator principle is the direct link between an economy's output and investments in production capacity. It can not only amplify an economic upswing but also introduce downturns. The expansion will eventually slow because savings do not keep pace with investments. This leads to financing problems, falling incomes, and hence a recession.
45 See Petersen and Strongin, 'Why are some industries more cyclical than others?', p. 190.
46 Ibid., p. 194.
47 See ibid., pp. 190–191.
48 See ibid., p. 191.
49 See Bils, Mark, 'Testing for contracting effects on employment', *The Quarterly Journal of Economics* 106.4 (1991): 1130.
50 See Carlton, Dennis W., 'The rigidity of prices.' *American Economic Review* 76.637–658 (1986): 655.
51 See Petersen and Strongin, 'Why are some industries more cyclical than others?', p. 192.
52 See ibid.
53 See ibid., pp. 194–196.
54 See Deleersnyder et al., *Weathering tight economic times.*
55 See Petersen and Strongin, 'Why are some industries more cyclical than others?', p. 190; see Deleersnyder et al., *Weathering tight economic times*, p. 4.
56 See Deleersnyder et al., *Weathering tight economic times*, p. 14.
57 See ibid., pp. 19–22.
58 See ibid., p. 20.
59 See Tan, Hao and John A. Mathews, 'Cyclical industrial dynamics: The case of the global semiconductor industry', *Technological Forecasting & Social Change* 77 (2010): 348–349.
60 See ibid., p. 349.
61 See Cuadrado-Roura, Juan R. and Alvaro Ortiz V.-Abarca, 'Business cycle and service industries: General trends and the Spanish case', *Service Industries Journal* 21, no. 1 (2001): 120.
62 See ibid., pp. 105–106.
63 See ibid., pp. 120–121.
64 This was for example done by IKEA with low price mass market furniture.
65 See Longair, Malcolm S., *Theoretical concepts in physics: An alternative view of theoretical reasoning in physics* (Cambridge: Cambridge University Press, 2003), pp. 38–40. And see: Kirkpatrick, Larry D. and Gregory E. Francis, *Physics: A conceptual world view*, 7th edn. (Belmont, CA: Brooks/Cole, Cengage Learning, 2010), p. 307.

66 See Kirkpatrick and Francis, *Physics: A conceptual world view*, pp. 304–306.
67 See for example: Ljung, Lennart, 'Perspectives on system identification', *Annual Reviews in Control* 34.1 (2010). Or see Keesman, Karel J., *System identification: An introduction*, Advanced Textbooks in Control and Signal Processing (London et al.: Springer, 2011).
68 This formulation is called *transfer function* or *system function*.
69 See Barlas, Yaman, 'Formal aspects of model validity and validation in System Dynamics', *System Dynamics Review* 12.3 (1996): 185.
70 See Schwaninger, Markus and Stefan Grösser, 'System dynamics as model-based theory building', *Systems Research and Behavioral Science* 25.4 (2008): 450. And see Größler, Andreas, Jörn-Henrik Thun and Peter M. Milling, 'System Dynamics as a structural theory in operations management', *Production and Operations Management* 17.3 (2008): 373. – System Dynamics was developed by Forrester. See for example: Forrester, Jay W., *Principles of systems*, 2nd edn (Cambridge, MA: Wright-Allen Press, 1968).
71 See Forrester, Jay W., *Industrial dynamics*, 6th printing 1969 ed. (Cambridge, MA: MIT Press, 1961) p. 51.
72 Ibid. – Emphases not in original.
73 For example if the pendulum is swung too hard, it will break.
74 See Sterman, John D., *Business dynamics: Systems thinking and modeling for a complex world* (Boston: Irwin/McGraw-Hill, 2000), p. 131.
75 See ibid., pp. 131–132. One of the models is for example: Sterman, John D., 'A behavioral model of the economic long wave', *Journal of Economic Behavior & Organization* 6.1 (1985): 36.
76 See Sterman, *Business dynamics*, pp. 129–130. And see Forrester, *Industrial dynamics*. And see Mass, Nathaniel J., *Economic cycles: An analysis of underlying causes* (Cambridge, MA: Wright-Allen Press, 1975).
77 See Senge, Peter M., *The fifth discipline: The art and practice of the learning organization*, 1st edn. (New York: Doubleday/Currency, 1990) pp. 378–379, pp. 389–392. And see: Sterman, *Business dynamics*, pp. 114–116.
78 See Senge, *The fifth discipline*, pp. 74–80.
79 Note: To be able to oscillate, a system must be at least second order, i.e. have two or more state variables. This insight is implicit in requiring an oscillating system to consist of a negative feedback loop with a delay because modelling a delay entails capturing the state of the system. Consequently, in addition to the delay at least one state variable has to be implemented, so the structure can produce oscillations. – For further detail see Sterman, *Business dynamics*, p. 290.
80 See ibid., pp. 663–664.
81 See Sterman, John D., 'Modeling managerial behavior: Misperceptions of feedback in a dynamic decision making experiment', *Management Science* 35.3 (1989): 334.
82 See Sterman, *Business dynamics*, p. 695.
83 See Cachon, Gérard P., Taylor Randall and Glen M. Schmidt, 'In search of the bullwhip effect', *Manufacturing & Service Operations Management* 9.4 (2007): 474–475.
84 Lee, Hau L., V. Padmanabhan and Seungjin Whang, 'The bullwhip effect in supply chains', *Sloan Management Review* 38.3 (1997): 93.
85 See Lee, Hau L., V. Padmanabhan and Seungjin Whang, 'Information distortion in a supply chain: The bullwhip effect', *Management Science* 50.12 (2004): 1875.
86 Forrester, Jay W., 'Industrial dynamics: A major breakthrough for decision makers', *Harvard Business Review* 36, no. 4 (1958): p. 40.
87 See Lee et al., 'The bullwhip effect in supply chains', pp. 93–94.
88 See Metters, Richard, 'Quantifying the bullwhip effect in supply chains', *Journal of Operations Management* 15.2 (1997): 97–98.

89 See Dejonckheere, J. et al., 'Measuring and avoiding the bullwhip effect: A control theoretic approach', *European Journal of Operational Research* 147.3 (2003): 567. Referring to: Forrester, 'Industrial dynamics: A major breakthrough for decision makers.' And Forrester, *Industrial dynamics*.

90 Forrester, 'Industrial dynamics: A major breakthrough for decision makers', p. 52.

91 See ibid., pp. 47–49.

92 See Sterman, 'Modeling managerial behavior.'

93 See ibid., pp. 326–327, System Dynamics Society, 'The beer game', 2013, web page, accessed: 15 Dec 2013.

94 See Sterman, 'Modeling managerial behavior', pp. 329–330.

95 See ibid., p. 334.

96 Ibid., p. 336.

97 See Sterman, *Business dynamics*, p. 751.

98 See ibid., p. 681.

99 See Steckel, Joel H., Sunil Gupta and Anirvan Banerji, 'Supply chain decision making: Will shorter cycle times and shared point-of-sale information necessarily help?', *Management Science* 50.4 (2004): 458–464.

100 See ibid., p. 463.

101 See Chen, Frank et al., 'Quantifying the bullwhip effect in a simple supply chain: The impact of forecasting, lead times, and information', *Management Science* 46.3 (2000): 436–442.

102 See ibid., p. 442.

103 See Smaros, Johanna et al., 'The impact of increasing demand visibility on production and inventory control efficiency', *International Journal of Physical Distribution & Logistics Management* 33.4 (2003): 336–354.

104 See Lee et al., 'Information distortion in a supply chain', pp. 1875–1886.

105 See ibid., pp. 1877–1878, pp. 1883–1884.

106 See ibid., pp. 1879–1881, 1884.

107 See ibid., pp. 1881–1882, 1884.

108 See ibid., pp. 1882–1885.

109 See Croson, Rachel and Karen Donohue, 'Behavioral causes of the bullwhip effect and the observed value of inventory information', *Management Science* 52.3 (2006): 328. – The authors use the Beer Distribution Game model to test the impact of a stochastical demand pattern on the bullwhip effect.

110 See ibid., p. 330.

111 See ibid., pp. 331–333.

112 Lyneis, James M. and Maurice A. Glucksman, 'Market analysis and forecasting as a strategic business tool.' In *Computer-Based Management of Complex Systems*, eds Milling, Peter M. and Erich O. K. Zahn (Springer Berlin Heidelberg, 1989).

113 Lyneis, James M., 'System Dynamics in business forecasting: A case study of the commercial jet aircraft industry,' *16th International Conference of the System Dynamics Society* (Québec City, Canada: 1998).

114 Lyneis, James M., 'System Dynamics for business strategy: A phased approach', *System Dynamics Review* 15.1 (1999).

115 Lyneis, James M., 'System Dynamics for market forecasting and structural analysis', *System Dynamics Review* 16.1 (2000).

116 Skinner, Steve and Elane Stock, 'Masters of the cycle', *Airline Business* 14.4 (1998).

117 Skinner, Steve et al., 'Managing growth and profitability across peaks and troughs of the airline industry cycle', in *Handbook of airline finance*, eds Butler, Gail F. and Martin R. Keller, 1st edn, An aviation week book (New York and others: McGraw-Hill, 1999).

118 Liehr, Martin et al., 'Cycles in the sky: Understanding and managing business cycles in the airline market', *System Dynamics Review* 17.4 (2001).

119 Jiang, Helen and R. John Hansman, 'An analysis of profit cycles in the airline indus-try', *Masters thesis*, Massachusetts Institute of Technology, 2004.

120 Jiang, Helen and R. John Hansman, 'An analysis of profit cycles in the airline industry', *6th AIAA Aviation Technology, Integration and Operations Conference (ATIO)*, (Wichita, KS: 2006).

121 Segers, Rafael, 'An analysis of external and internal drivers of profit cycles in the airline industry – An industry dynamics approach', Masters thesis, Cranfield University, 2005.

122 Sgouridis, Sgouris P., 'Symbiotic strategies in enterprise ecology: Modeling commercial aviation as an Enterprise of Enterprises,' PhD thesis, Massachusetts Institute of Technology, 2007.

123 Sgouridis, Sgouris et al., *Taming the business cycle in commercial aviation – Trade-space analysis of strategic alternatives using simulation modelling*, Massachusetts Institute of Technology: Working Paper Series, Cambridge, MA, 2008.

124 Pierson, Kawika, 'Modeling the cyclic nature of aggregate airline industry profits,' *27th International Conference of the System Dynamics Society*, (Albuquerque, NM: 2009).

125 Pierson, Kawika, 'Profit cycle dynamics,' PhD thesis, Massachusetts Institute of Technology, 2011.

126 Pierson, Kawika and John D. Sterman, 'Cyclical dynamics of airline industry earnings,' *System Dynamics Review* 29.3 (2013).

127 See Skinner and Stock, 'Masters of the cycle,' section 2.

128 See ibid., section 5.

129 'A wet lease is the leasing of an aircraft complete with cockpit and cabin crew, and other technical support. [...] The aircraft retains the paint scheme and logo of the lessor, although a temporary sticker can be used to show the lessee's name.' Definition by Morrell, Peter S., *Airline finance*, 3rd edn (Aldershot, England; Burlington, VT: Ashgate, 2007) p. 204.

130 See Skinner and Stock, 'Masters of the cycle', section 6.

131 See ibid., section 2.

132 Skinner et al., 'Managing growth and profitability across peaks and troughs of the airline industry cycle.'

133 See ibid., p. 26.

134 See ibid., p. 29.

135 See ibid.

136 See Lyneis, 'System Dynamics for market forecasting and structural analysis', p. 6.

137 See Lyneis and Glucksman, 'Market analysis and forecasting as a strategic business tool', p. 142. And see Lyneis, 'System Dynamics for business strategy', p. 64. And see Lyneis, 'System Dynamics for market forecasting and structural analysis', p. 9.

138 See Lyneis, 'System Dynamics for business strategy', pp. 63–64. Arrow polarities are not given in original.

139 Ibid., p. 63.

140 See Lyneis, 'System Dynamics for market forecasting and structural analysis', p. 7.

141 See ibid., p. 9.

142 See ibid., pp. 22–23.

143 See Liehr et al., 'Cycles in the sky', p. 320.

144 Ibid.

145 See ibid., pp. 315–316.

146 See ibid., p. 316.

147 See ibid., p. 320.

148 Ibid., p. 316.

149 See ibid., pp. 321–323.

150 Jiang and Hansman, 'An analysis of profit cycles in the airline industry', p. 16.

151 See Jiang and Hansman, 'An analysis of profit cycles in the airline industry', p. 46.

152 See Jiang and Hansman, 'An analysis of profit cycles in the airline industry', p. 5.

153 See ibid., p. 15.

154 See ibid., p. 9.

155 See ibid., p. 13.

156 See ibid., p. 11.

157 See ibid., p. 16.

158 See Segers, 'An analysis of external and internal drivers of profit cycles in the airline industry', p. 157.

159 See ibid., pp. 26–27.

160 See ibid., pp. 153–154.

161 See ibid., p. 144.

162 See ibid., pp. 142–143.

163 See ibid., pp. 145–147.

164 See ibid., p. 147.

165 Figure reprinted with the kind permission of Cranfield University. Source: ibid., 167.

166 Sgouridis et al., *Taming the business cycle in commercial aviation*, p. 14.

167 See ibid.

168 See Sgouridis, 'Modeling commercial aviation as an Enterprise of Enterprises', pp. 238–256.

169 See Sgouridis et al., *Taming the business cycle in commercial aviation*, pp. 5–6.

170 See ibid., pp. 14–15.

171 See ibid., p. 17.

172 See ibid., pp. 17–19.

173 Sgouridis formulates: fare price = [UnitCosts / (1+TargetProfitability)] * Loading EfctOnPrice * ProfitEfctOnPrice. See Sgouridis, 'Modeling commercial aviation as an Enterprise of Enterprises', p. 246.

174 Pierson, 'Profit cycle dynamics', p. 64.

175 See Pierson and Sterman, 'Cyclical dynamics of airline industry earnings', pp. 144–145.

176 Ibid., p. 145.

177 Ibid.

178 See ibid., p. 147.

179 See ibid., p. 149.

180 See ibid., pp. 137–138.

181 See model equations in supplementary material in: ibid.

182 See model equations in supplementary material in: ibid.

183 Only those System Dynamics models with documented equations can be evaluated. This excludes the studies by (first authors) Skinner and by Lyneis.

184 Again, only those System Dynamics models with documented equations can be evaluated. This excludes the studies by (first authors) Skinner and by Lyneis.

185 Pilarski, Adam M., *Why can't we make money in aviation?* (Aldershot, UK; Burlington, VT: Ashgate, 2007). – Non-scientific argumentation, largely based on work experience in the aviation industry.

186 Results counted for search terms 'profit cycle', 'boom and bust', 'profitability cycle' anywhere in title, abstract, or text body of the article.

187 As for academic journals: results counted for search terms 'profit cycle', 'boom and bust cycle', 'profitability cycle' anywhere in title, abstract or text body of the article.

188 Search terms anywhere in title, abstract, or text body of the article to find relevant paragraphs or chapters were 'cycle', 'cyclic', 'profit', 'profitability'.

189 O'Connell, John F. and George Williams, *Air transport in the 21st century: Key strategic developments* (Farnham, UK; Burlington, VT: Ashgate, 2011).

190 Morrell, *Airline finance*.

191 O'Connor, William E., *An introduction to airline economics*, 6th edn (Westport, CT: Praeger, 2001).

192 Wittmer, Andreas, Thomas Bieger and Roland Müller, *Aviation systems management of the integrated aviation value chain*, Springer texts in business and economics (Berlin; New York: SpringerLink, 2011).

193 Sheehan, John J., *Business and corporate aviation management*, 2nd edn. (New York: McGraw-Hill Education, 2013).

194 Flouris, Triant G. and Sharon L. Oswald, *Designing and executing strategy in aviation management* (Aldershot, UK; Burlington, VT: Ashgate, 2006).

195 Doganis, Rigas, *Flying off course – Airline economics and marketing*, 4th edn. (London and New York: Routledge, 2010).

196 Vasigh, Bijan, Ken Fleming and Liam Mackay, *Foundations of airline finance: Methodology and practice* (Farham, Surrey; Burlington, VT: Ashgate, 2010).

197 Harvey, Geraint, *Management in the airline industry* (London: Routledge, 2007).

198 Flouris, Triant G. and Ayse Kucuk Yilmaz, *Risk management and corporate sustainability in aviation* (Farnham, UK; Burlington, VT: Ashgate, 2011).

199 Clark, Paul, *Stormy skies: Airlines in crisis* (Farnham, UK: Ashgate, 2010).

200 Holloway, Stephen, *Straight and level: Practical airline economics*, 3rd edn. (Ashgate, 2008).

201 Delfmann, Werner, *Strategic management in the aviation industry* (Cologne; Aldershot, UK; Burlington, VT: Kölner Wissenschaftsverlag; Farnham, UK: Ashgate, 2005).

202 Belobaba, Peter, Amedeo R. Odoni and Cynthia Barnhart, *The global airline industry*, Aerospace series (PEP) (Chichester, UK: Wiley, 2009).

203 Pilarski, *Why can't we make money in aviation?*

204 International Air Transport Association (IATA), 'Publications > Economics > Market & Industry Issues > Profitability', 2014, web page, accessed: 3 Feb 2014.

205 See Pilarski, *Why can't we make money in aviation?*

206 'Overall, in good times everybody wants to finance aircraft. In bad times, there are too many powerful parties with too much to lose. The outcome is that financing seems to be always available.' In: ibid., p. 101.

207 Pilarski subsumes this under the chapter title 'Sexy industry drawing in dreamers and suckers', see: ibid., pp. 119–124.

208 Ibid., p. 154.

209 See ibid., pp. 155–158.

210 See ibid., p. 165.

211 See ibid., p. 187.

212 See ibid., pp. 179–186.

213 Ibid., pp. 197–198.

214 See ibid., p. 141.

215 See ibid., pp. 151–152.

216 'Wall street types have an abnormal fascination with capacity control believing with almost religious fervor that capacity constraint will necessarily lead to higher yields and more profit.' In: ibid., pp. 103–104.

217 See ibid., pp. 109–118.; 'One of these mistaken beliefs, in my opinion, is the statement that the industry is in dire need of consolidation. The almost universally accepted wisdom is that there is just too much competition and with at least some consolidation profitability would come to aviation.' In: ibid., p. 109.

218 Ibid., p. 206.

219 See ibid., p. 207.
220 See International Air Transport Association (IATA), *Profitability and the air transport value chain* (2013), pp. 14–29.
221 See International Air Transport Association (IATA), *Vision 2050* (Singapore 2011), pp. 31–37, 45.
222 See ibid., p. 46.
223 See International Air Transport Association (IATA), *Profitability and the air transport value chain*, p. 41.
224 See International Air Transport Association (IATA), *Vision 2050*, pp. 45–46, 53–54.
225 See Borenstein, Severin and Nancy L. Rose, *How airline markets work. . . Or do they? Regulatory reform in the airline industry* (2007), p. 34.
226 See Ben-Yosef, Eldad, *The evolution of the U.S. airline industry: Theory, strategy and policy*, Studies in industrial organization (Dordrecht: Springer, 2005) p. 112.
227 See Tretheway, Michael W. and W.G. Waters, 'Reregulation of the airline industry: Could price cap regulation play a role?', *Journal of Air Transport Management* 4.1 (1998): 48.
228 See Borenstein and Rose, *How airline markets work*, p. 33.
229 See Tretheway and Waters, 'Reregulation of the airline industry', p. 53.
230 See Button, Kenneth, 'Empty cores in airlines markets', *5th Hamburg Aviation Conference*, (Hamburg: 2002). And see Button, Kenneth, 'Liberalising aviation: Is there an empty core problem?', *Journal of Transport Economics and Policy* 30.3 (1996). – The original theory of the 'core' is documented in: Edgeworth, Francis Y., *Mathematical psychics – An essay on the application of mathematics to the moral science* (London: C. Kegan Paul & Co., 1881).
231 Button, 'Empty cores in airlines markets', pp. 3–4.
232 See ibid., p. 4. The 'Nash equilibrium' is documented in: Nash, John F., Jr., 'The bargaining problem', *Econometrica* 18.2 (1950). And in Nash, John F., Jr., 'Two-person cooperative games', *Econometrica* 21.1 (1953).
233 See Button, 'Empty cores in airlines markets', pp. 7 and 13. And see Button, 'Liberalising aviation', pp. 287–288.
234 Button (2002) references i.a.: Bittlingmayer, George, 'Did antitrust policy cause the great merger wave?', *Journal of Law and Economics* 28.1 (1985). And Pirrong, Stephen Craig, 'An application of core theory to the analysis of ocean shipping markets', *Journal of Law and Economics* 35.1 (1992). And Sjostrom, William, 'Antitrust immunity for shipping conferences: An empty core approach', *The Antitrust Bulletin* 38, no. Summer (1993). And Telser, Lester G., 'The usefulness of core theory in economics', *The Journal of Economic Perspectives* 8.2 (1994).
235 See Sjostrom, 'Antitrust immunity for shipping conferences: An empty core approach', p. 421.
236 See Button, 'Empty cores in airlines markets', p. 7.
237 See ibid., p. 10.
238 See Borenstein and Rose, *How airline markets work*, p. 35.
239 See ibid., pp. 40–43.
240 See ibid., pp. 35–40.
241 Ibid., p. 40.
242 See Chin, Anthony T. H. and John H. Tay, 'Developments in air transport: Implications on investment decisions, profitability and survival of Asian airlines', *Journal of Air Transport Management* 7.5 (2001): 329–330.
243 See ibid., p. 325.
244 See ibid., p. 329.
245 See Wojahn, Oliver W., 'Why does the airline industry over-invest?', *Journal of Air Transport Management* 19 (2012): 1–2.

246 See ibid., pp. 6–7.
247 See ibid., pp. 3–4.
248 See Werner, Frank M., 'Leverage and airline financial management', in *Handbook of airline finance*, eds Butler, Gail F. and Martin R. Keller, 1st ed. (New York: Aviation Week, 1999), p. 187.
249 See ibid., p. 188.
250 See ibid., pp. 195–196.
251 See ibid., p. 196.
252 See Garvett, Donald S. and Kyle J. Hilton, 'What drives airline profits? A first look', in *Handbook of airline finance*, eds Butler, Gail F. and Martin R. Keller, 1st edn. (New York: Aviation Week, 1999) p. 177.
253 See ibid., p. 178.
254 See ibid., pp. 179–180.
255 See ibid., p. 181.
256 Ibid.
257 See ibid., pp. 180, 184.
258 See Kahn, Alfred E., *Lessons from deregulation: Telecommunications and airlines after the crunch* (Washington, D.C.: AEI-Brookings Joint Center for Regulatory Studies: Distributed by Brookings Institution Press, 2004) p. 5.
259 See Rose, Nancy L., 'After airline deregulation and Alfred E. Kahn', 102.3 (2012): 376.
260 See Neidl, Raymond E., 'Current financial and operational trends in the airline industry', in *Handbook of airline finance*, eds Butler, Gail F. and Martin R. Keller, 1st edn. (New York: Aviation Week, 1999) p. 614.
261 See Neidl, Raymond E., 'Can the aviation industry shield itself from business cycles?', in *Handbook of airline finance*, eds Butler, Gail F. and Martin R. Keller, 1st edn. (New York: Aviation Week, 1999), p. 21.
262 Ibid.
263 See Neidl, 'Current financial and operational trends in the airline industry', p. 625.
264 See Adler, Nicole and Aaron Gellman, 'Strategies for managing risk in a changing aviation environment', *Journal of Air Transport Management* 21 (2012): 26.
265 Halsey, Ashley, 'Global airline profits expected to drop below 1% next year, industry official says', *The Washington Post*, 2011, web page, accessed: 18 Feb 2014.
266 Deseret News, 'Airline industry to present "perilous" financial picture', 2004, web page, accessed: 14 Feb 2014.
267 Reed, Ted, 'Airlines, not yet where they want to be, make 21 cents per passenger', Forbes.com, 2013 web page, accessed: 18 Feb 2014.
268 CAPA Centre for Aviation, 'Rising fuel costs dominate airline bottom lines', 2011, web page, accessed: 18 Feb 2014.
269 CAPA Centre for Aviation, 'High fuel prices and weak load factors erode SIA's profits', 2011, web page, accessed: 18 Feb 2014.
270 CAPA Centre for Aviation, 'Thai's profits drop in 1Q2011 as oil prices and external factors affect demand', 2011, web page, accessed: 18 Feb 2014.
271 CAPA Centre for Aviation, 'Gol's operating margin drops as Brazil's carriers refuse to raise fares', 2011, web page, accessed: 18 Feb 2014.
272 CNN Financial News, 'Airline 1Q losses mount', CNN Money Online, 2001, web page, accessed: 18 Feb 2014.
273 Isidore, Chris, 'US Air files Chapter 11 – again', CNN Money Online, 2004, web page, accessed: 18 Feb 2014.
274 Discussant, 'Why airlines fail – Too costly or bad management?', Airliners.net Forum, 2004, web page, accessed: 18 Feb 2014.
275 CNN Financial News, 'Airline 1Q losses mount', accessed: 18 Feb 2014.

276 Pearson, David, 'Air France-KLM Net Loss Widens', *The Wall Street Journal* Online, 2013, web page, accessed: 18 Feb 2014.

277 See Morrell, Peter S., 'Current challenges in a "distressed" industry', *Journal of Air Transport Management* 17.1 (2011): 16–17. And see: Franke, Markus, 'Innovation: The winning formula to regain profitability in aviation?', *Journal of Air Transport Management* 13.1 (2007): 21–23.

278 International Air Transport Association (IATA), *Press Release No. 28* (2004).

279 Veal, Sarah, 'How one airline cut costs and held onto profits', *The New York Times*, 1994, web page, accessed: 18 Feb 2014.

280 International Air Transport Association (IATA), *Cost structure – Irreconcilable differences?* (2010).

281 Peterson, Joel, 'American + U.S. Airways: A match made in heaven?', *Forbes* Online, 2013, web page, accessed: 18 Feb 2014.

282 Interview designs and how to select the appropriation method for a given research purpose are explained in, for example: Vogt, Paul W., Dianne C. Gardner and Lynne M. Haeffele, *When to use what research design* (New York: Guilford Press, 2012).

283 Roughly 50% of the participants represent German organisations, 30% American ones, and 20% are members of organisations with other nationalities.

284 See Porter, Michael E., 'Five forces in the airline industry,' in *Vision 2050*, ed. International Air Transport Association (IATA) (Report, 2011) p. 23.

3 System Dynamics model of airline industry profit development

3.1 Need for a System Dynamics analysis

In the previous chapter, potential airline profit cycle drivers were derived and categorised into general economic factors, airline industry environment features, and airlines' internal mechanisms. It was found that airline industry practitioners mainly hold general economic developments responsible for the profit cycle. In the following section their impact on airline profits will be examined empirically (see section 3.1.1). Results will reveal that the actual cycle drivers are complex. Hence, to assess the importance of general economic factors, as well as other categories' potential cycle drivers, a systemic analysis is required. As a method to address complex dynamic problems System Dynamics will be introduced (see section 3.1.2).

3.1.1 Complexity revealed in statistical examination of popular cycle driver hypotheses

Three popular hypotheses about what drives the airline profit cycle will be examined. As concluded in section 2.5, airline managers and the press focus on explaining the cycle by general economic developments, external shocks, and the fuel price. Their influence on airline profits will be statistically inspected.

The first hypothesis to be examined is that the airlines' profit cyclicality is merely the result of the general economic development. While it is true that airlines' demand develops with the general economy, statistical analyses reveal that economic fluctuations alone cannot explain the airline profit cycle. The correlation between the world's real GDP, as an indicator for economic development, and passenger numbers is almost perfect with $R^2 = 0.98$; between real GDP and revenue passenger kilometres (air kilometres sold to passengers) the correlation is $R^2 = 0.99$.[1] However, correlations between the world's GDP and world aggregate airline profits are below 0.4, mostly below 0.2, which means that less than 20% of the variance in airline profits can be explained by the variance in GDP. Table 3.1 summarises the calculated correlations.[2] Coefficients are based on 39 years (1971–2009) and include possible time lags of one, two, and three years between GDP and profit measures.[3]

The highest correlation is the one between annual real GDP growth and airlines' operating profitability with $R^2 = 0.36$. Their relation is shown in

Table 3.1 Correlations between global economic development (GDP) and worldwide airline profits

World data: Correlations between GDP and airlines' operating profit

based on years 1971–2009	op. profit	op. profit in t+1	op. profit in t+2	op. profit in t+3	real op. profit	real op. profit in t+1	real op. profit in t+2	real op. profit in t+3	op. profitability	op. profitability in t+1	op. profitability in t+2	op. profitability in t+3
GDP	0.09	0.16	0.21	0.20	0.01	0.04	0.06	0.06	0.06	0.03	0.02	0.01
real GDP	0.08	0.12	0.15	0.15	0.01	0.03	0.03	0.03	0.06	0.03	0.04	0.02
GDP growth p.a.	0.00	0.08	0.03	0.00	0.00	0.04	0.02	0.00	0.05	0.00	0.01	0.00
real GDP growth p.a.	0.11	0.04	0.09	0.02	0.18	0.01	0.06	0.03	0.36	0.01	0.04	0.05

	operating profit growth p.a.	operating profit growth p.a. in t+1	operating profit growth p.a. in t+2	operating profit growth p.a. in t+3	real op. profit growth p.a.	real op. profit growth p.a. in t+1	real op. profit growth p.a. in t+2	real op. profit growth p.a. in t+3	op. profitability growth p.a.	op. profitability growth p.a. in t+1	op. profitability growth p.a. in t+2	op. profitability growth p.a. in t+3
GDP	0.00	0.05	0.07	0.06	0.00	0.05	0.07	0.06	0.00	0.04	0.06	0.05
real GDP	0.00	0.04	0.04	0.05	0.00	0.04	0.04	0.05	0.00	0.04	0.04	0.04
GDP growth p.a.	0.04	0.01	0.02	0.00	0.04	0.01	0.02	0.00	0.04	0.01	0.02	0.00
real GDP growth p.a.	0.06	0.04	0.00	0.03	0.18	0.04	0.00	0.03	0.06	0.03	0.00	0.03

Figure 3.1. Similarity between real GDP growth and the operating profitability level is visible. Yet, an analysis of first differences reveals that both variables develop in the same direction in only 24 of the 39 years (62%). A comparison of real GDP growth and the change in operating profitability reveals that profitability changes are much larger. Hence, there is strong amplification in airline profits whose source remains to be detected.

It can be concluded that although the general economic development has a certain influence on airline profits it is by far not sufficient to explain the airline profit cycle.

The second hypothesis is that external shocks cause demand slumps and hence initiate airline profit downswings. Big crises for aviation since 1970 as well as world airline profits are shown in Figure 3.2.[4]

It can be observed that troughs in the airline profit cycle were preceded by or occur with a crisis. However, the shocks fail to explain all profit downturns. Table 3.2 lists crises and the beginnings of downturns, which are per definition

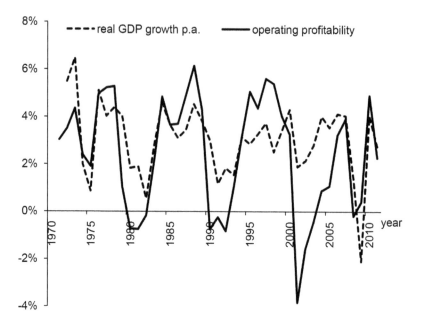

Figure 3.1 Relationship between global annual real GDP growth and airlines' operating profitability to revenues

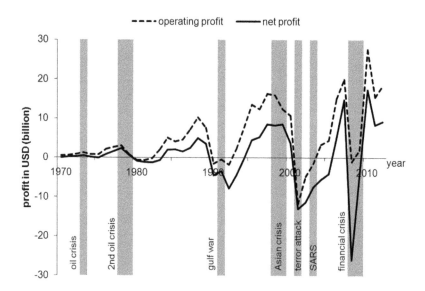

Figure 3.2 Financial results of worldwide airlines and international crises

Table 3.2 Time between beginning of profit downturn and crisis

Are shocks responsible for profit downturns?		
crisis	*downturn begins* *(after cycle peak in year x)*	*crisis initialised* *downturn?*
1973 oil crisis	1973	likely
1978/79 second oil crisis	1978	likely
1991 gulf war	1988 (3 years earlier)	no
1998/99 Asian financial crisis	1997 (1 year earlier)	likely
2001 9/11 terror attack	(4 years earlier, now upswing)	no
2003 near pandemic (SARS)	(in upswing)	no
2008/09 global financial crisis	2007 (1 year earlier)	likely

the profit cycle peaks. Four of the five downturns may have been introduced by a crisis because there is hardly or no time between shock and downturn. Yet, clearly, the profit downswing after 1988 was not initiated by a shock. The role of external shocks for the airline profit cycle therefore remains uncertain.

The third hypothesis is that the fuel price is the major airline profit cycle driver. For example, for US airlines in 2010 fuel expenses amounted to approximately a quarter of airlines' operating costs.[5] The hypothesis is that high market prices for fuel inevitably lead to low profits. Empirically, this finds no support. Correlations between fuel price and world airline operating profits for the years 1971–2009 are at most 0.20, as compiled in Table 3.3.[6] With $R^2 = 0.20$ the highest correlation is found between fuel price and operating profit two years later. Figure 3.3 shows that there is no visual relationship between fuel price and operating profit, except a counter-intuitive one: rising fuel prices since 2000 go along with on average rising instead of falling profits.[7] This means there must be compensatory factors which have a strong impact on airlines' profits. Altogether, it can be concluded that fuel price developments may have an influence on the airline profit cycle but are by far not sufficient to explain it.

The conclusion of the empirical analyses is that the general economy, external demand shocks, and the fuel price have influence on airline profits. However, each of them alone cannot explain the airline profit cycle. Likely, a combination of different drivers produces the cycle. The issue is complex: it involves many potential influencing factors; these are interdependent, and their relations are often non-linear and characterised by time delays.[8] Hence, to identify the airline profit cycle's drivers and suitable mitigation policies, a more comprehensive and systemic approach is necessary. It needs to allow testing the explanatory power of not only external influences from the general economy but also the airline industry environment and airline behaviour itself. Furthermore, the question why airline profits are cyclical needs to be explored

Table 3.3 Correlations between fuel prices and worldwide airline profits

World data: Correlations between fuel price and airlines' operating profit

based on years 1971–2009	op. profit	op. profit in t+1	op. profit in t+2	op. profit in t+3	real op. profit	real op. profit in t+1	real op. profit in t+2	real op. profit in t+3	op. profitability	op. profitability in t+1	op. profitability in t+2	op. profitability in t+3
fuel price	0.01	0.05	0.20	0.15	0.00	0.01	0.07	0.06	0.09	0.04	0.00	0.00
real fuel price	0.01	0.00	0.04	0.03	0.03	0.01	0.02	0.02	0.09	0.04	0.00	0.01
fuel price change p.a.	0.01	0.13	0.00	0.00	0.01	0.16	0.01	0.01	0.02	0.15	0.01	0.00
real fuel price change p.a.	0.00	0.11	0.00	0.00	0.01	0.15	0.01	0.00	0.01	0.15	0.01	0.00

	operating profit growth p.a.	operating profit growth p.a. in t+1	operating profit growth p.a. in t+2	operating profit growth p.a. in t+3	real op. profit growth p.a.	real op. profit growth p.a. in t+1	real op. profit growth p.a. in t+2	real op. profit growth p.a. in t+3	op. profitability growth p.a.	op. profitability growth p.a. in t+1	op. profitability growth p.a. in t+2	op. profitability growth p.a. in t+3
fuel price	0.01	0.00	0.10	0.03	0.01	0.00	0.09	0.02	0.01	0.00	0.07	0.02
real fuel price	0.05	0.02	0.01	0.00	0.04	0.02	0.01	0.01	0.05	0.02	0.00	0.01
fuel price change p.a.	0.00	0.05	0.04	0.05	0.00	0.05	0.04	0.05	0.01	0.05	0.04	0.06
real fuel price change p.a.	0.00	0.05	0.07	0.03	0.00	0.05	0.06	0.04	0.01	0.04	0.06	0.04

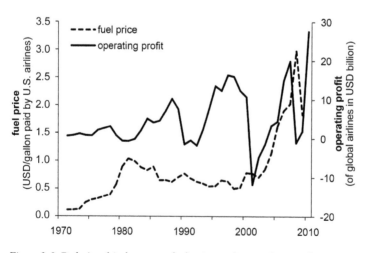

Figure 3.3 Relationship between fuel price and operating profit

over time which means analyses must account for the dynamics behind the airline profit cycle.

The methodology suitable to address the systemic and dynamic nature of the research problem is System Dynamics.[9] A System Dynamics model can capture the interrelated and entangled nature of the airline industry and can simulate different behaviour options for airlines under varying circumstances. It will thus yield not only a set of factors as a result but also the explanation why these particular factors cause and drive the profit cycle, and how they do that. This will give starting points for finding policies that dampen the system. A brief introduction to System Dynamics will be given in the following section.

3.1.2 System Dynamics as a method to address complexity

System Dynamics was developed by Jay W. Forrester in the late 1950s.[10] It applies to dynamically complex situations, i.e. situations in which the behaviour over time is important. System Dynamics models serve to better understand a dynamically complex situation and to find policies for avoiding or correcting undesirable behaviour.[11] Dynamic problems can arise in complex social, managerial, economic, or ecological systems – literally any dynamic systems characterised by interdependence, mutual interaction, information feedback, and circular causality.[12] First System Dynamics applications were the analyses of amplifying oscillations in supply chains (see also section 2.2.2).[13]

According to Milling, System Dynamics is a structural theory of a system. A system's structure causes its behaviour.[14] Consequently, all interactions that produce the dynamic behaviour in question need to be included in the system (closed boundary concept). Within its boundary the system consists of feedback loops. A feedback loop (see Figure 3.4) describes a circle in which a decision results in an action that changes the state of the system, information about which is the basis for future decision-making.[15] There are two kinds of feedback loops: balancing and reinforcing ones. A balancing feedback loop, also called 'negative' feedback loop, aims to achieve the balance between the actual and the desired state of the system. A reinforcing 'positive' feedback loop constantly reinforces its current condition. A system can be expressed as an interconnected combination of feedback loops. This way of formulating a system is inherently nonlinear.[16]

Although humans can conceptualise feedback loop systems, they generally lack the cognitive capability to deduce the consequent dynamic behaviour without assistance.[17] For example, it is difficult to grasp that over time different parts of the system structure may be active, and heavily influence the system behaviour (varying loop dominance).[18] Also, delays, for example for processing, production, or expectation formation, make the dynamics of a system difficult to gauge.[19] Mathematically formalising and simulating a feedback model compensates this human deficit and generates the system's behaviour over time.[20] The consequences of alternative decision rules and different circumstances can thus be derived. Furthermore, the rigorous mathematical model formulation necessary for computer simulations reveals decision makers' mental models.[21]

Flaws in the way decisions are made become explicit. Working with a System Dynamics model thus enhances decision makers' understanding of a problem and its potential solutions.[22] Besides, for example in a business context, a formal model offers a way to conserve experienced managers' insights about how the business works and what should be done in which scenario.[23]

The System Dynamics modelling process is iterative (see Figure 3.5).[24] The process steps illustrated below serve as an orientation. Insights gained in any step can lead to rethinking and redoing of another step. The modelling process starts by defining the problem to be solved. The second step is to gather information about the system and to generate initial hypotheses about the problem. The system boundary is selected and the identified feedback loops may be mapped in a causal loop diagram. The third step is to formulate a simulation model. In the fourth step, the validation process, different testing procedures help to determine whether the model is useful for its purpose. Results may lead to the revision of earlier steps. When confidence in the model's usefulness is gained, policy testing can be conducted.

Methodically, System Dynamics is based on several principles formulated by Forrester.[25] Elements of feedback loops are *levels* (= *stocks*) and *rates* (= *flows*). A level indicates the system's state or condition. It accumulates the results of actions in the system. An example is the water level in a bathtub. Levels can only be changed by rates, e.g. the water inflow and outflow. Rates (flows) are governed by decision rules, which may consist of *constant* values, e.g. a goal, and *auxiliary* variables, e.g. the discrepancy between level and goal.

The nomenclature and symbols used in the following model description are given in Figure 3.6.[26]

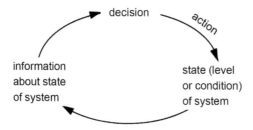

Figure 3.4 Feedback loop

Source: adapted from Forrester 1968, p. 43

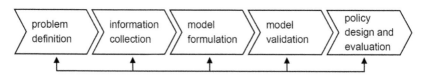

Figure 3.5 System Dynamics modelling process

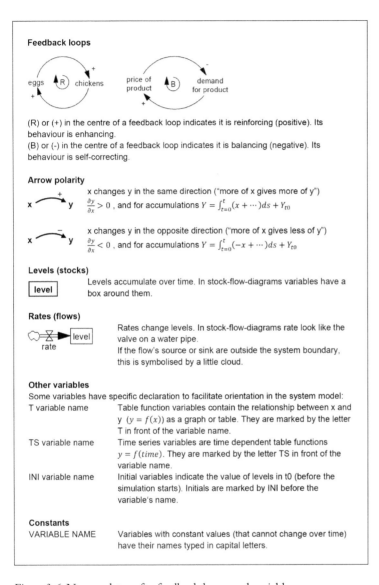

Feedback loops

eggs (R) chickens price of product (B) demand for product

(R) or (+) in the centre of a feedback loop indicates it is reinforcing (positive). Its behaviour is enhancing.
(B) or (-) in the centre of a feedback loop indicates it is balancing (negative). Its behaviour is self-correcting.

Arrow polarity

x changes y in the same direction ("more of x gives more of y")
$\frac{\partial y}{\partial x} > 0$, and for accumulations $Y = \int_{t=0}^{t}(x + \cdots)ds + Y_{t0}$

x changes y in the opposite direction ("more of x gives less of y")
$\frac{\partial y}{\partial x} < 0$, and for accumulations $Y = \int_{t=0}^{t}(-x + \cdots)ds + Y_{t0}$

Levels (stocks)

| level | Levels accumulate over time. In stock-flow-diagrams variables have a box around them.

Rates (flows)

Rates change levels. In stock-flow-diagrams rate look like the valve on a water pipe.
If the flow's source or sink are outside the system boundary, this is symbolised by a little cloud.

Other variables

Some variables have specific declaration to facilitate orientation in the system model:

T variable name — Table function variables contain the relationship between x and y $(y = f(x))$ as a graph or table. They are marked by the letter T in front of the variable name.

TS variable name — Time series variables are time dependent table functions $y = f(time)$. They are marked by the letter TS in front of the variable name.

INI variable name — Initial variables indicate the value of levels in t0 (before the simulation starts). Initials are marked by INI before the variable's name.

Constants

VARIABLE NAME — Variables with constant values (that cannot change over time) have their names typed in capital letters.

Figure 3.6 Nomenclature for feedback loops and variables

3.2 Outline of the airline profit cycle model

This section presents a System Dynamics model of airline industry profit cycles. As a starting point in section 3.2.1 the model's purpose is clearly defined and the resulting decisions about what to include in the modelled system and what to exclude from it (system boundary) are explained. Subsequently, in section 3.2.2, a rough outline of the model in the form of a causal loop diagram is given. This will facilitate orientation in the simulation model, which is presented in section 3.3. In section 3.4 the model's validity is examined, before it is calibrated for the US airline industry in Chapter 4.

3.2.1 System boundary

The purpose of the airline profit cycle model is to examine the impact of potential airline profit cycle drivers and mitigation measures, identified in Chapter 2, in model simulations.

The time horizon of the model encompasses several decades since a full swing of the profit cycle takes approximately ten years (see section 1.1). The central variable of the model is industry-wide aggregated airline profit. It is assumed that airlines seek to maximise profits and are able to do so in a deregulated industry environment. As shown in section 1.1 the US industry, which was already deregulated in 1978, exhibits the strongest airline profit cycle. It is concluded that to research the airline profit cycle a deregulated industry needs to be modelled.

The airline industry model will concentrate on *operating profits*, i.e. earnings before interest and tax (EBIT). They are the financial result of the airlines' core business, which is air transportation. As demonstrated in section 1.1, operating profits already exhibit the cyclicality that the model is intended to analyse. So the inclusion of income taxes, interest payments, currency exchange earnings, etc., which would be needed to derive *net profits*, would not add further value.

To derive key variables for the model, *operating profit* is decomposed into its components. It is the result of *operating revenue* minus *operating costs*.

operating profit = operating revenue – operating costs

The units airlines produce are seat miles, i.e. the distance of miles that each seat on a plane travels in the air. Seat miles made available to passengers by offering them on the market are called *available seat miles*. They quantify the supply side in the airline market. *Available seat miles* which are sold to passengers contribute to airlines' revenue. They are thus called *revenue passenger miles*. The price passengers pay for their tickets may include certain taxes that airlines have to pass on to the authorities. The part of the price which actually contributes to airline revenues, i.e. the revenue per seat mile sold, is called *yield*. *Operating revenue* is thus the product of *yield* and *revenue passenger miles*.

*operating revenues = yield * revenue passenger miles*

Operating costs are generated by personnel, fuel, aircraft rents and depreciation, etc.[27] They are calculated as the product of cost per unit produced, i.e. *unit cost per available seat mile*, and the quantity of *available seat miles*.

*operating costs = unit costs * available seat miles*

To be able to experiment with airline market dynamics, demand (*revenue passenger miles*), supply (*available seat miles*), and the price which brings them together (*yield*) need to be generated endogenously in the model. *Unit costs* need to be included as well, but may be only partly endogenous because airlines have, for example, no influence on fuel prices.[28]

Since the model is intended to generate industry-wide operating airline profit, the level of aggregation in the model is the industry level. This means all airlines based in a country (or region) will be examined as a whole.[29] Consequently, variables in the model will describe industry totals for demand and supply, and an average industry price level for an average product and service offer. Individual airlines are not modelled separately. Hence, the model is not designed to produce strategic recommendations for individual airlines. Insights will be gained on an industry level, and profit cycle mitigation suggestions for industry level decision makers will be given. These may be transferable to individual airlines, aircraft manufacturers, and other stakeholders.

Although in the model the airline industry is not disaggregated into individual airlines, their competition amongst each other is nonetheless captured.[30] It is reflected in the way they make their decisions. For example, airlines in a competitive environment are anxious to maintain or achieve a slim cost base, they feel a pressure to lower prices in order to fill their planes, and they are reluctant to reduce their capacity supply to defend their market shares. Airlines' decision processes will be explained in detail in section 3.3. The emergence of low-cost carriers as new competitors in the airline industry is represented in the model by an even higher pressure on airlines to reduce costs and prices, and a rise in ancillary yields[31].

Airlines may experience competition not only amongst each other but also with other modes of transportation. For example, high-speed trains with their frequent and dense network in Europe can be a threatening substitute to air travel. However, for most flights other transport modes do not offer passengers sufficiently similar qualities. 'It is obvious that geographic components, such as seas, impenetrable mountain ranges or even the mere distance of a trip, may complicate the presence or establishment of a given supply of adequate substitute modes.'[32] Since the model is going to be calibrated for the US airline industry, with all national and international traffic, competition with other modes of transportation is limited to certain routes and can be neglected from an industry perspective. Nonetheless, the attractiveness or quality of the air traffic service are captured in the model for possible alternative calibration choices. As suggested in previous modelling work the industry's service quality is approximated by the industry's *load factor*, i.e. the ratio of *revenue passenger miles* to *available seat miles* (see also section 3.2.1).[33] Higher load factors indicate a less comfortable flight experience and also an 'increased probability of delays due to the entire aircraft/airport system being close to capacity'.[34]

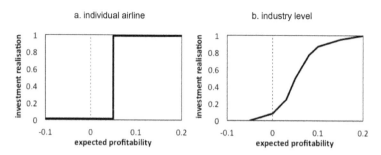

Figure 3.7 Example of decision distributions among airlines on industry level

Modelling from an industry perspective entails that decisions are often not answered with a clear yes or no. Each airline in the industry has different expectations, evaluation schemes, and endowments. What impact this has on the model shall be clarified with a fictive example. If an individual airline expects an investment to achieve more than 5% profitability, it will invest. For a lower profitability, the airline does not invest. Its behaviour is illustrated in Figure 3.7a. From an industry-level perspective the investment curve looks different (see Figure 3.7b). What one airline finds profitable enough, is not necessarily desirable for others. At 5% expected profitability, already more than half of the airlines choose to invest. At 10% average expected profitability, around 80% of the airlines invest. And at 20% even the most pessimistic airline invests. Some very optimistic airlines may still invest at an average expected profitability of −2%. However, at −5% no one seeks to invest anymore. The airline industry model developed in section 3.3 will take this macro view on decision rules.

A part of the airline industry is the air cargo business. For several reasons it will be regarded as implicit and will not be modelled explicitly. Only around 11% of global airline revenues are generated in freight transportation.[35] Besides, the way the cargo market works differs significantly from the airline industry's core business, passenger air transportation. Most cargo load (over 85%) is carried in the belly of passenger airplanes.[36] Hence, most cargo revenues would not be possible without the passenger business. An analysis of passenger and cargo revenues, illustrated in Figure 3.8, confirms that the two develop similarly over time.[37] Consequently, broadly speaking, air freight, passenger revenues, and cost base move in the same direction. Given the airline industry model's purpose is to examine profit cycle drivers, the cargo market seems well represented in a model focused on the passenger air transportation business.

In the model airlines' demand is not disaggregated into different fare classes, such as first, business, or economy class. The necessary industry data on yield or profitability in different fare classes is not publicly available. However, it is known that in terms of volume, premium and economy class exhibit similar reactions to income (GDP) changes.[38] In economic downturns both tend to

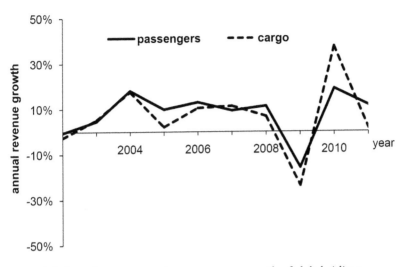

Figure 3.8 Annual passenger and cargo revenue growth of global airlines

decrease, in upturns they usually increase. There is no consensus as to which fare class reacts more strongly to income changes. Due to the similar behaviour of different fare classes and the lack of data, fare classes will not be modelled separately.

The airline industry model will contain several assumptions that need to be challenged in scenario simulations. In the base model aircraft manufacturers and lessors are assumed to guarantee adequate supply of ordered aircraft. So whilst airlines may need to wait for their orders they will eventually acquire them. Shortages in the lessors' or manufacturers' provision of aircraft are subject to scenario analyses.

The option to acquire aircraft on the used machine market is implicit in the model. If an aircraft is sold and bought within the same industry, the industry-level model does not need to account for it because it is merely a swap. If the transaction is conducted with a party outside the industry, this is represented in the model either by an aircraft retirement or by buying from a manufacturer or lessor, respectively.

The model boundary chart in Table 3.4 lists key aspects of the airline industry model and groups them into those which are calculated within the model (endogenous), those which feed into the model (exogenous), and those chosen to be excluded. How the airline industry model features the listed variables will be explained below.

3.2.2 Causal loop diagram of airline profitability dynamics

As an introduction to the airline industry model its basic structure will be outlined. This will facilitate orientation in the simulation model explained in subsequent sections.

Table 3.4 Model boundary chart with key variables of the airline industry model

endogenous	exogenous	excluded
• operating profit	• national income (GDP)	• corporate tax (net profit)
• operating revenues (ticket revenues and ancillary revenues)	• demand preferences	• currency exchange rates
• yield (revenue per mile)	• external shocks: financial crises, 9/11 terror attack, etc.	• interest payments on debt
• revenue passenger miles	• inflation	• lease capacity restrictions (in the model leases are always available, possibly with delay)
• operating costs	• taxes and fees (e.g. ticket taxes, security fees, airport departure tax)	• aircraft manufacturing restrictions (in the model aircraft are always available, possibly with delay)
• aircraft and labour costs	• non-ticket yield per mile (ancillary yield)	
• total variable costs	• fuel costs and other variable costs per mile	
• available seat miles	• subsidies, financing costs, and bankruptcy protection	
• desired seat capacity (fleet size and mix)	• maximum aircraft productivity (includes capacity and ability of airport and air traffic control infrastructure, airlines' network planning skills, aircraft's technological capabilities and evolution)	
• aircraft fleet owned, and leased		
• aircraft order rates		
• aircraft retirement rate, lease expiry rate		
• aircraft utilisation	• leasing share (part of desired seat capacity to be leased)	
• load factors (service quality)		
• airline decisions:		
• price setting		
• aircraft capacity planning		
• aircraft ordering		
• aircraft retirement policy		
• fleet utilisation adjustment		
• cost adjustment		
• expectations about:		
• prices		
• costs		
• load factors		
• profitability		

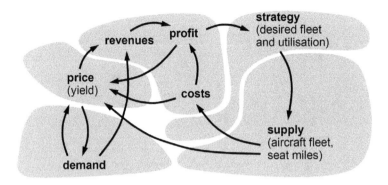

Figure 3.9 Outline of the airline industry model

Figure 3.9 features the airline industry model's basic relationships without going into detail. The shaded areas represent model parts. Profit is the result of revenues minus costs. Costs are generated by supply. Revenues are the product of price and demand. Price is mainly determined by the balance of demand and supply, as well as by profit and cost considerations. Airlines' supply of available seat miles is the result of their strategic decisions. These are based on profitability expectations as well as on current and expected market developments.

Using the same underlying relationships, Figure 3.10 offers more detail about the airline industry model.[39] This causal loop diagram will be presented below.

Airlines' operating profit is the result of operating revenue minus operating costs. Revenues depend on passenger demand and ticket prices. These are driven by competitive pressures, the ratio of demand to supply, costs, profitability expectations, and taxes and fees. Prices influence passenger demand which is in addition driven by general economic developments and crises, such as the 9/11 terror attack. Operating costs consist of a fixed and a variable component. Fixed costs are caused by the airlines' fleet, variable costs by airlines' supply of available seat miles. In case airlines expect their profitability to be inadequate, cost-cutting programs will be initiated. Based on profitability expectations, airlines determine the optimal utilisation of their aircraft. Also taking expected profitability into account as well as strategic considerations and financing conditions, airlines decide what fleet size and mix they desire for the future. By ordering and retiring aircraft airlines aim to adjust their current fleet to meet the desired supply level. Ordered aircraft will take a certain time (for production or lease preparation etc.) until they join the fleet.

As the causal loop diagram in Figure 3.10 visually suggests, the airline industry model is very interconnected. In the actual model the variable *real ticket yield*, for example, is element of 196 feedback loops.[40] The variable *expected profitability of new investments* is linked in 148 loops. Nonetheless, the model has only 124 net active equations (see Table 3.5) which makes it comparatively

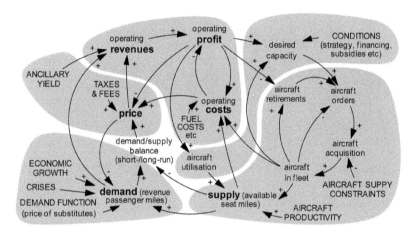

Figure 3.10 Causal loop diagram of the airline industry model

Table 3.5 Statistics of the airline industry model

Model statistics
(Statistics for the airline profit cycle model without scenario option variables.)

equations	203 total variables incl. system control parameters
	– 4 system control parameters
	= 199 variables
	– 52 defining constants (including initials)
	– 11 defining time series
	= 136 active equations
	– 12 duplicates that appear with real and nominal value
	= 124 net active equations
variables by type	
> stocks	23 = 13 regular + 10 implicit (*SMOOTH* functions)
>time series (TS)	11
>table functions (T)	4
connectedness*	843
>feedback loops	311
>causal links	
* as calculated by the SDM-Doc Tool	

---

small for a System Dynamics model.[41] The model is well within the range that Forrester defines as useful.[42]

A statistic summary of the airline industry model is given in Table 3.5, model details can be found in section 3.3. The System Dynamics software Vensim is used to visualise and simulate the model.[43]

3.3 Decision design and mechanisms in the model

The airline profit cycle model is structured into five modules. Each module calculates a key variable: demand, price, supply, cost, and profit which combines the previous four (see Figure 3.9 in preceding section). Though these modules are interdependent, as outlined in section 3.2.2, they will be explained separately, one at a time. Each module's description will close with a comparison of how the respective mechanisms are represented in previous airline industry models in the literature. The discussion is, of course, limited to studies which offer sufficient detail about their models. During the model presentation process in this section, the model overview given in Figure 3.10 in the previous section may provide orientation.

The airline profit cycle model is based on Sterman's commodity market model, which is designed as a generic model to explain cyclic fluctuations in a wide range of commodity industries.[44] A commodity is 'a raw material or primary agricultural product that can be bought and sold, such as copper or coffee'.[45] Hence, air travel is not a commodity. Nonetheless, since Sterman's model is generic many structural elements are useful starting points. Furthermore, the commodity market model has already been tested and successfully applied to an industry (pulp and paper).[46] It thus provides a robust basis for the airline profit cycle model.

3.3.1 Demand module

The demand airlines face in the market is expressed in terms of miles sold to passengers, i.e. *revenue passenger miles* (RPM). How these are calculated is explained in this section. Figure 3.11 outlines the process. The amount of miles sold depends primarily on their price. How prices affect sales is determined by the demand curve. It expresses how sensitive passengers react to price changes and how changes in economic growth affect air traffic demand. Generally, if prices fall, demand will increase, and if prices rise, demand will drop.[47] However, this does not happen immediately. Most passengers need time to consider travel alternatives and book their flights several weeks or months in advance. The result of the passengers' evaluation process is the amount of miles they wish to buy, i.e. the *industry demand*. If airlines have sufficient capacity on offer and there are no special influences (for example the 9/11 terror attack or the Olympics), airlines can serve their demand and realise *revenue passenger miles*.

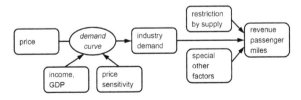

Figure 3.11 Outline of demand module

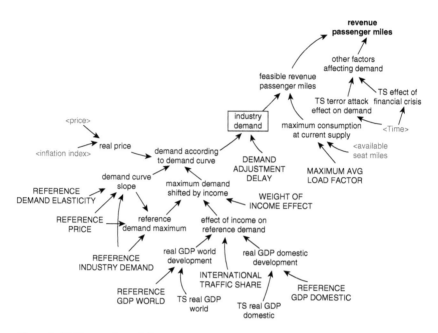

Figure 3.12 Demand module

Figure 3.12 displays the demand module's feedback structure in detail. To examine its underlying equations the *industry demand* will serve as a starting point.

The *industry demand* is the outcome of passengers' decision process. The results of their decisions and the time they need to take them are modelled separately. Passengers' decisions result is the *demand according to demand curve*. Their decision-making time is the *DEMAND ADJUSTMENT DELAY*. It aggregates the time passengers need to find and evaluate travel alternatives. This includes other modes of transport such as high-speed trains or inter-state buses. Also, most passengers book their flights several weeks or months in advance and not at the airport right before take-off. Hence, the *DEMAND ADJUSTMENT DELAY* is the time it takes until the *demand according to demand curve* becomes *industry demand*. In other words, the industry demand adjusts to *demand according to demand curve* and the *DEMAND ADJUSTMENT DELAY* is the speed of adjustment (see equation below).[48]

> *industry demand = INTEGRAL (demand according to demand curve – industry demand, demand according to demand curve$_{t0}$) / DEMAND ADJUSTMENT DELAY*

In the model a shorter formulation for this equation is used (see eq. 1).[49]

> *industry demand = SMOOTH (demand according to demand curve, DEMAND ADJUSTMENT DELAY)*   (1)

In some cases airlines may not be able to serve the entire *industry demand*. Due to safety regulation it is not possible to board more passengers on a flight than the aircraft has seats.[50] So, the amount of *feasible revenue passenger miles* is limited by the number of *available seat miles* (miles offered). Airlines' operational situation and competences might restrict boarding further so that the *MAXIMUM AVG LOAD FACTOR* airlines are capable of achieving on their flights is smaller than 100% (see eq. 2–3).

$$feasible\ revenue\ passenger\ miles = MIN\ (industry\ demand,$$
$$maximum\ consumption\ at$$
$$current\ supply) \qquad (2)$$

$$maximum\ consumption\ at\ current\ supply = available\ seat\ miles *$$
$$MAXIMUM\ AVG$$
$$LOAD\ FACTOR \qquad (3)$$

Furthermore, *feasible revenue passenger miles* may still not reflect the passengers that actually board the aircraft. There will be *other factors affecting demand* which are not captured by the demand function. These are psychological reactions to special events, such as people's sudden reluctance to fly after the 9/11 terror attack, or the diffuse fear and insecurity at the beginning of the financial crisis in 2008/9. The *other factors affecting demand* could also reflect the booking hype due to a World Cup or the Olympic games. In the airline industry model the *other factors affecting demand* are modelled as an exogenous time series (see eq. 4–5).

$$revenue\ passenger\ miles = feasible\ revenue\ passenger\ miles *$$
$$other\ factors\ affecting\ demand \qquad (4)$$

$$other\ factors\ affecting\ demand = 1 + (TS\ effect\ of\ financial\ crisis +$$
$$TS\ terror\ attack\ effect\ on\ demand) \qquad (5)$$

The core of the airline industry model's demand module is the demand function. As stated above, demand is a function of price. If price decreases, demand will increase; if price rises, demand will drop. Hence, the demand curve in the airline industry has a negative slope. The actual shape of the demand curve is not known. In the model it is assumed to be linear because a linear relationship is robust and clear to interpret.[51] (Also, model simulations at a later stage did not provide motivation to change the linearity assumption into a more complex formulation.) If flights were given away for free, there would be a certain maximum number of miles 'purchased'. At this maximum point people would have no interest to fly more, even though it were free. In case prices kept rising for some reason, they would eventually reach an amount at which nobody is willing to pay. This is the minimum point of the demand curve. In the model, the demand curve is defined by a reference point and the slope. The reference point is marked by the *REFERENCE PRICE* and the corresponding *REFERENCE INDUSTRY DEMAND* (eq. 6, preliminary formulation).

The *demand curve slope* is calculated based on the industry's REFERENCE DEMAND ELASTICITY as in equation 7. Elasticity is a construct often used in economics which expresses the relative changes of input and output.[52] For example, if a price change of -3% results in a demand increase of +6%, the demand elasticity is -2 = 6% / -3%.[53]

$$\begin{aligned} \textit{demand according to original demand curve} = {} & \textit{REFERENCE} \\ & \textit{INDUSTRY DEMAND} + \\ & \textit{demand curve slope} * (\textit{price} - \\ & \textit{REFERENCE PRICE)} \qquad (6) \end{aligned}$$

$$\begin{aligned} \textit{demand curve slope} = {} & \textit{REFERENCE DEMAND ELASTICITY} \\ & * \textit{REFERENCE INDUSTRY} \\ & \textit{DEMAND / REFERENCE PRICE} \qquad (7) \end{aligned}$$

The demand curve, which assigns a quantity sold to each price, can be interpreted as expressing passengers' willingness to pay. This is influenced by their income. Sterman's generic demand module, which has so far been the underlying concept here, does not include this influence.[54] If people's income increases, they have the option to spend more on flying because they may be willing to fly more or pay higher prices. In economic terms this means that an income increase shifts the demand curve outwards.[55] The demand curve will then indicate more demand for each price and higher prices for each demand level, respectively. At industry level, income is represented by the national income expressed by the gross domestic product (GDP). To shift the linear demand curve, only one point needs to be altered while the slope stays the same. For simplicity, the demand maximum where price is zero is chosen as the shifting point. This *reference demand maximum* is calculated in equation 8.

$$\begin{aligned} \textit{reference demand maximum} = {} & \textit{REFERENCE INDUSTRY} \\ & \textit{DEMAND} + \textit{demand curve slope} * \\ & (0 - \textit{REFERENCE PRICE}) \qquad (8) \end{aligned}$$

Therefore, the *maximum demand shifted by income* is a result of the *reference demand maximum* and the *effect of income on reference demand*, the strength of the effect being determined by the WEIGHT OF INCOME EFFECT (see eq. 9).

$$\begin{aligned} \textit{maximum demand shifted by income} = {} & \textit{reference demand maximum} \\ & * (\textit{effect of income on reference} \\ & \textit{demand} \wedge \textit{WEIGHT OF} \\ & \textit{INCOME EFFECT}) \qquad (9) \end{aligned}$$

The *effect of income on reference demand* is based on the development of GDP compared to a reference value. Since airlines operate in different world regions, different incomes influence their demand function. In the airline industry model, airlines' domestic and international traffic is distinguished. The two GDP developments contribute to the *effect of income on reference demand* according to their share of airlines' total traffic (see eq. 10–12).

$$
\begin{aligned}
\textit{effect of income on reference demand} = {} & \textit{real GDP domestic development} * \\
& \textit{(1 − INTERNATIONAL} \\
& \textit{TRAFFIC SHARE) + real} \\
& \textit{GDP world development} * \\
& \textit{INTERNATIONAL} \\
& \textit{TRAFFIC SHARE} \qquad (10)
\end{aligned}
$$

$$
\begin{aligned}
\textit{real GDP domestic development} = {} & \textit{real GDP domestic / REFERENCE} \\
& \textit{GDP DOMESTIC} \qquad (11)
\end{aligned}
$$

$$
\begin{aligned}
\textit{real GDP world development} = {} & \textit{real GDP world / REFERENCE} \\
& \textit{GDP WORLD} \qquad (12)
\end{aligned}
$$

The real, i.e. inflation adjusted, GDP values are taken instead of nominal GDPs because only an income change that is also a change in people's purchasing power can shift the demand curve. Besides, for consistency, not *price* but *real price* is taken to determine demand. For all variables in the airline industry model that require inflation adjustment an external time series of *inflation rate*s is inserted, and the corresponding inflation index is calculated in the model.[56]

Finally, the *demand according to demand curve*, already mentioned in equation 1, combines the influences of price and income (see eq. 13). Real income changes shift the demand curve while *real price* changes are movements along the curve. Regardless of price and income levels, demand may not fall below zero because negative passengers do not exist.

$$
\begin{aligned}
\textit{demand according to demand curve} = {} & \textit{MAX (0, demand curve slope} * \\
& \textit{real price + maximum demand} \\
& \textit{shifted by income)} \qquad (13)
\end{aligned}
$$

Comparison to other authors' modelling

Previous airline profit cycle models have used similar demand formulations. All include the positive influence of GDP on air traffic demand. In addition, Segers, Sgouridis, and Pierson incorporate the impact of price and the impact of external factors on demand.

Since Liehr et al. focus their study on aircraft capacity adjustment, their demand modelling is only peripheral.[57] They assume the number of passengers increases with GDP but is independent of price. Prices are only employed to allocate demand to different airlines.

Segers estimates demand econometrically using real GDP, yield, and dummies for external shocks such as 9/11 as explaining variables.[58]

Besides GDP, price, and external factors (such as 9/11), Sgouridis includes the influence of service quality on demand.[59] This implies that the quality of flying prevents people from buying plane tickets or encourages them to do so. However, people usually choose air travel not for the flight's sake but as transportation to their destination, and in most cases they have no competitive alternative to get there. So usually airlines' service quality does not determine if people fly; hence a change in service quality would not affect air travel demand.[60] Yet, on an individual airline level service quality certainly influences the allocation of demand between different airlines.

Pierson formulates air travel demand similar to Sgouridis as a multiplicative combination of effects.[61] There is a GDP effect, a price effect, the effect of exogenous influences, and the effect of service quality[62] on demand.

3.3.2 Price module

The price is the amount of money a customer has to pay for a product or service. How airlines' price-setting decision is represented in the airline industry model will be explained in this section. The price module's feedback structure is depicted in Figure 3.15 at the end of the section.

As an introduction Figure 3.13 outlines the price module: the price passengers pay for a ticket consists of ticket taxes and yield, i.e. the revenue per mile airlines earn. The yield comprises non-ticket revenues, such as extra baggage charges, and the actual ticket yield. The ticket yield is influenced by developments of demand and supply in the market, by revenue and profit considerations, as well as by costs and past experiences. How these factors determine the ticket yield, and hence price, will be explicated in detail in this section.

The *price* for a flight consists partly of taxes and fees that do not contribute to the airlines' revenues. Airlines are legally obliged to collect, for example, passenger facility charges, ticket taxes, security fees, and airport departure taxes, and pass them through to airports or government authorities.[63] Regulations vary between countries and over time.[64] From a modelling perspective, the question is whether taxes should be multiplicative or added to the ticket value. Roughly 30% of the tax to be paid on an average US ticket are percentage-based taxes; the majority is added.[65] Taxes in the airline industry model will thus be modelled as an add-on. Consequently, taxes do not decrease with price.

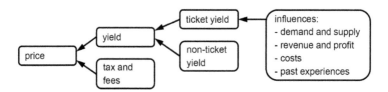

Figure 3.13 Outline of price module

Instead the tax share of price will increase when revenue per mile sold decrease in real terms, as it is the case in the US industry.[66] In the model, the time series *TS tax per mile* represents all pass-through taxes and fees for airlines. The other part of *price*, which is not a pass-through but contributes to airlines' revenue, is called *yield* (see eq. 14). It is the money earned per *revenue passenger mile*. Hence, *operating revenue* is the product of *yield* and *revenue passenger miles* (see eq. 15). It is assumed that airlines account for inflation during their yield planning processes so that all variables and expectations are expressed as 'real', i.e. inflation adjusted, values.

$$price = yield + TS\ tax\ per\ mile \qquad (14)$$

$$operating\ revenue = yield * revenue\ passenger\ miles \qquad (15)$$

$$real\ yield\ [= yield * inflation\ index] = real\ ticket\ yield + TS\ real\ non\text{-}ticket\ yield \qquad (16)$$

$$real\ ancillary\ revenue = TS\ real\ non\text{-}ticket\ yield * revenue\ passenger\ miles \qquad (17)$$

The airlines' *operating revenue* and hence the *yield* has two components: the money earned from ticket sales and non-ticket revenue, also called *ancillary revenue* (see eq. 16–17).[67] This has become increasingly relevant to the airline industry, especially to the low-cost segment that invented it.[68] Ancillary revenues are basically the result of two activities. The first is to 'unbundl[e] the traditional airline product and charg[e] for product attributes that were formerly encompassed within the ticket price or were available only to travellers in premium cabins'.[69] Examples are charges for call centres, credit card usage, priority check-in, seat assignment, checked baggage, lounge access, catering, and in-flight entertainment. The second activity is 'adding and charging for additional services beyond the core air transport product'.[70] Examples are travel insurance, airport parking, car hire, and bus and train tickets. In 2007 ancillary revenues accounted for approximately 0.5% of the world's airline operating revenues. Estimates for 2011 range between 3.6% and 5.6%, indicating the growing relevance of ancillary earnings.[71] The percentage of revenue made by non-ticket business varies among airlines.[72] Generally, it is expected to rise and become a vital revenue element for airlines.[73] The strategies and decision mechanisms behind ancillary revenue generation are still a work in progress in the airline industry. Several workshops and conferences are being held by practitioners around the world, yet to date there is no academic research on the topic.[74] For the airline industry model this means the generation of ancillary revenues cannot be modelled with confidence. Also, so far ancillary revenues are only a small part of airlines' operating revenue. Nonetheless, they will be included in the model to allow testing the impact of ancillary revenue on the airlines' profitability in model simulation experiments. Non-ticket yield will be inserted into the model as an external time series, i.e. *TS real non-ticket yield*.

When setting *ticket yield* airlines seek to maximise their revenue.[75] To achieve this they use two closely related activities: pricing and revenue management.[76] 'Pricing' is the process in which an airline determines which services are offered at what prices. For example, a Friday afternoon flight from New York to Miami may be offered at different prices depending on whether passengers want a return ticket, whether they fly business or economy class, whether they book well in advance, whether they change to a connecting flight in Miami, etc.[77] Among all these price offers the 'revenue management' process determines how many seats are made available for each particular offer. How these processes of developing price offers (pricing) and allocating seats to those price offers (revenue management) work to maximise airline revenues will be outlined in this section.

Since their implementation in the early 1980s, airlines' pricing and revenue management systems have become highly complex. At larger airlines not one but mostly two separate departments for pricing and revenue management handle the yield determination process.[78] The result is a large diversity of prices in the market. As Belobaba remarks: 'There are few facets of the airline business that generate as much discussion and confusion, among industry observers and consumers alike, as airline pricing and revenue management practices. [. . .] Together, [. . .][they] interact to create what can be a bewildering array of fare quotes for a consumer who simply wants to know how much it will cost to travel by air from one point to another.'[79]

The challenge in the airline industry model is to aggregate all those different ticket prices into one average industry price.[80] According to Sterman, in economic modelling the price-setting mechanism is 'one of the most difficult formulation challenges'.[81] Interviews with industry experts, i.e. practitioners and scholars, (see section 2.4.2) revealed that they know no satisfactory model of average industry yield.[82] Existing airline profit cycle models fall short to capture important aspects of airlines' yield determination. Details on this will be discussed at the end of this section, subsequent to the introduction of the price-setting process as it is implemented here in the airline industry model.

The starting point for airlines' pricing decisions is the *ticket yield* that airlines expect they should be able to generate. It reflects their belief about the equilibrium ticket yield which would clear the market. Airlines base this belief on past experiences, i.e. ticket yields they achieved in the past. So over time the airlines' *expected real ticket yield* gradually adjusts to the actual *real ticket yield* in the market (or rather to the *indicated real ticket yield* introduced below). The time it takes airlines to process a change and adjust their expectations is the *TIME TO ADJUST EXPECTED YIELD* (see eq. 18–19).

$$\text{expected real ticket yield} = INTEGRAL \text{ (change in expected real}$$
$$\text{ticket yield, INI YIELD}_{t0}) \tag{18}$$

$$\text{change in expected real ticket yield} = \text{(indicated real ticket yield} - \text{expected}$$
$$\text{real ticket yield) / TIME TO}$$
$$ADJUST \text{ } EXPECTED \text{ } YIELD \tag{19}$$

There is no restriction on the *real ticket yield*. Theoretically, airlines could give flights away for free or even start paying passengers for their journey. In 2006 Ryanair's chief executive O'Leary announced his vision that by the end of the decade more than half of their passengers would fly for free.[83] The lack in ticket revenues was to be compensated by non-ticket yields. In case ticket and non-ticket yields cannot cover *variable units costs* in the long run, an airline will become bankrupt. In the short run, however, it is possible to set *ticket yields* lower than *variable unit costs*, even when they are not subsidised by non-ticket yields (see eq. 20–22).

expected variable unit costs real = SMOOTH (variable unit cost real,
$$\text{TIME TO ADJUST VARIABLE}$$
$$\text{COST EXPECTATION)} \qquad (20)$$

minimum real ticket yield = expected variable costs real − TS real
non-ticket yield (21)

indicated real ticket yield = MAX (real ticket yield, minimum
real ticket yield) (22)

The actual *real ticket yield* can differ from the *expected real ticket yield* due to airlines' pricing decisions and revenue management activities (see eq. 23). The airlines' *expected real ticket yield* serves as an anchor for the *real ticket yield*.

real ticket yield = expected real ticket yield * effect of pricing on
yield * effect of revenue management on yield (23)

In the model, the effects on yield are linked by multiplication, not addition, because the effects are not clearly separable. Yield expectations, pricing, and revenue management decisions are strongly intertwined. In this multiplicative formulation an effect that equals 1 is neutral.

Figure 3.14 depicts the basic structure of the airline industry model's price-setting mechanism.

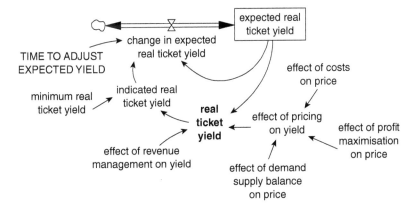

Figure 3.14 Basic ticket price-setting mechanism

The basic structure of the ticket price-setting mechanism produces a hill-climbing search as suggested in Sterman's commodity cycle model.[84] The process is called 'hill climbing' because the airlines' situation when it comes to determining yield can be compared to climbing a hill-top in a complete whiteout.[85] Without visibility hikers have to make careful steps in each direction to assess the ground's slope and find their way up the hill. Every few steps the checking process needs to be repeated. This procedure will guide hikers to their goal, provided the hill is smooth and has only one peak. The airlines' goal is to set the market-clearing price, i.e. to have the *expected real ticket yield* equal *real ticket yield*. If they charge more, they lose customers who find it too expensive; if they charge less, they lose revenue they could have earned. Unfortunately, like in a whiteout, airlines do not know where the market-clearing price lies. Demand and supply curves, i.e. the landscape, can also not be clearly specified. The hill-climbing structure offers an opportunity to build these uncertainties into the model and thus realistically reflect the airlines' behaviour. Pricing and revenue management processes, i.e. the hikers' careful steps, guide airlines towards their goal to precisely anticipate the market-clearing price. As in the hiking example, there is no guarantee that airlines will ever reach their goal. Depending on parameter values the hill-climbing structure can show very different behaviour. Illustrated with the hiking example, the landscape could, for example, be too flat to clearly detect a direction. Or hikers could be too aggressive and walk too many steps before reassessing their direction. As a result they could overshoot the peak or oscillate around it.

Having discussed the basic structure of the yield-setting process, the next step is to explain the *effect of pricing on yield*. Afterwards, the functioning of revenue management systems (*effect of revenue management on yield*) will be presented.

The effect of pricing on yield

In the pricing process an airline determines which services to offer at what price. To do this most airlines utilise a mix of three theoretical economic principles: cost-based pricing, demand-based pricing, and service-based pricing.[86] Tough competition in the market may force airlines to base prices on their costs. Demand-based pricing, on the other hand, does not regard the cost base. Here an airline seeks to charge every customer exactly what they are willing to pay. The different prices do not necessarily mean that the customers purchase different services. However, in service-based pricing airlines set different prices for different service offers.[87] While cost-based pricing reflects the degree of competition in the market, demand- and service-based pricing are more concerned with matching supply and demand as well as possible. Given a certain offer (supply), airlines seek to find profit-maximising prices. The airlines' pricing decision process is thus subject to costs, to the demand supply balance, and to the overall goal to maximise profits (see equation 24). How exactly they influence the price, and yield respectively, will be explored below.

$$\begin{aligned}
\textit{effect of pricing on yield} = \;&\textit{effect of costs on price} * \textit{effect of demand}\\
&\textit{supply balance on price} * \textit{effect of profit}\\
&\textit{maximisation on price} \quad\quad\quad\quad\quad\quad\quad (24)
\end{aligned}$$

The effect of costs on price

Competition in the market forces airlines to keep their cost situation in mind when setting their prices. The *real ticket yield* is thus not only based on the *expected ticket yield* but may also need to be based, at least partly, on expected costs (see equation 25). This depends on the degree of monopoly power which an airline is able to exploit in its pricing decisions.[88] An airline's potential monopoly power is reflected in the price-cost margin, i.e. (costs − price) / price = (costs / price) − 1. In perfectly competitive markets the price-cost margin would be zero. A margin towards -1 implies that the airline has monopoly power.

$$\begin{aligned}
\textit{effect of costs on price} = \;&\textit{1 + SENSITIVITY OF PRICE TO}\\
&\textit{COSTS* ((forecast real total unit}\\
&\textit{costs / expected real ticket yield) − 1)} \quad\quad (25)
\end{aligned}$$

The *SENSITIVITY OF PRICE TO COSTS* expresses how strongly airlines can exercise their expected monopoly power, or rather how much the competitive situation in the market will depress their yield expectations in the pricing process. Hence, the *SENSITIVITY OF PRICE TO COSTS* determines how strongly costs are incorporated into the pricing process. If the cost information is irrelevant for the pricing process, the *SENSITIVITY OF PRICE TO COSTS* equals 0. If, on the contrary, the market is highly competitive and airlines are forced to concentrate on costs and ignore whatever yield they may have achieved in the past, the *SENSITIVITY OF PRICE TO COSTS* equals 1. Hence, the *effect of costs on price* adjusts the anchor that *real ticket yield* has in *expected real ticket yield* and moves it towards *expected real total unit costs*. In the extreme case of perfect competition the *effect of cost on price* would lower *expected real yield* completely to the *expected real total unit costs*, which means that airlines would make zero operating profit. The competitive situation and thus the tendency to focus on costs has been aggravated by the increased presence of low-fare airlines.[89] However, airlines have certain routes in their networks and certain departure times in their schedules that are less competitive than others. So in reality the airline market is not perfectly competitive which means that the *SENSITIVITY OF PRICE TO COSTS* will be below 1.[90]

The effect of demand supply balance on price

The second market pressure influencing the pricing process is the expected development of demand and supply. In economic theory the fundamental influence on price is the balance of demand and supply.[91] If the demand for a product is larger than its supply, its price rises. In case there is excess supply, the price falls. Airlines have neither perfect information about the demand curve nor the supply structure. Each airline will gain experience in the industry and form its own expectations about demand developments and competitors' supply strategies. For each origin-destination market airlines assess their potential demand, its price elasticity and willingness to pay.[92] In the model this expected demand potential is represented by the *expected demand according to demand curve* which implies no restrictions on demand by substitutes, supply shortages, or other factors affecting demand but price and income (see demand module construction in section 3.3.1). Besides the future demand potential, airlines evaluate their competitors' moves and strategies. They analyse whether those seek to gain market share, to leave, or to enter certain markets. In that way, airlines form an expectation about the future supply in the industry. The ratio between the expected demand potential and expected supply is the *expected demand supply balance* (see eq. 26).

$$\text{expected demand supply balance} = \text{expected demand according to}$$
$$\text{demand curve} \, / \, \text{expected supply} \qquad (26)$$

This balance is compared to a reference situation. The *reference demand supply balance* is set to equal the airlines' maximum load factor. Consequently, in the reference situation the supply that airlines can provide clears the market and matches exactly the potential demand (see eq. 27 – 28). If airlines expect the demand potential to be higher than the expected supply, they will set higher prices. If they expect the balance to be lower, prices will be reduced to generate the additional demand needed to match the expected supply.

$$\text{relative demand supply balance} = \text{expected demand supply balance}$$
$$/ \, \text{reference demand supply balance} \qquad (27)$$

$$\text{reference demand supply balance} = \textit{MAXIMUM AVG LOAD}$$
$$\textit{FACTOR} \qquad (28)$$

The strength of the *effect of demand supply balance on price* is indicated by the *SENSITIVITY OF PRICE TO DEMAND SUPPLY BALANCE* (see eq. 29). A standard formulation of effects is used by specifying the effect as a power function of the normalised input.[93]

$$\text{effect of demand supply balance on price} = \text{relative demand supply balance}$$
$$\textit{\textasciicircum SENSITIVITY OF}$$
$$\textit{PRICE TO DEMAND}$$
$$\textit{SUPPLY BALANCE} \qquad (29)$$

The effect of profit maximisation on price

The third pressure influencing an airline's pricing decision is its own profit situation. Making profit is a primary objective of airline pricing.[94] The question is what airlines consider to be an adequate profit level. State-owned airlines may target only a break even whereas others seek to achieve target rates of return for their shareholders or even aim to make additional savings for new investments. Besides, while some airlines are more concerned with current profitability, others will focus more on long-term profits.[95] 'Thus even the profit objective in airline pricing may have different implications for different airlines.'[96] In the airline profit cycle model, airlines compare their current profit situation to a target. If current profitability falls below the target, there is a pressure to increase price and ensure margins. Whenever profitability exceeds the target, the pressure on price is not necessary. In detail, the mechanism works as follows: it takes airlines a little *TIME TO PERCEIVE PROFITABILITY* because different information needs to be processed, aggregated, reported etc. (see eq. 30–31).

$$\text{perceived profitability} = INTEGRAL \text{ (change in perceived profitability, INI PROFITABILITY)} \qquad (30)$$

$$\text{change in perceived profitability} = \text{(profitability to revenues − perceived profitability) / TIME TO PERCEIVE PROFITABILITY} \qquad (31)$$

The currently *perceived profitability* is compared to the *profitability target*. The target is set based on the *profitability trend* and possibly augmented by a *STRETCH GOAL*, which serves as a buffer to ensure the *profitability target* will be met in the end (see eq. 32).[97] The *profitability trend* is based on the profitability values the airline achieved in the past. It updates to new profitability information taking some time to perceive a change in the profitability trend (see eq. 33–34). In the case of an airline that has been making losses in the past, so that the *profitability trend* may have become negative, it is assumed that the airline will seek to achieve at least break even. The *profitability target* is thus restricted to be non-negative (see eq. 32).

$$\text{profitability target} = MAX \text{ (0, profitability trend + STRETCH GOAL)} \qquad (32)$$

$$\text{profitability trend} = INTEGRAL \text{ (change in profitability trend, INI PROFITABILITY TREND)} \qquad (33)$$

$$\text{change in profitability trend} = \text{(profitability to revenues − profitability trend) / TIME TO PERCEIVE PROFITABILITY TREND} \qquad (34)$$

The difference between the *profitability target* and the currently *perceived profitability* is the *profitability performance gap* (see eq. 35). If this is positive, which means the current profitability exceeds the target, there is *profitability pressure on price*.[98] In case the *profitability performance gap* is negative, the airline does not meet the target and pressure to increase prices is exercised. The bigger the gap, the fiercer the pressure will be (see eq. 36). How sensitive the pricing process reacts to profit pressures is expressed by the strength of the overall *effect of profit maximisation on price* (see eq. 37).

$$profitability\ performance\ gap = perceived\ profitability -$$
$$profitability\ target \qquad (35)$$

$$profitability\ pressure\ on\ price = 1 + MAX\ (0,\ profitability\ performance$$
$$gap *(-1)) \qquad (36)$$

$$effect\ of\ profit\ maximisation\ on\ price = profitability\ pressure\ on\ price$$
$$^\wedge SENSITIVITY\ OF\ PRICE$$
$$TO\ PROFIT\ PRESSURE \qquad (37)$$

The effect of revenue management on yield

Having determined the price for their offers, airlines need to decide how many seats to allocate to each offer. Imposing booking limits on different fare classes is necessary because leisure (discount) and business (full-fare) passengers typically wish to travel at the same times, for example on Friday afternoons.[99] The booking limits on the lower fare seats make sure that there is a quantity of seats reserved for passengers with higher willingness to pay. 'The main objective of YM [= yield or revenue management] is therefore to **protect seats** for later booking, high-fare business passengers.'[100] At the point where revenue management systems interfere all flights are already scheduled, their capacities are fixed, and their price offers are determined. The revenue management mechanism is thus short-term oriented. It 'is the airline's "last chance" to maximise revenues'.[101] Airlines use computer systems to automatically exercise their revenue management.[102] They compare current bookings for a future flight to past booking data for the exact same flight. This historic information has been collected by the computer database over the past decades. Based on the comparison an estimate for the demand and revenue for each booking class is generated. Mathematical models with elaborate optimisation algorithms then calculate the optimal revenue maximising booking limits for each class. Demand and revenue estimations and the optimisation calculations are repeated in regular intervals during the flight booking period, in some cases even daily.

For inclusion in the airline profit cycle model the detail and diversity of the revenue management process needs to be aggregated at industry level. The airlines' *load factor* indicates how much of the capacity offered is currently booked. A short *TIME TO PERCEIVE LOAD FACTOR CHANGE* is needed to compile and process the information in revenue management systems. What airlines base their decisions on is thus the *perceived load factor* (see eq. 38). This is compared to the *expected load factor*. The load factor expectation is based on historical bookings and is adjusted to the current bookings, taking its *TIME TO ADJUST LOAD FACTOR EXPECTATION*s (see eq. 39–40).

$$
\begin{aligned}
perceived\ load\ factor = &\ SMOOTHI\ (load\ factor,\ TIME\ TO \\
&\ PERCEIVE\ LOAD\ FACTOR \\
&\ CHANGE,\ INI\ PERCEIVED\ LF) \quad\quad (38)
\end{aligned}
$$

$$
\begin{aligned}
expected\ load\ factor = &\ INTEGRAL\ (change\ in\ expected\ LF, \\
&\ INI\ EXPECTED\ LF) \quad\quad\quad\quad\quad\quad (39)
\end{aligned}
$$

$$
\begin{aligned}
change\ in\ expected\ LF = &\ (load\ factor - expected\ load\ factor)\ / \\
&\ TIME\ TO\ ADJUST\ LOAD \\
&\ FACTOR\ EXPECTATION \quad\quad\quad (40)
\end{aligned}
$$

The deviation between perceived and expected load factor is expressed in the *load factor performance gap* (see eq. 41). Assuming that revenue management systems work well, this gap will indicate the effect revenue management has on airlines' yield (see eq. 42).[103] If there are more seats filled than expected, i.e. if the gap is positive, the airlines' ticket yield will be higher. If airlines did not receive as many bookings as expected for the different fare classes, i.e. if the gap is negative, the ticket yield will be lower. This happened for example after the 9/11 terror attack when many people were suddenly reluctant to fly and bookings fell severely short of the expected level. How the load factor performance gap translates into ticket yield changes, is expressed by the *SENSITIVITY OF YIELD TO REVENUE MANAGEMENT* (see eq. 42).

$$
\begin{aligned}
load\ factor\ performance\ gap = &\ (perceived\ load\ factor - expected \\
&\ load\ factor)\ /\ expected\ load\ factor \quad (41)
\end{aligned}
$$

$$
\begin{aligned}
effect\ of\ revenue\ management\ on\ yield = &\ (1 + load\ factor\ performance\ gap) \\
&\ ^\wedge\ SENSITIVITY\ OF \\
&\ YIELD\ TO\ REVENUE \\
&\ MANAGEMENT \quad\quad\quad\quad\quad\quad (42)
\end{aligned}
$$

Comparison to other authors' modelling

How the airlines' price and yield determination processes are implemented in the airline industry model has been described above. The price mechanisms used in previous research on the airline profit cycle are different in several respects.

Liehr et al. model price as a result of load factors and competition.[104] The degree of competition is external to the model and therefore cannot change no matter what happens in the industry. Apart from the competition effect, prices in the model are an instantaneous result of the current load factor as predetermined in a table function. This immediate response excludes the industry's pricing process completely. Besides, the table function suggests that the airline industry had one target load factor that stays the same for all times and a predefined price range that has nothing to do with costs or other industry factors. Altogether, Liehr et al.'s price modelling seems 'structurally parsimonious' as the authors claim.[105]

Segers' price-setting mechanism is similar to Liehr at al.'s approach. In his model, price has only very limited endogenous influence.[106] The ratio of actual to desired load factor determines a small part of yield changes. The major influence on price is an exogenous negative constant which is intended to reflect the effect of competition on price. Thus, in Segers' model price almost inevitably has to decline, regardless of the circumstances in the industry.

Sgouridis formulates price as a basic cost plus model.[107] Unit costs are adjusted by profitability expectations, load factor expectations, and current profit margins.[108] All three adjustment factors are exogenous to the system. Therefore, apart from the unitcosts, all variables influencing the development of price in Sgouridis' model are predetermined by external data. The various dynamics which impact the airlines' yield are not represented.

Pierson's version to model the price-setting mechanism incorporates more endogenous feedback from other parts of the system.[109] Altogether, the price-setting mechanism is more detailed then in previous work and can thus be discussed more elaborately. The current ticket price adjusts to the indicated ticket price with a very short delay. The indicated ticket price is based on the ticket price and influenced by three factors: the industry's profit margin, demand supply balance, and costs.[110] While the profit margin and cost effects are endogenous, the demand supply balance effect is exogenously driven. In Pierson's model the current load factor is compared to the normal load factor which is an exogenous time series.[111] It is fitted to the historical load factor development. Historically, load factors were rising. In a scenario in which the industry is nearly in equilibrium and load factors stagnate or rise only slightly, there would be no reason for hugely rising 'normal' load factors. The assumption that the normal load factor has no connection to industry developments is not realistic. It serves as a target for the current load factor and needs to change with the airlines' experience. The simulated price changes resulting from this price-setting

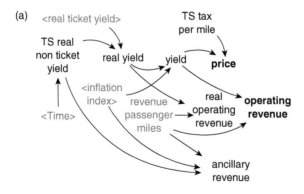

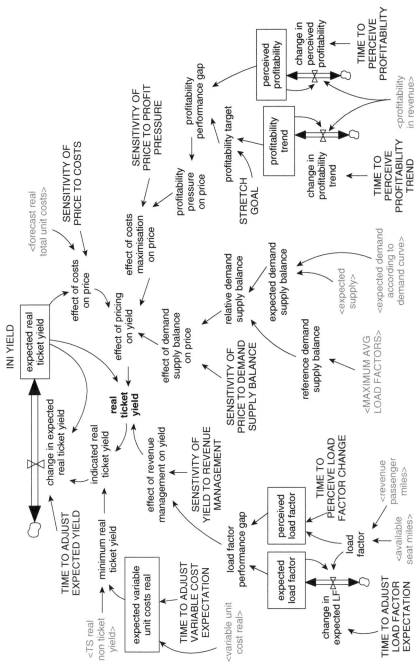

(b)

Figure 3.15 Price module

mechanism are thus questionable. Besides, what Pierson's price-setting mechanism lacks is a medium- or long-term influence. All influences on the ticket price are current values so that the whole process 'lives in the moment'.[112] In reality, airlines plan strategically, and set and publish most of their fares many months before the actual flight. Hence, it seems incorrect to assume this purely instantaneous price response. The appropriateness of Pierson's price-setting mechanism is thus problematic.

3.3.3 Supply module

Airlines' business purpose is to provide available seat miles. How much traffic airlines offer is subject to their fleet planning, route planning, and schedule planning.[113] In the fleet planning process airlines determine 'what type of aircraft to acquire, when and how many of each'.[114] It is the strategic decision with the longest range. Route and schedule planning are medium-term decisions. In the route planning process airlines decide 'where to fly the aircraft profitably, subject to fleet availability constraints'.[115] The decisions how often and at what times to fly each route, given operational and aircraft limitations, are a result of the scheduling process.[116] Fleet, route, and schedule planning are interdependent. The existing aircraft fleet is the basis for airlines' route and scheduling choices. Meanwhile, decisions to add new routes to the network often require additional aircraft.

In the following paragraphs the airlines' planning processes determining their supply of available seat miles will be explained and translated into model equations. The model structure is outlined in Figure 3.16. The amount of *available seat miles* an airline offers depends on its fleet (*total fleet,* consisting of *owned aircraft* and *leased aircraft*), its *production capacity* (the maximum productivity of its aircraft), and how much the fleet is actually used (*capacity utilisation*). The size of the *total fleet* depends on the airline's *desired capacity*. The strategic planning process behind this *desired capacity* is the starting point to introduce the airline industry model's supply module.

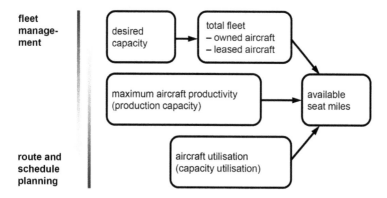

Figure 3.16 Outline of supply module

Desired capacity of the aircraft fleet

The strategic decisions around aircraft fleet size and composition have large impact on airlines' long-term operational and economic performance.[117] Aircraft are typically depreciated over a period of 10 to 15 years. Their operating life can last more than 30 years.[118] Fleet planning needs to deal with the uncertainty inherent in such a long time period. Meanwhile, the acquisition of a new aircraft involves a huge capital investment. 'In 2008, prices for a typical twin-engine, narrow-body, 150-seat aircraft that might be used for short- to medium-haul domestic services ranged from $50 to $60 million per unit [=aircraft]. The purchase price of a long-range, wide-body aircraft such as the Boeing 747-400 with over 400 seats exceeds $225 million per unit, and the Airbus 380 aircraft, which can seat up to 600 passengers on long-haul flights, has a list price of over $300 million per unit [. . .], although most airlines pay much less than the list price due to discounting.'[119] How fleet planning is reflected in the airline industry model's feedback structure is depicted in Figure 3.17.

The fleet planning process starts by defining the desired aircraft capacity. This *desired capacity* is measured in seats and aggregates the airlines' desired number and size of aircraft. Airlines' current *total fleet* may be desired to be

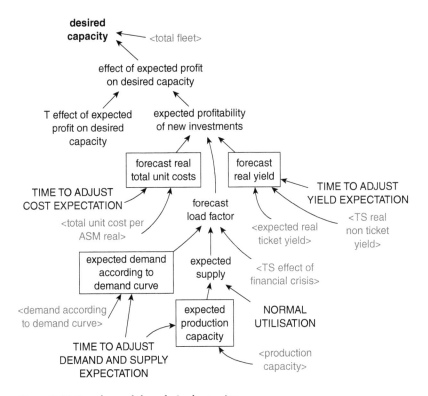

Figure 3.17 Supply module – desired capacity

enlarged, downsized, or to stay the same. Airlines base that decision about fleet size and aircraft mix on business case calculations.[120] They estimate the future *expected profitability of new investments* in the fleet (see eq. 43–45). How this expected profitability translates into desired aircraft purchases is indicated by the table function *T effect of expected profit on desired capacity* (see graph eq. 45). At zero expected future profitability, investments would stagnate. Since not all airlines and investors have exactly the same profitability expectations, some may choose to invest, others to divest, so overall the *desired capacity* in the industry would stay the same. If the *expected profitability of new investments* is positive, *desired capacity* increases. While expected profitability is positive but moderate, the attractiveness of investments is also moderate. Incumbents may seek to enlarge their market shares and thus enlarge their fleets, while potential new entrants might expect higher returns elsewhere and choose not to invest. When the expected future profitability in the industry exceeds expected returns of alternative investments, the desired capacity level rises greatly – and eventually reaches saturation, representing the market's limits to financing and absorption of new capacity. Consequently, the positive part of the table function is S-shaped. The negative part is also S-shaped. In case the industry is expected to be unprofitable, subsidies and favourable bankruptcy protection may at first prevent too many market exits.[121] However, when expected future profitability reduces further, airlines will be forced to shrink their business or leave the market – until even the most optimistic investors believe the industry to be so unprofitable in the future that they choose to abandon it.

$$desired\ capacity = total\ fleet * effect\ of\ expected\ profit\ on\ desired\ capacity \tag{43}$$

$$effect\ of\ expected\ profit\ on\ desired\ capacity = T\ effect\ of\ expected\ profit\ on\ desired\ capacity\ (expected\ profitability\ of\ new\ investments) \tag{44}$$

$$T\ effect\ of\ expected\ profit\ on\ desired\ capacity = (-0.5,0),\ (-0.4,0.1),\ (-0.2,0.8),\ (0.1,0.97),\ (0,1),\ (0.15,1.05),\ (0.35,1.18),\ (0.5,1.2)$$

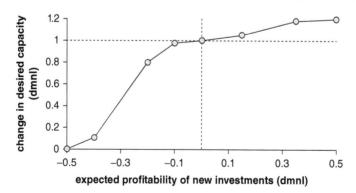

(45)

The *expected profitability of new investments* consists of forecasts for yield, total unit costs, and the potential load factor (see eq. 46). Profitability is calculated as revenues minus costs (= profit), relative to revenues. On a unit level, profitability equals revenue per mile sold (= yield) minus unit cost per mile sold, relative to revenue per mile sold. Since unit costs are calculated based on miles offered, not miles sold, they need to be adjusted by the *forecast load factor*, i.e. the expected quantity of miles sold compared to miles offered (see eq. 46).[122]

expected profitability of new investments = *ZIDZ (forecast real yield –*
  ZIDZ (forecast real total unit
  costs, forecast load factor),
  forecast real yield)   (46)

The *forecast real yield* is based on past yields, specifically on yield expectations which are constantly updated by the actual *real yield* achieved in the market (consisting of ticket and non-ticket yield). The time it takes to identify the trends, compile the yield forecast, and the frequency with which this is done, is reflected by the *TIME TO ADJUST YIELD EXPECTATION* (see eq. 47).

forecast real yield = *SMOOTHI (expected real ticket yield + TS real*
  non-ticket yield, TIME TO ADJUST YIELD
  EXPECTATION, expected real ticket
  yield + TS real non-ticket yield)   (47)

The *forecast real total unit costs* is based on the actual *total unit cost per ASM real*. The forecast is adjusted to new information, trends are updated, and cost projections calculated. This needs the *TIME TO ADJUST COST EXPECTATION* (see eq. 48).

forecast real total unit costs = *SMOOTHI (total unit cost per ASM real,*
  TIME TO ADJUST COST
  EXPECTATION, total unit cost per
  ASM real)   (48)

The *forecast load factor* depends primarily on the expected ratio of demand and supply. The *expected demand according to demand* curve builds on airlines' past experience with demand and updates beliefs taking the *TIME TO ADJUST DEMAND AND SUPPLY EXPECTATION*s (see eq. 49).[123] The *expected supply* is a function of the *expected production capacity* which is the maximum number of seat miles the fleet will be able to produce. This is estimated building on past experiences with *production capacity* limits. Incorporating the current information in the estimation process takes the *TIME TO ADJUST DEMAND AND SUPPLY EXPECTATION* (see eq. 50–51). To calculate the *expected supply* level the *expected production capacity* needs to be adjusted with the assumed aircraft utilisation. The fleet cannot always work at its absolute maximum, which requires best weather, extra shifts for employees, postponed maintenance, etc. It is thus assumed that the fleet will be used as usual (*NORMAL UTILISATION*), meaning the aircraft will need the usual number of maintenance days etc. (see eq. 50).

expected demand according to demand curve = SMOOTHI (demand
according to demand curve,
TIME TO ADJUST
DEMAND AND SUPPLY
EXPECTATION,
INI EXPECTED
DEMAND)   (49)

*expected supply = expected production capacity * *
NORMAL UTILISATION   (50)

expected production capacity = SMOOTHI (production capacity,
TIME TO ADJUST DEMAND
AND SUPPLY EXPECTATION,
INI PRODUCTION CAPACITY)   (51)

The *forecast load factor* does not only depend on the expected demand supply ratio. It also takes special circumstances into account that can be foreseen but are not captured by the demand curve.[124] This could be demand-increasing events, such as a World Cup, or devastating events like the financial crisis. (Given the planned calibration of the model for the US airline industry between 1985 and 2010, the *effect of the financial crisis* is already included here.) An event like the 9/11 terror attack, which airline management expects has an only temporary effect, is not incorporated into the planning process (see eq. 52).

*forecast load factor = expected demand according to demand curve * *
(1+ effect of financial crisis) / expected supply   (52)

Owned fleet management

Having determined their *desired capacity* level, airlines need to adjust their *total fleet* correspondingly. The *total fleet* consists of *owned aircraft* and *leased aircraft* (see eq. 53). What part of their desired aircraft acquisitions airlines decide to buy and how much they lease is a very individual decision that depends on several factors. These are financial aspects such as cost comparisons and tax issues as well as flexibility considerations.[125] The availability of desired aircraft from lessors and manufacturers may also be relevant.[126] Most of these factors are external to the airline industry model (see section 3.2.1: System boundary). Hence the lease or buy decision is not modelled explicitly. The ratio between leased and owned aircraft is inserted as time series *TS leasing share*. Desired leased and owned capacities are derived accordingly (see eq. 54–55). This section will focus on adjustments of the owned fleet, the subsequent section will address leased aircraft fleet management.

$$total\ fleet = leased\ aircraft + owned\ aircraft \tag{53}$$

$$desired\ capacity\ leased = desired\ capacity * TS\ leasing\ share \tag{54}$$

$$desired\ capacity\ owned = desired\ capacity * (1 - TS\ leasing\ share) \tag{55}$$

Aircraft pass through an ageing chain depicted in Figure 3.18. Each year a certain number of aircraft is ordered (*order rate*). It takes manufacturers some time, i.e. the average *CAPACITY ACQUISITION DELAY*, to process orders, manufacture the aircraft, and deliver them to the airlines. In reality, some aircraft will be delivered a little earlier, others later than the average *CAPACITY ACQUISITION DELAY* implies. To capture this technically, the process is modelled as a 3rd order material delay.[127] Formulated explicitly, the variable *aircraft on order* consists of three exemplary process stages, *AO1*, *AO2*, and *AO3*, that each contribute a fraction to the *CAPACITY ACQUISITION DELAY* (see eq. 56–64).

$$aircraft\ on\ order = AO1 + AO2 + AO3 \tag{56}$$

$$AO1 = INTEGRAL\ (order\ rate - R1,\ AO3_{t0}) \tag{57}$$

$$R1 = AO1\ /\ DL \tag{58}$$

$$AO2 = INTEGRAL\ (R1 - R2,\ AO3_{t0}) \tag{59}$$

$$R2 = AO2\ /\ DL \tag{60}$$

$$AO3 = INTEGRAL\ (R2 - acquisition\ rate,\ Ini\ backlog\ owned_{t0}) \tag{61}$$

$$Ini\ backlog\ owned = INI\ BACKLOG * (1 - TS\ leasing\ share) \tag{62}$$

$$DL = CAPACITY\ ACQUISITION\ DELAY\ /\ 3 \tag{63}$$

$$acquisition\ rate = AO3\ /\ DL \tag{64}$$

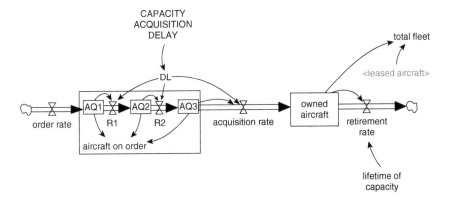

Figure 13.18 Ageing chain for aircraft in ownership

The acquired aircraft (*acquisition rate*) enlarge the quantity of *aircraft owned*. After their service life the aircraft are retired (*retirement rate*) (see eq. 65–66).

$$\text{owned aircraft} = INTEGRAL \text{ (acquisition rate} - \text{retirement} \\ \text{rate, Ini owned}_{t0}) \qquad (65)$$

$$Ini\ owned = INI\ TOTAL\ AIRCRAFT * (1 - TS\ leasing\ share) \qquad (66)$$

In the following paragraphs the different decisions in airlines' owned fleet management process will be explained in detail. The corresponding model structure is presented in Figure 3.19. Starting point is the order planning process. The underlying structure for modelling it is the ordering decision mechanism in Sterman's commodity cycle model.[128]

In the order planning process airlines determine how many aircraft orders they place at what time. An airline can choose to place a firm order or to purchase an option. 'A firmly-ordered aircraft is contractually committed, whereas an optioned aircraft is subject to a future and separate negotiation.'[129] The main benefit of optional purchases for an individual airline is the shorter waiting time between (firm) order and aircraft acquisition. Modelling this on an industry level, it does not matter which airline receives which spot on the waiting list. An order option not exercised would simply be a thought discarded in the planning process.[130] Hence, in the *order rate* in the airline profit cycle model represents firm orders and exercised options. It is thus positive by definition (see eq. 67).

$$\text{order rate} = MAX\ (0,\ indicated\ orders) \qquad (67)$$

Result of the order planning process is the number of *indicated orders*. To determine this, airlines calculate the deviation between the aircraft capacity they have (*aircraft owned*) and the *desired capacity owned* (see eq. 70). The *CAPACITY ADJUSTMENT TIME* reflects how often the discrepancy is checked and resolved. It includes the time needed until decisions are prepared and taken by airline management during the capacity planning process. To arrive at their *desired acquisition rate* airlines also take into account that some aircraft may soon need be retired and replaced. For simplicity the *expected retirement rate* is set to equal the actual *retirement rate*. In reality, however, not all airlines may know precisely and immediately how much capacity other airlines discard from the market (see eq. 68–69).

$$\text{desired acquisition rate} = \text{expected retirement rate} + \text{adjustment} \\ \text{for capacity} \qquad (68)$$

$$\text{expected retirement rate} = \text{retirement rate} \qquad (69)$$

$$\text{adjustment for capacity} = \text{(desired capacity owned} - \text{owned aircraft)} / \\ CAPACITY\ ADJUSTMENT\ TIME \qquad (70)$$

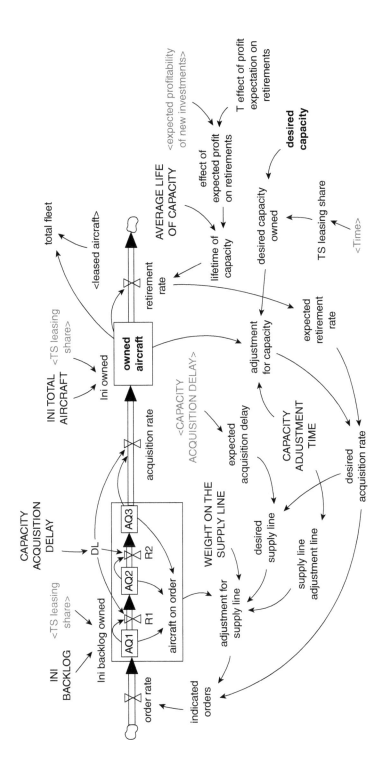

Figure 3.19 Fleet management for owned aircraft

Airlines have an expectation how long it will take until an ordered aircraft is delivered and ready to be used in their fleet. This *expected acquisition delay* is, for simplicity, set to equal the actual *CAPACITY ACQUISITION DELAY* (see eq. 71).

$$\text{expected acquisition delay} = CAPACITY\ ACQUISITION\ DELAY \qquad (71)$$

Based on the *expected acquisition delay* and taking into account how many *aircraft on order* they already have, airlines calculate their *desired supply line*. It is the amount of aircraft capacity airlines desire to have in the supply line, i.e. on order, to ensure the *desired acquisition rate* (see eq. 72).[131] The difference between the *desired supply line* and actual *aircraft on order* is cleared in the *supply line adjustment time* (see eq. 73). It is assumed that project managers handle all adjustment aspects simultaneously so that the *supply line adjustment time* equal the *CAPACITY ADJUSTMENT TIME* (see eq. 74).

$$\text{desired supply line} = \text{expected acquisition delay} * \text{desired acquisition rate} \qquad (72)$$

$$\text{adjustment for supply line} = (\text{desired supply line} - \text{aircraft on order}) * WEIGHT\ ON\ THE\ SUPPLY\ LINE\ /\ \text{supply line adjustment time} \qquad (73)$$

$$\text{supply line adjustment time} = CAPACITY\ ADJUSTMENT\ TIME \qquad (74)$$

Since the airline market and the aircraft manufacturing market are not completely transparent, there may be confusion about the amount of *aircraft on order* in the entire industry. Managers will not have complete knowledge about all competitors' actions.[132] Or airline managers might ignore the supply line, for example when shareholders press for expansion in profitable times. The degree to which airlines account for the supply line, or disregard it due to lacking information or ignorance, is captured by the *WEIGHT ON THE SUPPLY LINE*.[133] If airlines are fully aware of the capacity volumes in the supply line the *WEIGHT ON THE SUPPLY LINE* equals 100%. In case airlines failed completely to account for the supply line, the *WEIGHT ON THE SUPPLY LINE* would be 0%. In the model, the *WEIGHT ON THE SUPPLY LINE* blurs the supply line information and thus reduces its impact on the ordering decision (see eq. 73).[134]

Altogether, the order planning process resulting in *indicated orders* is an anchoring and adjustment process.[135] The *desired acquisition rate* is the anchor and it is adjusted by the *adjustment for the supply line* (see eq. 75). Given the industry's supply situation is not fully transparent (*WEIGHT ON THE SUPPLY LINE* < 100%) the adjustment process would be insufficient. The role of the anchor would be stronger and the felt necessity for adjustments would be weaker. This means in prosperous years where the *desired acquisition rate* is high, airlines will tend to keep ordering, partly ignoring all the aircraft that are already on order. In consequence, overcapacity would emerge when the *desired acquisition rate* stabilised or even drops.

indicated orders = desired acquisition rate + adjustment for supply line   (75)

If many aircraft are ordered at once and aircraft manufacturers' production capacities are exceeded, airlines will probably need to wait longer for delivery. In the airline industry model a manufacturing capacity limit is incorporated as an option which can be switched on and off in simulation experiments. This has been done to account for the different strategies the two big aircraft manufacturers, Airbus and Boeing, have exhibited in the past. Their world-wide order and delivery developments are displayed in Figure 3.20.[136] Boeing followed the airlines' order cycle with its aircraft production capacity. Airbus, on the contrary, chose a smooth production capacity expansion.

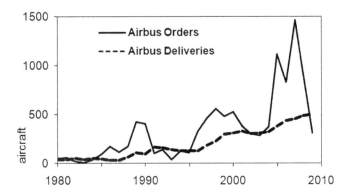

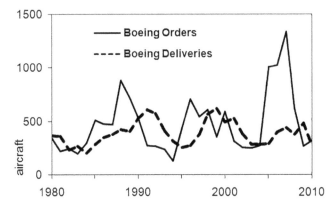

Figure 3.20 Aircraft orders and deliveries of Airbus and Boeing

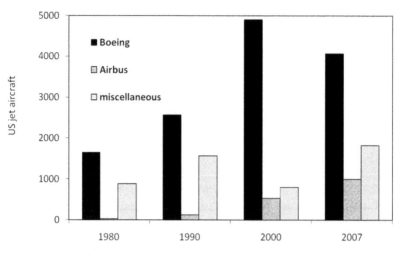

Figure 3.21 US jet aircraft fleet by manufacturers[137]

Since the airline industry model will be calibrated for the US industry where the majority of aircraft are Boeings (see Figure 3.21), it can be assumed that the aircraft manufacturers' production capacity is adapted to incoming orders. Hence, the aircraft acquisition is not limited. To simulate a potential manufacturing strategy change towards smoother capacity adjustment, a constraint to the manufacturers' production capacity can be switched on. The airlines' aircraft acquisition rate is then restricted by the *MANUFACTURERS' MAXIMUM FINISHING RATE* (see eq. 64a). Consequently, when aircraft orders exceed manufacturers' capabilities, orders pile up and airlines need to wait longer for the delivery of their aircraft.[138]

$$\begin{aligned} \text{acquisition delay} = {} & \text{IF THEN ELSE (SWITCH limit} \\ & \text{manufacturing} = 1,\ \text{MIN (MANUFACTURERS} \\ & \text{MAXIMUM FINISHING RATE, AO3/DL),} \\ & \text{AO3 / DL)} \end{aligned} \qquad (64a)$$

The acquired aircraft spend their service lifetime in the fleet and are afterwards retired (see eq. 77). Depending on their age and condition, aircraft may be recycled or sold to airlines in other markets. An airline's decision to dispose of an aircraft depends mainly on its profitability.[139] The higher fuel and maintenance costs of older aircraft need to be outweighed against the investment in newer models. The marketing appeal of newer aircraft, their fit to planned fleet changes, and their carbon and noise emissions may also influence the decision. All these aspects are usually translated into financial terms so that in the end economic arguments dominate the decision-making process. When airlines expect unprofitable times and hence desire to reduce their capacity, aircraft are more easily retired. When airlines expect a profitable period and feel the need to enlarge their fleet, older aircraft are likely to be kept in service a little longer. Consequently, the service *lifetime of capacity* will vary with airlines' profit expectations (see eq. 76). The *effect of expected profit on retirements*, which alters the *AVERAGE LIFE OF CAPACITY*, depends on the *expected profitability of new investments* as defined in the table function *T effect of profit expectation on retirements* (see eq. 77–79). The function is S-shaped and has a lower and an upper limit (see graph eq. 79). The lower limit means that aircraft would not be retired before they are depreciated. At the upper end there is a technological limit to prolonging the aircraft's service lifetime.[140]

$$retirement\ rate = owned\ aircraft\ /\ lifetime\ of\ capacity \tag{76}$$

$$lifetime\ of\ capacity = effect\ of\ expected\ profit\ on\ retirements \\ *\ AVERAGE\ LIFE\ OF\ CAPACITY \tag{77}$$

$$effect\ of\ expected\ profit\ on\ retirements = T\ effect\ of\ profit\ expectation\ on \\ retirements\ (expected\ profitability \\ of\ new\ investments) \tag{78}$$

$$T\ effect\ of\ profit\ expectation\ on\ retirements = (-0.5,0.2),\ (-0.35,0.3), \\ (-0.1,0.7),\ (0,1),\ (0.1,1.3), \\ (0.2,1.6),\ (0.3,1.8),\ (0.5,2)$$

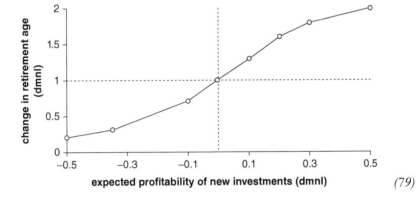

$$(79)$$

Leased fleet management

Since the mid-1980s leasing instead of owning aircraft has become increasingly popular among airlines.[141] The general idea is that aircraft leasing offers more flexibility, requires less up-front capital investment, and allows more frequent fleet renewal.[142] Newer aircraft may result in marketing and cost advantages. The major role of aircraft leasing in the airline industry was highlighted by the International Air Transport Association (IATA) in 2010 when it announced that leasing companies now own approximately one third of the world's aircraft.[143] 'Leasing has become a strategic source to many of the world's airlines, where a common rule of thumb today is taking delivery of around 1/3 of aircraft capacity under operating leases.'[144] Among US airlines the share of leased aircraft is even higher, with 46% in 2009 of which 88% are operating leases (as opposed to capital leases or other types).[145]

Operating leases are termed between one and seven years, usually for five years.[146] After expiry the lessee usually has the offer to extend the lease for a further two to four periods.[147] Throughout the lease, the aircraft remains in the lessor's ownership but maintenance is nonetheless to be paid by the lessee.[148]

The flexibility leasing offers in terms of fleet adjustment compared to buying aircraft starts with faster deliveries. Still, after signing the lease some time is needed until the airline can actually utilise the aircraft. It needs to be configured with the airline's paint scheme, interior, and avionics.[149] Gavazza states in 2010 that '[a]lmost all operating lessors' purchases of new aircraft have a designated lessee at the time of the order. In fact, the first speculative order was placed by GECAS only in the late 1990s, and the number and size of speculative orders have remained small in recent years.'[150] This implies that there is a significant planning period on the lessors' side between the lease agreement and the actual acquisition.

The degree of flexibility an airline obtains by leasing its aircraft is a result of the comparatively short timeframe (e.g. lease period five years, aircraft service lifetime 25 years) in which the aircraft causes the airline expenses. In a crisis situation, such as the 9/11 terror attacks, airlines may be interested in early lease returns to reduce capacity to slumped demand. While Morrell states that operating leases 'can be returned to the lessor at relatively short notice and without major penalty',[151] Vasigh et al. and industry analysts emphasise that airlines need to expect the continuation of lease payments until the end of the contracted period – even if they return the aircraft early.[152] Regarding the vast overcapacities of many US airlines after the 9/11 shock, the latter statement seems convincing. Moreover, interviews with industry experts (introduced in section 2.4.2) confirmed that early lease returns are very costly. Fleet experts pointed out that regardless on the periodic lease payments, an early return would cause additional costs because the aircraft will need to be returned in immaculate condition which requires time and money for intensive technological maintenance and mandatory checks. For the airline industry model, it is thus assumed that the continuation of lease payments until the end of the lease period as well as the penalty and extra maintenance costs make early lease returns futile. Hence, the option will not be implemented in the model.

Interviewed experts held conflicting opinions about whether or not lease contracts usually include aircraft utilisation restrictions, such as a minimum or maximum usage. The existence of these special terms is undoubted but their content and commonness is unclear. In the airline industry model it will thus be assumed that leases can be used in the same way as owned aircraft.

Whether leasing is more or less expensive then owing an aircraft depends on the lessors' and airlines' particular financing and tax situation. Likely, an airline leasing its aircraft will pay more over the long term because the lessor will require its margin to cover the aircraft's long-term costs and compensate for the risks involved with aircraft release and residual value.[153] In contrast, the A4A Airlines for America argues that leasing 'can be a less expensive way to acquire aircraft, since high-income leasing companies can take advantage of tax credits. In such cases, the tax savings to a lessor can be reflected in the lessor's price.'[154] For the airline industry model, the costs associated with leasing and owing aircraft are thus assumed to be the same.

In the model, the aircraft leasing process is similar to the owned fleet management. The ageing chain is presented in Figure 3.22 (see eq. 80–86). Leased aircraft are ordered (*order rate leasing*) and augment the quantity of *lease orders placed*. The lessor then needs time to process orders, and to maintain, customise, and deliver the aircraft. This is the *LEASE ACQUISITION TIME*. Like with aircraft manufacturers it is possible that lessors are confronted with more aircraft orders than they can provide for. To test the impact of that constraint in model simulations, a limit, i.e. the *LESSORS' MAXIMUM DELIVERY RATE* can be switched on (see eq. 83–83a). Per contract a lease expires after the *AVERAGE LEASE PERIOD*. It is assumed to be fixed because lease contracts are generally fixed agreements and an early exit is usually very costly (see discussion above).

$$\text{order rate leasing} = MAX\ (0,\ \text{indicated orders leasing}) \tag{80}$$

$$\text{lease orders placed} = INTEGRAL\ (\text{order rate leasing} - \text{lease acquisition} \\ \text{rate, Ini lease backlog}_{t0}) \tag{81}$$

$$\text{Ini lease backlog} = INI\ BACKLOG * TS\ \text{leasing share} \tag{82}$$

$$\text{lease acquisition rate} = \text{lease orders placed} /\ LEASE \\ ACQUISITION\ DELAY \tag{83}$$

$$\text{lease acquisition rate} = IF\ THEN\ ELSE(SWITCH\ \text{limit} \\ \text{leasing} = 1,\ MIN(LESSORS\ MAXIMUM \\ DELIVERY\ RATE,\ \text{lease orders placed} / \\ LEASE\ ACQUISITION\ DELAY), \\ \text{lease orders placed} /\ LEASE \\ ACQUISITION\ DELAY) \tag{83a}$$

$$\text{leased aircraft} = INTEGRAL\ (\text{lease acquisition rate} - \text{lease expiry} \\ \text{rate, Ini leased}_{t0}) \tag{84}$$

$$\text{Ini leased} = INI\ TOTAL\ AIRCRAFT * TS\ \text{leasing share} \tag{85}$$

$$\text{lease expiry rate} = \text{leased aircraft} /\ AVERAGE\ LEASE\ PERIOD \tag{86}$$

How many leases airlines order depends on the *desired capacity leased*. Taking the *leased aircraft* they already have and the soon *expected lease expiry rate* into account airlines calculate their *desired acquisition rate leasing*. Depending on the transparency of the supply chain, airlines adjust their ordering behaviour. With incomplete information about the supply chain or with an aggressive ordering attitude airlines will order too much capacity compared to their actual desired

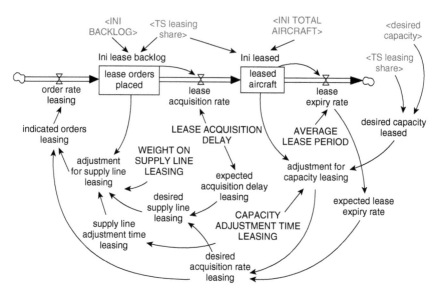

Figure 3.22 Ageing chain and fleet management for leased aircraft

supply line. The model equations for these mechanisms are given below (see eq. 87–94; for a more detailed explanation see the similar description for ordering owned aircraft).

adjustment for capacity leasing = (desired capacity leased − leased aircraft) /
CAPACITY ADJUSTMENT
TIME LEASING (87)

expected lease expiry rate = lease expiry rate (88)

desired acquisition rate leasing = expected lease expiry rate + adjustment
for capacity leasing (89)

desired supply line leasing = expected acquisition delay leasing ∗
desired acquisition rate leasing (90)

expected acquisition delay leasing = LEASE ACQUISITION DELAY (91)

supply line adjustment time leasing = CAPACITY ADJUSTMENT
TIME LEASING (92)

adjustment for supply line leasing = (desired supply line leasing − lease
orders placed) ∗ WEIGHT ON
SUPPLY LINE LEASING/
supply line adjustment time leasing (93)

indicated orders leasing = desired acquisition rate leasing +
adjustment for supply line leasing (94)

The fleet's production capacity (maximum aircraft productivity)

With their *total fleet* (= *owned aircraft* + *leased aircraft*) airlines have a certain *production capacity* in terms of seat miles they can realise per year. The time series *TS maximum aircraft productivity* indicates the maximum number of miles an aircraft can fly in a year (see eq. 95). Reaching the maximum implies that the weather is perfect, airports are not congested, the crew works overtime, maintenance is postponed if possible and so on. The fleet's *production capacity* also reflects airport capacity and ability, air traffic control infrastructure, airlines' network planning skills, and the aircraft's technological capabilities and evolution. Advances towards larger aircraft sizes, longer flight distances, or faster operations all increased the maximum aircraft productivity over the last decades.

$$production\ capacity = TS\ maximum\ aircraft\ productivity * total\ fleet \qquad (95)$$

Aircraft utilisation

The aircraft *capacity utilisation* indicates how much of the maximum *production capacity* airlines plan to use. It is the result of extensive route and schedule planning processes in which airlines determine where and when to fly with their current fleet in the season.[155] In their planning airlines expect normal circumstances, i.e. average weather conditions, usual airport and air traffic control performance, standard maintenance effort and so on. Route and schedule planning comprises strategic considerations and network optimisation calculations, the overall objective being profitability.[156] Result is the *NORMAL UTILISATION*, already mentioned in the 'desired capacity' section in eq. 50.[157]

In reality, not everything works as planned. Short-term adjustments to the planned *NORMAL UTILISATION* are necessary to react to disruptions and changes in short-run profitability expectations. Hence, airlines need to re-optimise their flight schedules frequently. The time adjustments take is the *UTILISATION ADJUSTMENT TIME* (see eq. 102).[158] To determine short-run profitability on route or even flight level is a difficult task because most of airlines' costs are fixed costs (see section 3.3.4) and are thus not easy to assign to a single route or flight. From a network perspective it may be beneficial to offer a flight which does not cover its costs, for example to generate feeder traffic for international flights.[159] In the network as a whole, however, an airline's operating performance needs to achieve at least break even to be profitable.

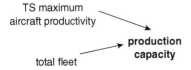

Figure 3.23 Supply module – aircraft productivity

To calculate the *operating performance gap* the difference between the airlines' actual *load factor*, representing their operating performance, and the *break even load factor* is calculated (see eq. 96). The *break even load factor* is computed based on the airline's *perceived real yield* and *perceived total unit cost per ASM real* (see eq. 97). Perceptions of yield and costs are frequently adjusted to the changing environment (see eq. 98 and 99).

$$operating\ performance\ gap\ =\ perceived\ load\ factor\ -\ perceived\ break\ even\ load\ factor \tag{96}$$

$$perceived\ break\ even\ load\ factor\ =\ perceived\ total\ unit\ cost\ per\ ASM\ real\ /\ perceived\ real\ yield \tag{97}$$

$$perceived\ real\ yield\ =\ SMOOTHI\ (real\ yield,\ TIME\ TO\ PERCEIVE\ YIELD\ CHANGE,\ INI\ PERCEIVED\ REAL\ YIELD) \tag{98}$$

$$perceived\ total\ unit\ cost\ per\ ASM\ real\ =\ SMOOTHI\ (total\ unit\ cost\ per\ ASM\ real,\ TIME\ TO\ PERCEIVE\ UNIT\ COST\ CHANGE,\ INI\ PERCEIVED\ TOTAL\ UNIT\ COST) \tag{99}$$

If an airline performs better than planned and enjoys high short-run profitability, it will seek to exploit the favourable situation and offer more seat miles than originally planned. This is feasible in a limited time frame where aircraft maintenance can be postponed and employees can be asked to work extra shifts. If an airline's current performance is unprofitable, flights may be cancelled so that altogether aircraft utilisation is reduced.[160] (Simultaneously, to return to profitability airlines will use price policies to generate more revenue, as explained in section 3.3.2, and they will aim to lower costs, which will be examined in the subsequent section).

The table function *T effect of operating performance gap on utilisation* indicates how much airlines change their aircraft *capacity utilisation* compared to the planned *NORMAL UTILISATION* given the airline's *operating performance gap* (see eq. 100–103). The more the *load factor* exceeds break even, the higher the airlines' motivation to increase aircraft utilisation up to the limit (see graph for eq. 101).[161] Whenever the load factor falls below the break even level, capacity is reduced. The worst flights and routes may be cancelled first. If the airline still does not return to break even, efforts may become more aggressive and aircraft may be grounded. The table function has an S-shape because not all airlines in the industry will have exactly the same cost structure. While some already struggle below their break even, others will still be working profitably. The lower the industry's average load factor drops below average break even, the fewer airlines will still be able to be profitable. At some point even the last ones will need to make major short-term capacity reductions.

indicated capacity utilisation = NORMAL UTILISATION
$$* \ T \ effect \ of \ operating \ performance \ gap$$
$$on \ utilisation \ (operating \ performance \ gap) \qquad (100)$$

T effect of operating performance gap on utilisation = $(-0.3,0)$, $(-0.25,0.1)$,
$$(-0.2,0.6), \ (-0.1,0.88),$$
$$(0,1), \ (0.1,1.08),$$
$$(0.3,1.15)$$

(101)

change in capacity utilisation = (*indicated capacity utilisation* − *capacity utilisation*) / UTILISATION ADJUSTMENT TIME   *(102)*

capacity utilisation = INTEGRAL (*change in capacity utilisation*, *indicated capacity utilisation*$_{t0}$)   *(103)*

The utilisation of the leased aircraft in the fleet might differ from the utilisation determined above due to contract restrictions, e.g. maximum or minimum usage requirements (see above, section 'aircraft leasing'). The impact of these restrictions will be tested in scenarios with a separate *leased aircraft utilisation*.

Figure 3.24 depicts the model structure for aircraft utilisation.

The result: available seat miles

The result of airlines' fleet planning (*desired capacity*) and their fleet management is their *total fleet* (*owned aircraft* and *leased aircraft*). This has a certain *production capacity*. The number of *available seat miles* airlines offer depends on their *capacity utilisation* (see eq. 104).

available seat miles = *production capacity* * *capacity utilisation*   *(104)*

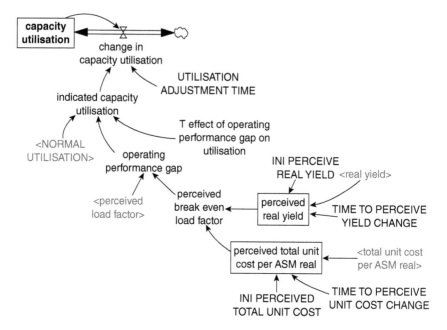

Figure 3.24 Supply module – aircraft utilisation

Figure 3.25 Supply module – available seat miles

In case leasing contracts include specific minimum or maximum usage requirements, these will be inserted into the model with a separate *leased aircraft utilisation* applied to the *leased aircraft*.

Comparison to other authors' modelling

Previous models of the airline profit cycle use the same basic supply structure as presented above: an aircraft ageing chain. Aircraft are ordered and will be delivered after the manufacturing lead time. They then stay in service until retirement. In terms of implemented decision rules and details, different authors' supply modelling varies. The main differences between previous approaches and the presented airline industry model will be outlined.

The aircraft ordering mechanism in Liehr et al.'s model differs most from the above presented airline industry model.[162] Liehr et al.'s order decision process does not take already placed aircraft order into account. Neither does it consider replacements for aircraft close to retirement. How much capacity airlines order depends on their current load factor compared to its target. If the load factor exceeds its target and the airline is profitable, enough capacity to fill the load factor gap will be ordered. Additionally, an order for twice the expected market growth will be placed. Unfortunately, Liehr et al. do not explain their model's ordering mechanism in detail. Aircraft retirement and utilisation both do not vary with profitability. The option to lease rather than buy aircraft is not implemented.

For Segers the amount of aircraft ordered depends on capacity and demand forecasts, not on profitability expectations.[163] After several profitable years airlines are assumed to become optimistic and order even more than forecasts indicate. Likewise, after consecutive unprofitable years they become pessimistic and order less. Once aircraft are in the market their utilisation depends on load factor performance towards an exogenous target, not on profitability. Following that logic, a rather empty flight with a full business class and correspondingly high revenue would be cancelled. Segers does not include leasing.

According to Sgouridis aircraft orders depend on a comparison of desired and actual capacity. How much capacity airlines desire is determined by demand forecasts combined with an exogenous target load factor.[164] When ordering, airlines take the existing fleet, due retirements, and all or just a share of already placed orders into account. Similarly to Segers, Sgouridis implements a profit effect on ordering behaviour, so profitable periods lead to additional orders and vice versa. This implies that airlines calculate a desired aircraft order and then, just because they are profitable, change the number afterwards to add more (even though they calculated they do not need more). Aircraft utilisation adjustment is exogenous in Sgouridis' model but retirements depend on profitability. Since Sgouridis' focus is not only on airlines but also on aircraft manufacturers, their aircraft production rate is endogenous.

Pierson's way of modelling airline supply is very similar to the above presented airline industry model.[165] A difference is that Pierson's desired capacity is based on demand forecasts and an exogenous target load factor, not on profitability. Besides, aircraft retirements are also independent of profit consideration. They are purely based on age. In the aircraft ordering process Pierson includes the option to cancel aircraft orders but does not assign costs to it, though according to interviews with airline managers, cancelling a contracted aircraft order is highly costly. Pierson does not include leasing.

3.3.4 Cost module

Airlines' aircraft acquisition and utilisation decisions have several financial implications. They induce operating costs. The cost module's feedback structure is depicted in Figure 3.28 at the end of this section.

The airlines' *total operating costs real* are the sum of all their variable and fixed costs (see eq. 105).

$$total\ operating\ costs\ real = sum\ variable\ costs\ real + sum\ fixed\ costs\ real \qquad (105)$$

Variable costs vary with the level of output, i.e. *available seat miles*, whereas fixed costs do not.[166] The division of costs into variable and fixed depends on the timeframe.[167] In the long run all costs are variable and airlines are entirely free of commitments. In the very short run, for example right before take-off, an airline's costs for aircraft, labour, fuel, and other items are all fixed and can no longer be influenced. In the airline industry model the unit of time is years; short-term decisions in the model, for example aircraft utilisation adjustments, can be taken within a few weeks. So the term 'variable costs' will be used for e.g. fuel costs and landing fees. Fixed costs are for example the costs of aircraft ownership or leasing, and labour costs. Contracts and other obligations do not allow a total avoidance of those fixed costs within a few weeks whereas fuel costs and landing fees could be prevented in that timeframe.

The division of airlines' costs into variable and fixed is a very general representation of their sophisticated cost accounting practices. However, since these vary significantly depending on for example the purpose of the account, the company, or the regulatory requirements, the rough division into only variable and fixed costs serves the objective to model the industry on an aggregate level. A categorisation of costs into variable and fixed is given in Table 3.6 (see appendix A for details). It is based on a cost accounting scheme by Holloway (see Figure 3.26).[168]

Figure 3.27 provides an indication of what impact each cost item has on airlines' total operating costs in the US airline industry.[169] Fuel and labour costs each account for a quarter of airlines' costs. Airlines' costs of rents and ownership (incl. depreciation) represent only around 7% of total operating costs.

Table 3.6 Classification of costs into variable and fixed

Cost classification	
variable	*fixed*
fuel	labour
food and beverages	aircraft rent and ownership
landing fees	non-aircraft rent and ownership
maintenance material	professional services
passenger commissions	aircraft insurance
communication	non-aircraft insurance
(transport-related expenses)	advertising and promotion
	utilities and office supplies
	(other operating expenses)

Cost categories as in ATA cost index, assigned according to Holloway. Find details in appendix A.

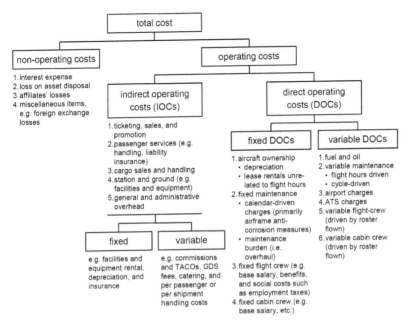

Figure 3.26 Holloway's airline cost classification scheme (Holloway 2008, p. 274)

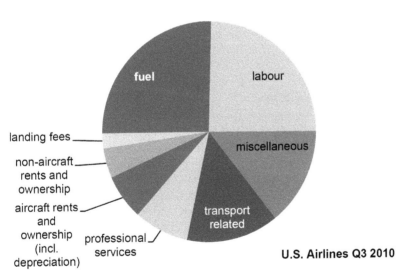

Figure 3.27 Operating cost items of US airlines in 3rd quarter of 2010

The total of all variable costs, i.e. the *sum variable costs real*, is calculated by multiplying *available seat miles* by the unit cost they cause, i.e. the *variable unit cost real* (see eq. 106). By far the largest variable cost block for airlines are fuel costs (see Figure 3.27). They are external to the airline industry, which means airlines cannot influence them. In the airline industry model fuel and other variable costs are thus external time series (see eq. 107).

$$sum\ variable\ costs\ real = variable\ unit\ cost\ real * available$$
$$seat\ miles \tag{106}$$

$$variable\ unit\ cost\ real = TS\ real\ fuel\ cost\ per\ ASM + TS\ other$$
$$variable\ cost\ per\ ASM\ real \tag{107}$$

The airlines' *sum fixed costs real* depends on the number of seats in the total fleet multiplied by all fixed costs that are accounted to it (see eq. 108). These are mainly the costs of labour, and aircraft rent and ownership costs. The underlying assumption here is that labour, as well as other fixed costs, scale with the aircraft fleet size. This is straightforward as far as for example aircraft leasing and ownership costs, flight personnel, and aircraft insurance, are concerned. The remaining fixed costs blocks, such as infrastructure costs and general management staff, are also assumed to be larger for airlines with bigger fleets. Airlines with larger fleets and thus more operations will need for example more airport terminals, maintenance stations, and employees to run their business. Depending on their efficiency individual airlines may require less or more than the average fixed costs for the same amount of available seat miles.

$$sum\ fixed\ costs\ real = fixed\ unit\ cost\ real * total\ fleet \tag{108}$$

$$fixed\ unit\ cost\ real = overhead\ unit\ cost\ real$$
$$= INTEGRAL\ (change\ in\ overhead\ real\ unit\ cost,$$
$$INI\ FIXED\ UNIT\ COST_{t0}) \tag{109}$$

In line with the general approach to cost accounting in the airline industry model, the terms 'fixed costs' and 'overhead costs' are used interchangeably (see eq. 109). The development of overheads depends strongly on the airlines' profit situation. It takes the *TIME TO ADJUST PROFITABILITY EXPECTATIONs* to perceive change in the profitability (see eq. 115). In unprofitable times airlines will seek to cut costs. Even an expected profitability below a certain (positive) target level may induce pressure to reduce costs. If airline managers expect an unsatisfactory financial performance, they usually initialise internal initiatives to 'slim down' and 'economise' the company. However, not every desired fixed cost level is attainable in reality. There is a *MINIMUM FIXED UNIT COST REAL*. For example, even if all aircraft in the airlines' fleet were fully depreciated, they would still incur costs due to mandatory aircraft maintenance checks. The leased aircraft would still not be rented out for free. Also, there is a minimum wage that airlines will need to pay their employees to prevent them from taking other jobs in other industries that offer better conditions. In some countries there may even be legal obligation to pay a certain wage minimum. Hence, the *desired fixed unit cost real* is not to fall under the cost minimum (see eq. 111). The desired overheads may, however, increase in profitable times. In a financially successful period, labour unions will pressure airlines to raise wages or improve working conditions, for example by reducing working hours and consequently hiring more people. Besides, airlines will tend to make additional investments in infrastructure or will be willing to accept higher aircraft lease rates. The relationships explained above are captured in the table function *T effect of expected profitability on overheads* which expresses how *expected profitability* translates into a level of *desired fixed unit costs real* (see eq. 112–114, with graph).[170] The *effect of expected profitability on overheads* thus indicates the pressure on overheads to change either way.

Resolving the difference between the desired and actual overhead level will take some time, i.e. the *FIXED UNIT COST ADJUSTMENT TIME* (see eq. 110). It reflects infrastructure and service contract adjustment times as well as labour contract negotiation periods.

$$\text{change in overhead real unit cost} = \text{(indicated fixed unit cost real} - \text{overhead unit cost real)} / \textit{FIXED UNIT COST ADJUSTMENT TIME} \quad (110)$$

$$\text{indicated fixed unit cost real} = MAX \text{ (desired fixed unit cost real,} \\ \textit{MINIMUM FIXED UNIT COST REAL)} \quad (111)$$

$$\text{desired fixed unit cost real} = \text{overhead unit cost real} * (1 + \text{effect of expected profitability on overheads)} \quad (112)$$

$$\text{effect of expected profitability on overheads} = T \text{ effect of expected profitability on overheads (expected profitability)} \quad (113)$$

$$T \text{ effect of expected profitability on overheads} = (-0.5, -0.6), (-0.2, -0.2), \\ (-0.1, -0.09), (0, -0.015), \\ (0.025, 0), (0.1, 0.03), \\ (0.2, 0.05), (0.5, 0.1)$$

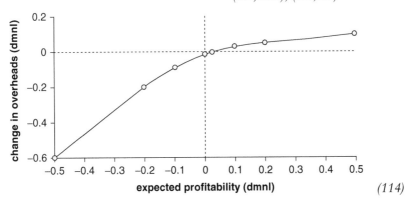

$$(114)$$

$$\text{expected profitability} = SMOOTH \text{ (profitability to revenues,} \\ \textit{TIME TO ADJUST PROFITABILITY EXPECTATION)} \quad (115)$$

Having calculated the variable, fixed, and total costs, an additional indicator can be computed. Dividing the *total operating costs real* by the number of *available seat miles* yields the *total unit cost per ASM real* (see eq. 116).

$$total\ unit\ cost\ per\ ASM\ real = total\ operating\ costs\ real\ /\ available\ seat\ miles \tag{116}$$

To grant a quick and comprehensive overview over the airlines' financial situation in the model, the cost module is formulated twice: first in real terms, then in nominal values by multiplying fixed unit costs and the variable unit cost components by inflation. Apart from the inflation adjustment the equations for the real and the nominal structure are the same (see eq. 117–123).

$$fuel\ cost\ per\ ASM = TS\ real\ fuel\ cost\ per\ ASM\ *\ inflation\ index \tag{117}$$

$$other\ variable\ cost\ per\ ASM = TS\ other\ variable\ cost\ per\ ASM\ real\ *\ inflation\ index \tag{118}$$

$$overhead\ unit\ cost = overhead\ unit\ cost\ real\ *\ inflation\ index = fixed\ unit\ cost\ per\ seat \tag{119}$$

$$variable\ unit\ cost\ per\ ASM = fuel\ cost\ per\ ASM + other\ variable\ cost\ per\ ASM \tag{120}$$

$$sum\ variable\ costs = variable\ unit\ cost\ per\ ASM\ *\ available\ seat\ miles \tag{121}$$

$$sum\ fixed\ costs = fixed\ unit\ cost\ per\ seat\ *\ total\ fleet \tag{122}$$

$$total\ operating\ costs = sum\ variable\ costs + sum\ fixed\ costs \tag{123}$$

Comparison to other authors' modelling

How previous airline industry models address costs varies from treating them as completely exogenous to employing endogenous cost control. In Liehr et al.'s model the focus is on aircraft capacity adjustment. In consequence, costs and profit are not made endogenous.[171] Segers assumes airlines become more efficient in several unprofitable years and they become slightly less efficient in profitable periods.[172] This productivity control together with exogenous unit costs results in total costs. Sgouridis employs more detail by distinguishing three types of costs: fuel, aircraft ownership, and other operating expenses.[173] As his attention is not only on airlines but also on aircraft manufacturers, aircraft prices are endogenous. Cost-cutting efforts are included for manufacturers, not for airlines. Pierson's model also incorporates a limited cost control mechanism: wages depend on airline profitability.[174] However, all other costs, including aircraft ownership costs, are summarised as variable cost per mile. That means with no miles flown aircraft come for free. In his model the comprising variable unit cost cannot be reduced.

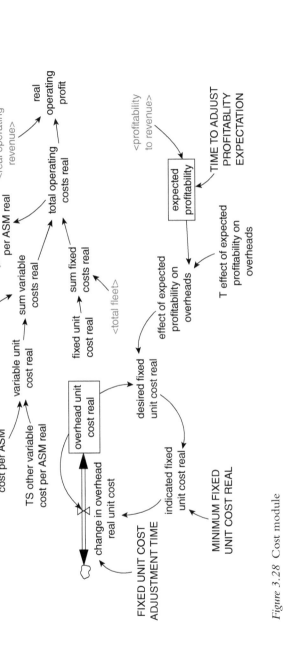

Figure 3.28 Cost module

3.3.5 Consolidation of modules to full model: profit calculation

Calculating the operating profit brings all modules of the airline industry model together. The module's feedback structure is presented in Figure 3.29.

Operating profit is defined as *operating revenue* minus *operating costs* (see eq. 124 and 125). Common profit indicators, such as the *profitability to revenues* and the *operating margin*,[175] are also computed in equations 126–127.[176] (Technical note: Because of its small size the profit module is programmed on the same model view as the cost module.)

$$operating\ profit = operating\ revenue - total\ operating\ costs \tag{124}$$

$$real\ operating\ profit = real\ operating\ revenue - total\ operating\ costs\ real \tag{125}$$

$$profitability\ to\ revenues = ZIDZ\ (operating\ profit,\ operating\ revenue) \tag{126}$$

$$operating\ margin = XIDZ\ (operating\ revenue, total\ operating \\ costs,\ 1000000)\ \_with\ 1,000,000\ as\ placeholder \\ for\ 'infinitely\ large'\ if\ costs\ are\ zero \tag{127}$$

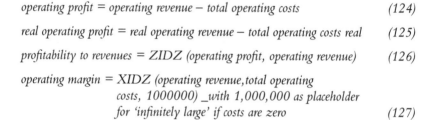

Figure 3.29 Profit calculation in the airline industry model

3.4 Validation of model structure

Validating a model means to determine whether it fits its purpose. Sterman emphasises: 'All models are wrong, so no models are valid or verifiable in the sense of establishing their truth. The question [. . .] is never whether a model is true but whether it is useful.'[177] Hence, the aim of the validation process is to gain confidence in the model's usefulness.[178] This is the prerequisite to conduct model experiments and derive convincing policy recommendations.

The validation process is iterative (see introduction to the modelling process in section 3.1.2). Test results lead to revise parts of the model which then need to be tested again. System Dynamics literature suggests sets of validation tests, for example by Forrester and Senge,[179] Barlas,[180] and Sterman.[181] The airline profit cycle model designed above has been validated along Sterman's framework.[182] During the modelling building process his suggested tests were frequently conducted and have led to several improvements. Many validation tests are not clearly distinguishable. Often one action may be needed for different tests, for example expert interviews.

Expert interviews played a central role in the model validation process. They were used to determine the adequacy of the system boundary and model structure. This implied checking if all important problem aspects are endogenous, if the model is consistent with the experts' knowledge about the system, and if the implemented decision rules describe actors' actual behaviour. The model was discussed at different stages. The pool of interviewees was the same as described in section 2.4.2. As part of their expert interview on potential airline profit cycle drivers and mitigation measures, each interviewee was questioned about how things work (decision rules and model structure) in his or her area of expertise. For example, a head of pricing department gave insights into pricing and yield management, a chief fleet manager approved how an airline's capacity planning is represented in the model, etc. Most experts wished more detail be added to 'their' model part. However, they expressed that all relevant functionalities are included, and model structure and decision rules correspond with their knowledge about the system.

The system's response to extreme conditions was part of the expert discussions. First, the system's plausible reaction to extreme conditions was defined. Then it was checked if the system behaved accordingly. In case simulation results did not meet expectations, it was discussed whether the discrepancy was due to flaws in the model or misguided expectations in the first place. Hence, the extreme condition tests became a key part of the model building process, and in consequence increased experts' confidence in the model's results.

The 'family member test', which requires to calibrate the model for a related system to see if that works as well, has not been conducted. The reason is that sufficient data for other markets than the US airline industry is not publicly available. It can, however, be argued that the family member test is nonetheless passed successfully since the airline industry model is based on Sterman's commodity cycle model which has already been well applied to the pulp and paper industry.[183]

Results of further validation tests will be presented as part of the following sections. Parameter assessment, for example, is a crucial part of the model calibration in section 3.5, behaviour reproduction is examined in section 3.6, and sensitivity analyses are essentially scenario analyses discussed in sections 4.1–4.5.

3.5 Calibration of the model for the US airline industry

3.5.1 Reasons for market and time frame choice

The model is calibrated for US passenger airlines with their systemwide activity, which means their national and international traffic. The underlying assumption when calibrating the model for US air carriers is that while changes occur in the modelled market segment, the rest of the world remains stable. Which impact changes in the 'outside world', i.e. the industry environment and the general economy, have on the US airline industry will be simulated in sections 4.3 and 4.4.

There are several reasons for choosing to calibrate the airline profit cycle model for the US carriers:

- The US airline industry shows most cyclicality in their profits (see section 1.1).
- The US market is one of the largest and most relevant world markets. In 2010 25% of the world's scheduled seats departed in the United States, 26% in the Far East (incl. India and China) and 25% in Europe. The United States has the largest domestic market.[184]
- Data availability for US airlines is comparatively good because they are legally obliged to report operational and financial information to the US Department of Transportation (further detail in subsequent section 3.5.2).

To research the US airline industry's dynamics it is helpful to choose a timespan for calibration in which no major structural changes occurred that would need to be incorporated. The US airline industry was already deregulated in 1978.[185] In the mid-1980s the US airline market was well transitioned, low-cost carriers were establishing their market position (e.g. People Express, Southwest), yield management systems developed, and Airbus was close to introducing its narrow-body family and thus becoming one of the two major airplane manufacturers.[186] Consequently, the model is calibrated to the situation at the end of 1984 so simulations start in January 1985. From this starting point simulations can run for as long as data for the model's external time series is available. For example gross domestic products (GDP) or fuel prices need to be inserted. A consistent dataset is available until 2010. It will be introduced in the subsequent section 3.5.2.

The US airline industry 1985–2010

To provide background to the US airline industry, the developments of key variables between 1985 and 2010 are depicted in Figure 3.30.[187]

In this period the US airline industry is a growing business. Airlines' supply of seat miles and passengers' demand for air transport both more than doubled within the respective timespan. Meanwhile, airlines increased their efficiency. Real costs per seat mile offered sank from approximately 8 to 6 cents. More elaborate network planning and yield management systems further enhanced efficiency gains. As a result, average load factors rose from approximately 60% to 80%. While traffic grew and unit costs decreased, airlines' real yields have dropped since the market is open to price competition. Altogether they fell by

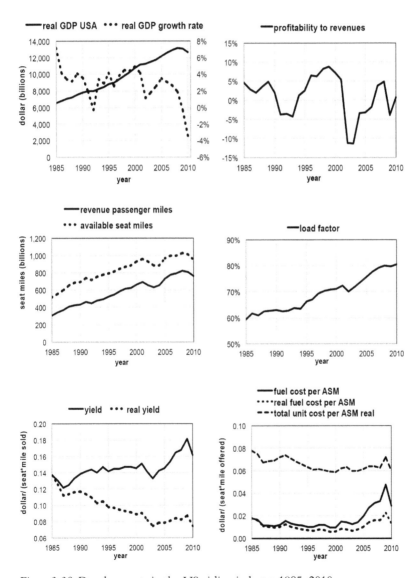

Figure 3.30 Developments in the US airline industry 1985–2010

over 40% between 1985 and 2010, from approximately 14 to 8 cents per seat mile sold. After 2001 yields seem to have stabilised at the lower level.

Financially the US airlines' situation in 1985 was successful. Profitability to revenues was at 5% and airlines managed to sustain it until 1989. In the early 1990s losses were being made before profitability reached a new record level in the late 1990s. After the terror attacks in 2001, airlines suffered losses again. In 2007 airlines succeeded to return to being profitable, but were set back by the fuel price peak in 2008 and the outbreak of the financial crisis. Nonetheless airlines managed to regain profitability in 2010.

The industry's environment between 1985 and 2010 was challenging. Several crises shook the economy: the gulf war in 1990/1, the terror attack on 11 September, 2001, and the outbreak of the financial crisis in late 2008. Moreover, the fuel price peaked in 2008. During the year it increased by more than 70% and then released back to normal.[188] From a modelling perspective, these extreme conditions can be seen as natural experiments to test the model's performance and build confidence that the implemented decision rules reflect reality (see section 3.4 on model validation).

3.5.2 Consistent industry data base for model parameterisation and reference time series

Having chosen to calibrate the airline profit cycle model for US airlines, necessary datasets need to be compiled. Basically, two sets of data are required. The first set is needed to compare model simulations to what really happened in the industry in the past. This set is called reference data or historic data. It contains the historic development of key variables, most of which have already been shown in Figure 3.30 in the previous section. The reference dataset is not essential for the feasibility of model simulation but for the model validation process, i.e. behaviour reproduction tests (see section 3.4). Second, the input dataset for the model is needed. Required data inputs have already been specified while developing the model's equations in section 3.3. They are listed in appendix C. The following types of data are required:

- time series data for external influences that change over time
- constants for external influences that remain the same over time
- initial values for levels in $t_0 =$ January 1985

The dataset to calibrate the airline profit cycle model needs to meet several requirements. First, it needs to be complete. A System Dynamics model simulation will not work if inputs for even one variable are left blank. In some cases it is thus necessary to estimate variable values. The impact of a change in those estimated values will be examined to determine if it may be useful to dedicate more resources into developing a more precise estimate. Second, data inputs have to be credible and reliable. Data preferably comes from an objective source with an industry-wide perspective. Unfortunately, one source does not cover all inputs needed in the airline industry model so that data from different sources has to be combined. The challenge is thus, third, to keep the dataset consistent.

The most complete, reliable, and consistent source of data about US airlines is the 'ATA Cost Index for US Passenger Airlines'. The last freely available version was published in 2011. Publisher of the dataset was the American Air Transport Association (ATA), renamed as Airlines for America (A4A) in December 2011.[189] The A4A is America's oldest and largest airline trade association; its members and affiliates transport more than 90% of US airline passenger and cargo traffic.[190] After the name change the Cost Index file was removed from the website's open access content, the 2011 file being the last available version. This file is used to calibrate the airline profit cycle model. It contains data until the end of 2009 and some 2010 estimates. Consequently, the model can be calibrated until January 2010.

The ATA Cost Index is primarily derived from information which the US Department of Transportation (DOT) collects in Form 41.[191] US federal law requires most American passenger and cargo airlines to report financial and operating information to the DOT.[192] Form 41 contains data of large certified US air carriers with operating annual revenues of USD 20 million and more. Between 1990 and 2014, 146 carriers have made filings. US carriers are included with all their traffic, domestic and international. Non US-owned airlines' business in the United States is not incorporated.[193] Appendix B offers further background information on the ATA Cost Index.

For many of the model's input variables, the ATA Cost Index does not provide the exact corresponding time series. These are derived based on data offered. For example, yield is calculated as operating revenue divided by revenue passenger miles. And cost positions are aggregated according to the scheme proposed in section 3.3.4 and appendix A.

The ATA Cost Index does not cover the model's entire input and reference data needs. Hence, several additional data sources are employed:

- GDP data: United Nations Statistics Office
- Inflation data: World Bank
- Taxes (per seat mile): US National Bureau of Economic Research report by Borenstein[194]
- Price elasticity of demand: Intervistas report (meta-study prepared for the IATA)[195]
- Share of domestic and international travel: DOT's Bureau of Transportation Statistics[196]
- Typical aircraft lease period: Morrell[197]
- Other data: expert interviews and sensitivity tests

As last stated, 'other' variables, which can neither be calibrated based on the ATA Cost Index nor on sources listed above, needed to be assessed by aviation experts. Interview partners presented in section 2.4.2 were engaged in the parameter discussion in two cases.

First, experts were consulted when data availability for a variable was insufficient. Some data is for example only publicly available for a selection of airlines, and not for the industry as a whole back to 1985. Here, experts scaled and completed the time series. Variable calibrated by this procedure are for example:

- Ancillary revenue: Data sources: DOT's Bureau of Transportation Statistics (not reported separately),[198] Amadeus/Ideaworks report, Oxford Economics report.[199] Discussion result: Starting in 1995 with the emergence of low-cost carriers ancillary revenues grow slowly, they increase after the 2001 crisis as a source of additional revenue for financially distressed airlines, and reach approximately 10% of US airlines' total operating revenue in 2010.
- Share of leased aircraft: Data sources: DOT's Bureau of Transportation Statistic and Gritta/Lippman.[200] Discussion result: Values are interpolated to form a smooth S-shaped growth curve.

Second, when no data was available, experts were asked to contribute esti-mates for variables in their particular area of expertise. They contributed insights about how long processes take in airline management to calibrate delays and adjustment times. In order to check how much accuracy is required for a particular variable, sensitivity tests are conducted (as intro-duced in section 3.4 and shown in sections 4.3–4.5). Experts also indicated, for example, how sensitive the price-setting mechanism should react to the different pressures influencing it, and gave a range for each pressure. To calibrate those price sensitivities, parameter values were mathematically opti-mised to generate the best fit between simulated and historic yield as well as profitability.[201] A similar procedure was applied to calibrate the effect of non-economic demand shocks on revenue passenger miles.

Retrieved variable values for input and reference data as well as their sources are listed in appendix C. The subsequent section will focus on one type of input variables, namely the time series, because they insert behaviour into the model.

3.5.3 Historic data time series affecting model dynamics

Prior to discussing model simulations and the behaviour of certain variables, it is crucial to examine behaviour which is implied in the dataset. For example, if *revenue passenger miles* decrease sharply in 2001, this is due to the 9/11 terror attack and people's consequential reluctance to fly. This demand slump is not generated by model mechanisms.

The model's external time series, listed in appendix C with their data sources, are:

1   inflation rate
2   economic developments (GDP)
3   demand shocks' non-economic component (e.g. reluctance to fly after 9/11 terror attack, or panic after financial crisis outbreak 2008/9)
4   ticket taxes (simplified as add-on on yield)
5   ancillary yields (non-ticket revenues per mile, e.g. travel insurance)
6   variable unit costs (e.g. fuel)
7   aircraft productivity maximum (reflects technology, network planning, etc.)
8   share of leased aircraft (lease or buy decision not modelled)

Figure 3.31 depicts these time series. None of the time series exhibits the cyclicality observed in profitability. The airline industry's profit cycle is thus not inserted externally but generated within the system by model mechanisms.

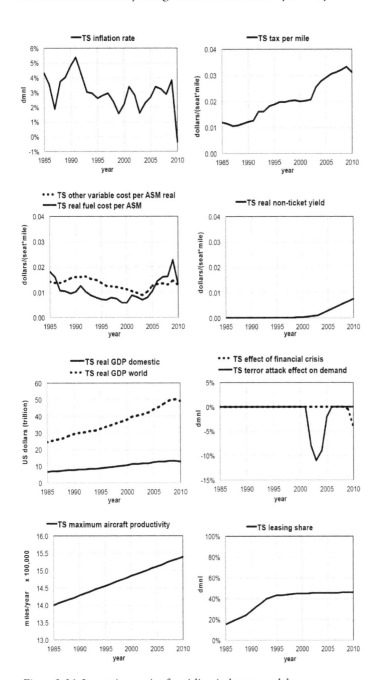

Figure 3.31 Input time series for airline industry model

3.6 Confidence in the model's behaviour and results

In this section the model's base run will be presented. The base run is the simulation run the model creates given the input data described in the previous section 3.5. Comparing the base run to the historic reference data is essential to create confidence in the model (see Behaviour Reproduction test as part of the validation process in section 3.4). If the base run simulation matches historic data, it confirms the dynamic hypothesis, i.e. the model.[202]

Table 3.7 Model fit statistics

	standard error measures						Theil's statistics			significance	
variable	coefficient of correlation (dmnl) *r*	coefficient of determination (dmnl) *R²*	mean absolute percent error *MAPE*	mean square error (units^2) *MSE*	root mean square error (units) *RMSE*	bias (dmnl) U_M	unequal variation (dmnl) U_S	unequal covariation (dmnl) U_C	probability of random result in two-tail t-test *P(T<t)*	statistically significant difference *yes/no*
operating profit	0.95	0.90	13%	2.39E+18	1.54E+09	0.00	0.00	1.00	98%	no
profitability	0.94	0.88	12%	3.42E-04	1.85E-02	0.01	0.00	0.99	88%	no
real operating profit	0.94	0.89	13%	9.47E+17	9.73E+08	0.00	0.00	1.00	97%	no
total unit cost per ASM real	0.97	0.95	2%	3.49E-06	1.87E-03	0.53	0.02	0.45	23%	no
total op. cost real	0.97	0.94	3%	4.18E+18	2.05E+09	0.01	0.11	0.88	90%	no
real operat. revenue	0.96	0.93	3%	4.33E+18	2.08E+09	0.01	0.02	0.97	88%	no
fixed unit cost real	0.97	0.94	2%	1.97E+06	1.40E+03	0.56	0.01	0.43	18%	no
available seat miles	0.99	0.98	3%	8.19E+20	2.86E+10	0.20	0.16	0.65	68%	no
real yield	0.98	0.96	3%	1.25E-05	3.54E-03	0.00	0.09	0.91	97%	no
real price	0.97	0.94	3%	1.88E-05	4.33E-03	0.20	0.14	0.66	48%	no
revenue passenger miles	1.00	1.00	1%	7.93E+19	8.90E+09	0.00	0.01	0.99	100%	no

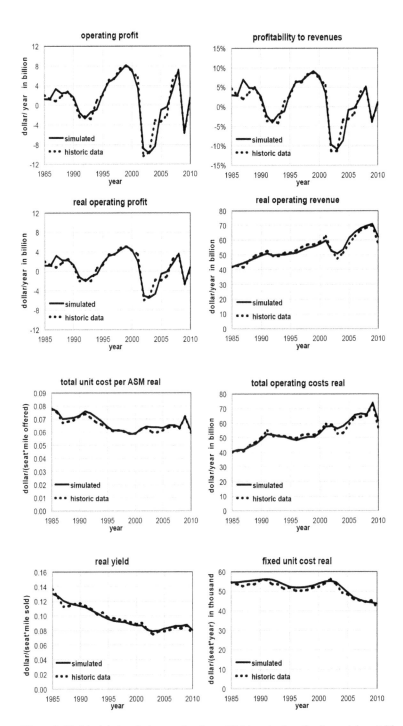

Figure 3.32 Model simulation vs. 'real world' historic data for financial variables

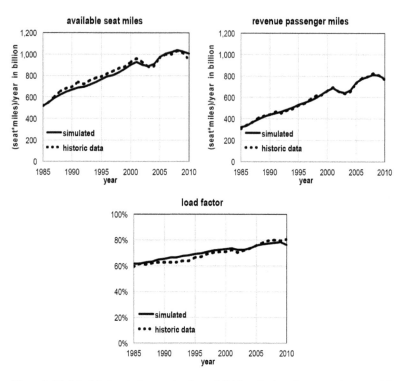

Figure 3.33 Model simulation vs. 'real world' historic data for operating variables

Figures 3.32 and 3.33 show the model's base run compared to historic time series for key variables. By nature the model is a representation of the real system and does not include all its complexity. Hence, a certain deviation between simulated and historic behaviour can be expected. Sterman suggests statistic measures to determine how well the two match.[203] These indicators are computed in Table 3.7 for all key variables. They reveal no statistically significant deviation between modelled and historic 'real world' behaviour.

Notes

1 Pearson's coefficient for linear correlations based on years 1970–2011. Data sources: For real GDP: UN Statistics, 'World. GDP, at constant 2005 prices – US Dollars', web page, accessed: 14 Nov 2013. For demand: A4A Airlines for America, 'World airlines: Annual results. Traffic and operations 1929–present', web page, accessed: 21 Nov 2014.

2 Based on Pearson's correlation coefficient.

3 Data sources: For GDP: UN Statistics, 'World. GDP, at current prices – US Dollars', web page, accessed: 14 Nov 2013. For real GDP: UN Statistics, 'World. GDP, at constant 2005 prices – US Dollars', accessed: 14 Nov 2013. For airline profits: A4A Airlines for America, 'World airlines: Annual results. Financial results 1947–present', web page, accessed: 15 Nov 2013. For inflation adjustment:

UN Statistics, 'World. GDP, Implicit Price Deflators – US Dollars. Implicit Price Deflator (2005=100)', web page, accessed: 14 Nov 2013. – Profitability calculated as ratio of profit to revenue.

4 Data source: A4A Airlines for America, 'World airlines: Annual results. Financial results 1947–present', accessed: 15 Nov 2013. Crises chosen as in: Airbus, *Global market forecast 2013–2032* (2014), p. 3.

5 Data source: A4A Airlines for America (formerly ATA Air Transport Association), 'ATA Cost Index for US Passenger Airlines, 3rd quarter 2010', 2011, web page, accessed: 23 Feb 2011.

6 Based on Pearson's correlation coefficient. The fuel price is the fuel expense paid by US airlines as indicated in: ibid. Inflation adjusted by the World Bank's consumer price index CPI (2000=100) given in 'ATA Cost Index'. Further data sources: For GDP: UN Statistics, 'World. GDP, at current prices – US Dollars', accessed: 14 Nov 2013. For real GDP: UN Statistics, 'World. GDP, at constant 2005 prices – US Dollars', accessed: 14 Nov 2013.

7 Data sources: For fuel: A4A Airlines for America (formerly ATA Air Transport Association), 'ATA Cost Index for US Passenger Airlines, 3rd quarter 2010', accessed: 23 Feb 2011. For GDP: UN Statistics, 'World. GDP, at current prices – US Dollars', accessed: 14 Nov 2013.

8 According to Milling complexity has three dimensions: the number of elements or variables (variety), the number of connections between those elements (connectivity), and the type of connections (function). Complex problems have many elements which are strongly interconnected and their connections are non-linear and often involve time delays. See Milling, Peter M., 'Kybernetische Überlegungen beim Entscheiden in komplexen Systemen', in *Entscheiden in komplexen Systemen*, ed. Milling, Peter M. (Berlin: Duncker & Humblot, 2002), pp. 11–12.

9 See Milling, Peter M., *Der technische Fortschritt beim Produktionsprozeß: Ein dynamisches Modell für innovative Industrieunternehmen* (Wiesbaden: Gabler, 1974), pp. 55–57. For a discussion of pros and cons of different potential methods, see for example: Sgouridis, Sgouris P., 'Symbiotic strategies in enterprise ecology: Modeling commercial aviation as an Enterprise of Enterprises', PhD thesis, Massachusetts Institute of Technology, 2007, pp. 226–231.

10 See Forrester, Jay W., *Industrial dynamics*, 6th printing 1969 edn. (Cambridge, MA: MIT Press, 1961). And see Forrester, Jay W., *Principles of systems*, 2nd edn. (Cambridge, MA: Wright-Allen Press, 1968). For a history of the field see: Forrester, Jay W., 'The beginning of System Dynamics', System Dynamics Society Meeting (Germany: Stuttgart, 1989). And see Sterman, John D. and David C. Lane, 'Jay Wright Forrester', in *Profiles in operations research: Pioneers and innovators*, eds. Assad, Arjang A. and Saul I. Gass, International Series in Operations Research & Management Science (New York: Springer, 2011).

11 See Forrester, Jay W., 'System Dynamics and the lessons of 35 years', in *A systems-based approach to policymaking*, ed. Greene, Kenyon B. (Springer US, 1993) p. 199.

12 See directly Richardson, George P., 'System Dynamics', in *Encyclopedia of operations research and management science*, eds. Gass, Saul and Carl Harris (Kluwer Academic Publishers, System Dynamics Society, www.systemdynamics.org/what-is-s/, accessed: 30 Jan 2014, 1999/2011).

13 See Forrester, *Industrial dynamics*.

14 See Milling, Peter M., 'Leitmotive des System-Dynamics-Ansatzes', *Wirtschaft swissenschaftliches Studium (WiSt)* 13.10 (1984): 507. – Similarly, Richardson and Pugh suggest to think of models as dynamics hypothesis of a system. See Richardson, George P. and Alexander L. Pugh, *Introduction to System Dynamics modeling with DYNAMO*, MIT Press/Wright-Allen series in System Dynamics (Cambridge, MA: MIT Press, 1981), p. 55.

15 See Forrester, *Principles of systems*, p. 4.3.

16 A case study illustrating the difference between thinking in linear process terms or in feedback systems is given in Senge, Peter M., *The fifth discipline: The art and practice of the learning organization*, 1st edn. (New York: Doubleday/Currency, 1990), pp. 70–73.

17 See Lane, David C., 'Should System Dynamics be described as a "hard" or "deterministic" systems approach?', *Systems Research and Behavioural Science* 17 (2000): 4. And see Sterman, John D., 'Modeling managerial behavior: Misperceptions of feedback in a dynamic decision making experiment', *Management Science* 35.3 (1989): 334–336.

18 For example see Ford, David N., 'A behavioral approach to feedback loop dominance analysis', *System Dynamics Review* 15.1 (1999): 3.

19 For example see Senge, Peter M., *The fifth discipline: The art and practice of the learning organization*, Rev. and updated. ed. (New York: Doubleday/Currency, 2006), pp. 88–91.

20 See Forrester, Jay W., 'Industrial dynamics – After the first decade', *Management Science* 14.7 (1968): 399–401, 414. And see Milling, Peter M., 'Systems research and corporate policy making', in *Advances in information systems research*, eds Lasker, George E., Tetsunori Koizumi, and Jens Pohl (Windsor, Ontario: The International Institute for Advanced Studies, 1991).

21 See Strohhecker, Jürgen, 'System Dynamics als Managementinstrument [System Dynamics as a management instrument]', in *System Dynamics für die Finanzindustrie: Simulieren und Analysieren dynamisch-komplexer Probleme* eds. Strohhecker, Jürgen and Jürgen Sehnert (Frankfurt: Frankfurt-School-Verlag, 2008), pp. 30–33.

22 See Größler, Andreas, Frank H. Maier, and Peter M. Milling, 'Enhancing learning capabilities by providing transparency in business simulators', *Simulation Gaming* 31.2 (2000).

23 See Morecroft, John D.W., 'System Dynamics and microworlds for policymakers', *European Journal of Operational Research* 35 (1988): 314, 317.

24 See Sterman, John D., *Business dynamics: Systems thinking and modeling for a complex world* (Boston: Irwin/McGraw-Hill, 2000), pp. 86–89. Forrester emphasises the process perspective in Forrester, Jay W., '"The" model versus a modeling "process"', *System Dynamics Review* 1.1 (1985). – The literature offers many similar versions of process division and step labels. There is however a general consensus about the modelling process itself.

25 See Forrester, *Principles of systems*.

26 Partly taken from Zimmermann, Nicole, *Dynamics of drivers of organizational change* (Wiesbaden: Gabler, 2011), p. 12.

27 More information on airlines' cost structure will be presented in section 3.3.4.

28 Some airlines, namely the 'gulf carriers', are said to have cheaper access to fuel. Yet, Emirates responds: 'We buy fuel from BP, Shell and Chevron in Dubai and worldwide at market rates.' This is supported by the research institute CAPA. It finds Emirates' cost advantage is mainly due to lower labour costs. – Emirates, *Airlines and subsidy: Our position* (2012). And see: CAPA Centre for Aviation, 'Unit cost analysis of Emirates, IAG & Virgin; about learning from a new model, not unpicking it', 2014, web page, accessed: 23 Feb 2015.

29 In section 1.1 the 'global airline industry' was defined as comprising all airlines around the world providing scheduled or non-scheduled air transportation, with their airlines' passenger and cargo transportation as well as ancillary businesses. Narrowing the 'airline industry' definition down to a geographic region or country

can be done in two ways: 1) only the traffic operated within that area, no matter what airline operates it; and 2) only the airlines based in the area, including all their national and international traffic. The airline industry model works for both definitions. In section 3.5 the model will be calibrated for US airlines, following the second industry definition.

30 Areas of inter airline competition concern for example service quality, flight departure times, and frequencies on each route. See Douglas, Evan J., 'The pricing and competitive strategies of US airlines', *Journal of Applied Business Research* 5.2 (1989): 23.

31 Ancillary revenues are non-ticket revenues, for example credit card fees or baggage charges. For details see section 3.3.2 on modelling the components of the average airline industry price.

32 Brons, Martijn et al., 'Price elasticities of demand for passenger air travel: A meta-analysis', *Journal of Air Transport Management* 8.3 (2002).

33 See Sgouridis, 'Symbiotic strategies in enterprise ecology', p. 50. And see Pierson, Kawika, 'Profit cycle dynamics', PhD thesis, Massachusetts Institute of Technology, 2011, p. 41.

34 See Belobaba, Peter, 'Overview of airline economics, markets and demand', in *The global airline industry*, eds Belobaba, Peter, Amedeo R. Odoni and Cynthia Barnhart (Chichester, UK: Wiley, 2009), pp. 67–68.

35 Own calculations based on systemwide global commercial airline revenues (total, passengers, cargo) for 2001 to 2011. Data sources: for 2001–2003 Sgouridis, 'Symbiotic strategies in enterprise ecology', p. 50; for 2004 onwards see International Air Transport Association (IATA), *Fact sheet: Industry statistics, March 2010* (2010).

36 Own rough calculation; data source: International Air Transport Association (IATA), *Fact sheet: Industry statistics, September 2013* (2013).

37 Own calculations based on systemwide global commercial airline revenues (total, passengers, cargo) for 2001 to 2011; data sources: for 2001–2003 International Air Transport Association (IATA), *Cargo e-chartbook* (Q4 2010), p. 3., starting 2004 International Air Transport Association (IATA), *Fact sheet: Industry statistics, March 2010*.

38 See Intervistas, *Estimating air travel demand elasticities* (Prepared for IATA, 2007), p. 36. And see Pearce, Brian, 'The state of air transport markets and the airline industry after the great recession', *Journal of Air Transport Management* 21 (2012): 5.

39 Notation as introduced in Figure 3.6 on page 93: an arrow with a '+' indicates development in the same direction, '–' stands for development in the opposite direction.

40 Automatically counted within System Dynamics modelling software Vensim. SDM-Doc Tool provides a higher number: 749 loops. Tool available at: System Dynamics Society, 'The SDM-Doc tool', web page, accessed: 15 Dec 2014. For further information see Martinez-Moyano, Ignacio J., 'Documentation for model transparency', *System Dynamics Review* 28, no. 2 (2012).

41 System Dynamics model size categories are not consistently defined. A **small** model has 200–400 equations (Lyneis), less than 200 equations (Hines/Johnson), 100–200 equations (Morecroft), 7–8 major feedback loops (Ghaffarzadegan et al.). To be **useful** a model must have at least 20–30 equations (Lyneis), and less than 400 equations (Morecroft). – See Lyneis, James M., 'System Dynamics for business strategy: A phased approach', *System Dynamics Review* 15.1 (1999): 45–46. And: See Hines, James H. and Dewey W. Johnson, 'Launching System Dynamics', *Proceedings of the 12th International Conference of the System Dynamics Society*, (Stirling,

Scotland: 1994), pp. 85–86. And: see Morecroft, John D. W., 'The feedback view of business policy and strategy', *System Dynamics Review* 1.1 (1985): 16. And: see Ghaffarzadegan, Navid, John Lyneis, and George P. Richardson, 'How small System Dynamics models can help the public policy process', *System Dynamics Review* 27.1 (2011): 23.

42 According to Forrester, 'significant models for the answering of top-management questions [generally] range in size between 30 and 3,000 variables'. See Forrester, *Industrial dynamics*, p. 61.

43 Ventana Systems, *Vensim* (System Dynamics modelling software).

44 See Sterman, *Business dynamics*, pp. 798–824 and p. 841.

45 Oxford Dictionaries, 'Definition of "commodity"', web page, accessed: 31 July 2013.

46 See Sterman, *Business dynamics* pp. 24–28.

47 For example: See Mankiw, N. Gregory, *Principles of macroeconomics*, 6th edn. (Cengage Learning, 2012), p. 67.

48 Separated by a comma, the variable's initial value in t=0 is given.

49 A *SMOOTH* function is commonly used in System Dynamics modelling to represent expectations. The equation *expected demand = SMOOTH(demand, time to form expectations)* is a short formulation for *expected demand =INTEG((demand-expected demand)/ time to form expectations, demand$_{t0}$)*. Hence, there is a level variable implicit in the *SMOOTH* formulation.

50 See US Code of Federal Regulations, '§ 121.311 (b) and § 121.317 (f)', web page, accessed: 15 Oct 2013.

51 See Sterman, *Business dynamics*, pp. 812–813.

52 See Mankiw, *Principles of macroeconomics*, pp. 90–92. In his book Mankiw adopts the 'common practice of dropping the minus sign and reporting all price elasticities of demand as positive numbers' (p. 91). To avoid confusion, the airline industry model uses the mathematically correct formulation. For price P and demand D the demand elasticity $\varepsilon = (dD/D) / (dP/P) = (dD/dP) * (P/D)$. The demand curve slope s is defined as $s = dD/dP$. It is the same for all points on the linear demand curve. Therefore, for the reference point (Pr, Dr) and reference elasticity εr the demand curve slope can be calculated as $sr = s = dDr/dPr = (dDr/dPr) * (Pr/Dr) * (Dr/Pr) = \varepsilon r * (Dr/Pr)$.

53 On a linear demand curve the elasticity will change with price. When the price is lower than the reference level, a price change of 1% will entail a weaker demand reaction compared to the reference level (demand is more inelastic). When price is higher, the demand reaction will be stronger (demand is more elastic).

54 See Sterman, *Business dynamics*, pp. 811–813.

55 See Mankiw, *Principles of macroeconomics*, p. 70.

56 Equations for the inflation module are: inflation index = INTEGRAL (inflation index change, 1$_{t0}$); inflation index change = inflation index * TS inflation rate / REPORTING PERIOD.

57 See Liehr, Martin et al., 'Cycles in the sky: Understanding and managing business cycles in the airline market', *System Dynamics Review* 17.4 (2001): 324–330.

58 See Segers, Rafael, 'An analysis of external and internal drivers of profit cycles in the airline industry – An industry dynamics approach', *Masters thesis*, Cranfield University, 2005, pp. 31–47.

59 See Sgouridis, 'Modeling commercial aviation as an Enterprise of Enterprises', pp. 238–240.

60 In case there is a competitive alternative to air travel, it seems logical to include service quality in the model, for example in the European short-haul market where airlines are faced with a dense and frequently served high-speed train network.

61 See Pierson, 'Profit cycle dynamics', pp. 40–43. And see Pierson, Kawika and John D. Sterman, 'Cyclical dynamics of airline industry earnings', *System Dynamics Review* 29.3 (2013): 131–137 and supplementary download model.

62 Pierson limits service quality to the aspect of airport congestion and resulting flight delays.

63 See Holloway, Stephen, *Straight and level: Practical airline economics*, 3rd edn. (Ashgate, 2008), pp. 126–127.

64 In the US market '[i]n the 1980s, the entire ticket tax was a percentage of the ticket value. The passenger facility charges were added in the early 1990s, the segment tax in 1997 and the September 11 security fee in early 2002, all based on the number of flights the passenger boards, regardless of the fare paid.' – In: Borenstein, Severin, *On the persistent financial losses of US airlines: A preliminary exploration* (2011), pp. 4–5.

65 See A4A Airlines for America, *Government-Imposed Taxes on Air Transportation*, 2013, web page, accessed: 9 Oct 2013.

66 See Borenstein, *On the persistent financial losses of US airlines*, pp. 4–5.

67 See Holloway, *Practical airline economics*, p. 188.

68 See Oxford Economics in partnership with Amadeus, *The travel gold rush 2020: Pioneering growth and profitability trends in the travel sector* (November 2010), pp. 14–16.

69 Holloway, *Practical airline economics*, p. 188.

70 Ibid., p. 189.

71 The first large-scale ancillary revenue report was issued by IdeaWorks and Amadeus in 2007. Only 23 airlines disclosed ancillary revenues of in sum $2.45 billion. In 2011 50 airlines reported $22.6 billion. Given the world airlines' operating revenues of $509.8 billion in 2007 and $618.1 billion in 2011, the approximate share of ancillary revenues was 0.5% in 2007 and 3.6% in 2011. IdeaWorks and Amadeus published an estimate of 5.6% for 2011. – See IdeaWorks and Amadeus, 'Press release: Ancillary revenue reported by airlines grew to €18.23 billion in 2011 and jumped 66% in two years', 23 July 2012, web page, accessed: 8 Oct 2013. And for operating revenue data see A4A Airlines for America, 'Annual financial results: World airlines', web page, accessed: 8 Oct 2013.

72 In 2012 low-cost airlines, such as JetBlue or Southwest, reached around 7%, traditional airlines, e.g. Air Canada or Etihad, 3%. Major US carriers, e.g. American or United, generated approx. 10% ancillary revenue while the industry's ancillary revenue champions, e.g. AirAsia, easyJet, and Spirit Airlines, reached up to 20%. – See IdeaWorks and Amadeus, 'Press release: Airline ancillary revenue projected to reach $36.1 billion worldwide in 2012', 29 Oct 2012, web page, accessed: 8 Oct 2013.

73 See O'Connell, John F., 'Ancillary revenues: The new trend in strategic airline marketing', in *Air transport in the 21st century: Key strategic developments*, eds O'Connell, John F. and George Williams (Farnham, UK; Burlington, VT: Ashgate, 2011), p. 147.

74 See IdeaWorks and Amadeus, 'Press release: Airline ancillary revenue projected to reach $36.1 billion worldwide in 2012', accessed: 8 Oct 2013.

75 See Belobaba, Peter, Amedeo R. Odoni and Cynthia Barnhart, *The global airline industry*, Aerospace series (PEP) (Chichester, UK: Wiley, 2009), p. 88.

76 See ibid.

77 Holloway uses five dimensions to 'make sense of sometimes highly complex passenger tariff structures': class of service, time of travel, booking restrictions, bundling, and distribution channel. See Holloway, *Practical airline economics*, pp. 147–148.

78 See ibid., p. 129.

79 Belobaba et al., *The global airline industry*, p. 73.

80 For information on price dispersion in the airline industry see for example: Borenstein, Severin and Nancy L. Rose, 'Competition and price dispersion in the US airline industry', *Journal of Political Economy* 102, no. 4 (1994).

81 Sterman, *Business dynamics* p. 813.

82 Research on airline yield often takes a more micro perspective and examines for example the different prices charged to passengers on the same route. See, for example, Borenstein and Rose, 'Competition and price dispersion in the US airline industry.'

83 See Maier, Matthew, 'A radical fix for airlines: Make flying free', CNN Money, 2006, web page, accessed: 10 Oct 2013.

84 See Sterman, *Business dynamics*, pp. 813–818.

85 For a detailed explanation of the hill-climbing optimisation procedure: see ibid., pp. 537–539.

86 See Belobaba et al., *The global airline industry*, p. 76.

87 See ibid., pp. 76–78.

88 See Holloway, *Practical airline economics*, p. 157. Note: Holloway defines the price-cost margin as *(price- cost) / price*, so his results have the opposite algebraic sign.

89 In fact Belobaba observes that '[t]he presence of a low-fare airline in an O-D market [= origin-destination market] is perhaps one of the most important determinants of average fare levels'. See Belobaba et al., *The global airline industry* p. 76.

90 For an analysis of on route competition see: Azzam, Mark and Eva-Maria Cronrath, 'Airline network structures and development strategies', *13th Annual World Conference of the Air Transport Research Society (ATRS)*, (Abu Dhabi: 2009).

91 See Mankiw, *Principles of macroeconomics*, pp. 77–83.

92 See Belobaba, 'Overview of airline economics, markets and demand', p. 61.

93 This formulation is commonly used because taking logs of the equation results in the log-linear model that can be estimated by linear regression. See Sterman, *Business dynamics*, pp. 526–527.

94 See Doganis, Rigas, *Flying off course – Airline economics and marketing*, 4th edn. (London/ New York: Routledge, 2010), p. 252.

95 See ibid.

96 Ibid.

97 Stretch goals are found to be fairly common in practice, see: Sitkin, Sim B. et al., 'The paradox of stretch goals: Organizations in pursuit of the seemingly impossible', *Academy of Management Review* 36.3 (2011): 546.

98 The *profitability pressure on price* equals 1 which means the effect is neutral.

99 See Belobaba, 'Overview of airline economics, markets and demand', p. 61.

100 Belobaba et al., *The global airline industry*, p. 88. Emphasis as in original.

101 Ibid., p. 89.

102 For an introduction into revenue management see: Belobaba, Peter, 'Application of a probabilistic decision model to airline seat inventory control', *Operations Research* 32.2 (1989).

103 The assumption here is that airlines focus on revenue maximisation not on load factor maximisation. Hence, if on a flight more seats are booked than the revenue management system expected (i.e. if the load factor is higher than expected), total

revenue and thus yield is higher. Under a load factor maximisation approach, the higher load factor would not necessarily imply greater total revenue because the maximisation system may have lowered prices strongly to achieve the high load factor.

104 Liehr et al., 'Cycles in the sky', p. 320.

105 See ibid., pp. 318, 326–327.

106 See Segers, 'An analysis of external and internal drivers of profit cycles in the airline industry', pp. 119–123.

107 Sgouridis formulates: fare price = [UnitCosts / (1+TargetProfitability)] * Loading EfctOnPrice * ProfitEfctOnPrice. See Sgouridis, 'Symbiotic strategies in enterprise ecology', p. 246.

108 See ibid.

109 Pierson formulates: Indicated Ticket Price per Seat Mile = Ticket Price * Effect of Demand Supply Balance on Price * Effect of Margin on Price * Effect of Costs on Price. See Pierson, 'Profit cycle dynamics', p. 43, pp. 128–131.

110 See ibid., p. 128.

111 The longest delay being 2.6 weeks (Time to Adjust Ticket Prices = 0.05 years). See ibid., p. 121.

112 See ibid., p. 131.

113 See Belobaba et al., *The global airline industry* p. 153.

114 Ibid.

115 Ibid.

116 See ibid.

117 See Clark, Paul, *Buying the big jets: Fleet planning for airlines*, 2nd edn. (Aldershot, UK; Burlington, VT: Ashgate, 2007), pp. 11–12, 171.

118 See Belobaba et al., *The global airline industry*, p. 154.

119 Ibid.

120 See Clark, *Buying the big jets: Fleet planning for airlines*, pp. 211–228. – Clark adds that 'in reality, once the numbers have been crunched, emphasis has to shift to other fundamental areas that all contribute to the business case. The list of items to take into consideration is endless.' Among others synergies with existing fleet, timing, or politics are mentioned. Clark stresses the importance of personal relationships and trust for fleet purchasing decisions. See ibid., pp. 231–232.

121 Borenstein and Rose have investigated the US airline market and emphasise that 'Chapter 11 bankruptcy filings do not equate with an airline shutting down. Although some of the carriers that have entered bankruptcy have been liquidated, the majority have emerged to operate as publicly-held companies or been merged into another airline, generally with operations disrupted for little or no time.' – Borenstein, Severin and Nancy L. Rose, *How airline markets work. . . Or do they? Regulatory reform in the airline industry* (2007), p. 19.

122 The Vensim formula ZIDZ(*A,B*) stands for 'Zero If Divided by Zero (otherwise *A/B*)'. It means that *A* is divided by *B*; if *B* is zero, the formulation returns zero. See Ventana Systems, *Documentation for Vensim* (2013).

123 The *demand according to demand curve* is chosen instead of revenue passenger miles because the latter demand variable was possibly already subject to capacity constraints. See section 3.3.1 for an introduction to the model's demand module.

124 Some of the *other factors affecting demand* (see section 3.3.1) might appear here if they can be foreseen by the management.

125 See Morrell, Peter S., *Airline finance*, 3rd edn. (Aldershot, UK; Burlington, VT: Ashgate, 2007) p. 207.

126 See Clark, *Buying the big jets: Fleet planning for airlines*, p. 231.
127 For further information about delay structures and their behaviour see: Sterman, *Business dynamics*, pp. 409–467.
128 See ibid., pp. 805–807.
129 Clark, *Buying the big jets: Fleet planning for airlines*, p. 12.
130 From a manufacturer's point of view aircraft order options can be challenging when it comes to production capacity planning. Reliable forecasts how many options will be confirmed and how many cancelled are essential to ensure their business success.
131 Example: An airline's *desired acquisition rate* is to receive ten new aircraft per year. The *expected acquisition delay*, i.e. the time between order placing and actual acquisition of the aircraft, is two years. Consequently, the airline's *desired supply line*, i.e. the total number of aircraft on order, equals *2 years * 10 aircraft = 20 aircraft.*
132 See Sterman, 'Modeling managerial behavior', p. 337.
133 The idea is introduced in: Sterman, *Business dynamics*, p. 693.
134 Example continued: The airline still has a *desired acquisition rate* of ten new aircraft per year, the *expected acquisition delay* is still two years, and consequently the *desired supply line*, i.e. the desired number of aircraft on order, is 20 aircraft. Let there be already 15 *aircraft on order*. Besides, airlines have a strategic fleet planning process that takes 1 year (*CAPACITY ADJUSTMENT TIME* =1 year). The resulting *order rate* would be *desired acquisition rate* of 10 aircraft per year plus the *adjustment for supply line* = (20 aircraft − 14 aircraft) / 1 year = 6 aircraft / 1 year = 6 aircraft/year; the *order rate* = 10 + 6 = 16 aircraft per year. Now, if the supply line is not fully transparent in the industry and not every airline knows what all others have ordered, the *WEIGHT ON THE SUPPLY LINE* is only, say, 50%. Thus, only half of the aircraft on order and half of the desired supply line will be taken into account. The *adjustment for supply line* = (20 aircraft − 14 aircraft) * 50% / 1 year = 6 aircraft * 50% / 1 year = 3 aircraft/year. The *order rate* = 10 + 3= 13 aircraft per year.
135 See Sterman, *Business dynamics*, pp. 678, 534.
136 Data sources: Boeing, 'Orders and deliveries', 2010, web page, accessed: 18 Aug 2010. Note: Cargo and small regional aircraft included. And: Airbus, 'Historical orders and deliveries 1974–2009', 2010, web page, accessed: 8 Sept 2010.
137 Data source: The Airline Monitor, *United States jet aircraft fleet – Status as of December 31, 2007 and selected earlier years* (July 2008).
138 Sgouridis (2007) and Lyneis (2000) suggest an alternative way of modelling this: They include a feedback on the *CAPACITY ACQUISITION DELAY*. It varies with the amount of *aircraft on order* compared the manufacturers' capacity. – The solution presented above is thus a 'shortcut' to experiment with manufacturing constraints while keeping the model as small as possible.
139 See Belobaba et al., *The global airline industry*, p. 158.
140 Assuming an average aircraft service lifetime of 25 years, the lower limit would be a depreciation period as short as five years, and the technological upper limit would be 50 years.
141 See Gavazza, Alessandro, 'Asset liquidity and financial contracts: Evidence from aircraft leases', *Journal of Financial Economics* 95.1 (2010): 83.
142 See Belobaba et al., *The global airline industry*, p. 157.
143 See International Air Transport Association (IATA), *Special report: Opportunities in aircraft leasing* (2010).
144 Gibson, William, *Aircraft lessor prospects and lease valuation for airlines* (International Air Transport Association (IATA), October 2008), p. 2.

145 Own calculation. Data source: US Department of Transportation (US DOT), Bureau of Transportation Statistics, 'Schedule B-43 Inventory, number of seats by aircraft status (capital lease, operating lease, owned)', web page, accessed: 10 Sept 2013.

146 See Morrell, *Airline finance* p. 200.

147 See ibid., pp. 200–201.

148 See ibid., p. 201.

149 See Vigeant-Langlois, Laurence, 'Overview of the aircraft leasing industry', (CIT Aerospace, April 2011), vol., p. 11.

150 Gavazza, 'Asset liquidity and financial contracts: Evidence from aircraft leases', p. 83.

151 Morrell, *Airline finance*, p. 200.

152 See Vasigh, Bijan, Reza Taleghani and Darryl Jenkins, *Aircraft finance: Strategies for managing capital costs in a turbulent industry* (Ft. Lauderdale, FL: J. Ross Pub., 2012), p. 276. And see Conklin & de Decker, 'Lease pros and cons – The things you should know', web page, accessed: 13 Sept 2013.

153 See Oum, Tae Hoon, Anming Zhang, and Yimin Zhang, 'Optimal demand for operating lease of aircraft', *Transportation Research Part B: Methodological* 34.1 (2000): 18.

154 A4A Airlines for America, 'Chapter 4: Airline economics', web page, accessed: 13 Sept 2013.

155 For more information on route planning, schedule planning, and schedule optimisation find an introduction in: Belobaba et al., *The global airline industry*, chapters 6, 7, and 9.

156 See, for example: Lederer, Phillip J. and Ramakrishnan S. Nambimadom, 'Airline network design', *Operations Research* 46.6 (1998): 785.

157 For example: In terms or days which an aircraft is available for service the maximum per year, i.e. the *production capacity*, is 365. An interviewed fleet expert estimated that each aircraft annually needs 60 days for mandatory maintenance checks. Hence the *NORMAL UTILISATION* can be estimated as (365-60)/365=83%.

158 Belobaba et al., *The global airline industry* p. 253.

159 See Pels, Eric, 'Airline network competition: Full-service airlines, low-cost airlines and long-haul markets', *Research in Transportation Economics* 24, no. 1 (2008): 68.

160 Holloway, *Practical airline economics*, p. 557.

161 The limit can be calculated as maximum capacity utilisation (100%) divided by *NORMAL UTILISATION*. The maximum utilisation is 100% because the *production capacity* is defined as the absolute maximum supply.

162 See Liehr et al., 'Cycles in the sky', pp. 324–330.

163 See Segers, 'An analysis of external and internal drivers of profit cycles in the airline industry', pp. 49–83.

164 See Sgouridis, 'Symbiotic strategies in enterprise ecology', pp. 240–244.

165 See Pierson, 'Profit cycle dynamics', pp. 40–57. And see Pierson and Sterman, 'Cyclical dynamics of airline industry earnings', pp. 131–137 and supplementary model.

166 See Holloway, *Practical airline economics*, p. 266.

167 See Morrell, *Airline finance*, p. 9.

168 See Holloway, *Practical airline economics*, p. 274.

169 Data source: A4A Airlines for America (formerly ATA Air Transport Association), 'ATA Cost Index for US Passenger Airlines', 3rd quarter 2010, accessed: 23 Feb 2011.

170 See Borenstein and Rose, *How airline markets work*, pp. 36–37. – Not only labour contracts but also aircraft lease rates and ownership costs depend on airlines' profitability. In unprofitable times, aircraft manufacturers and lessors tend to reduce their

rates in order to make at least some money rather than none, and thus avoid rushing financially distressed airlines into bankruptcy. Also, unprofitable airlines who are willing to sell aircraft to cut capacity reduce aircraft prices in the market. In profitable times, however, when capacity additions are generally required, aircraft rents and ownership costs usually rise

171 See Liehr et al., 'Cycles in the sky', pp. 324–330.

172 See Segers, 'An analysis of external and internal drivers of profit cycles in the airline industry', pp. 85–116.

173 See Sgouridis, 'Symbiotic strategies in enterprise ecology', pp. 244–246.

174 See Pierson, 'Profit cycle dynamics', pp. 40–57. And see Pierson and Sterman, 'Cyclical dynamics of airline industry earnings', pp. 131–137 and supplementary model.

175 Morrell defines operating margin = operating revenue / total operating costs. In case total operating costs are zero, the operating margin is infinitely high (set to equal 1000000). See Morrell, *Airline finance*, p. 56.

176 Technical note: ZIDZ = compute zero if divided by zero. XIDZ = compute value x if divided by zero.

177 Sterman, *Business dynamics*, p. 890.

178 See Größler, Andreas, 'Modelltests [Model tests]', in *System Dynamics für die Finanzindustrie: Simulieren und Analysieren dynamisch-komplexer Probleme*, eds. Strohhecker, Jürgen and Jürgen Sehnert (Frankfurt: Frankfurt-School-Verlag, 2008), p. 254.

179 Forrester, Jay W. and Peter M. Senge, 'Tests for building confidence in System Dynamics models', *TIMS Studies in the Management Science* 14 (1980).

180 Barlas, Yaman, 'Formal aspects of model validity and validation in System Dynamics', *System Dynamics Review* 12.3 (1996).

181 Sterman, *Business dynamics*, pp. 845–891.

182 See ibid., pp. 858–861. – Note: Sterman's 'System Improvement Test' cannot yet be conducted. Its leading question is whether the modelling process helped change the system for the better. This could only be answered if derived airline profit cycle mitigation measures were already implemented and in place for a significant period of time.

183 See ibid., pp. 824–829.

184 Data source: Official Airline Guide (OAG) flight schedules database, publishes nonstop passenger departures, accessed 23 Nov 2010.

185 See 'The Airline Deregulation Act, signed on October 24, 1978'. United States Federal Aviation Administration, A Brief History of the FAA, www.faa.gov/about/history/brief_history, accessed: 14. Dec. 2011. – 'The most important effect of the Act, whose laws were slowly phased in, was on the passenger market. For the first time in 40 years, airlines could enter the market or (from 1981) expand their routes as they saw fit. Airlines (from 1982) also had full freedom to set their fares. In 1984, the CAB was finally abolished since its primary duty, that of regulating the airline industry, was no longer necessary.' US Centennial of Flight Commission, 'Deregulation and its consequences', web page, accessed: 17 Nov 2014.

186 See Sgouridis, Sgouris et al., *Taming the business cycle in commercial aviation – Tradespace analysis of strategic alternatives using simulation modelling*, Massachusetts Institute of Technology: Working Paper Series, Cambridge, MA, p. 12.

187 Data sources: A4A Airlines for America (formerly ATA Air Transport Association), 'ATA Cost Index for U.S. Passenger Airlines, 3rd quarter 2010', accessed: 23 Feb 2011. For GDP: UN Statistics, United States. 'GDP, at constant 2005 prices – US Dollars', web page, accessed: 27 Jan 2012. For inflation: World Bank, United States. Inflation consumer prices, annual %, web page, accessed: 29 Nov 2012.

188 Peak at 353 USD cents/gallon in 3rd quarter 2008 compared to 206 USD cents/ gallon in 3rd quarter 2007 and 192 USD cents/gallon in 3rd quarter 2009. Data source: A4A Airlines for America (formerly ATA Air Transport Association), 'ATA Cost Index for US Passenger Airlines, 3rd quarter 2010', accessed: 23 Feb 2011.

189 See A4A Airlines for America, 'Air Transport Association changes name to Airlines for America (A4A), 2011', web page, accessed: 5 June 2013.

190 See A4A Airlines for America, 'About A4A', web page, accessed: 5 June 2013.

191 See A4A Airlines for America (formerly ATA Air Transport Association), 'ATA quarterly cost index for US passenger airlines: Methodology', web page, accessed: 13 Dec 2011.

192 Form 41 Financial Reports contain financial information on large certified US air carriers, i.e. carriers that hold Certificates of Public Convenience and Necessity issued by the DOT authorizing the performance of air transportation with annual operating revenues of $20 million or more. Reported financial information includes balance sheet, cash flow, employment, income statement, fuel cost and consumption, aircraft operating expenses, and operating expenses. This data is collected by the Office of Airline Information in the DOT's Bureau of Transportation Statistics. – See US Bureau of Transportation Statistics (BTS), 'Data profile: air carrier financial reports (Form 41 financial data)', web page, accessed: 5 June 2013.

193 The Federal Aviation Act requires that an applicant for an air carrier Certificate of Public Convenience and Necessity be a citizen of the United States. Furthermore, it requires that the president and two thirds of the board of directors be US citizens, and that at least 75% of the voting stock be owned or controlled by US citizens. – Dempsy, Paul Stephen, *Airline regulation: The US example* (McGill University, 2009), p. 6.

194 In the report figure 2 shows the development of the average tax as a share of the base ticket price. Using ATA Cost Index yield data this percentage tax is transformed into a tax per seat mile. – Data source: Borenstein, *On the persistent financial losses of US airlines*, pp. 4–5.

195 See Intervistas, *Estimating air travel demand elasticities*, summary pp. 1–5. – Demand elasticities in the report are generic. They consist of a base elasticity for national, pan-national, or route level analysis, a multiplier for geographic aviation markets, and short and long haul adjustment.

196 Own calculation. Chosen to be a constant value because international traffic shares vary only within 10 %-points in 1985–2010. Data source: US Bureau of Transportation Statistics, 'Table T1: US air carrier traffic and capacity summary by service class', web page, accessed: 8 Aug 2011.

197 Operating leases (the most frequent leasing type) last five years on average. See Morrell, *Airline finance*, p. 200.

198 In February 2009 the BTS reacted on the growing popularity of non-ticket revenue making by publishing a directive how to report ancillary revenues. They are not summarised in one account but divided among several existing ones. Hence, for model calibration only a range of ancillary revenues can be derived. – See US Bureau of Transportation Statistics, 'No. 289 – Reporting ancillary revenues on Form 41', 2009, web page, accessed: 2 Oct 2013.

199 See Amadeus and IdeaWorks, *Amadeus guide to ancillary revenue* (2010).

200 Data sources: US Bureau of Transportation Statistics, 'Air Carrier Financial: Schedule B-43 Inventory', web page, accessed: 10 Sept 2013. And: Gritta, Richard and Ellen Lippman, 'Aircraft leasing and its effect on air carriers debt burdens: A comparison over the past several decades', *Journal of the Transportation Research Forum* 49.3 (2010).

201 Optimization based on a Powell search modified for Vensim simulation, with a maximum of 1,000 iterations and a pass limit of two (number of times the optimizer will run through an entire Powell search). For more information see Ventana Systems, 'Optimization options', web page, accessed: 20 May 2014. And see: Powell, Michael J. D., 'An efficient method for finding the minimum of a function of several variables without calculating derivatives', *Computer Journal* 7.2 (1964).

202 See Ford, Andrew, *Modelling the environment: An introduction to System Dynamics modelling of environmental systems* (Washington DC: Island Press, 1999), p. 176.

203 See Sterman, John D., 'Appropriate summary statistics for evaluating the historical fit of System Dynamics models', *1st International Conference of the System Dynamics Society*, (Chestnut Hill, MA USA: 1983). See also Sterman, *Business dynamics*, pp. 874–880.

4 Examination of airline profitability dynamics in model experiments

In this section the airline industry model developed in Chapter 3 will be used to conduct simulation experiments in order to answer the research questions posed in Chapter 1:

1 Why are airline profits cyclical?
2 What are the causes and dynamics that determine the profit cycle's shape?
3 How can the situation be improved?

First, in section 4.1 the cycle's origin will be detected. Then, in sections 4.2–4.5 the potential cycle causes, drivers, and mitigation measures identified in Chapter 2 will be tested for their impact on the airline profit cycle. In section 4.6 the results will be summarised.

4.1 Identification of cycle origin area

In this section the origin of the airline industry's profit cycle will be identified. First, in section 4.1.1, it is examined if the origin is within the airline indus-try or if oscillations are merely a product of external dynamics such as GDP growth, fuel price fluctuations, or shocks. The result is that the profit cycle's origin must be inside the airlinze industry. Hence, in sections 4.1.2–4.1.3 the airline industry model is inspected piece by piece to detect the airline profit cycle's origin. Results are summarised in section 4.1.4.

4.1.1 The model's capability to sustain a steady state

Economic research, presented in section 2.1.1, focuses on the concept of equi-librium. Mankiw defines an 'equilibrium as a situation in which various forces are in balance – and this also describes a market's equilibrium. At the equilib-rium price, the quantity of the good that buyers are willing and able to buy exactly balances the quantity that sellers are willing and able to sell.'[1] At the equilibrium point a system is stable. However, an equilibrium may or may not emerge.[2] In this section it will be tested if the airline industry model can be balanced into equilibrium, i.e. whether airline profitability can theoretically be steady. Furthermore, in case an equilibrium point is found, scenario simulations will assess its sensitivity towards changes in the system. Questions to be examined are whether the system regains its balance, how long that takes, and how much the change drives the system away from its equilibrium point.

If a system is in equilibrium, it does not mean that nothing changes within. Sterman illustrates this with a practical example: 'If water drains out of your tub at exactly the rate it flows in, the quantity of water in the tub will remain constant and the tub is in equilibrium. Such a state is termed a **dynamic equilibrium** since the water in the tub is always changing. **Static equilibrium** arises when all flows into and leaving a stock are zero.'[3] Consequently, the dynamic equilibrium is also referred to as steady state. It requires that for each stock the net rate of change must be zero. Transferred to the airline industry a static equilibrium, in which for example aircraft were never retired, does not make sense. Yet, a dynamic equilibrium, in which inflows and outflows of stocks such as aircraft, price, and demand are in balance, may exist.

To find a potential steady state for the airline industry model, a step approach will be applied. First, it will be examined whether the industry is already in equilibrium and its cyclicality is merely due to external factors. Then, second, in case the industry was not in equilibrium at the starting point of simulations in 1985, it will be investigated whether an alternative set of initial values can create a steady state. Third, the stability of the possibly discovered equilibrium can be tested.

Step 1: Stable general economy and industry environment

Set-up: All time series inserting dynamics into the model are set constant at their initial value. (Since this is a theoretical scenario, the time axis is neutrally labelled. Year 0 corresponds to 1985. The 'base run' given for comparison is the model's reproduction of developments in the US airline industry, introduced in section 3.6.)

Result, see Figure 4.1: Although all influences on the airline industry are kept stable, airlines' profitability still exhibits a cycle. Therefore, the US airline

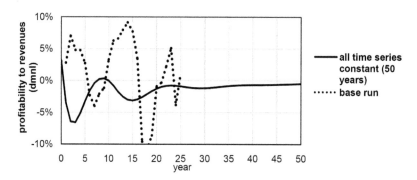

Figure 4.1 Simulation with all external time series constant at their initial 1985 values

industry was not in a steady state in 1985. Furthermore, it can be concluded that the airline profit cycle must be driven by industry mechanisms because profitability oscillates for many years although all external factors are perfectly stable. Third, the fact that after several years profitability finds an equilibrium implies that there must be cycle mitigating mechanisms in the industry, too. It also shows that a dynamic equilibrium (a steady state) for the airline industry exists.

Step 2: Find a steady state generating initial value set (external factors still stable)

Set-up: As in the previous step, all time series inserting dynamics into the model are set constant and treated as initials. Now, initial values are experimented with to find a set which renders all net rates equal to zero (inflow = outflow). During the search process all parameter values are still restricted by logical limits, for example aircraft load factors cannot exceed 100%. Methods applied to find a suitable set of initial values are model optimisation (already introduced in 3.3.2) and the principle of nested intervals (when inserting long-run equilibrium values as new initial values). The search process required many iterations.

Result, see Figure 4.2: An equilibrium is found at zero profitability. This is in line with economic theory which states that in a perfectly competitive market all payers make zero profit in equilibrium.[4] However, it cannot be concluded that the airline industry is a perfectly competitive market. First, because there may well be other equilibrium points for the airline industry. Second, because zero aggregate industry profit does not reveal the distribution of profits among individual airlines. And third, in reality state interventions such as subsidies or market exit barriers imply the market is not perfectly competitive. These imperfections are built into the model (see section 3.3.3). The zero profitability equilibrium point should thus not be interpreted in the light of competitive theory. The parameter set used to initialise the model is listed in Appendix C.

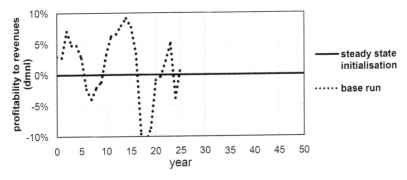

Figure 4.2 Simulation with an initialisation parameter set generating a steady state

Step 3: Determine whether the discovered equilibrium is stable or unstable

Having discovered that the airline industry is able to sustain a steady state, the question remains whether the established equilibrium is stable or unstable (see section 2.2.1). According to Forrester '[a] stable system is one that tends to return to its initial conditions after being disturbed. It may overshoot and oscillate [. . .], but the disturbances decline and die out. In an unstable system that starts at rest, an initial disturbance is amplified, leading to growth or to oscillations whose amplitude increases.'[5] Hence, to test the stability of the airline industry's equilibrium, a 'disturbance' needs to be inserted.

Set-up: A sudden demand shock disturbs the steady state. Real GDP growth declines by –10% for the duration of 1 year in year t = 5.

Result, see Figure 4.3: The inserted disturbance causes profitability to oscillate around the equilibrium value. The cycle's amplitude is diminishing. Some time after the disturbance oscillations die out and the airline industry returns to its steady state. Hence, according to Forrester's definition the airline industry's equilibrium is **stable**.

Conclusion: Origin of oscillations inside the industry

An external disturbance, such as a GDP shock, can cause profitability oscillations that last many years before a stable profitability level is regained. The mechanisms responsible for the oscillation must be within the airline industry. They remain to be identified.

The building block of a system which is able to generate oscillations is a negative (=balancing) feedback loop with delay (see section 2.2.1). Figure 4.4 shows the airline industry model's causal loop diagram (as presented earlier in section 3.2.2, Figure 3.10) complemented by delay markers, i.e. double lines crossing the arrow. They indicate for example reporting and perception delays, delays for expectation building or decision making, or physical delays. The longest delay in the airline industry model is the aircraft service lifetime,

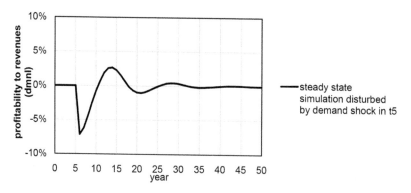

Figure 4.3 Simulated equilibrium is temporarily disturbed

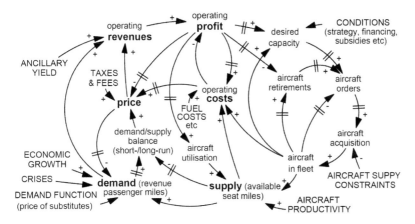

Figure 4.4 Airline industry model causal loop diagram with delay markers

which is the time an aircraft stays in the fleet until it is retired. The causal loop diagram shows that the majority of relationships in the system involve delays. Hence, the cycle generating feedback loop cannot easily be spotted.

To identify the profit cycle's origin a loop knock-out analysis will be conducted. This is a routine procedure in System Dynamics to isolate the mechanism in a model which causes a certain behaviour.[6] The model will be confronted with an external shock to start oscillations. Then mechanisms in the model, i.e. feedback loops, can be switched off (one after the other, all at once, or in combination) and their effects on cyclicality can be observed.

The airline industry model consists of more than 200 feedback loops.[7] The model's most important mechanisms are shown in the casual loop diagram in Figure 4.4, which still contains over 30 feedback loops.[8] In consequence, only a relevant selection of loop knock-outs will be presented in the following analysis. It will start with feedback loops concerning the airline industry's supply and costs in section 4.1.2, and will then examine the airlines' interaction with the market in section 4.1.3.

4.1.2 Potential cycle origins on cost and supply side

The following loop knock-out analyses will examine key feedback loops concerning the airline industry's cost and supply generation. The aim is to identify the airline profit cycle's origin.

To trigger the profit cycle, the airline industry model is given a demand shock in the form of a sudden real GDP growth rate decline of −10% for the duration of one year in year t = 5. In the following simulation experiments, the highlighted feedback loops are simulated while all other feedback loops in the model are switched off. For each presented simulation a brief simplified description of the mechanisms in question is given. Full explanations of the model's mechanisms can be found in section 3.3. Background information on the notation of feedbacks is given in Figure 3.6 on p. 89. (Reminder: 'x →⁺ y' means that x and y develop in the same direction, e.g. if x get bigger, y will get bigger. 'x →⁻ y' means that x and y develop in opposite directions, e.g. if x gets bigger, y will get smaller.)

Feedback structure 'cost cutting'

Set-up, see Figure 4.5: When airlines make losses they seek to reduce costs to improve their profit situation. In profitable times costs tend to rise. Labour unions are likely to negotiate higher wages or benefits, which augment the airlines' cost base and reduce profit. Also, aircraft tend to be more expensive in profitable than in unprofitable times.

In short: cost →⁻ profit →⁺ cost (balancing feedback)

Result, see Figure 4.6: There is no cycle in profitability. Consequently, this feedback does not cause cyclicality.

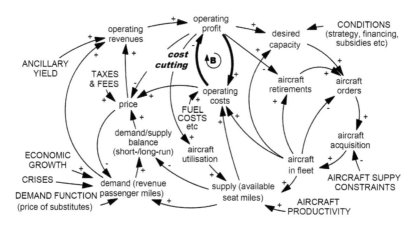

Figure 4.5 Cost-cutting feedback loop

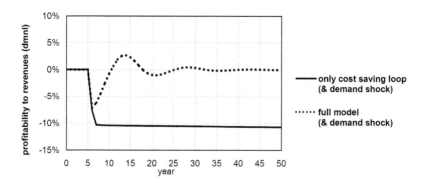

Figure 4.6 Cost-cutting feedback loop simulation result

Feedback structure 'short-run cost reduction by aircraft utilisation adjustment'

Set-up, see Figure 4.7: Depending on their profit situation airlines can decide to use their aircraft more or less intensively. For example, after a demand shock empty flights can be cancelled. In boom times or for special events airlines aim to expand their short-run supply.

In short: profit →⁺ aircraft utilisation →⁺ supply →⁺ costs →⁻ profit (balancing feedback)

Result, see Figure 4.8: There is no profitability cycle. Hence, aircraft utilisation adjustment is not the airline profit cycle's origin.

Feedback structure 'fleet management'

Set-up, see Figure 4.9: Fleet management encompasses several mechanisms. Airlines and investors determine how much capacity growth they desire. This depends on the airline industry's profitability. If a fleet expansion is chosen,

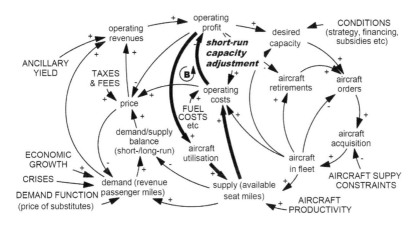

Figure 4.7 Aircraft utilisation adjustment feedback loop

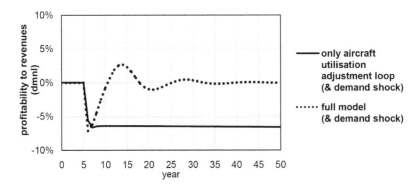

Figure 4.8 Aircraft utilisation adjustment feedback loop simulation result

the added aircraft will augment the airlines' cost base by causing fixed costs and usage-dependent variable costs. (Aircraft usage does not change in this scenario.) Costs alter the airlines' profit situation and thus the desired amount of capacity. The bigger the industry already is, the more airlines and investors seek to participate. This means the same desired capacity growth rate creates more growth in absolute terms the bigger the industry (multiplier effect). The actual aircraft order size depends on due aircraft replacements and the existing fleet including already placed orders.

In short:

1   Interaction between profit and fleet management: 1a. aircraft costs (fixed costs): profit →⁺ desired capacity →⁺ aircraft orders →⁺ aircraft acquisition →⁺ aircraft in fleet →⁺ costs →⁻ profit (balancing loop); 1b. aircraft usage costs (variable costs): profit →⁺ desired capacity →⁺ aircraft orders →⁺ aircraft acquisition →⁺ aircraft in fleet →⁺ supply →⁺ costs →⁻ profit (balancing loop)
2   Multiplier effect: desired capacity →⁺ aircraft orders →⁺ aircraft acquisition →⁺ aircraft in fleet →⁺ desired capacity (reinforcing loop)
3   Aircraft order sizing: 3a. Replacing retired aircraft (aircraft lifecycle): aircraft orders →⁺ aircraft acquisition →⁺ aircraft in fleet →⁺ aircraft retirements →⁺ aircraft orders (reinforcing loop); 3b. Accounting for existing fleet: aircraft orders →⁺ aircraft acquisition →⁺ aircraft in fleet →⁻ aircraft orders (balancing feedback)

Results, see Figure 4.10: There is a small cyclic movement in profitability. The inserted demand shock causes a deep trough. The industry recovers and after nine years (in t = 14) becomes more profitable than before. Another nine years later (in t = 23) airlines make losses again, and so on. The profitability cycle's period is 19 years (peak to peak), its amplitude 10.7 %-points. After 21 years profitability returns to stability.

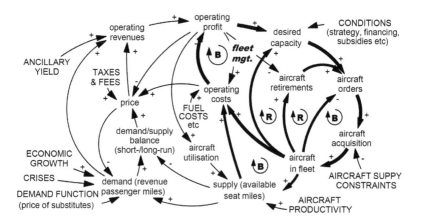

Figure 4.9 Fleet management feedback loops

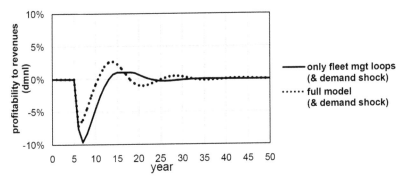

Figure 4.10 Fleet management feedback loops simulation result

In comparison, giving the same demand shock to the full model causes more cyclicality than the fleet management simulation. The trough in the full model simulation is less deep, the recovery faster, the first profit peak higher. The following losses are deeper, and so on. The full model's profitability cycle of 14 years is five years shorter than the fleet management simulation's. However, the amplitude of 9.8 %-points is ca. 1 %-point smaller. Profitability also returns to stability at 0% but needs 24 years for the transition process which is three years longer than in the fleet management simulation.

In the following section the fleet management process will be examined further to identify the profit cyclicality's origin. For this purpose the aircraft order sizing mechanism, which is at the heart of fleet management, will be studied more closely.

Feedback structure 'aircraft order sizing' as part of fleet management

Set-up, see Figure 4.11: The airline industry seeks to achieve its desired capacity level. How many aircraft need to be ordered depends on the existing fleet, due replacements, and already placed orders. The scenario does not include cost effects nor revenue changes. Hence the shock, which is necessary to start potential oscillations, is not the demand shock inserted in previous simulations but a shock in *desired capacity*,[9] in size in line with the demand shock.[10]

In short: See 'fleet management' scenario under (3.): a. Replacing retired aircraft (aircraft lifecycle): aircraft orders →[+] aircraft acquisition →[+] aircraft in fleet [+] aircraft retirements →[+] aircraft orders (reinforcing loop); b. Accounting for existing fleet: aircraft orders →[+] aircraft acquisition →[+] aircraft in fleet →[-] aircraft orders (balancing feedback)

Result, see Figure 4.12: There is a cycle in the fleet size. (Given the set-up, a change in profitability cannot be observed but a change in the aircraft fleet.) It is stronger than in the full fleet management simulation, with shorter period and bigger amplitude. Concretely, the aircraft order sizing cycle's period of six years (see solid line) is much shorter than the 19 years period in the previous scenario (see dash-dotted line).[11] The amplitude from 1st trough to 1st peak is

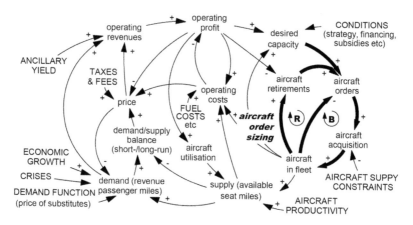

Figure 4.11 Aircraft order sizing feedback loops

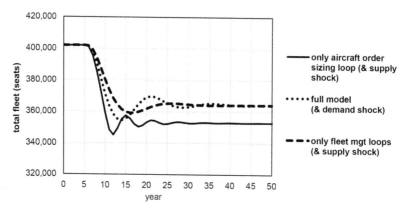

Figure 4.12 Aircraft order sizing feedback loops simulation result

with 12,300 seats in the aircraft order sizing scenario almost twice as big as in the previous fleet management simulation with 6,200 seats. Still, a difference of 12,300 seats means only ca. 1.6 %-points profitability change.[12] The return to a stable aircraft number in the fleet takes 26 years, which is four years longer then the fleet management scenario.

To track the profit cycle's origin further, the aircraft order sizing mechanism's two components will be examined in the next scenarios.

Feedback structure 'aircraft lifecycle' as part of fleet management's aircraft order sizing

Set-up, see Figure 4.13: The aircraft order sizing mechanism examined above is reduced further to an aircraft's lifecycle only. This mechanism ensures that

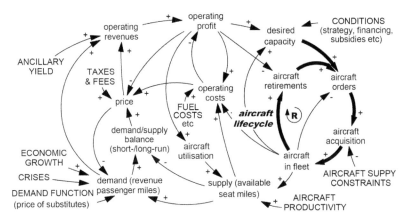

Figure 4.13 Aircraft lifecycle feedback loops

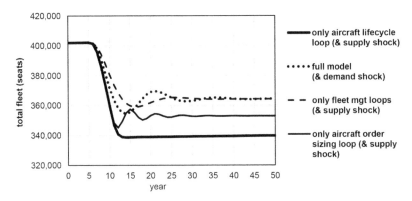

Figure 4.14 Aircraft lifecycle feedback loops simulation result

retired aircraft are replaced by new ones, provided the same or more capacity is desired. The process takes already placed orders into account. The previously introduced supply shock is given to start potential oscillations.

In short: aircraft orders →⁺ aircraft acquisition →⁺ aircraft in fleet →⁺ aircraft retirements →⁺ aircraft orders (reinforcing loop)

Result: There is no cycle.

Feedback structure 'accounting for existing fleet' as part of fleet management's aircraft order sizing

Set-up, see Figure 4.15: The set-up is the same as in the 'aircraft order sizing' scenario. The only difference is that aircraft are not retired anymore.

In short: aircraft orders →⁺ aircraft acquisition →⁺ aircraft in fleet →⁻ aircraft orders (balancing feedback)

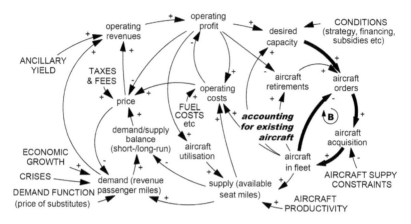

Figure 4.15 Accounting for existing aircraft feedback loop

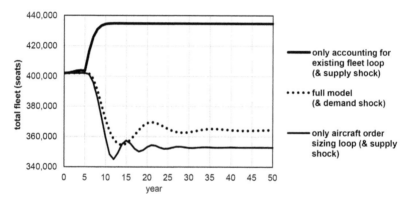

Figure 4.16 Accounting for existing aircraft feedback loop simulation result

Result, see Figure 4.16: There is no cycle. Aircraft capacity develops to a stable higher level.[13]

The question why the aircraft order sizing scenario revealed a clear cycle remains to be answered in further analyses in the following section.

Further analysis of the 'aircraft order sizing' feedback structure

Previous experiments discovered that the process of sizing aircraft orders causes oscillations. As soon as the inserted shock causes the airline industry's desired capacity level to diverge from the actual one, a cycle emerges. Yet, the aircraft order sizing feedback's components, (1) the mechanism to ensure aircraft retirement replacements and (2) the mechanism to account for the existing fleet, *alone* do *not* produce cyclic behaviour. It is the combination of the two feedback loops that generates oscillations.

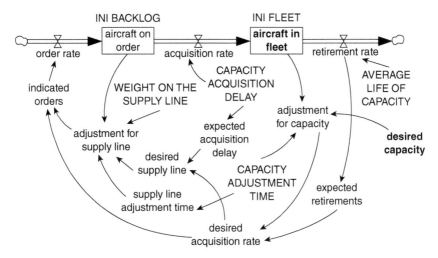

Figure 4.17 Stock and flow structure behind 'aircraft order sizing' feedback

Figure 4.17 presents the explicit model structure of the aircraft order sizing feedback loops. To achieve more clarity, the structure is slightly simplified; a full description can be found in section 3.3. A similar formulation has already been used in other System Dynamics models. These are for example Sterman's Beer Game model,[14] Forrester's production distribution model,[15] Meadows's commodity cycle model,[16] as well as previous airline industry models. Cycle causes and amplification mechanisms in these models have been summarised in Chapter 2. They will be tested and discussed in this section.

According to systems theory the structural prerequisite for oscillations is a balancing feedback loop with a delay.[17] This structural element exhibits its goal-seeking behaviour when the goal deviates from the system's state. Results oscillate around the goal because of the delay between action and effect. In their airline industry models Liehr et al., Jiang/Hansman and others find the delay between placing aircraft orders and their actual delivery to be a main reason for the airline profit cycle; all implying that a longer delay time entails a stronger cycle.[18] Their intuition is, the longer the delay time, the greater the chance that the aircraft to be acquired will not correspond with the amount needed at the time of acquisition. Hence, a longer delay likely creates a bigger mismatch between supply and demand, and a stronger profit cycle. In the airline profit cycle model developed here the *CAPACITY ACQUISITION DELAY* represents the discussed delay time. Its impact on cyclicality will be tested.

Set-up: In the 'aircraft order sizing' scenario the *CAPACITY ACQUISITION DELAY* of two years is first doubled then halved from year t = 5 onwards.

Result, see Figure 4.18: Changes in the *CAPACITY ACQUISITION DELAY* do have an impact on cyclicality. As expected, a longer timespan

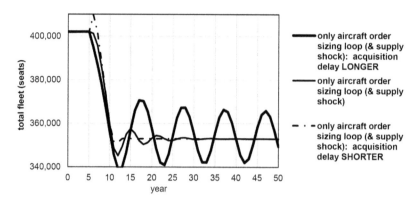

Figure 4.18 Simulation results for 'aircraft order sizing' feedback with varying capacity acquisition delay

between aircraft ordering and acquisition results in increased oscillations. A shorter *CAPACITY ACQUISITION DELAY* almost eliminates oscillations. The cycle's amplitude (1st trough to 1st peak) for a doubled delay time is in terms of profitability 4.0 %-points, which is still less than the full model's reaction amplitude of 9.8 %-points.[19] Nonetheless, the *CAPACITY ACQUISITION DELAY* is a sensitive factor and cycle driver.

Sterman points out that for a negative feedback loop with a delay to actually oscillate it is necessary that the delay in the system must be at least partially ignored.[20] From experiments with a production distribution system called the Beer Game, Sterman concludes that when placing orders, people regularly fail to account properly for the supply line, i.e. units already on order.[21] To mitigate and eliminate oscillations in the system, Sterman consequently proposes decision makers should fully account for the supply line. The impact of the degree to which the supply line is incorporated into the planning decisions, i.e. the *WEIGHT ON THE SUPPLY LINE*, in the aircraft order sizing process will be tested in the airline industry model.

Set-up: In the 'aircraft order sizing' scenario the variable *WEIGHT ON THE SUPPLY LINE*, which usually equals 50%, is set to 100%. Hence, the supply line is fully taken into account.

Result, see Figure 4.19: The scenario alteration dampens cyclicality but does not eliminate it. In light of the initial expectation that 100% weight on the supply line ensures the absence of cyclicality, it may seem surprising that the 'aircraft order sizing' structure still exhibits cyclic behaviour. The reason is the timing of acquisitions, technically the type of delay, which determines the aircraft *acquisition rate*'s shape. While Sterman's model assumes that most orders can quickly be fulfilled out of inventory stocks (first order delay), the airline profit cycle model expects aircraft to mainly be produced on demand so that airlines often have to wait the production lead time and longer to acquire their ordered aircraft (third order delay).[22] The difference in actual and expected timing of acquisitions leads to inaccuracies in the order planning process. Managers expect the cutback to be sufficient, though actually they have cut back a little too much already because aircraft are acquired a little later then they expected. Consecutively, the same mistake makes them order too much, then again too little, and so on until the system finds its new equilibrium after 21 years. Unfortunately, a mechanism solving the timing issue and hence providing a 'perfect' expectation for the acquisition rate by 'perfectly' accounting for the supply line seems to hit the limits of System Dynamics computer simulation. A solution was not found in the literature, neither did interviewed System Dynamicists provide an answer. Consequently, the timing issue is left to be addressed by future research. Here the assumption stands that fully accounting for the supply line in terms of volume and timing would make the oscillations disappear completely. This assumption, however, seems highly theoretical since in reality there may always be disruptions, inaccuracies in information flows, or unforeseen circumstances. Inaccuracies in aircraft order planning can thus be identified as a cycle driver.

Forrester discovers in his production distribution model that stability can be achieved by adjusting inventory more gradually. The speed with which deciders chose to act on inventory and supply line deficits is found to be one of the sensitive factors in his model.[23] If it takes long to place orders or if orders are rarely placed, aircraft capacity in the industry will adjust more gradually and oscillations in the system will be damped. This finding is underlined by Meadows' commodity cycle model which shows that the system is more stable if production does not react strongly to price changes.[24] Transferred to the airline profit cycle model this means cyclicality would depend on the *CAPACITY ADJUSTMENT TIME.* The intuition behind this would be that a mismatch between supply and demand, and hence the profit cycle, can best be prevented when the ordering process is given more time. On an industry level

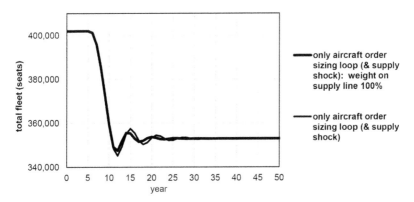

Figure 4.19 Simulation results for 'aircraft order sizing' feedback with full weight on the supply line

aircraft capacity would consequently adjust more gradually, whereas spontaneous frequent decision making would result in stronger profitability oscillations. This will be tested in the following simulation.

Set-up: In the 'aircraft order sizing' scenario the *CAPACITY ADJUSTMENT TIME* of 1 year is first doubled than halved. To avoid distortions the weight on the supply line remains at 100%.

Result, see Figure 4.20: Changing the *CAPACITY ADJUSTMENT TIME* changes the cycle. As expected, prolonging the planning time results in less cyclicality. In fact, oscillations are hardly recognisable anymore when the *CAPACITY ADJUSTMENT TIME* is doubled. Shortening the adjustment time makes the cycle more pronounced. Compared to the result of doubling the *CAPACITY ACQUISITION DELAY* (see simulation above) the amplification here is smaller. Doubling the delay between aircraft ordering and acquisition gives an amplitude of 4.0 %-points profitability change (1st trough to 1st peak), while halving the time with which deciders act on capacity deficits results in an amplitude of only 1.6 %-points.[25]

In conclusion, the aircraft order sizing structure is found to generate oscillations. That means the mismatch between airlines' actual and desired capacity is an origin of cyclicality in the airline industry. In further analyses three factors which amplify the cycle have been identified.

The first cycle driver is the *CAPACITY ACQUISITION DELAY (CAD)*, i.e. the time period between ordering and acquiring an aircraft. With a longer delay time chances rise that ordered aircraft do not match the amount actually required in the future. The mismatch between desired and actual capacity then results in a profitability cycle. A longer delay makes oscillations more pronounced.

The second cycle driver can be understood as a more refined version of the first finding. Accounting correctly for the *CAD* when planning aircraft orders and the resulting supply line will diminish the profit cycle. On the other

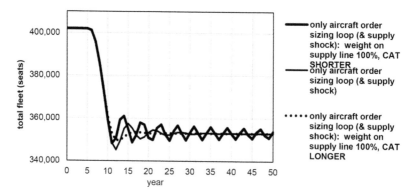

Figure 4.20 Simulation results for 'aircraft order sizing' feedback with varying capacity adjustment time

hand, inaccuracies in the order planning process, which are bound to occur in reality, will increase the mismatch between desired and actual capacity and thus the profit cycle.

The third factor driving the airline profit cycle is the *CAPACITY ADJUSTMENT TIME (CAT)* which indicates how often deciders act on capacity needs. A shorter adjustment time means airlines plan and process orders faster. This enhances oscillations because quick and frequent decision making means the industry acts with full force even on only temporary market changes. Given the delay between ordering and delivery, this may result in a huge mismatch between desired and actual capacity at the time the ordered aircraft enter the market. If each airline takes more time to prepare order decisions, the industry as a whole will adjust capacity more gradually. Hence, a longer *CAT* dampens the profit cycle.

Among the three factors the capacity acquisition delay has the largest lever in this limited feedback loop simulations. Which impact each factor actually has in the airline industry will be assessed by full model simulations in the next sections.

In the following section the loop knock-out analyses will be continued. Further amplifying mechanisms have yet to be discovered. They are expected to be present because even big changes in the cycle causing aircraft order sizing structure, such as doubling the capacity acquisition delay, do not cause huge oscillations.[26] Consequently, there must be further cycle drivers or additional cycle causes in the remaining model feedbacks.

4.1.3 Price determination as potential oscillator

Loop knock-out analyses in the previous section focused on the airline industry's cost and supply side. In this section the analysis will be completed by examining airlines' interaction with the market, i.e. the industry's price and demand side. The central element of interaction between supply and demand is the ticket price. Depending on price, customers decide whether to buy a ticket or not (see section 3.3.1). Hence, airlines' price determination process (introduced in section 3.3.2) will be inspected in this section. The analysis will be conducted in the same way as in the previous section. The price-setting mechanism will be divided into its components to assess each key feedback loop separately.

Feedback structure 'cost orientation of price'

Set-up, see Figure 4.21: In the price determination process costs can serve as an anchor. In one extreme, prices are set as a mere mark-up on costs. In the other, costs do not influence price setting at all. Costs are incurred by airlines' fleet management as described above.

In short: 1. cost $\rightarrow^+$ price $\rightarrow^+$ revenue $\rightarrow^+$ profit $\rightarrow^+$ desired capacity $\rightarrow^+$ aircraft orders $\rightarrow^+$ aircraft acquisition $\rightarrow^+$ aircraft in fleet ($\rightarrow^+$ supply) $\rightarrow^+$ costs (reinforcing loop); 2. all mechanisms described under 'fleet management'

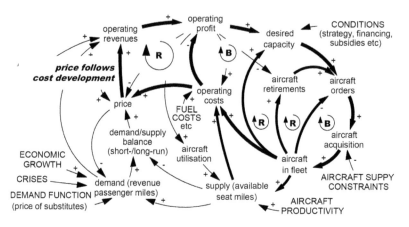

Figure 4.21 Feedback loops for cost orientation of price

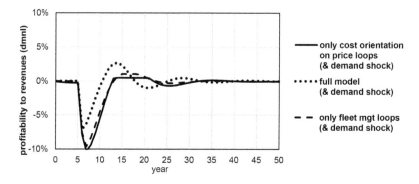

Figure 4.22 Simulation result for cost orientation of price feedback loops

Result, see Figure 4.22: The simulated profitability is in line with the cycle which the 'fleet management' loop creates on its own. So, the 'cost orientation of price' does not add new dynamics and is thus not a cycle driver. However, the option to adjust costs in the short run was not yet accounted for.

Set-up addition, see Figure 4.23: To incorporate short-run cost adjustment, the mechanisms allowing airlines to vary aircraft utilisation according to their current profitability situation is added.

In short: The above, plus the mechanism described under 'short-run cost reduction by aircraft utilisation adjustment' (illustrated in Figure 4.7)

Results, see Figure 4.24: Having included the 'aircraft utilisation' loop means that almost the full model is active. This includes the fleet management part. The simulated profitability cycle strongly resembles the 'fleet management' scenario's profitability. Hence, no new dynamics are added, no further cycle cause is found.

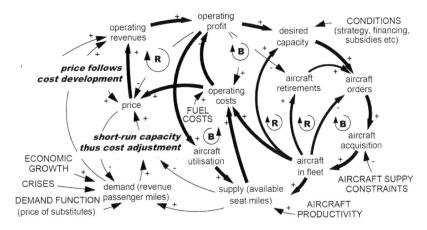

Figure 4.23 Feedback loops for cost orientation of price with additional short-run
cost adjustment

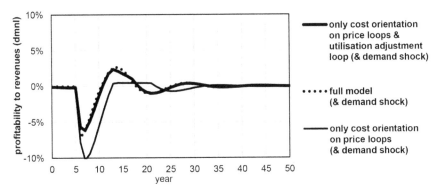

Figure 4.24 Simulation result for cost orientation of price with additional short-run
cost adjustment

Feedback structure 'profit pressure on price'

Set-up, see Figure 4.25: An airline's profit situation has an impact on prices.
If losses are being made, airlines feel pressure to make more revenue and thus
to increase prices. In reality, this pressure may often be overpowered by other
components of the price-setting process, for example by the idea to stimulate
additional demand by lowering prices. The profit pressure is however part of
airlines' price-setting considerations.

In short: price $\to^+$ revenues $\to^+$ profit $\to^-$ price (balancing loop)

Results, see Figure 4.26: There is no cycle.

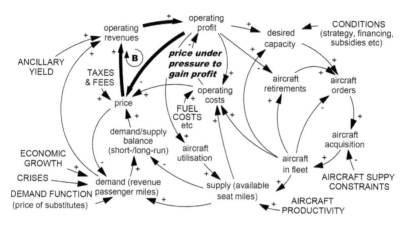

Figure 4.25 Profit pressure on price feedback loop

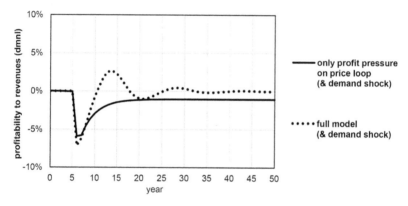

Figure 4.26 Profit pressure on price feedback loop simulation result

Feedback structure 'short-run demand stimulation by price'

Set-up, see Figure 4.27: To increase revenues airlines can not only raise prices (as in the mechanism above), they may also try to generate additional demand. To stimulate demand, prices are reduced when aircraft are not full enough. When the desired load factor is reached, airlines rise prices to earn more revenue.

In short: price →⁻ demand →⁺ short-run demand/supply balance →⁺ price (balancing feedback)

Results, see Figure 4.28: There is no cycle.

It is noteworthy that the airlines' attempt to stimulate demand after the shock causes profitability to decrease particularly quickly and severely. In this scenario short-run demand stimulation by price is the only alternative available to airlines

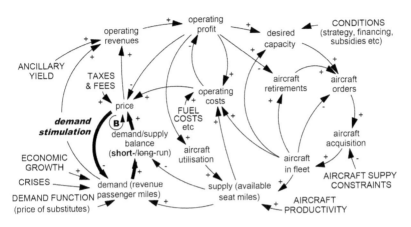

Figure 4.27 Feedback loop for demand stimulation by price

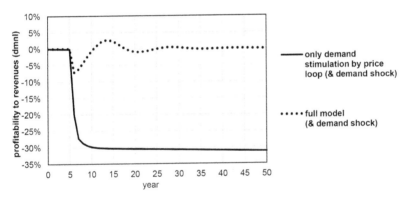

Figure 4.28 Feedback loop simulation result for demand stimulation by price

to deal with the demand shock. Thus, airlines reduce prices sharply and immediately. The resulting profitability is even lower than –30%, which is a four
times stronger reaction than is shown by the full model (–7% profitability).

Feedback structure 'revenue management'

Set-up, see Figure 4.29: Airlines use revenue management to maximise revenue
in the short run while filling the aircraft.[27] Revenue management combines
two mechanisms which have been examined before, 'short–run demand stimulation by price' and 'fleet management'. Both alter their part of the demand/
supply balance, which links them as highlighted in the diagram. The aircraft
capacity, which the 'fleet management' mechanism provides, is taken as given.

Flights are already scheduled and now need to be filled. To fit demand to that capacity, airlines make short-run price adjustments using the 'demand stimulation by price' mechanism. (On the supply side there is no short-run adjustment mechanism involved in revenue management.)

In short: See scenarios 'short-run demand stimulation by price' and 'fleet management'; plus: short-run demand/supply balance $\to^+$ price $\to^-$ demand $\to^+$ revenues $\to^+$ profit $\to^+$ desired capacity $\to \ldots \to$ supply $\to^-$ short-run demand/supply balance (reinforcing feedback)

In previous scenarios it was found that the 'fleet management' structure, more precisely the 'aircraft order sizing' mechanism, generates mild oscillations (see Figure 4.10). The simulation of 'short-run demand stimulation by price' did not produce any profitability cycle but had immediate and severe profitability consequences (see Figure 4.28).

Results, see Figure 4.30 and Figure 4.31: Profitability is strongly cyclical. The cycle's amplitude of 36 %-points (1st trough to 1st peak) is 3.6 times

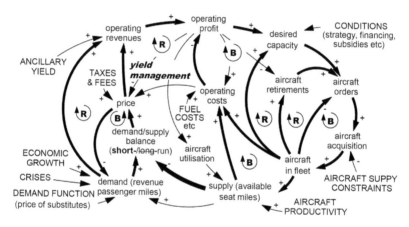

Figure 4.29 Revenue management feedback loops

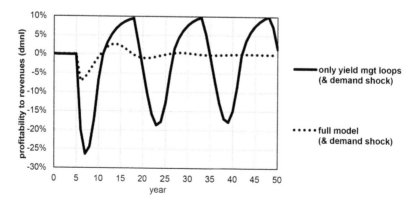

Figure 4.30 Revenue management feedback loops simulation result

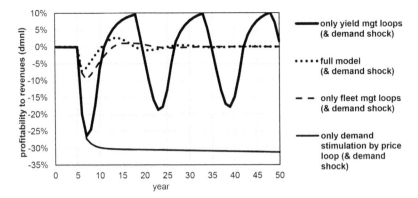

Figure 4.31 Revenue management feedback loops simulation result (compared to 'fleet management' and 'demand stimulation by price')

bigger than the amplitude of 10 %-points generated by the full model. Besides, it is 3.4 times larger than the amplitude created in the 'fleet management' feedback simulation. Though separately the 'fleet management' and 'short-run demand stimulation by price' did not produce a severe profitability cycle, their combination does. The mild oscillations created in the 'fleet management' area are magnified by the strong reactions in the 'short-run demand stimulation by price' model part. Revenue management is thus identified as a key amplifier for the airline profitability changes.

Feedback structure 'effect of long-run market expectations on price'

Set-up, see Figure 4.32: The previous scenario 'revenue management' focused on the short-term balance between demand and supply. In the pricing process the long-term demand supply balance is of interest. Airlines analyse market trends and incorporate their findings in the price-setting process.

In short: Feedback loops are the same as in the scenario 'revenue management', the difference being that, rather than the very short-term supply demand balance, more long-term market expectations are in focus: long-run demand/supply balance →⁺ price →⁻ demand →⁺ revenues →⁺ profit →⁺ desired capacity → ... → supply →⁻ long-run demand/supply balance (reinforcing feedback)

Results, see Figure 4.33: There is clearly a cycle in profitability. Profitability is more cyclic than in the fleet management scenario. As in the revenue management scenario, the interaction of demand and supply amplifies the industry's inherent aircraft capacity oscillation7d to the revenue management simulation the profitability cycle here is much less pronounced. Its period is longer and its amplitude smaller. Concretely, the cycle's amplitude of 16 %-points (1st trough to 1st peak) is 1.6 times bigger than the amplitude generated by the full model's simulation, 1.5 times bigger than in the fleet management scenario, but less than half as big (0.4 times) as in the revenue

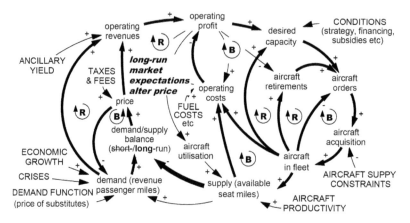

Figure 4.32 Feedback loops for long-term expectations' effect on price

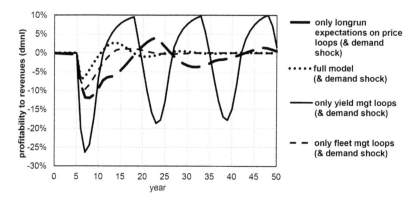

Figure 4.33 Feedback loops simulation results of only long-term expectations' effect on price

management simulation. The profitability cycle's period of 24 years (1st peak to 2nd peak) is 1.7 times longer than the full model's simulated cycle, 1.3 times longer than in the fleet management scenario, and 1.6 times longer than in the revenue management scenario.

4.1.4 Summary of feedback loop analysis results

Loop knock-out analyses show that the airline profit cycle's origin lies in the 'fleet management' feedback, more precisely in the 'aircraft order sizing' process. The mismatch between desired and actual aircraft capacity is the sources of cyclicality. The level of desired capacity mirrors expectations about demand and supply, as well as about yield and cost developments. When a disturbance causes desired and actual capacity to diverge, airlines introduce corrective actions. Several factors cause these actions to be unsuitable so that airlines overshoot their goal, which again entails corrective actions, and the cycle emerges.

Within the 'aircraft order sizing' structure, three cycle driving factors were identified: the capacity acquisition delay (i.e. the time period between ordering and actually acquiring an aircraft); the accuracy of aircraft order planning (i.e. how much the supply line is taken into account); and the capacity adjustment time (i.e. the time deciders take to act on capacity needs). All three can contribute to a mismatch between desired and actual capacity, which results in profitability oscillations. First, a long capacity acquisition delay causes corrective action to come too late and is hence likely to create a mismatch of desired and actual capacity. Second, incorrectly accounting for the capacity acquisition delay in the order sizing process by neglecting aircraft orders that have already been placed also adds to the mismatch. Third, taking capacity decisions based on short timeframes results in overreacting to singular events, and thus contributes to the desired and actual capacity mismatch.

Overall, the profitability cycle generated by the fleet management feedback structure is broadly in line with the full model simulation result. The 'fleet management' profitability cycle has an amplitude which is only 1%-point bigger than the full model's cycle amplitude of 9.8%-points. However, the waves of the fleet management profitability cycle are five years longer than the full model ones. This difference is due to fleet management's interaction with other parts of the model. Their dynamics will be explored in subsequent sections.

Combining fleet management with a mechanism for short-run demand stimulation by price is a structural representation of airlines' revenue management. Its simulated profitability amplitude is 3.6 times larger than the full model's cycle amplitude. Revenue management is clearly a cycle amplifier. A similar long-term orientated price-setting approach also has an amplifying effect, yet much weaker in comparison to the revenue management.

To illustrate the dynamics in the amplification process, the example of a demand shock will be discussed. Airlines react to the sudden lack of demand by lowering prices to stimulate sales and cover their fixed costs. The marginal costs of taking an additional passenger on board are almost negligible so it makes sense to sharply reduce prices. As a result not only the diminished demand but also the reduced prices push revenues downwards, and thus aggravate the profitability downswing. Once the first supply cutbacks take effect, airlines are able to achieve higher load factors again, and hence prices move upwards. Amplification now works to exaggerate prices up to the point where they become too expensive to fill the aircraft. Additionally, based on high revenues too many new aircraft are ordered and augment the airlines' cost base. Their financial situation deteriorates, and the cycle continues.

Next steps

Per definition loop knock-out analyses focus on simulating only a certain model part. Simulation results with the full model may reveal that a factor has a much bigger or smaller impact. With all mechanisms working at once, some effects may be compensated by others. How big the impact of each cycle driving factor on the airline profit cycle actually is will be assessed by full model simulations in the next sections.

4.2 Approach to scenario analysis and sensitivity assessment

In subsequent sections 4.3–4.5 the impact which potential cycle drivers and mitigation measures (derived in Chapter 2) have on the airline profit cycle will be assessed in model experiments. This section will introduce the analysis procedure.

There are two ways to conduct scenario analyses: The 'building up' and the 'stripping down' approach.

Starting point for the building up approach is an equilibrium situation in which everything is stable (see section 4.1.1). This assumes that change occurs neither in the airline industry nor in any external factors, such as the fuel price or the general economy. Certainly, this is unrealistic and abstract. However, the advantage of conducting scenario analyses in a stability setting is that it allows us to observe the effect of one change while everything else remains untouched. While this separation is not possible in reality, where many factors vary at the same time, the equilibrium model setting allows us to isolate each variation and assess its impact.

The stripping down approach builds on historic facts. The starting point is the situation as it was in reality in the US airline industry from 1985 onwards. Clearly, that is not an equilibrium setting. Therefore, the impact of a change in one factor is difficult to assess since there will be other interfering influences.

In line with the academic purpose of this study the building up approach, i.e. a stability setting, is chosen for scenario analyses.[28] This will ensure a more thorough understanding of which factors influence airline industry profitability and how they do that. Interviewed experts (see section 2.4.2) found the reality setting much easier to grasp than the highly theoretical stability setting. Beginning the analysis with counter-factual 'what would have happened in the industry if . . . ' scenarios was perceived as enlightening. Hence, in Chapter 5 a reality setting will be used to illustrate key findings.

In the following sections the potential airline profit cycle drivers and mitigation measures compiled in section 2.5 will be tested for their impact on the airline industry's profitability (see Figure 4.34). First, general economic factors, such as GDP or fuel price developments, will be inspected. Afterwards, the influence of the airline industry environment, e.g. industry regulations or aircraft manufacturers' behaviour, will be assessed. Finally, the impact of

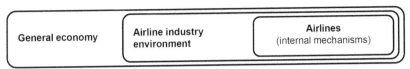

Figure 4.34 Categorisation of airline profit cycle drivers and mitigation measures as in section 2.5

airlines' behaviour, e.g. their aircraft ordering or price-setting mechanisms, will be examined. The research questions formulated in section 1.3 will guide the testing process:

1   Why are airline profits cyclical?
2   What are the causes and dynamics that determine the cycle's shape?
3   How can the situation be improved?

In model experiments, developments over a period of 50 years are simulated. There is no rule in System Dynamics to determine the 'correct' time horizon for simulation.[29] As a rule of thumb the simulation period should contain at least three cycles.[30] The observed period of the airline profit cycle is 10–11 years (see section 1.1) which means that 50 simulated years would contain almost five complete cycles. Another rule of thumb is 'to set the time horizon several times as long as the longest time delays in the system, and then some'.[31] The largest time constant (delay) in the model is the aircraft service lifetime of 25 years, which can be prolonged to a maximum of 50 years. Accordingly, a period much longer than 50 years would need to be simulated. A third rule of thumb asks 'to measure the transient time as four times the sum of time constants around the dominant loop'.[32] The sum of all time constants in the model is ca. 50 to 75 years (due to the variability of aircraft service lifetime). Finally, to ensure model validity no major structural changes may occur throughout the simulation period.[33] Such structural stability is likely to be present for 50 years. Given the industry in its current form has existed for approximately 25 years, a simulation period which covers twice that age seems reasonable. Overall, the simulation period has to be in line with the model's purpose, include the origins of the problem and its symptoms, and allow enough time to observe direct and indirect effects of potential policies.[34] Experiments have shown that the relevant behaviour can be observed within the selected 50-year time period.

Simulation experiments can be compared by the resulting impact on airline industry profitability. In case there is a cycle, its amplitude and period will be measured. If they change over time, the first amplitude and period are taken. The amplitude is measured from extreme value to extreme value (not from peak or trough to mean value) to include more information. The cycle period is measured from peak to peak. In case the cycle diminishes and resolves into stability, the number of years this stabilising process takes is

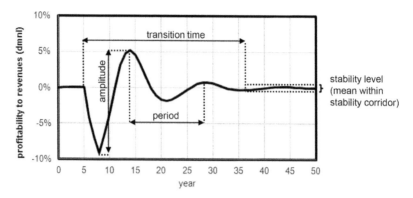

Figure 4.35 Illustration of measures capturing cyclicality

counted. Stability is considered to be reached when profitability deviates less than +/− 0.5 %-points from the stability level (which means a variation of less than 1 %-point). The stability level is the average profitability in the last 20 simulated years, from t = 30 to t = 50. The described cyclicality measures are illustrated in Figure 4.35.

4.3 Influence of general economic factors on airline profits

Potential cycle causes, drivers, and mitigation measures identified in Chapter 2 in the category 'general economic factors' are listed below (see Figure 4.36, categorisation introduced in section 2.5). In this section their influence on airline industry profitability will be tested. First, changes on the demand side will be explored in section 4.3.1, then supply side changes in section 4.3.2.
    potential cycle causes and drivers:

- general economic development (national income)
- external shocks (terror attacks, wars, diseases, weather, etc.)
- fuel price fluctuations

potential mitigation measures:

- none (because airlines cannot influence the general economic factors. Airlines' options to cope with them will be discussed in section 4.5 on airline behaviour.)

4.3.1 Developments of national income and demand shocks

In different scenarios stable and unstable demand developments are tested. Stable developments are for example constant GDP growth rates. Unstable developments are a business cycle or demand shocks. The equilibrium model calibration, which is used for scenario testing, assumes stability, i.e. no GDP growth and no crises. Scenario changes are inserted in year t = 5.

Constant GDP growth

Scenario set-up: Real GDP grows by 3%/ 5%/ 1% per year. Three per cent annual growth is approximately the historic average in the United States since 1985. Five per cent and 1% are selected to examine the effect of bigger and smaller growth, respectively.

Results, see Figure 4.37: The first profit reaction to economic growth is positive. After the change is inserted, profitability oscillates. The cycle's period is 13/ 17/ 14 years. The cycle's amplitude is 8/ 9.7/ 2.9 %-points and diminishes quickly. A stable profitability level is regained after 21/ 27/ 13 years when the industry has processed the change. The stability level of profitability is positive with 4.2%/ 5.8%/ 1.5%. It can be concluded that a higher GDP growth rate entails a higher peak profit, more time needed to stabilise profitability, and a higher profitability level in equilibrium.

Two observations are striking. First, although the GDP development is constant, profitability oscillates for many years. Consequently, the initial GDP growth increase, when the scenario is inserted in year t = 5, causes a cycle. It augments

Figure 4.36 Focus on the general economy's influence

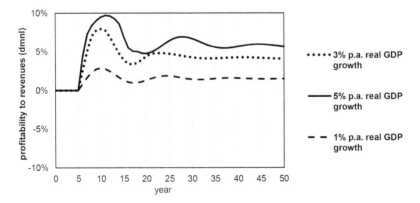

Figure 4.37 Constant GDP growth scenario

the desired industry's desired capacity level so it diverges from the actual one (see cycle origin in section 4.1.4). Second, the scenario shows that the stability level of profitability can be positive; it does not necessarily need to be zero.

Business cycle

Scenario set-up: The fundamental real GDP growth rate is 3% per year. This is varied by a sine wave with a period of ten years and an amplitude of half the fundamental growth rate. Thus real GDP growth varies between +1.5% and 4.5% per year.

Results, see Figure 4.38: Overall, profitability is positive. It exhibits a strong and lasting cycle. There is no stability within the simulated 50 years. Between the first and the second cycle the amplitude diminishes slightly. As in the previous 'constant GDP growth' scenario the airline industry's first reaction to the sudden positive demand development is strongest. The profitability cycle's amplitude is 7.3 %-points. Its period is ten years which corresponds with the inserted business cycle period. Comparing the business cycle (real GDP growth rate) to the resulting profitability cycle, a time lag of three years can be observed. Profitability peaks three years later than GDP.

It becomes evident that the business cycle translates into airline industry profitability. The industry even amplifies the cyclic input. The economic growth variation amplitude of 3 %-points results in approx. 7 %-points profitability change. The cycle period, however, is not amplified but the same (ten years). There is a three-year phase lag, between the business cycle and the airline profit cycle. Reasons for the phase lag remain to be detected.

Demand shocks by economy

Scenario set-up 'positive event': A positive event, e.g. the Olympics, causes special economic growth. For the duration of 1 year / 1 quarter of a year the

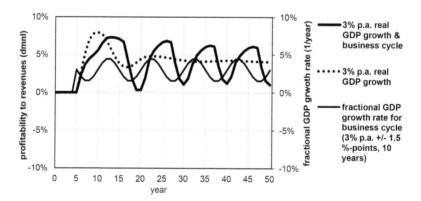

Figure 4.38 Business cycle scenario

usual real GDP growth of 0% rises to +10%. (These assumptions are extreme to better illustrate the dynamics.)

Scenario set-up 'negative event': A negative event, e.g. the outbreak of the financial crisis, can lead a severe economic downturn. For the duration of 1 year/ 1 quarter of a year real GDP slumps by –10%. Before and after the crisis growth is 0%.

Results, see Figure 4.39: Positive and negative events show symmetric results. The positive event leads to a profitability peak, the negative event to a trough. Amplitudes are 10.5/ 3.2 %-points for a positive event and 9.8/ 2.7 %-points for a negative event. In all cases profitability oscillates with diminishing amplitude and resolves to 0% profitability per year. The stable profitability level is reached after 11 years if the event is short (1 quarter of a year). It takes 19 years after a positive 1-year event and 24 years after a negative 1-year event to return to stable profits.

Remarkable is that, as a consequence of cyclicality, the positive event does not only have positive consequences. It causes profitability losses in later years. A second observation is that the existence of the airline industry's self-stabilising mechanism is again confirmed. However, with a process time of at least ten years, the mechanism seems rather slow.

Demand shocks due to other factors

The *other factors affecting demand* combine all influences on airlines' demand which do not constitute the demand curve.[35] Among these other factors are for example the fear after a terror attack, a volcano eruption, or distress after an economic crisis. Airlines consider most of the shocks, which are summarised among *other factors affecting demand*, as temporary. However, for example the psychological component of economic shocks may be considered to be longer lasting and thus needs to be taken into account for aircraft ordering and retirement decisions. The airline industry's reaction to different demand shocks will be examined in the following three scenarios.

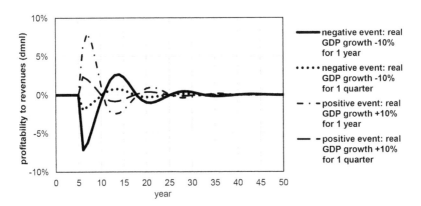

Figure 4.39 Demand shocks with roots in the economy

Demand shock scenario 1: 'Temporary vs. lasting shock'

Set-up: A lasting and a temporary shock are simulated separately. First, in the time series *TS lasting effect on demand* a shock of size –2.5% for the duration of one year is inserted. Second, the same is done with *TS temporary effect on demand*.

Results, see Figure 4.40:[36] Both shocks produce the same profitability collapse. After the slump, profitability oscillates slightly towards a stability level at 0%. A minor difference between the two shocks is observable in the industry's rebound reaction after the profitability trough. The temporary shock reaction leads to a slightly smoother profit development. The lasting shock creates an amplitude of 9.7 %-points in profitability and a period of 16 years, the temporary shock yields 9.2 %-points amplitude and a 17-year period. Overall, all other things equal, it does not make a big difference in terms of profitability whether airlines regard a shock as temporary or lasting.

Demand shock scenario 2: 'Extreme demand shock'

Set-up: To test the models' behaviour under extreme conditions, demand is very sharply reduced. In *TS temporary effect on demand* a shock which cuts potentially sold revenue passenger miles by –10% for the duration of one year is inserted. This means that no matter what airlines do, during that year demand will always end up being 10% less than it normally would be. Hence, this scenario is far from being realistic.

Result, see Figure 4.41: The demand drop is so severe that the industry desires to shut down. As all efforts to regain profitability are in vain, the industry's desired capacity level falls to zero. Five years after the crisis only 5% of demand can still be served. After the industry's breakdown there is no economic growth nor any other positive sign to recover profitability and convince potential new investors to enter the market. So the shutdown is completed.

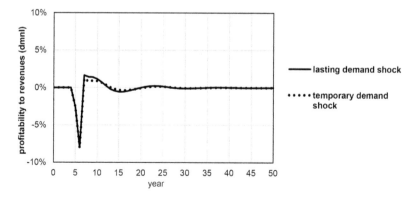

Figure 4.40 Demand shocks due to other factors

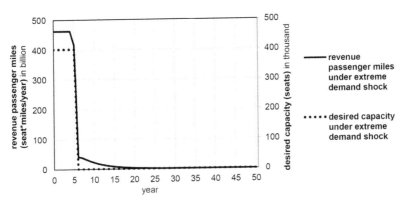

Figure 4.41 Extreme demand shock scenario for demand shocks by other factors

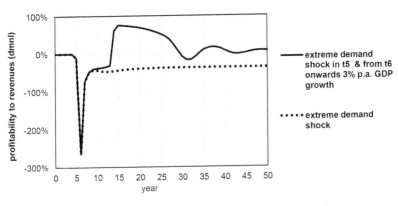

Figure 4.42 Extreme demand shock with subsequent GDP growth

If the crisis was followed by a positive economic growth period, the situation would change. Assuming a constant real GDP growth of 3% per year after the shock year t = 5, the industry will find back to profitability within ten years (see Figure 4.42). In this case airlines would at first benefit vastly from low fixed costs and high yields until the industry matures and stabilises again around zero profitability.

Demand shock scenario 3: 'Chain of external shocks'

Set-up: A chain of temporary shocks hits the airline industry. *TS temporary effect on demand* is set to reduce demand by 2.5% for the duration of 1 year and to repeat that reduction every 10 years, starting in year t = 10. In a second simulation the same set-up is used for *TS lasting effect on demand*.

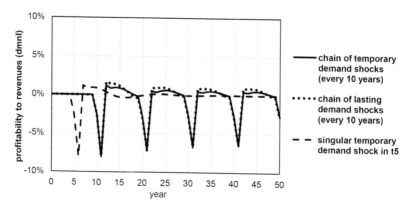

Figure 4.43 Chain of negative external events

Results, see Figure 4.43: For each separate shock profitability develops as described in the 'temporary vs. lasting shock' scenario above. The difference is that the cycle does not have the time to develop due to the disruption by the next crisis. Profitability thus exhibits the enforced period of ten years. This shows that external events can disguise the airline industry's ability to return to stability. A series of events can make the industry's profitability development look chaotic or enforce a regular pattern. A profitability 'cycle' could thus be the result of a series of events rather than industry mechanisms. Yet, previous experiments, in which only constant developments or singular events are inserted, have proven that the airline industry exhibits a profitability cycle which is driven by mechanisms within the industry (see also section 4.1).

Conclusion

Model experiments have revealed that economic developments and demand shocks strongly influence the airline profit cycle.

Every change in the economy (GDP) causes a profitability cycle in the airline industry. Economic changes alter air traffic demand and yields that airlines can achieve. Hence, they alter the airlines' desired capacity level and cause it to diverge from their actual capacity. This mismatch between actual and desired capacity was identified as the profit cycle's origin in section 4.1. Simulations confirmed that a continuous change in GDP, such as the business cycle, is not necessary to make profitability swing.

Stable positive economic growth results in a positive long–run profitability level in the airline industry. However, a GDP growth change in a positive direction does not only have positive consequences. A year with exceptionally high economic growth also starts a profit cycle. First, profitability peaks but shortly afterwards airlines' profitability declines, and so on.

Negative demand shocks also result in cyclic profitability. This means shock-dependent profitability losses are followed by a rebound phase with positive profits. All other things equal, it does not make a big difference in profitability whether airlines regard a shock as temporary or as lasting.

The shape of the airline profit cycle varies with a demand shock's intensity. Stronger shocks entail stronger reactions, i.e. longer-lasting cycles with higher amplitudes. There is no obvious connection between the cycle period and shock size. Most likely, the period is determined by the industry's internal mechanisms which will be examined in section 4.5.

The economy's business cycle translates into airline profitability. It swings with the business cycle's period. However, there is a time delay between an economic boom and an airline industry profitability peak of approximately three years. The mechanisms in the airline industry that cause this delay remain to be detected.

The industry can stabilise itself and achieve a constant equilibrium profitability level. The adjustment process to get there often takes more than 11 years in experiments. In reality, GDP growth is likely to change frequently within that period so that profit stability is unlikely to be reached. The industry will step from one adjustment phase into the next.

4.3.2 Fuel price developments

Besides economic developments, fuel price fluctuations are often mentioned to be driving the airline profit cycle. This will be tested in the following model experiments. By simulating stable and unstable fuel price developments, the fuel price's impact on airlines' profit cyclicality will be assessed. Stable developments are price increases that persist afterwards (step change) or continuous price increases by a certain annual percentage. An unstable development is a fuel price peak, which occurred for example in 2008 when prices rose by more than 70% within the year, and then dropped back to normal.[37]

Persisting fuel price increase

Scenario set-up: In year t = 5 the real fuel cost per available seat mile (ASM) of 0.018 USD in the equilibrium model increases to 0.023 US dollar/ASM and then persists at the new level. Historically, within the model's calibration timespan i.e. since 1985, 0.023 US dollar/ASM were the highest fuel costs level airlines were exposed to. In a second simulation the fuel price increases to an even higher level of 0.028 US dollar/ASM. In a third simulation, the price increase to 0.023 US dollar/ASM occurs less suddenly, with a five-year ramp up time from t = 5 until t = 10.

Results, see Figure 4.44: A fuel price increase causes severe losses in the first place. After the shock airline profitability oscillates around the stability level of 0% with diminishing amplitude. The increase to 0.023 US dollar/ASM causes a first amplitude of 9.1 %-points in profitability, the larger rise

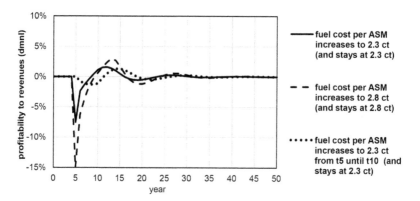

Figure 4.44 Persisting fuel price increase

to 0.028 US dollar/ASM results in a swing twice as large with 18.0 %-points amplitude. The increase to 0.023 US dollar/ASM which happens steadily over five years causes an amplitude of only 2.6 %-points. The fact that airlines have time to adjust to the change makes their profitability issues much smaller. Within four, five, or seven years after the price increase the industry has processed the change and profitability becomes positive. Afterwards airlines' cost-saving efforts result in higher profits for a while until airlines become unprofitable again, and so on. The industry reaches stability after 15/24/13 years. The profit cycle's period of approximately 14 years is the same in all three simulations, which indicates that the same cost adaption mechanisms are at work. Depending on the size and suddenness of the occurring fuel price change airlines need more or less time to process the initial shock. A big shock takes more recovery time than a small one; a smooth fuel price increase takes more recovery time than a sudden one, but the smooth increase leads to much smaller profitability losses.

Continuous fuel price increase

Scenario set-up: The fuel price (real fuel cost per ASM) increases continuously by 1% per year, starting in year t = 5. In a second simulation, it grows by 3% per year.

Results, see Figure 4.45: A continuous price increase of 1% per year does not lead to visible changes in profitability. (They are smaller than the model's accuracy.) Airlines are able to process the fuel price change even though it is not small compared to previous scenarios (see Figure 4.46). The continuous fuel price increase of 3% per year leads to a price of 0.069 US dollar/ASM in year t = 50, which is almost three times the initial value. This is too much to process for the airline industry. In year t = 15 the industry almost

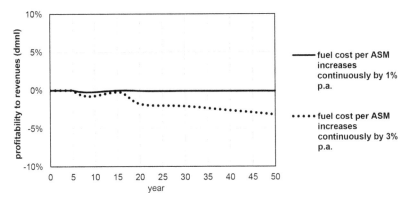

Figure 4.45 Continuous fuel price increase

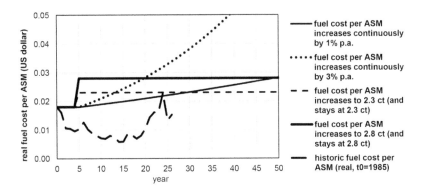

Figure 4.46 Comparison of simulated fuel price increases

reaches its zero profitability stability level again but the exponentially rising fuel price keeps pressuring airlines. They improve their efficiency, raise prices to compensate additional costs, and reduce capacity due to deteriorating profitability. However, their efforts are not sufficient and the industry's profitability diminishes further while the fuel price continuous to rise.

Fuel price peak

Scenario set-up: There is a fuel price peak in year t = 5. For the duration of 1 year the fuel cost per ASM is 0.023/ 0.028 USD instead of the usual 0.018 USD.

Results, see Figure 4.47: A one-year fuel price peak causes a mild cycle with severe losses in the first two years after the shock. For the lower peak price

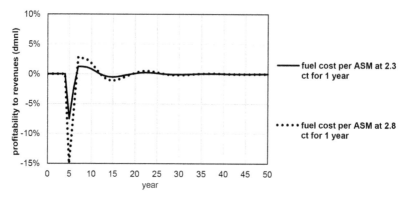

Figure 4.47 Fuel price peak

the cycle's first amplitude is 8.7 %-points profitability whereas the higher peak leads to an even higher amplitude of 17.8 %-points. After the fuel price shock airlines work to compensate the additional costs by increasing their efficiency, cutting unprofitable capacity, and raising prices as much as possible. Efforts pay off and after two years they enjoy a small profitability peak. The profitability cycle diminishes quickly and the industry regains stable profitability at 0% after 6 / 13 years. Both cycles exhibit the same 15 year-period. This indicates that the same coping mechanisms are at work, which was already discovered in the 'persistent fuel price increase' scenario.

Conclusion

The impact of fuel price developments on the airline profit cycle has been assessed in experiments. A fuel price change causes a cycle. This means fuel price changes, even if they occur in only one year, cause several subsequent years of cyclic profitability. The reason is that fuel price changes alter the business case which determines airlines' desired capacity level. The consequent mismatch between desired and actual capacity results in a cycle (see section 4.1).

The profit cycle's amplitude after a fuel price change depends on its suddenness and size. As expected, a big price increase causes more losses and takes longer to recover from. If the fuel price increases not abruptly but over a couple of years, the transition phase back to stable profitability may take slightly longer but the cycle's amplitude is much smaller. Airlines are able to process the smoother change better. They manage to increase efficiency, cut unprofitable capacity, and raise prices to compensate for the augmented costs. However, airlines can only handle a certain degree of continuous fuel price increases.

Whether the fuel price changes abruptly or smoothly, the resulting airline profit cycle's period is approximately 14–15 years. This must be the result of airlines' coping strategies, which will be explored in section 4.5 on airlines' behaviour.

4.3.3 Summary for general economic factors

General economy factors such as GDP developments, demand shocks, and fuel price fluctuations have a strong impact on the airline profit cycle. A change in the general economy initiates a cycle. As a consequence, even a temporary change in the general economy has lasting effects on airlines' profitability.

The time the airline industry needs to stabilise itself after a change in the general economy is in most experiments longer than ten years. In reality, the general economy is likely to change frequently during that time, and initialise cycles. Hence, unless the airline industry's cycle mitigation mechanisms (which have yet to be detected) are strengthened thoroughly, profit stability is unlikely to be reached.

The economy's business cycle translates into airlines' profits. The business cycle's period reappears in airline profits. Its amplitude is magnified in the airline industry by mechanisms which remain to be identified.

The airline profit cycle's shape after a general economy change depends on the size and suddenness of the event. The airline industry is generally more successful in processing continuous changes than sudden ones. Stable positive GDP growth leads to higher long-term profitability for airlines. A sudden fuel price increase can lead to four times more losses than an increase of the same size which happens over a few years.

A simulation compares the impact of a fuel price change to a GDP growth change (see Figure 4.48). In the equilibrium model a persisting fuel price

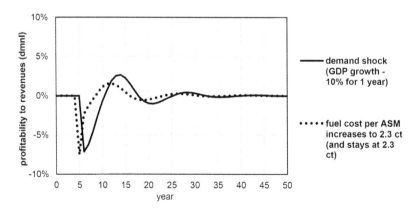

Figure 4.48 Impact of fuel price change compared to economic growth change

increase by ca. 30% causes similar first year losses as a real GDP growth drop of −10% for one year.[38] Both profit cycles exhibit a similar period and amplitude. However, the airline industry recovers more quickly from the fuel price change. Four years after the fuel price change, but not until six years after the economic shock, the industry becomes profitable again.

In case a change in the general economy was too big for the airline industry, it could theoretically shut down (see Figure 4.41: Extreme demand shock scenario). This shows that the model produces plausible results under extreme conditions. Furthermore, it reveals that the system's steady state, discovered in section 4.1.1, is only *locally* stable (see definitions in section 2.2.1), which basically means that the system can break and does not necessarily always regain its equilibrium state.

Which mechanisms in the airline industry and its environment emphasise and mitigate profit cyclicality remains to be analysed in subsequent sections.

4.4 Impact of airline industry environment on airlines' financial performance

In this section the airline industry environment's influence on the airline profit cycle will be assessed. Potential profit cycle drivers and possible mitigation measures in the industry environment have already been identified in Chapter 2. They are repeated in Table 4.1 (see also supplementary Figure 4.49). In the following section the listed factors will be tested for their impact on airline profit cyclicality in model simulation experiments.

The analysis will focus on cycle drivers, since knowledge about them is the prerequisite for designing suitable cycle mitigation measures. Hence, regulatory action such as price limits will be addressed at a later stage, in section 4.5. The airline industry's 'market structure' listed as a potential cycle driver in Table 4.1 will not be discussed separately but as part of other scenarios. The industry's fragmentation is, according to IATA, the result of high market exit barriers.[39] These will be addressed in section 4.4.2. Destructive competition, which describes a severe case of price competition, will be investigated in section 4.5.6 on price-setting policies. Whether or not the airline industry has an empty core cannot be examined because to 'directly test for the existence of an empty core is not possible'.[40]

As in previous analyses a demand shock of −10% real GDP growth for one year in year t = 5 will be inserted to start oscillations. This demand shock will serve as a reference to compare different simulations. (For a discussion of the 'demand shock' scenario see section 4.3.1.)

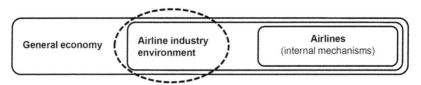

Figure 4.49 Focus on the airline industry environment's influence

Table 4.1 Cycle drivers and mitigation measures in the airline industry environment

Airline industry environment	
cycle driver	• investors' behaviour: easy access to capital, accurate forecasts • regulation: high taxes, bankruptcy law (high barriers to exit), government airline ownership, market liberalisation • high fixed costs (long aircraft long service lifetime, labour contract duration, unions) → slow adjustment, low marginal costs • aircraft manufacturers' behaviour: responsive production, production lead time • market structure: fragmented / empty core / destructive competition • non-changeable features: based on durable good (aircraft), non-storable product, imperfect information • demand features: price sensitive, herding behaviour amplifies demand changes, commoditisation (flying becomes normal)
mitigation measure	aircraft manufacturers: • slow production adaptation, order limits, big buffers in production (longer supply line adjustment time), produce to sales not to orders • more reliable on-time delivery • shorten lead times regulation: • minimum price, fixed price • airline ownership privatisation • allow consolidation, limit competition versus more competition • lower barriers to market exit (less bankruptcy protection)

4.4.1 Investors' behaviour

It is argued that investors' behaviour strongly influences the airline profit cycle.[41] Even though the airline industry's return on investment overall does not cover their costs (see section 1.2), investors keep financing new aircraft. Critics state this easy access to capital causes overcapacities in the industry which results in negative profitability.[42] Pearce finds that even during the recession in 2009 the world's airlines have expanded their fleet by 1%,[43] which leads Wohjan to conclude that the airline industry 'is adjusting to recessions not by shedding capacity but by underutilizing a still growing fleet'.[44] The question is how airline profitability would develop if investments in the airline industry were conducted more hesitantly, that means if access to capital was not as easy. This will be tested in the following simulations.

Scenario set-up: More difficult access to capital implies that investors expect higher profits to finance the same amount of capacity. In the model, the relationship between profitability expectations and the desired capacity level is expressed in the table function *T effect of profits on desired capacity*.[45] In this scenario the function is first altered to have investors invest more speculatively and aggressively, so they expect less profitability to finance the same aircraft capacity. Then the function is changed to have investors invest more cautiously, assuming they expect more profitability to desire the same aircraft capacity. In the first simulation the desired capacity expansion at each profitability level is doubled, in the second simulation it is halved. How investors choose to withdraw their support depends on bankruptcy regulations, which will be examined in the subsequent section. The usual demand shock is inserted to start oscillations.

Results, see Figure 4.50: Easier access to capital, i.e. more aggressive investment behaviour, results in a stronger airline profit cycle. In the first years after the demand shock airlines suffer losses and do not make new investments. Afterwards, in the profitable phase airlines start to invest, and the consequences of more and less aggressive investment behaviour become visible. The industry profitability develops positively when financing new aircraft is more difficult. The cycle expires 15 years after the shock without airlines making any more losses (only around year t = 24 profitability equals -0.2%). In contrast, speculative and aggressive investing, which implies giving airlines easy access to capital, results in a more pronounced profitability cycle compared to the demand shock reference. In the profitable phase around year t = 14 airlines invest heavily which leads to overcapacities, higher costs, and losses thereafter. The second profitability through is reached in year t = 19 with -2.2%. The cycle's period of 12 years is shorter than the reference's 14-year period.

In conclusion, easy access to capital (speculative and aggressive investors' behaviour) amplifies the airline profit cycle. More difficult access to capital (less aggressive, more cautious investor behaviour) eliminates the cycle after the after-shock rebound peak. Hence, if investors expect more profitability from their investments, they will achieve better profitability, all other things equal.

4.4.2 Market exit barriers

It is stated that the airline industry's high barriers to exit the market are responsible for the profit cycle.[46] When unprofitable airlines that would actually need

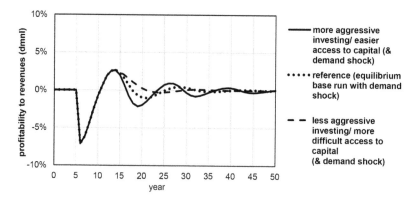

Figure 4.50 Investors' behaviour – airlines' access to capital

to cease business are kept in the market, this causes overcapacities leading to losses. Exit barriers can have an official regulatory nature, as for example the US chapter 11 bankruptcy law which allows unprofitable airlines to continue operations. Also, official or indirect subsidies disguise airlines' actual financial position. Moreover, government-owned airlines, which are not obligated to be profitable, distort the market. Critics argue the airline industry's financial performance would be much better in a fully liberalised market with low barriers to exit.[47] This will be examined in the following experiment.

Scenario set-up: Loss-making airlines need to reduce their capacity. When losses are too big, airlines go out of business. In the model the relationship between expected profitability and airlines' capacity is expressed in the table function *T effect of profits on desired capacity*.[48] In an industry with low barriers to exit a small loss already entails big capacity cutbacks. High barriers to exit mean high protectionism, so big losses result in only moderate capacity cutbacks. The table function *T effect of profits on desired capacity* is altered accordingly.[49] The usual demand shock starts oscillations.

Results, see Figure 4.51: The airline industry exhibits much more profit cyclicality with lower barriers to exit which imply more market liberalisation, less government-owned not-for-profit airlines, less bankruptcy protection, or less subsidies. The simulated profitability cycle has an amplitude of 15.3 %-points and a period of 11 years. Though the cycle's amplitude is diminishing, airline profitability does not return to a stability level within the simulated 50 years. The reason is that due to the easier market exit the level of desired capacity in the industry changes more drastically. The industry recovers more quickly from the demand shock and profits in the rebound phase are much higher due to the more severe shake out. Over time profits made in upswings are bigger than losses made in downturns. So facilitating market exits makes the airline industry on average more profitable but also more unstable.

Against expectations, higher barriers to exit stabilise airlines' profitability. There is hardly a cycle, only a small rebound peak of 0.7% after the demand shock, after which the industry becomes stable at 0% profitability.

In conclusion, the airline industry's exit barriers have a significant impact on the airline profit cycle. They can amplify or stabilise it. High barriers to exit (i.e. extensive bankruptcy protection, subsidies, and not-for-profit governmental airline ownership) stabilise airline profits whereas low exit barriers (i.e. market liberalisation) lead to more cyclic profitability. It is to note that though the liberalised industry is more cyclic, its profitability level on average over time is higher than in the protected industry.

4.4.3 Taxes on flight tickets

Airline industry lobbyists often claim flight ticket taxes significantly reduce airline profits.[50] In the US airline industry ticket taxes and fees have been rising over the years and amount to roughly 27% of yield in 2014.[51]

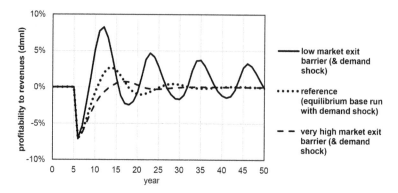

Figure 4.51 Market exit barriers

Scenario set-up: In the model, ticket taxes are an add-on on airlines' yield.[52] This is a simplification of reality but serves to get an impression of the overall impact of taxes augmenting the consumer price. In the equilibrium model calibration, the initial ticket tax is zero. In a first simulation, a high ticket tax of 0.02 USD per seat mile, which equals approximately 30% of yield, is injected. In the second simulation the same tax of 0.02 USD per seat mile is implemented over a timespan of ten years, increasing steadily during that time. In the third simulation a more realistic 3% tax increase of 0.002 USD per seat mile is inserted.

Results, see Figure 4.52: Tax increases trigger the airline profit cycle. However, a normal tax increase in the range of 3 %-points has hardly any influence on airline profitability. It causes a profitability cycle with an amplitude of only 1 %-point. If airlines knew about the tax increase in advance, consequences would be even milder. The unrealistic sudden tax increase of 30% has a much larger impact on profitability. The effect is similar to the reference demand shock's profit impact. When taxes are not suddenly increased by 30% but are given a 10-year ramp up time, airlines' profitability is much less affected. The cycle's amplitude is 3.5 %-points instead of 9.9 %-points. Both cycles have a period of 15 years and converge to the stability level of 0% profitability.

In conclusion, a tax increase of 3% causes hardly any profit cyclicality. Furthermore, introducing a tax increase not at once but over time helps to stabilise profitability. Consequently, against expectations, tax increases (within a reasonable range) have only moderate impact on airlines' profit cyclicality.

4.4.4 Demand characteristics

Experts and literature often underline the impact of air traffic demand characteristics on the airline profit cycle. The airline industry is found to have a

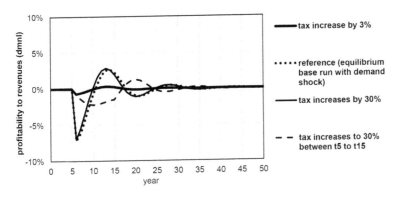

Figure 4.52 Tax increases

price sensitive demand.[53] While the IATA claims this price sensitivity depresses yields and leads to a generally low profitability, industry cycle research suggests a price sensitive demand mitigates cyclicality.[54] Airline customers' price sensitivity is further enhanced by a commoditisation of the airline product in mature markets such as the United States.[55] Another airline demand feature which is argued to deteriorate airlines' profitability is customers' herding behaviour. It is said to aggravate profit cycle swings.[56] In model experiments all three aspects will be examined for their impact on airline profitability.

Scenario 'price sensitivity of demand'

Set-up: How sensitive demand reacts on price changes is expressed by the price elasticity of demand.[57] Changing the price elasticity means changing customers' willingness to pay (find demand function modelling explained in section 3.3.1). The model's *REFERENCE DEMAND ELASTICITY* is −1, which means that for example a +5% price change results in a (−1 * 5% =) −5% demand change. First, a 50% higher, then a 50% lower price sensitivity is simulated. Since demand features change over time, elasticities will start transforming in year t = 5 and the process will be completed in year t = 10. The model is given the usual demand shock to start oscillations. To validate results both simulations are repeated with a more realistic demand pattern, i.e. the business cycle examined in section 4.3.1, instead of the demand shock.

Results, see Figure 4.53 and Figure 4.54: A change in the price sensitivity of demand destabilises the airline industry. It causes airline profitability to cycle, no matter if the change is an increase or a decrease.

A more price sensitive demand facilitates the industry's recovery from the shock. Airlines' attempts to stimulate demand by lowering prices work well on the price-sensitive customer base. Within three years airlines regain profitability, having reached their trough at -4.8% profitability. After 23 years profitability is stable again. In the demand shock reference profitability returns within six years, its bottom point being -7.1%. Stability is reached after 19 years. A lower price sensitivity of demand results in a deep trough of -10.6%. The industry needs seven years to regain profitability and 20 years to become stable again.

In a business cycle setting, there is a big difference between increasing and decreasing price sensitivity of demand in the first ten years. The industry's equilibrium price is a low price. So when customers become more price sensitive in year t = 5 their demand rises at the given price level. Hence, the higher price sensitivity of demand leads to higher profitability in the first ten years because airlines are able to exploit high load factors and raise prices. A less price sensitive demand results in fewer revenue passenger miles being sold at the given price. Load factors deteriorate and airlines need to make great efforts to reanimate the insensitive demand with price reductions.

In summary, though airline organisations complain about a high price sensitivity of demand, it is in the airline industry's current state (with its low price level) beneficial for airlines' profitability.

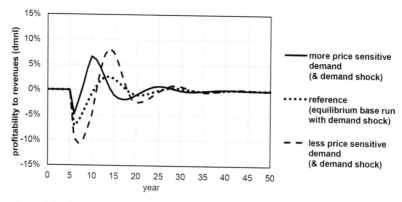

Figure 4.53 Price sensitivity of demand (demand shock)

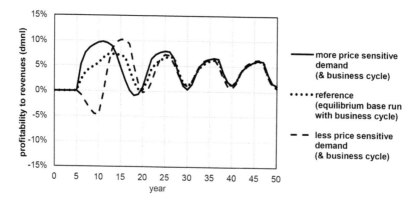

Figure 4.54 Price sensitivity of demand (business cycle)

Scenario 'commoditisation of air travel'

The commoditisation trend, which industry analysts observe in mature airline markets such as the United States, is stated to deteriorate airlines' profitability.[58] Commoditisation of the air travel product means customers value air travel increasingly less than other products. This implies that customers become more price sensitive. The effect of an underlying increasing air travel commoditisation trend will be examined in the following section.

Set-up: The price elasticity of demand rises by 1% per year. This means it starts at −1 in year t = 5 and equals -1.6 in year t = 50. The business cycle used in the previous section is inserted to simulate realistic conditions.

Result, see Figure 4.55: Against analysts' claims, increasing price sensitivity of demand leads to more stable and higher profitability. Compared to the business cycle reference the average profitability in the long run is approximately 1 %-point higher and the cycle amplitude is 1.7 %-points smaller. The reason is that the GDP increase shifts the demand curve outwards so more seat miles are sold at the same price. Rising load factors allow airlines to increase prices slightly. Given the increased price sensitivity of demand, the slight change has a big lever so sales rise further. In downturns the increasing size of the lever assists airlines to keep a higher price level because they need only small reductions to reanimate demand.

Consequently, as in the previous scenario, against airline organisations' claims, the commoditisation trend is not negative for the airline industry profitability in its current (low price level) state. On the contrary, commoditisation leads to a higher average profitability level.

Scenario 'customers' herding behaviour'

The airline profit cycle is argued to be driven by herding behaviour.[59] It describes the phenomenon that an individual tends to do what the group does. When many people fly, even more people will fly. For example, because business

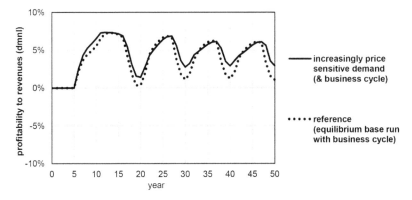

Figure 4.55 Commoditisation (increasing price sensitivity of demand)

partners expect a return visit or families decide to explore a holiday destination friends told them about. Likewise, when people are reluctant to fly, for example after a terror attack, many others will follow their lead. Altogether, this reinforcing mechanism makes demand more rigid to change the current development direction. What impact increased herding behaviour has on airlines' profitability will be assessed in the following section.

Set-up: To simulate the rigidity of demand the time it needs to react to changes, i.e. the *DEMAND ADJUSTMENT DELAY*, is prolonged. First, the usual demand shock is inserted to start oscillations. Then the simulation is repeated in a business cycle setting.

Results, see Figure 4.56 and Figure 4.57: A more rigid demand mitigates the profitability effect of a shock. The shock is a short event. If people are slow to react, the worst of the shock is already over before they decide to act on the circumstances. Hence, the profitability cycle's amplitude is only 7.8 %-points which is 2 %-points less than in that of the reference run. Faced with a business cycle, a customer base with herding behaviour leads to a more pronounced profitability cycle with approximately 1 %-point more amplitude than the reference run. Herding is a reinforcing mechanism. Confronted with gradual developments, such as the business cycle, it reinforces the development direction which leads to higher peaks and lower troughs.

In reality, changes in the airline industry's environment are a mix of rapid and gradual developments. Thus, against expectations, herding behaviour cannot be confirmed to drive the airline profit cycle. Depending on the environmental change it may well serve to stabilise airlines' profitability.

4.4.5 Aircraft manufacturers' behaviour

Aircraft are essential for airlines to supply air transportation. It was found in section 4.1 that fleet management is the airline profit cycle's origin. Aircraft manufacturers create the environment for airlines' fleet management decisions.

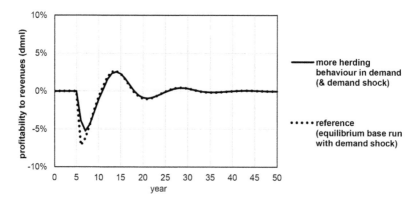

Figure 4.56 Herding behaviour (demand shock)

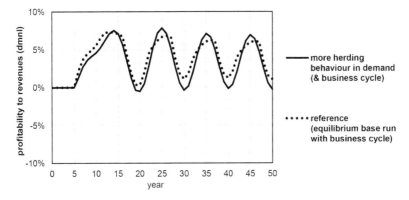

Figure 4.57 Herding behaviour (business cycle)

Manufacturers set the aircraft price, and their technology fundamentally determines an aircraft's service lifetime. Moreover, manufacturers' processes and production capacities determine airlines' aircraft *CAPACITY ACQUISITION DELAY*, i.e. the time it takes from ordering to receiving an aircraft. What impact aircraft manufacturers' behaviour has on the airline profit cycle will be tested in the following scenarios.

Scenario 'aircraft price (fixed unit cost)'

The airline industry's high level of fixed costs is argued to be a reason for its profit cyclicality.[60] In this scenario the profitability impact of more and less expensive aircraft will be examined. (Airlines' cost-cutting actions or aircraft leasing options will be explored in section 4.5 on airline behaviour.)

Set-up: Aircraft prices, or costs respectively, are a part of airlines' fixed costs. Since the model does not differentiate between different fixed cost components (see section 3.3.4), the airlines' fixed unit costs are varied as a whole in this scenario. Alterations thus also comprise labour costs etc., and will lead to results which are more pronounced than they would be if only the aircraft cost component was changed. In the first simulation aircraft prices rise by 30%. In the second simulation they fall by 30%. Aircraft prices or fixed costs, respectively, change over a period of five years starting in year t = 5. The cost change is inserted in the variable *change in overhead real unit cost*. Thus, the change does not only concern new aircraft but also the existing fleet.

Results, see Figure 4.58: A rise in fixed costs, though spread over five years, triggers the airline profit cycle. Its amplitude is 7.3 %-points. The cycle's period is 14 years. After 26 years the industry has returned to its stability value of 0% profitability. This means airlines have adjusted their supply and ticket prices to the new cost level.

During the five years when fixed costs fall by 30%, airlines enjoy a profitability peak. This is followed by a downswing because the additional profits

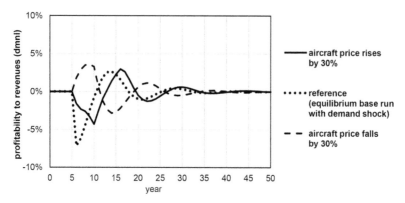

Figure 4.58 Aircraft price (fixed unit cost)

lead to more investment in new capacity. When capacity becomes larger than demand, profitability swings downwards. Profitability continues to oscillate until the industry finds stability again in year t = 25.

In summary, the effect of aircraft price changes on the airline profitability is moderate. If aircraft prices changed significantly (+30% in five years), airlines' profitability would still be 2.5 %-points better than after the usual demand shock. A massive aircraft price reduction (−30% in five years) would only result in +3 %-points profitability.

Scenario 'aircraft service lifetime'

A short aircraft service lifetime means that aircraft need to be replaced more often. Hence, the fixed costs, which aircraft represent for airlines, are not fixed as long. This flexibility increase is stated to mitigate airlines' profit cyclicality.[61]

Set-up: The aircraft service lifetime, i.e. the *AVERAGE LIFE OF CAPACITY*, which is assumed to be 25 years in the equilibrium model, is simulated to be half as long (12 years). In a second simulation it is assumed to be twice as long (50 years).

Results, see Figure 4.59: An abrupt change of aircraft's service lifetime triggers a cycle in airline profitability. Considering the diversity of the airline industry's capacity in terms of aircraft types and ages, such a sudden and huge change in the service lifetime seems unrealistic. However, even these dramatic changes do not entail large profitability cycles. Halving the service lifetime results in a cycle with 5.1 %-points amplitude. This is only half as much as the demand shock profitability cycle's amplitude of 9.8 %-points. Doubling the service lifetime leads to only 2.5 %-points amplitude. After approximately 12 years the airline industry has processed the change and profits are back at their stable zero profitability level.

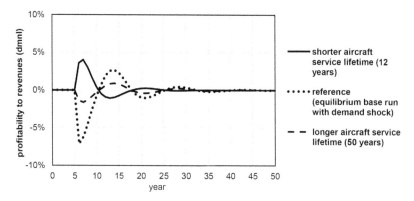

Figure 4.59 Aircraft service lifetime

Altogether, the impact of changes in aircraft service lifetime, and hence in the industry's fixed cost base, is only moderate compared to other factors.

Scenario 'capacity acquisition delay'

It is often stated that the long lead time between aircraft ordering and delivery increases profit cyclicality.[62] Experiments in section 4.1.2 with an isolated fleet management model part confirmed this finding. Yet it remains to be discovered how and how much the capacity acquisition delay, i.e. the time between aircraft order and delivery, will impact airline profitability if all dynamics of the industry are at work in the full model.

Set-up: The *CAPACITY ACQUISITION DELAY (CAD)* in the equilibrium model is two years. In two simulations the delay will be halved to one year and doubled to four years. The usual demand shock will start oscillations.

Results, see Figure 4.60: Against expectations a shorter delay time amplifies the airline profit cycle, a longer delay time dampens it. Halving the *CAD* results in an amplitude of 13.1 %-points profitability which is only 3.3 %-points more than the profitability amplitude created by the demand shock alone. Doubling the *CAD* makes the cycle's amplitude smaller; it is 7.7 %-points profitability. Also, the longer *CAD* leads to a smoother cycle in terms of cycle period. The doubled *CAD*'s cycle exhibits a period of 16 years whereas the short *CAD* simulation's period of 14 years is in line with the demand shock reference's cycle period.

Receiving ordered aircraft later is beneficial for the airline industry's profitability because it inhibits airlines' capacity expansion. From an isolated fleet management perspective a prolonged aircraft acquisition delay leads to more planning mistakes and more instable results (see section 4.1.2). Yet, in the airline industry as a whole airlines' easy access to capital leads them to order more

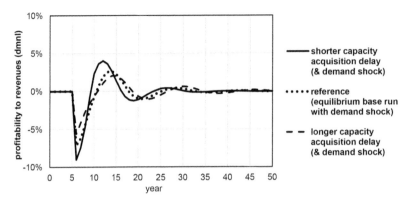

Figure 4.60 Capacity acquisition delay

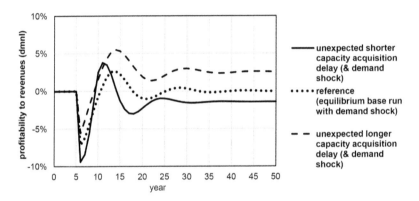

Figure 4.61 Unexpected capacity acquisition delay change

than is good for them with regard to profitability. So the prolonged capacity acquisition delay is a helpful constraint.

The simulations above assume airlines immediately learn about increased lead times. However, aircraft production may take longer than even the manufacturer expects. The impact of the *CAD* being constantly longer than airlines expect will be tested.

Set-up: As above, the *CAD* of two years is first halved, then doubled, and the usual demand shock is inserted. Additionally, the *expected acquisition delay* is kept constant at two years.

Results, see Figure 4.61: If the *CAD* is permanently shorter than expected, airlines' profitability becomes negative in the long-run. Stability is reached at -1.4%. When airlines persistently underestimate the *CAD*, i.e. when it is longer than expected, profitability stabilises at +2.4%.

Consequently, to mitigate the airline profit cycle the aircraft manufacturers' lead times should be long, ideally even longer than airlines expect. If airlines receive their aircraft too late, this involuntary capacity constraint results in a higher long-run profitability level for airlines.

Scenario 'buffers in production'

Inventory buffers in the aircraft production process are said to mitigate cyclicality.[63] This will be tested in the following experiment.

Set-up: The model is altered so there is always sufficient inventory to fulfil the majority of aircraft orders immediately. This assumption is highly unrealistic because aircraft production is lengthy and costly. Consequently, large numbers would not be produced to stock. To simulate buffered production the model is set up with a first order delay which replaces the third order delay structure for aircraft production (see sections 3.3.3 and 4.1 for background).

Result, see Figure 4.62: The buffered production leads to a 0.4 %-points less cyclic airline profitability than the reference. Stable profits are reached after 18 years, which is one year earlier than in the demand shock reference simulation.

Consequently, it hardly makes a difference whether there are buffers in the aircraft production process or not. As shown in the previous scenario, it is much more important whether or not airlines expect the changed aircraft delivery pattern.

Scenario 'aircraft manufacturer production limits'

Production limits for aircraft manufacturers are said to deteriorate airline profitability. Especially in boom times when airlines order plenty of new capacity, aircraft production limits would cause airlines to miss out on extra revenues.[64]

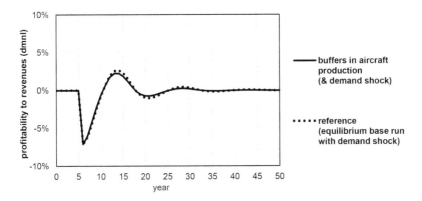

Figure 4.62 Buffers in aircraft production

On the other hand, previous airline profit cycle research found that slow aircraft production adaptation mitigates the cycle.[65] Slow adaptation is merely a softer version of a production restriction, which does not allow adaptation at all. Instead of production limits some researchers postulate aircraft order limits.[66] For manufacturers it is essentially the same whether they are not allowed to take orders or not allowed to produce ordered aircraft.

A production to sales, which some supply chain researchers suggest to mitigate the profit cycle, does not make sense for aircraft manufacturers.[67] Their product is translated into a service and this transition from aircraft to revenue passenger miles is influenced by many strategic considerations. Having to estimate all these factors, it cannot be assumed that a produce-to-sales strategy achieves better results than a production to orders.

A set of experiments will be used to determine whether aircraft manufacturers' slow or restricted production adaptation mitigates or amplifies the airline profit cycle.

Set-up: For the first simulation aircraft manufacturers' production capacity is limited to -10% of the normal aircraft delivery rate. So starting in year t = 5 the airlines' aircraft *acquisition rate* has a maximum value of 12,300 seats/year. In the second simulation, in addition to the manufacturers' limitation, lessors' ability to deliver aircraft is also restricted to -10% of the normal delivery rate. The usual demand shock is inserted to start oscillations. Subsequently, both simulations are repeated without the demand shock.

Results, see Figure 4.63 and Figure 4.64: Given the demand shock airline profits start to cycle. After the shock, when the industry becomes profitable again, airlines start ordering aircraft and the industry enjoys a profitability peak in year t = 14. Then smoothly without further downswings profitability returns to its stability level in year t = 20. The delivery restriction has eliminated the cycle. In the second set of simulations without the initial demand shock, both the manufacturers' and the lessors' limitations push the airline industry to a higher stable profitability level. The transformation process takes

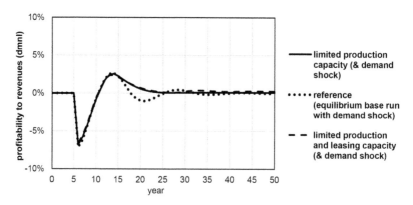

Figure 4.63 Limited production and leasing capacity (with demand shock)

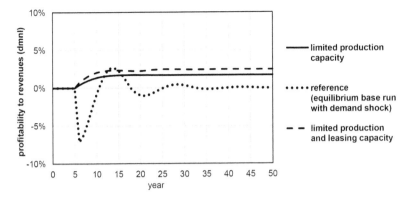

Figure 4.64 Limited production and leasing capacity (no demand shock)

approximately five years. The new sustained profitability is 1.7% if only manu-facturers are restricted and 2.5% if lessors are limited, too.

It can be concluded that restricting the inflow of new capacity into the air-line industry stabilises airlines' profitability in boom times because it prevents overcapacity. It does not take away from the boom's profitability peak, and it prolongs the profitable phase. However, delivery restrictions cannot dampen a shock-induced downswing. They only become effective in profitable times.

How realistic it would be to call for an aircraft delivery limit remains ques-tionable. During the restricted periods aircraft orders would pile up over years which would make capacity enlargements for manufacturers, lessors, or poten-tial new market entrants increasingly attractive.

4.4.6 Perfect information

Supply chain research regards information flow problems as a main driver of cyclicality.[68] Consequently, information-sharing concepts and improving fore-casting are often stated to mitigate cyclicality.[69] The importance of forecast and information accuracy for airlines' profit cyclicality will be assessed in this experiment.

Set-up: First, information flows in the industry are simulated to be per-fect. In an industry with perfect information, expectations always turn out to be correct. The expected values equal current values. All expectation and perception times in the model listed in Table 4.2 are set to be very short (0.0625 years) and the weights on the supply line are 100%. Second, imper-fect information, i.e. slow information flows, is simulated. All expectation and perception times in the model are doubled and the supply line information is not available (*WEIGHTs ON THE SUPPLY LINE* = 0%). The usual demand shock starts oscillations.

Table 4.2 Variables altered in 'perfect information' scenario

Variables altered in 'perfect information' scenario	
supply module	*TIME TO ADJUST COST EXPECTATION*
	TIME TO ADJUST EXPECTED YIELD
	TIME TO ADJUST DEMAND AND SUPPLY EXPECTATION
	TIME TO PERCEIVE UNIT COST CHANGE
	TIME TO PERCEIVE YIELD CHANGE
	WEIGHT ON THE SUPPLY LINE
	WEIGHT ON THE SUPPLY LINE LEASING
price module	*TIME TO ADJUST YIELD EXPECTATION*
	TIME TO ADJUST VARIABLE COST EXPECTATION
	TIME TO ADJUST LOAD FACTOR EXPECTATION
	TIME TO PERCEIVE LOAD FACTOR CHANGE
	TIME TO PERCEIVE PROFITABILITY
	TIME TO PERCEIVE PROFITABILITY TREND
cost module	*TIME TO ADJUST PROFITABILITY EXPECTATION*

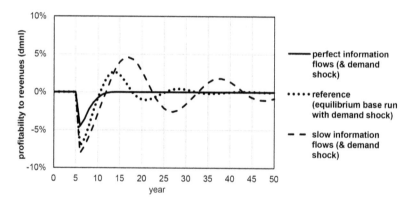

Figure 4.65 Perfect and imperfect information

Results, see Figure 4.65: The airline profit cycle disappears when information flows are perfect. Moreover, the effect of the demand shock is mitigated. In the trough airline have a profitability of -4.5%, which is 2.7 %-points more profitable than in the reference demand shock simulation. Only six years after the shock profitability returns to stability, without any cyclic movement or rebound effect.

Slow information flows aggravate the airline profit cycle. Its amplitude of 12.7 %-points profitability is much higher than the reference's amplitude of 9.8 %-points. The profit cycle's period of 21 years is longer than the reference's 14-year period. Within the simulated 50 years the industry does not return to stability.

In conclusion, simulations confirm supply chain research's finding that improved information flows and accurate forecasts diminish cyclicality. More insights about which forecasts and expectations airlines should strive to perfect in order to best mitigate their profit cyclicality will be examined in section 4.5 on airlines' behaviour.

4.4.7 Technological progress

Innovations are argued to be causing an industry cycle.[70] In the airline industry an innovation could be a new type of aircraft such as the extra large Airbus 380, the invention of hub network structures, or a major regulatory change requiring more aircraft checks. The impact of these factors on airline profitability will be examined in the following experiments.

Scenario 'aircraft availability'

An aircraft is not always available to fly. By law it needs to pass several maintenance tests at regular intervals. Their effect on airlines' profitability will be tested.

Set-up: In the model an aircraft's normal availability for service is expressed as *NORMAL UTILISATION*. In two simulations it is altered by +/- 5 %-points. This corresponds to approximately +/- 20 service days, which is a third of the normal maintenance amount.

Result, see Figure 4.66: The innovation causes a small cycle. It has a period of approximately 14 years and diminishes quickly. Stability at 0% profitability is regained after ca. 15 years. An aircraft availability increase leads to a profitability downturn because it suddenly creates overcapacity in the market. Correspondingly, an availability decrease leads to a profitability peak. The simulated cycle amplitudes are about half as big as the reference demand shock run's profitability amplitude of 9.8 %-points.

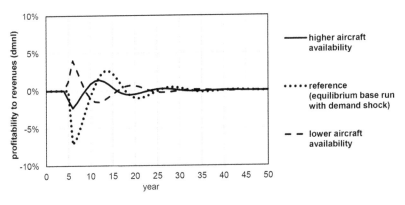

Figure 4.66 Aircraft availability for service (normal utilisation)

Scenario 'innovation increasing aircraft productivity'

The amount of miles an aircraft can fly per year depends for example on its size and on the airlines' network planning skills. Innovations, such as the bigger A380 aircraft or an aircraft with an immensely longer range, strongly change the aircraft's mile production capability. Its effect on airlines' profitability will be assessed in the following simulation.

Set-up: The *TS maximum aircraft productivity* increases by 10%. The transition is completed within five years, from t = 5 to t = 10. As in the previous scenario no demand shock is injected.

Result, see Figure 4.67: An innovation which increases aircraft's maximum productivity causes a profitability cycle. The introduction of the innovation leads to a cycle downturn because the productivity gain generates overcapacity. The simulated 10% maximum productivity increase within five years hits the industry significantly, though not as strongly than a demand shock of -10% real GDP growth during one year (i.e. the usual demand shock). The cycle amplitude is 5.2 %-points and its period is 15 years. The industry regains stability at 0% profitability after 21 years.

Against common belief, an innovation in the airline industry is not necessarily positive for airlines' profitability. The first profitability reaction to an innovation is negative because the innovation increases aircraft productivity which leads to overcapacities in the market.

4.4.8 Summary for airline industry environment factors

In this section the results of experiments with airline industry environment factors will be summarised. Identified airline profit cycle causes, measures that eliminate the cycle, and changes that strongly impact the cycle's shape are listed in Tables 4.3– 4.5.

Several factors in the airline industry environment can cause airline profits to oscillate. Most of them trigger only small or moderate cycles compared to

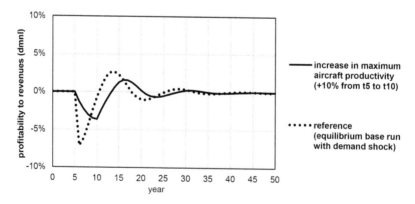

Figure 4.67 Innovation increasing aircraft productivity

the reference simulation (which is usually a demand shock with -10% real GDP growth in one year). These are tax increases, variations in the aircraft manufacturers' lead time, aircraft price changes, and innovations in technology which affect aircraft performance.

Simulated changes in customers' price sensitivity generate profitability cycles which are much larger than the reference cycle. Price sensitivity changes also result in the largest profitability cycle amplitudes among all experiments with airline industry environment factors.

Low barriers to market exit do not cause a profit cycle but intensely enhance cyclicality in terms of amplitude, period, and transition time. High exit barriers such as bankruptcy protection laws or subsidies can eliminate the profit cycle completely.

Easy access to capital shortens the profitability cycle's period and prolongs its transition time but has only a comparatively small impact on amplitude. The profit cycle could be eliminated if access to capital was more difficult for airlines.

Aircraft manufacturers could eliminate the airline profit cycle by limiting their aircraft delivery volume or by adapting production very slowly. In the long run this behaviour would even lead to a higher stable profitability level in the airline industry. However, though this behaviour is beneficial for the airline industry, it is questionable whether it is in the aircraft manufacturers' best interest. In case aircraft manufacturers' lead time (which is the same as airlines' capacity adjustment delay (CAD)) becomes prolonged and airlines permanently fail to anticipate this, profitability in the airline industry reaches a higher level of stable profits.

In a world with perfect information the airline profit cycle would not exist. Imperfect information flows prolong the profit cycle's period, which is a damping feature. However, overall they enhance cyclicality because the transition phase to regain stability is extremely long. If information flows are simulated to be twice as slow as they currently are in the industry, the resulting profitability does not become stable within the simulated 45 years.

Table 4.3 Cycle causes in the airline industry environment

Cycle causes (These changes in the airline industry environment cause a cycle.)	
more cyclic than reference	• price sensitivity of demand higher/lower
less cyclic than reference	• tax increase
	• aircraft price (fixed costs) higher/lower
	• aircraft service lifetime shorter/longer
	• innovation in normal utilisation higher/lower
	• innovation in aircraft productivity
	• capacity acquisition delay shorter/longer expected/unexpected

Table 4.4 Cycle eliminators in the airline industry environment

Cycle eliminators	
(These airline industry environment changes eliminate or extremely dampen cyclicality.)	
without rebound	• perfect information • limited aircraft delivery (without demand shock)
one rebound after the demand shock	• hard access to capital / less aggressive investing • higher barriers to market exit • limited aircraft delivery (and demand shock)

Table 4.5 Cycle shape definers in the airline industry environment

Cycle shape definers
(These factors change the cycle's shape. Only the most influential factors are selected.)

	drivers	dampers
amplitude[1]	• lower price sensitivity of demand (92%, 104%) • lower market exit barriers (56%) • innovation in fleet productivity (46%)	• perfect information (no cycle, -54%)
period[2]	• lower market exit barriers (-21%) • easy access to capital / more aggressive investing (-14%)	• slow information flow (50%) • higher price sensitivity of demand (and business cycle) (40%) • longer capacity acquisition delay (CAD) (14%) • CAD change unexpected (14%)
transition time[3]	• easy access to capital / more aggressive investing (53%) no transition after demand shock: • lower barriers to market exit • slow information flow	• limited aircraft delivery (without demand shock) (no cycle, -79% / -74%) • perfect information (no cycle, -68%)
stability value[4]	negative profitability in steady state: • CAD change unexpected shorter (-1.4%)	positive profitability in steady state: • CAD change unexpected longer (2.6%) • limited aircraft delivery (without demand shock) (no cycle, 1.7% / 2.4%)

1 A *driver*'s amplitude is more than 40% bigger than the reference's, a *damper*'s more than 40% smaller.

2 A *damper*'s period is more than 10% longer than the reference's, a *driver*'s more than 10% shorter.
3 A *driver*'s transition time is more than 40% longer than the reference's, a *damper*'s is > 40% shorter.
4 These factors cause the profitability stability value to deviate from zero.

4.5 Airlines' behaviour as driver of cyclicality

The airlines' own influence on the profit cycle will be examined in a last set of experiments. Literature review and expert interviews in Chapter 2 revealed that while airline managers tend to see the profit cycle's causes outside the industry, researchers mainly see them within (see Figure 4.68). In particular, airlines' fleet management and price setting are suspected to strongly impact the profitability. In structural analysis in section 4.1 fleet management was already found to be the airline profit cycle's origin, and the airlines' price-setting mechanism was assumed to be an amplifier. How much changes in airlines' fleet management and price-setting policies actually impact the industry's profitability remains to be assessed in the following section. Moreover, other potentially cycle-driving or mitigating airline behaviour derived in Chapter 2 will be examined in scenario simulations.

Section 2.5's list of key potential cycle drivers and mitigation measures is repeated in Table 4.6. The first argument that 'management mistakes' causes the profit cycle is omitted from scenario testing because it is not concrete enough to be translated into a simulation set-up.

As in the previous section a demand shock of -10% real GDP growth for one year in year t = 5 will be inserted to start oscillations. The demand shock simulation (see section 4.3.1) will also serve as reference to compare scenarios. In some cases instead of the demand shock a business cycle will be injected (as in the 'business cycle' scenario in section 4.3.1.). The business cycle is loosely based on GDP developments in reality in the United States. The fundamental real GDP growth rate is 3% per year. It is changed by a sine wave with a period of ten years and varies between +1.5% and 4.5% GDP growth per year.

4.5.1 Aircraft capacity planning

How much aircraft capacity airlines desire is a strategic decision with long-term impact on operational and economic performance. The decision is based on forecasts as well as management considerations. Forecasting inaccuracies in the planning process and airlines' high market share targets are said to drive the airline profit cycle.[71] Which impact changes in airlines' desired capacity planning process have on the industry's profitability will be assessed in the following experiments.

Scenario 'forecasts for the business case'

Forecasts about future developments of costs, yields, demand and supply are necessary to calculate the business case which determines airlines' desired aircraft capacity (see section 3.3.3 for details). Forecast inaccuracies in airlines'

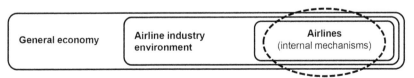

Figure 4.68 Focus on the impact of airlines' behaviour

Table 4.6 Cycle drivers and mitigation measures in the category 'airline behaviour'

Airline behaviour	
cycle driver	• business model experimentation, management mistakes
	capacity adjustment
	• planning (limited forecasting horizon, forecast errors, trend extrapolation, market share targets)
	• aircraft ordering (pro-cyclical investment, long order processing time, misperception of delays)
	• capacity management (inflexible)
	• aircraft retirement (no divestment in unprofitable times due to sunk costs and cutting costs and aircraft value develops with airline industry profits)
	• misperception of delays
	price setting
	• rigid prices
	versus:
	• flexible, quickly adjusting prices (extensive yield management)
	• short-term demand stimulation by price
	cost adjustment
	• restructuring costs
	• slow labour cost adjustment due to contract negotiations
mitigation measure	• avoid management mistakes
	• improve knowledge about cycle
	capacity adjustment:
	• planning (improve risk management by including crisis and cyclicality in plans, buffers for forecast inaccuracy, coordinate forecasting in alliance and prevent protective action)

- slow aircraft capacity adjustment
- reduce processing times
- capacity reduction
- aircraft ordering (slow, steady, profit independent, counter-cyclical, take supply line into account, based on demand forecast not market share target)
- leasing (to avoid high fixed costs and long aircraft service lifetime)
- capacity utilisation (flexible)
- aircraft retirement (responsive, steady, counter-cyclical)

price setting:
- prompt adjustment, more elaborate yield management

versus:
- less elaborate yield management (less extreme price discrimination for more customer satisfaction)
- focus on long-term profit maximisation
- no demand stimulation by price

cost adjustment (cost reduction):
- consolidation (efficiency gains, vertical integration, scale and scope economies)
- restructuring (more efficient, lower cost)
- outsourcing (e.g. catering), code-sharing (spilt route costs)
- network optimisation: more efficient network planning (e.g. hubbing), specialisation on market segments
- prevent productivity decrease after consecutive profitable years
- variable capacity and labour contracts (→ leasing)
- no labour decrease in contractions

planning processes are said to magnify the airline profit cycle.[72] Inaccuracies are for example caused by a limited forecasting horizon. Lyneis argues that a trend extrapolation is an unsuitable forecasting method for the airline industry because it neglects its cyclicality.[73] Sgouridis finds that a long-term trend extrapolation aggravates cyclicality slightly but increases airlines' overall profitability.[74] What impact long-term trend extrapolation forecasting and perfectly accurate forecasts for the business case have on airline profitability will be examined in this scenario.

Set-up: To simulate long-term trend extrapolation in the business case, expectation adjustment times are doubled.[75] In a second simulation they are cut by half to generate a more short-term oriented trend extrapolation forecasting for comparison. In a third simulation expectations are formed almost perfectly accurately, which means they almost equal current conditions. Therefore, expectation adjustment times are set extremely short (= 0.0625 years). Expectation adjustment times are the *TIME TO ADJUST COST EXPECTATION*, the *TIME TO ADJUST YIELD EXPECTATION*, and the *TIME TO ADJUST DEMAND AND SUPPLY EXPECTATION*. The usual demand shock is inserted to start oscillations.

Results, see Figure 4.69: Long-term trend extrapolation in business case forecasts result in a bigger profit cycle. Its amplitude is 11.0 %-points which is 1.2 %-points larger than the demand shock reference. Stability is not reached within the simulated 45 years. The more short-term oriented forecast leads to a cycle amplitude of 9.4 %-points. The difference between the two approaches is clearer in terms of cycle period. Long-term forecasting prolongs the cycle's period to 20 years compared to the reference's 14 years, whereas the short-term forecasting shortens the cycle period to 12 years.

Perfectly accurate business case forecasts eliminate the airline profit cycle. Only four years after the demand shock airlines' profitability reaches its stability level of 0% again. In the 'perfect information' scenario in section 4.4.6 it was found that perfect information eliminates the cycle. This scenario now reveals that not all information flows in the industry need to be perfect to eradicate the profit cycle. Perfect accuracy is only required in forecasts which feed into the business cases in airlines' capacity planning process.

The experiment suggests that it is not helpful, in fact harmful, if airlines rely on past trends. Since trend extrapolation is a popular forecasting technique, this finding needs to be challenged.[76]

The forecasting procedure will be confronted with two more elaborate demand patterns. Since the airline industry is characterised by operational growth, an increasing demand will be tested. Additionally, as the airlines' environment is volatile, a business cycle will be inserted.

Set-up: The expectation adjustment times are varied as before. First, a growing demand pattern is simulated as in the 'constant demand growth' scenario in section 4.3.1. Real GDP increases by 3% per year, which is approximately the US historic average since 1985. Second, as a fluctuating demand pattern the usual business cycle is inserted.

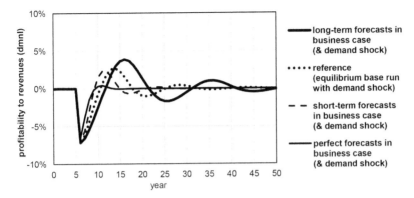

Figure 4.69 Business case adjustment time (single demand shock)

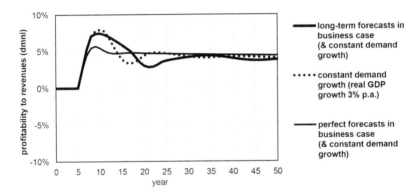

Figure 4.70 Business case adjustment time (constant demand growth)

Results, see Figure 4.70 and Figure 4.71.[77] The constant demand growth simulation confirms the result above that short-term oriented forecasting leads to more stable profitability. Only seven years after the GDP growth rate change, airlines' profitability is stable again whereas the process takes 20 years with long-run trend forecasts.

In contrast, given a volatile demand pattern like the business cycle, airlines' profitability benefits from long-term trend extrapolation. Profitability is overall less cyclic. The cycle's amplitude is 6.9 %-points (and only 2.9 %-points from 2nd minimum to following maximum) compared to 7.5 (4.7) %-points with short expectation formation times.

In conclusion, which forecasting approach results in more stable profitability depends on the nature of developments. The business case requires forecasts for yield, costs, demand, and supply developments. If these change rarely with sudden events followed by long constant phases, airline profitability will be more stable with a short-term oriented forecasting approach. If, on the other

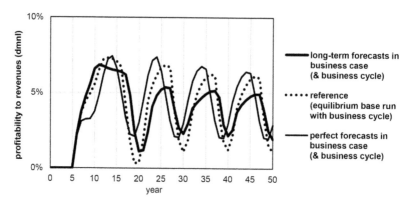

Figure 4.71 Business case adjustment time (business cycle)

hand, changes in business case inputs are volatile, the long-term forecasting approach leads to more stable profits. Since airlines' business environment is generally volatile, the industry benefits from long-term forecasting in the capacity planning process.

Overall, the impact of expectation formation times on the profit cycle is high. In a volatile business environment long-term oriented forecasting dampens the profit cycle, reducing its amplitude by 38%. Furthermore, perfectly accurate forecasts for the business case formulation in the capacity planning process eliminate airlines' profit cyclicality after a demand shock, and dampen it when faced with a business cycle.

Scenario 'delivery forecasts'

The model assumes airlines are well informed about the delivery schedule for ordered aircraft and plan their addition to the fleet correctly. Changes in aircraft manufacturers' delivery schedules are immediately accounted for. However, in reality aircraft may be delivered years later than originally contracted. What impact errors in delivery planning have on the airlines' profit situation, what difference it makes if airlines constantly misjudge the delivery timing, and if planning with a time buffer is beneficial, will be tested in the following experiment.

Set-up: Airlines plan an aircraft acquisition delay of three years (*expected acquisition delay*) instead of the two years manufacturers actually need (*CAPACITY ACQUISITION DELAY*). Airlines could do so because they like to plan with a buffer or because they constantly underestimate the manufacturers' performance. In a second simulation, the situation is reversed. The *expected acquisition delay* is one year while the actual *CAPACITY ACQUISITION DELAY* remains two years long. Manufacturers deliver their aircraft constantly later than airlines expect. Meanwhile, the simulation assumes that airlines do

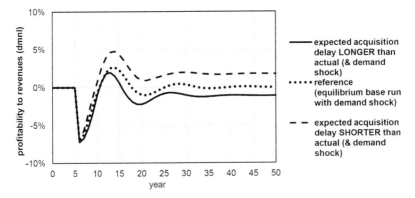

Figure 4.72 Delivery forecasts (expected and actual acquisition delays diverge)

not learn and do not adapt their expectations. The model is given the usual demand shock to start oscillations.

Results, see Figure 4.72: The stable profitability level in both simulations is notably different. Planning with a buffer results in a lower profitability level of −1.1% whereas expecting the delay to be shorter entails a positive stable profitability level of 1.8%. In terms of amplitude and period the profitability cycle does not react much to the different delivery forecast approaches. Planning with longer than actual delays results in a cycle amplitude of 9.2 %-points profitability and a period of 14 years. Stability is reached after 18 years. Expecting the delivery delay shorter than it is leads to an amplitude of 11.8 %-points and a 16-year period. Profits become stable again after only 19 years.

Consequently, airlines' approach to aircraft delivery forecasting largely impacts their long-term profitability. Expecting the time it takes to receive ordered aircraft to be longer than it actually is results in losses. The reason is that when calculating the *desired supply line* the time buffer in the capacity process leads to higher orders. These result in overcapacity in the industry which deteriorates the airlines' cost base and their yields, and hence translates into lower profitability. From an industry perspective it is thus advisable to believe in manufacturers' delivery schedules or even plan with early deliveries to be prepared for the not-yet-desired capacity additions.

Scenario 'market share targets'

Airlines' desire to expand market shares is argued to lead to overcapacities in the industry which result in cyclic profitability.[78] Whether airlines' high market share targets enhance the profit cycle will be tested in the following section.

Set-up: Having higher market share targets influences airlines' capacity investment decision. For each expected profitability level airlines desire some additional capacity to meet their ambitious market share growth targets.

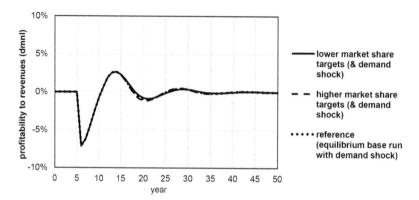

Figure 4.73 Market share targets

An addition of 10% is simulated. So, for example, instead of a 20% capacity increase, airlines with higher market share target desire 22% capacity expansion. In a second simulation, for comparison, a 10% reduction is simulated which means airlines would drastically decrease their market share targets and decide to shrink. The table function *T effect of expected profit on desired capacity* is altered accordingly.[79] The usual demand shock starts oscillations.

Results, see Figure 4.73: Higher or lower market share targets which change the desired capacity adjustment in the range of 10% hardly influence airline profitability. Both simulations have the same amplitude and period than the reference, and need the same 19 years to regain stability. Hence, to produce a notable impact on airlines' profitability, airlines' market share targets in aggregate need to be much higher or lower than simulated.

4.5.2 Aircraft ordering policies

In literature, long aircraft order processing times and pro-cyclical ordering behaviour are stated to be major cycle drivers.[80] To mitigate the profit cycle, counter-cyclic or steady ordering behaviour is advised. The supply line should be taken into account. Processing times should be shortened according to some authors, while others suggest slower ordering mechanisms. The following experiments will clarify how different aircraft ordering behaviour influences airlines' profitability.

Scenario 'profit dependence of aircraft ordering'

Aircraft orders depend on airlines' profitability (see sections 1.2 and 3.3.3). In profitable times orders are placed, whereas in unprofitable times new aircraft orders are reduced to a minimum. This pro-cyclic ordering behaviour is argued to cause capacity to fluctuate between overcapacity and shortage which results in cyclical profits.[81] Individual airlines are suggested to gain an advantage over their competitors by counter-cyclic ordering. The airline profit cycle model does not take an individual airline but instead follows an industry perspective. On an industry level, it does not make sense to assume counter-cyclic ordering. First, because not all airlines would agree to invest heavily in unprofitable times. Second, the collective counter-cyclic action would change the profit cycle itself so that counter-cyclic would become pro-cyclic.

The following experiment will clarify how a profit-**in**dependent order policy influences airline profitability. Some authors argue this steady aircraft ordering would mitigate the airline profit cycle.[82]

Set-up: The *order rate* is constant at its equilibrium value. So no matter what order size (*indicated orders*) airlines calculate, they will not act on it but instead constantly order 13,700 seats/year. Hence, neither profit nor other aspects influence aircraft orders. The usual demand shock is inserted to start oscillations. In a second simulation a usual business cycle is inserted instead.

Results, see Figure 4.74 and Figure 4.75: The steady aircraft ordering policy eliminates oscillations. After the shock, stable profitability is regained

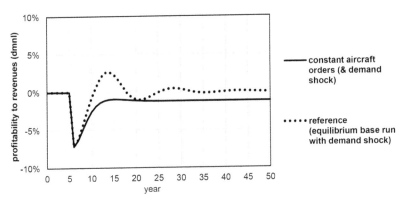

Figure 4.74 Steady aircraft ordering (demand shock)

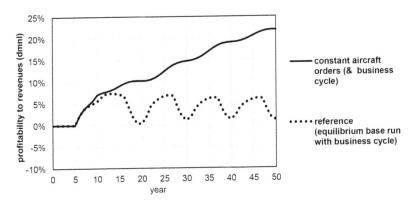

Figure 4.75 Steady aircraft ordering (business cycle)

within seven years. The stability level is −1.2%. This profitability level provokes only slight divestment. Hence, very slowly (more slowly than visible in the graph) capacity is reduced and profitability develops towards 0%. Combined with a business cycle the forcefulness of steady aircraft ordering becomes more evident. Since airlines do not sufficiently react to the rising demand, a capacity shortage emerges. This results in rising yields and hence increasing profits for airlines.

In summary, steady aircraft ordering eliminates the cycle. What profitability level airlines achieve with this policy depends on the development of demand. If less than the steadily ordered aircraft are needed, airlines will become unprofitable; if more is required, they make profits.

Scenario 'speed of aircraft order adjustment'

Not only steady but also slow aircraft ordering is said to dampen the airlines' profit cycle.[83] In contrast, previous airline profit cycle researchers claim that aircraft order processing times need to be faster to mitigate the cycle.[84] However, in section 4.1 fast aircraft order adjustment, i.e. a short *CAPACITY ADJUSTMENT TIME (CAT)*, was already found to be a cycle driver. The following experiment will show how large the impact of *CAT* changes on airline profitability is.

Set-up: In two simulations the *CAT* is first doubled then halved. The usual demand shock is inserted to start oscillations.

Results, see Figure 4.76 and Figure 4.77: A longer order processing time dampens the cycle. The doubled *CAT* almost eliminates it. Rapid decision making, on the other hand, amplifies the profit cycle. Its amplitude is with 12.5 %-points profitability much higher than the 9.8 %-points of the demand shock reference. Also, its period of ten years is much shorter then the reference's 14 years. In the business cycle setting, the amplifying effect of responsive capacity ordering becomes even more evident. Responsive ordering amplifies the airline industry's profitability cycle by +64%, while slow and gradual capacity enlargements almost eliminate cyclicality (amplitude reduced by −59% to the business cycle reference). Moreover, the slow ordering policy leads to a higher average profitability level.

In conclusion, against statements of some previous airline profit cycle researchers, quick and responsive capacity ordering behaviour is not beneficial for airlines' profitability.[85] With slow and gradual capacity enlargement, the airline profit cycle can be intensely mitigated and the average profitability level can be increased.

Scenario 'planning with buffers'

The aircraft ordering process may include buffers.[86] Either time buffers can be implemented or order volumes can be stocked up. Both buffer versions will be tested for their impact on airline profitability.

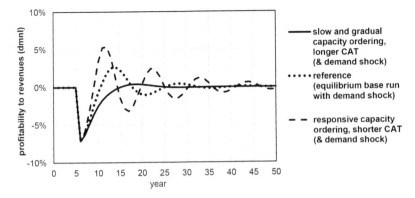

Figure 4.76 Capacity ordering adjustment time (demand shock)

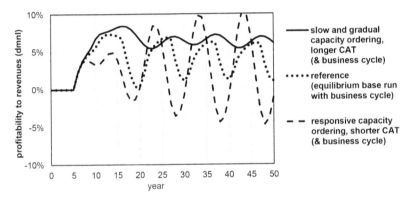

Figure 4.77 Capacity ordering adjustment time (business cycle)

Set-up **'time buffer'**: To be on the safe side airlines plan that the time it takes until they receive their ordered aircraft is longer than it actually is. The *expected acquisition delay* is set to be 50% longer than the actual *CAPACITY ADJUSTMENT DELAY*. First, the usual demand shock is inserted, then the usual business cycle is injected to validate results.

Results, see Figure 4.78 and Figure 4.79: A time buffer amplifies the profit cycle. After the shock when aircraft arrive earlier than planned, they deteriorate rising load factors and thus dampen airlines' profitability increase. Profitability settles at −1.1% and recovers only very slowly in the speed of divestment. Faced with a business cycle, the dynamics a time buffer creates become more apparent. The time buffer leads airlines to believe the supply line was longer so they put more aircraft on order to achieve their desired acquisition rate of x aircraft per year. The extra orders deteriorate load factors. This drives prices down and profitability suffers until the next demand upswing. At that time the

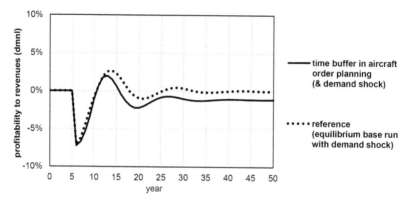

Figure 4.78 Aircraft order planning with time buffer (demand shock)

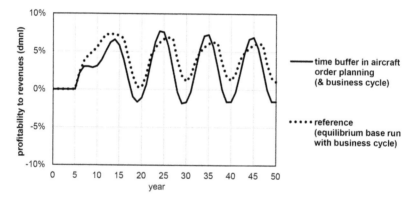

Figure 4.79 Aircraft order planning with time buffer (business cycle)

extra capacity is useful to exploit additional profits. In the following demand downswing the situation reverses, and so on. Hence, a time buffer amplifies profit cyclicality. The amplitude of 9.6 %-points is bigger than the reference's 7.3 %-points.

The finding that a time buffer in order delivery time scheduling results in more pronounced cyclicality is in line with system theory which claims oscillations arise if a delay time in the system is not correctly accounted for.[87] Planning with a buffer is a deliberate choice to incorrectly estimate the delay time.

Set-up **'volume buffer'**: To ensure sufficient capacity supply, airlines decide to order 20% more than they calculated to need. In the model this volume buffer is a multiplier to *indicated orders*. The usual demand shock is inserted to start oscillations. In a second simulation the usual business cycle is applied.

Results, see Figures 4.80 and 4.81: The volume buffer amplifies airline profit cyclicality. The cycle's amplitude is 8.1 %-points compared to the business

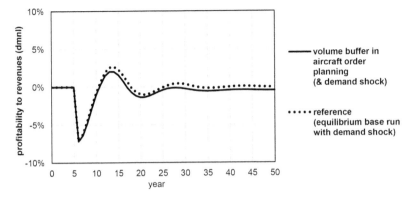

Figure 4.80 Aircraft order planning with volume buffer (demand shock)

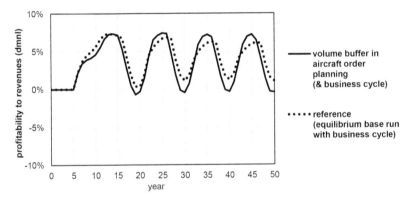

Figure 4.81 Aircraft order planning with volume buffer (business cycle)

cycle reference's 7.3 %-points profitability. The effect and its explanation are the same as for the time buffer examined above.

Hence, not only time buffers but also volume buffers in airlines' aircraft ordering process amplify the airline profit cycle.

Scenario 'weight of supply line in order planning'

The term 'weight of supply line' is used to express to what extent airlines take into account aircraft orders already placed but not yet delivered (= orders in the supply line) in their order planning process. System research claims, if airlines fully account for the supply line in the order determination process (i.e. full weight on the supply line), the profit cycle would be dampened.[88] If the capacity acquisition delay was the only delay in the system, giving full weight on the supply line should eliminate the cycle.

The incomplete weight on the supply line was already identified as a cycle driver in section 4.1.[89] In the following experiment, the size of its impact on airline profitability will be examined.

Set-up: The *WEIGHT ON THE SUPPLY LINE* is set to 100%, which means airlines fully consider all aircraft in the supply line in their order sizing process. In a second simulation the weight is set to 0%, which means airlines ignore all aircraft orders they have placed but not yet received at the time of planning. To ensure no interference with the aircraft leasing sector the leasing option is switched off. All aircraft in the industry are owned. The usual demand shock is inserted to start oscillations. In a second set of simulations the usual business cycle is injected to confirm the effects.

Results, see Figures 4.82 and 4.83: Whether there is full or no weight on the supply line hardly makes a difference for airlines' profitability. Clearly, the cycle does not disappear. In the demand shock scenario the 100% weight translates into an *adjustment for the supply line* which reduces the *desired acquisition*

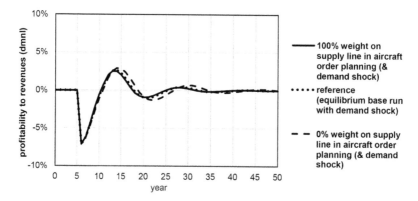

Figure 4.82 Weight on the supply line in aircraft order planning (demand shock)

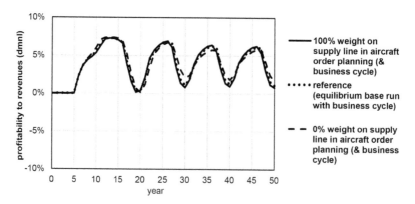

Figure 4.83 Weight on the supply line in aircraft order planning (business cycle)

rate by 27%. However, due to the demand shock the *desired acquisition rate* is very small, so in absolute terms the supply line adjustment is very small. In the business cycle simulations, when demand rises and there is on-going need for additional capacity, full *adjustment for the supply line* is in the first trough still only 6% of the *desired acquisition rate*.

In consequence, the decision to fully or not at all take placed orders into account when ordering new aircraft impacts airlines' profitability only marginally. The amount of aircraft on order is simply too small compared to the existing fleet and cost base to have a significant influence.

4.5.3 Aircraft utilisation strategies

Each season airlines determine their route and schedule planning. In the short run they may have to deviate from their plans. Airlines can cut their supply in case their current operating performance falls severely, as it did for example after the 9/11 terror attack. Likewise, if for example the Olympics increase demand in an area temporarily, more seat miles can be offered. Some airline profit cycle research and aviation experts advise to keep capacity as flexible as possible to mitigate cyclicality.[90] The following experiment will examine the impact of more and less aggressive short-run capacity utilisation adjustments on airlines' profitability.

Scenario 'short-run aircraft utilisation adjustment'

Set-up: The table function *T effect of operating performance gap on utilisation* determines how airlines' current operating performance translates into capacity changes. This will be altered to reflect a 50% more aggressive adjustment behaviour. In a second simulation capacity utilisation adjustment is completely switched off. The usual demand shock starts oscillations.

Results, see Figure 4.84: Without the opportunity to cancel flights, airlines' profitability suffers enormously after a shock. In the subsequent upswing airlines earn very high profits because they benefit from the former shakeout. The profitability cycle amplitude of 29.7 %-points emphasises how much instability the absence of short-run capacity utilisation adjustments inserts in the industry. Within the simulated 50 years the industry does not regain stability. In contrast, the simulation of a 50% more aggressive utilisation adjustment yields almost the same result as the reference run. Only a slight cycle damping effect is visible. This means that the airline industry's current aircraft utilisation policy already exploits this management tool's full potential. The profitability cycle's amplitude is 7.6 %-points, and stability at 0% is retrieved after 18 years. All three simulation have cycle periods of 14 years.

In conclusion, airlines' current practice to adjust their aircraft utilisation to market needs in the short run dampens the airline profit cycle. Without this short-term fleet utilisation adjustment, airline profits would be much more cyclical.

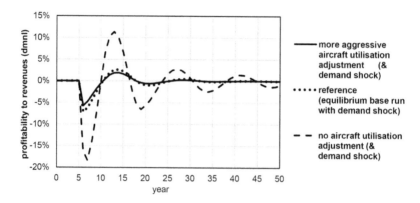

Figure 4.84 Short-run capacity utilisation adjustment

4.5.4 Aircraft retirement practice

Previous research on airline profit cyclicality found that profit-dependent aircraft retirements dampen the cycle.[91] This policy means that in profitable times, when more capacity is needed, older aircraft should stay in service. In unprofitability times when capacity reductions are desired, aircraft retirements should be accelerated. This is a common practice in the airline industry. In the following experiments its impact on the airline profit cycle will be examined. Moreover, the influence of longer or shorter aircraft service lifetimes will be tested.

Scenario 'profit-dependent aircraft retirement'

Set-up: How airlines' profitability expectations translate into aircraft service lifetime changes is captured in the table function *T effect of profit expectation on retirements*. In a first simulation this will be altered so airlines' retirement policy is 50% more aggressive, i.e. more responsive to profitability expectations. For a second simulation the profit-dependence of aircraft retirements will be switched off completely. The usual demand shock will start oscillations.

Results, see Figure 4.85: Adjusting the aircraft service lifetime depending on profitability dampens the cycle. The more aggressive profit-dependent retirement policy improves airlines' financial situation only slightly compared to the reference run, which suggests that airlines already exploit this management tool's potential. The profitability cycle's amplitude is 8.7 %-points. Stability is reached at 0% after 17 years. In contrast, a stable profit-independent retirement policy results in less stable profitability. The cycle's amplitude is 12.3 %-points and stability is regained after 33 years. Both simulations have a cycle period of 15 years.

The overall impact of retirement adjustment policies is moderate. The cycle's amplitude varies by 2.5 %-points compared to the reference run. The stability level can be reached two years earlier with an even more aggressive profit-dependent aircraft retirement policy.

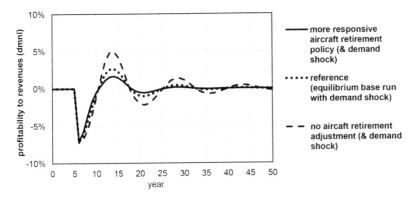

Figure 4.85 Profit-dependent aircraft retirement

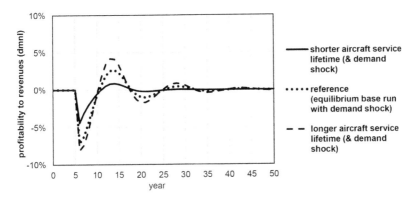

Figure 4.86 Aircraft service lifetime

Scenario 'aircraft service lifetime'

The impact of airlines' strategic decision how long to operate their aircraft will be examined.

Set-up: The *AVERAGE LIFE OF CAPACITY* is calibrated to be 25 years in the model. It will first be prolonged then reduced by 50%. (The usual profit-dependent retirement adjustment policy will stay in place.)

Result, see Figure 4.86: A long aircraft service lifetime aggravates the profit cycle, a short lifetime dampens the cycle significantly. After the shock profitability does not drop as much as in the reference run. The profitability amplitude is 5.3 %-points, which is 4.5 %-points less than the reference run. Stability is regained after 12 years within the first cycle. The longer aircraft service lifetime results in 12.3 %-points profitability and reaches stability after 26 years, the cycle period being 14 years.

The choice of the regular aircraft service lifetime largely impacts airlines' profitability. A short average operating life for aircraft dampens the cycle significantly. This suggests that instead of buying aircraft, a more extensive use of aircraft leasing could mitigate the profit cycle. This will be examined in the next section.

4.5.5 Aircraft leasing

Literature and industry practitioners recommend aircraft leasing.[92] It allows airlines to be more flexible with their capacity adjustment so they can achieve a better match between their supply and demand. To assess the impact of aircraft leasing on airline profit different aspects of aircraft leasing will be examined in the following model experiments. Simulations will be conducted in two settings (implemented from t = 0): In the first setting all aircraft in the industry are leased, in the second all are owned. In each setting the effect of a demand shock or a business cycle on profitability will be compared (inserted in t = 5).

In the model it is assumed that leased and owned aircraft incur roughly the same costs and have no special utilisation requirements (see section 3.3.3). The difference between the leased and the owned part of the fleet is that leased aircraft operate on five-year contracts while owned aircraft usually stay in service for 25 years (see section 3.3.3 for lease contract and aircraft retirement assumptions).

Scenario 'aircraft leasing as alternative to buying'

Set-up: In the first simulation all aircraft are leased. In a second simulation all aircraft are owned. The usual demand shock is inserted. To confirm results, simulations are repeated with the usual business cycle instead of the demand shock as disturbance.

Results, see Figure 4.87 and Figure 4.88: When the airline industry experiences a demand shock it hardly makes a difference in profitability whether the fleet is leased or owned. The profitability cycle amplitude is 9.7 %-points for the all-leased fleet and 9.8 %-points for an all-owned fleet. Cycle periods are 15 years (all leased) and 14 years (all owned). In both cases stable profitability is regained after 19 years.

Given a business cycle, it hardly matters for profitability whether the fleet is leased or owned. Yet, there is a slight difference in the profitability cycle's long-term amplitude. From the 2nd trough to the subsequent peak the all-leased simulation's amplitude is 5.3 %-points, the all-owned simulation's is 6.7 %-points. The long-run profitability average in the all-leased simulation is 0.3 %-points higher if all aircraft are owned.

In summary, by leasing instead of buying their fleet, airlines can ameliorate their profitability situation slightly. Overall, the profitability impact of the decision to lease or buy is small. A reason may be that the usual lease contract period of five years is too long to achieve the necessary degree of flexibility. This will be examined in the next scenario.

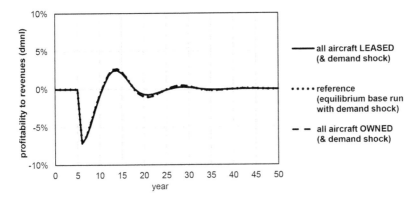

Figure 4.87 Aircraft leasing as alternative to buying (demand shock)

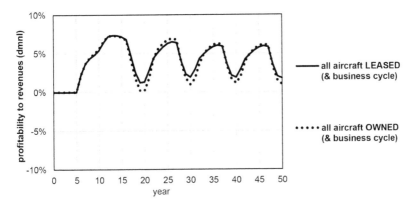

Figure 4.88 Aircraft leasing as alternative to buying (business cycle)

Scenario 'aircraft lease period'

The usual contract period of aircraft leases in the airline industry is five years.[93] In this scenario the effect of longer or shorter lease periods on airlines' profitability will be examined. Some researchers explicitly suggest to employ very short-term leases.[94]

Set-up: All aircraft are leased. First, a very short lease period of one year is simulated, then a longer ten-year contract. The results of both simulations are compared to the previously simulated effects of five-year contracts. The usual demand shock is inserted. The simulations are repeated with the usual business cycle instead of the demand shock.

Results, see Figure 4.89: There is hardly a difference between a 5-year contract and a 10-years contract. The 10-year contract results in a slightly more pronounced cyclicality, its amplitude being 0.4 %-points bigger.

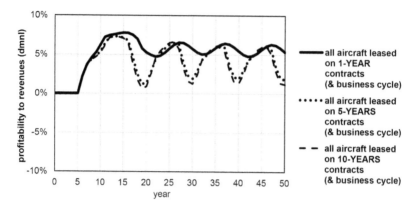

Figure 4.89 Aircraft lease period (part 1/2)

In a business cycle environment one-year lease contracts dampen the airline industry's cyclicality strongly. Its long-term cycle amplitude (from 2nd trough to subsequent peak) is 1.8 %-points which is very small compared to usual five-year contract's amplitude of 5.3 %-points. Moreover, the one-year contract's average profitability level of 5.6% is higher than the usual five-year contract's 4.2% average.

If a demand shock is simulated, having an all leased fleet with one-year contracts eliminates cyclicality. There is only a small rebound peak after the shock before profitability becomes stable again.

In conclusion, very short-term leasing is extremely positive for airline profitability. It can eliminate the profit cycle and significantly dampen the effects of external fluctuations such as a business cycle while achieving a higher level of profitability.

Next, it will be assessed if contract durations longer than one year can achieve similarly good cycle damping while maintaining high profitability.

Set-up: Using the set-up above, two additional contract length, a two-year and a three-year contract period, are simulated.

Result, see Figure 4.90 (for better visibility the graph displays only t = 25 to t = 50): The shorter the lease contract period, the more stable the industry's profitability. The difference in long-term profitability amplitude (2nd trough to subsequent peak) between a five-year and a three-year contract as well as between a three-year and a two-year contract is each only 0.9 %-points. Meanwhile, the difference between a two-year and a one-year contract is 1.7 %-points.

Consequently, very short-term capacity leasing contracts with a duration of less than two years can significantly dampen the cycle. However, aircraft lease contract periods of less than two years are not customary in the aviation industry.[95]

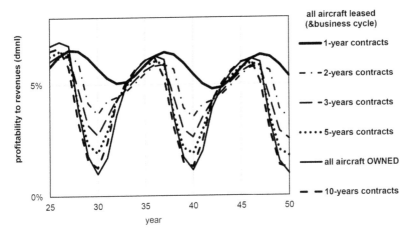

Figure 4.90 Aircraft lease period (part 2/2)

If leasing contracts had a duration of more than two years, the resulting profitability would still be than if the fleet was owned. In the case that leasing contracts were longer than ten years, the average profitability would not be better than if all aircraft were owned.

It should be noted that in the simulated scenarios aircraft unit costs are not varied with lease contract length. In reality, very short-term lease contracts are probably more expensive than longer ones because lessors will require a premium to compensate for their higher risks and flexibility. Thus, in the next experiment short-run leases will be more expensive.

Set-up: As above, an all-leased fleet operating on one-year contracts is simulated. In addition, it is assumed that lessors make one-year leases 100% more expensive than the usual five-year contracts. It is further assumed that it takes 25 years (one aircraft service lifetime) to transform the whole fleet into one-year leases. In the model, the *MINIMUM FIXED REAL UNIT COST* is doubled over a ramp up time of 25 years between t = 5 and t = 30.

Results, see Figure 4.91: Compared to the usual five-year lease contracts one-year leases still dampen the airline profit cycle if a risk premium is included. However, during the 25 years long fleet transformation phase the airline industry's profitability is lower because airlines need to cope with the increasing cost base. When the transformation is completed, airline's profitability remains on a high level of more than 5% average profitability. Though faced with a business cycle, profitability only cycles with an amplitude of only 2.0 %-points, which is low compared to the five-year leases' amplitude of 5.3 %-points.

In conclusion, one-year leases are a means to dampen the airline industry's profit cyclicality. Airlines' profitability will suffer during the fleet transformation phase but stabilise at a high level afterwards.

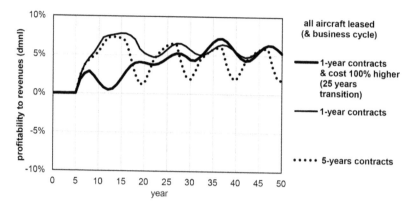

Figure 4.91 Very short-term aircraft lease contracts and their additional costs

Scenario 'utilisation restriction for leased aircraft'

Aircraft lease contracts may include restrictions such as minimum or maximum usage. The impact these restrictions have on airline profitability will be examined in this scenario.

Set-up **'minimum usage'**: The all-leased setting will be used. Aircraft have a mandatory utilisation minimum. It is calculated as percentage of the *NORMAL UTILISATION* which assumes aircraft are available for service on approximately 300 days per year. In the first simulation a 94% minimum is tested, which means aircraft utilisation could be reduced up to 20 days to 280 days if airlines saw short-term need for capacity utilisation adjustment. In a second simulation a stricter limit of 97%, which corresponds to ten days tolerance, is simulated.

Results, see Figure 4.92: A 20-day tolerance in aircraft utilisation reduction yields approximately the same profitability pattern as the reference's unrestricted utilisation. The stricter ten-day tolerance exhibits a much deeper trough, resulting in an amplitude of 17.0 %-points compared to the unrestricted simulation's 9.7 %-points. Consequently, the ten-day tolerance is not sufficient to react to the severe demand shock. In case external circumstances require to reduce utilisation, such a minimum utilisation requirement results in severe profitability problems for the airline industry.

Set-up **'maximum utilisation'**: The set-up above is altered to test a maximum restriction instead of the minimum usage requirement. For the first simulation the maximum utilisation allowed equals the planned one (100% of *NORMAL UTILISATION*). In the second simulation ten days of maintenance can be postponed (103% of *NORMAL UTILISATION*).

Results, see Figure 4.93: Profitability benefits if airlines are not allowed to make extra use of their capacity in the upswing phase after the demand shock. The reason is that the restriction allows airlines to raise prices which results in

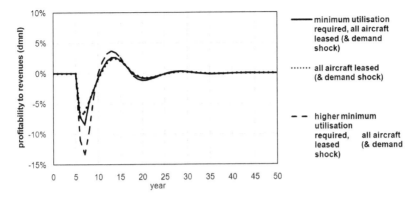

Figure 4.92 Minimum utilisation restriction for leased aircraft

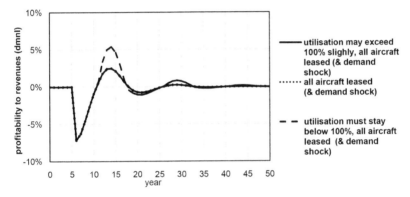

Figure 4.93 Maximum utilisation restriction for leased aircraft

better profitability than if they had been able to serve the additional demand with extra capacity. The cycle amplitude reaches 12.6 %-points compared to the unrestricted utilisation's 9.7 %-points. If airlines have a ten-day tolerance to increase their aircraft utilisation, there is no difference to the unrestricted case, which means that the limit is not touched.

In conclusion, a minimum utilisation requirement for leased aircraft deteriorates profitability further in downcycles. A maximum utilisation restriction enhances profitability in upcycles. Hence, to achieve a more stable and higher profitability, the usage of leased aircraft should ideally be free to reduce but usage increases should be limited.

4.5.6 Price-setting mechanism

As an introduction to experiments with alternative price-setting policies, it is briefly summarised how airlines' complex price-defining mechanisms are represented in the airline industry model. Details can be found in section 3.3.2. The price-setting process consists of two phases: the 'pricing' in which airlines decide which service to offer at what fare, and the seat allocation in which elaborate mathematical systems, i.e. revenue management systems, allocate seats to each fare.

- In the pricing process, when setting fares, airlines' starting point is their expectation of the market clearing price which they gather from past experiences. Additionally, three factors influence the pricing process. First, airlines are guided by their cost base, at least to a certain degree. At the extreme, airlines could base prices fully on their costs and ignore their past price experiences. Second, medium to long-term expectations about the developments of demand and supply are considered in the process. Third, there is a profit pressure on price. Whenever profitability falls below the airlines' target there is a pressure to restore margins, i.e. to raise prices. To what extent each of these three influences impacts the actual price is in the model expressed by the sensitivity of price to each influence.
- Once the fares are set, airlines need to allocate an amount of seats to each fare with the aim to maximise overall revenue and hence profit. This is done by revenue management systems. Their work is very short-term oriented. Within minutes they adjust price offers for each flight and place them in the market.

Whether price setting should be short-term oriented is still an open debate in the literature, among industry practitioners, and in previous airline profit cycle research (see Chapter 2). The speed of price adjustments has increased significantly with the application of revenue management systems. Some argue that the extensive use of revenue management allows airlines to maximise profits.[96] Pierson and Sterman find in their airline industry model that full concentration on revenue management stabilises the airline profit cycle significantly.[97] On the contrary, Sgouridis derives with his model that short-term demand stimulation by price increases instability because it creates the illusion of overcapacities.[98] Industry practitioners add that revenue management's price discrimination deteriorates customer satisfaction.[99] They call for a more long-term approach to profit maximisation. Some even suggest regulation to slow price changes down.[100] The issues whether a short-term or long-term focus in price setting is more favourable for the airline industry's profitability will be examined in subsequent experiments.

The cycle origin identification analysis in section 4.1 has revealed that airlines' current price-setting mechanism, which relies heavily on revenue management, is potentially a strong cycle amplifier. Its actual impact on airline profits will be tested in the following scenarios.

In addition, the impact of cost or profit pressure on price as well as the influence of the increasingly important ancillary revenues on the airline profit cycle will be examined.

Scenario 'only revenue management'

To assess the impact of revenue management on airline profitability the following tests are conducted.

Set-up: Airlines' price setting is entirely determined by revenue management. All other influences on price are ignored, meaning that pricing departments do not give any new impulse. In the model the *effect of pricing on yield* is set constant at its neutral value 1. In a second simulation in addition the aggressiveness in revenue management is increased by inserting a higher value for the *SENSITIVITY OF YIELD TO REVENUE MANAGEMENT*. The usual demand shock starts oscillations.

Results, see Figure 4.94: There is hardly a difference in simulated profitabilities. The airlines' usual price-setting policy, the simulated 'only revenue management' policy, and the even more aggressive 'only revenue management' rule, all have approximately the same outcome. The reason is that airlines compensate mistakes in price setting by fleet utilisation adjustments.

To assess the impact of different price policies, it is necessary to switch off the option to adjust aircraft capacity in the short run in the following price experiments.

Revised set-up: Simulations above are repeated while airlines' short-run capacity utilisation adjustment is prohibited. So the impact of price decisions is not perturbed. The 'no utilisation adjustment' simulation serves as a reference (see section 4.5.3).

Results, see Figure 4.95: Compared to the 'no utilisation adjustment' reference (dashed line) a full concentration on revenue management makes airline profitability much worse. The effort to stimulate demand after the shock by lowering prices results in a record profitability low of −24.8%, even worse (−26.2%) when revenue management is executed more aggressively. The reference case exhibits a trough at −18.4%. The amplitude of an 'only revenue management' policy is with 32.8 %-points, and 35.5 %-points in the more

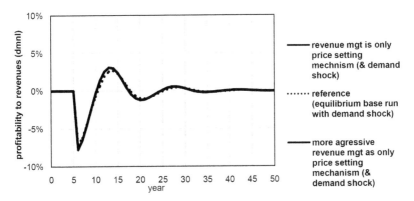

Figure 4.94 Only revenue management with compensation by utilisation adjustment

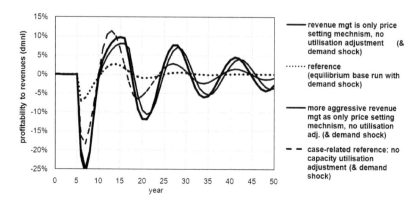

Figure 4.95 Only revenue management

aggressive version, very large, even compared to the reference's 29.7 %-points. All simulations have a cycle period of approximately 14 years.

In conclusion, by focusing only on revenue management in the price-setting process airlines intensely increase their profit cyclicality. Simulations in a business cycle environment underline this finding.

Scenario 'no (little) revenue management'

In this scenario the profitability impact of an abolishment of revenue management will be assessed. Additionally, the consequence of making only little use of revenue management systems will be simulated.

Set-up: In a first simulation airlines abstain completely from revenue management. Price setting is only subject to the influence of pricing (explained in section 3.3.2). In the second simulation pricing and revenue management are both working but revenue management is not used much. The *SENSITIVITY OF YIELD TO REVENUE MANAGEMENT* is reduced. As in the previous scenario the usual demand shock is inserted and aircraft utilisation adjustment is prevented.

Results, see Figure 4.96: A price-setting policy without revenue management almost eliminates the profit cycle. After the demand shock there is only a small rebound peak of 0.8% before profitability returns to stability at 0%. Correspondingly, a less aggressive revenue management usage mitigates the situation compared to the 'no utilisation adjustment' reference. The amplitude is only about half as large, with 16.9 %-points compared to 29.7 %-points. The period of 16 years is two years longer.

When revenue management has no influence in airlines' price-setting processes, there is hardly a cycle in profitability anymore. When only little revenue management is employed, profitability is much more stable than in the reference case.

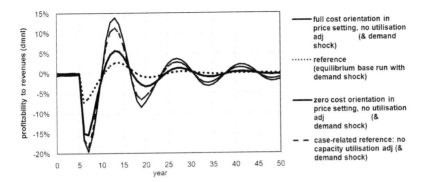

Figure 4.99 Cost orientation in pricing

with market clearing prices (see section 3.3.2 for more details). In the airline industry cost orientation is low and airlines rely on past experiences instead. In this scenario the impact of zero and full cost orientation on airline profitability will be explored.

Set-up: The *SENSITIVITY OF PRICE TO COSTS* is first simulated to be 0 (none) then simulated to equal 1 (full). The usual demand shock is inserted and aircraft utilisation adjustment is switched off.

Results, see Figure 4.99: More cost orientation mitigates the profit cycle. Full orientation on costs results in a cycle amplitude of 21.0 %-points, compared to 29.7 %-points in the 'no utilisation adjustment' reference.

Cost-oriented price-setting compensates for some of the amplification produced by revenue management. Cost adjustments take significantly more time than revenue management systems need for price alterations. So if prices are anchored closely to total unit costs, they cannot change as fast. In consequence, the profit cycle is successfully dampened.

Comparison of 'profit pressure' and 'cost orientation' in pricing

Compared to the stronger profit pressure in the scenario before last the cost orientation policy is not as successful to counteract losses after the demand shock. However, in a business cycle setting the cost orientation policy dampens cyclicality much more than the profit pressure policy (see Figure 4.100).[102] Since cost adjustments are slow compared to the price adjustments, the increased cost orientation almost eliminates cyclicality in the volatile business cycle environment. Yet, the average profitability level is lower than when the profit pressure policy is applied. The enhanced focus to achieve profitability targets does not limit the cycle peaks and is thus able to reach a higher profitability

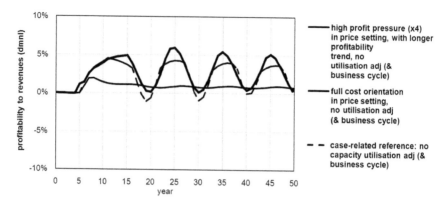

Figure 4.100 Cost orientation vs. profit pressure in pricing

average. How volatile profitability remains depends primarily on the observation period which the profitability trend is based on, i.e. *TIME TO PERCEIVE PROFITABILITY TREND.*[103]

Scenario 'long-term market developments in pricing'

Expectations about future demand and supply developments influence the pricing process. Airlines form their expectations based on many years of experience with demand development and competitors' supply strategies. For each origin–destination market they assess their potential demand, its price elasticity and willingness to pay. It will be tested what impact these more long-term market considerations in the pricing process have on airline profitability.

Set-up: The *SENSITIVITY OF PRICE TO DEMAND SUPPLY BALANCE* is emphasised (quadrupled). In a second simulation long-term market considerations are eliminated from the pricing process. The usual demand shock is inserted and aircraft utilisation adjustment is switched off. The simulation is repeated in the business cycle setting used above.

Results, see Figure 4.101 and Figure 4.102: Long-term market considerations in the pricing process hardly impact airline profitability. After a demand shock there is only 1%–point difference in the cycle amplitudes of the 'no utilisation adjustment' reference, the simulation with eliminated market trend orientation, and the simulation with quadrupled influence of long-term market developments. In a business cycle setting the increased impact of long-term market trend amplifies the cycle. Yet, compared to a price-setting mechanism which emphasises short-term market developments, i.e. revenue management, the amplification is small. This confirms previous results of the model structure analysis in section 4.1.3.

In summary, compared to other pricing elements the impact of long-term market developments in pricing, though four times as strong as usually in the industry, is small.

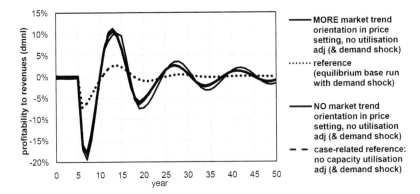

Figure 4.101 Emphasis on long-term market developments in pricing

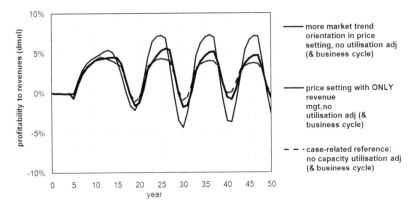

Figure 4.102 More long-term market trend orientation in business cycle setting

Scenario 'increasing ancillary yield'

Ancillary sales allow airlines to generate additional revenue with every pas-senger (see section 3.3.2). How an increase in non-ticket yields impacts airline profitability in the long run will be tested in the following scenario.

Set-up: Non-ticket yield rises in a linear fashion to one third of the original ticket yield. The usual demand shock is inserted.

Results, see Figure 4.103: Whether or not airlines make ancillary sales, hardly changes their profitability. The cycle amplitude is 0.1 %-point smaller than in the demand shock reference simulation. In both cases stability is regained after 19 years. However, the ancillary yield results in a stable profit-ability level of 0.2%.

In summary, when non-ticket yields rise to one third of the original ticket price, airlines' long-run profitability gains only 0.2 %-points. The effect is so

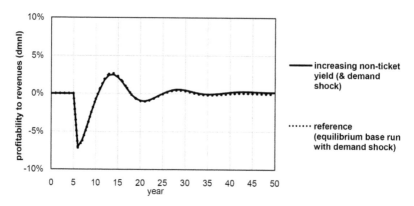

Figure 4.103 Increasing ancillary yields

small because as ancillary yield increases, ticket yield decreases. The reason is that once airlines start making additional revenues through ancillary activities, they are willing to reduce ticket yields in order to make more sales. The revenue management mechanism, which is mainly responsible for this behaviour, thus reduces the positive effect which ancillary revenues could have.

Conclusion for airlines' price-setting policies

Model experiments in this section contribute to the debate about whether a short-term oriented price-setting approach is beneficial. Simulations revealed that the extensive use of revenue management as a short-term price policy strongly amplifies the airline profit cycle. Without revenue management there would not be a profit cycle after a demand shock. Less revenue management usage could dampen the cycle significantly. These findings confirm previous airline profit cycle research by Sgouridis, and contradict conclusions by Pierson and Sterman.[104]

Airlines will probably not refrain from using revenue management systems because doing so may entail loosing market shares to competitors. Two measures are found to compensate for revenue management's negative effects. First, compensation is achieved when airlines give profitability targets more weight in the price-setting process and emphasise achieving target margins. This will push yields upwards. Second, a more cost-oriented price-setting approach can mitigate the profit cycle even more strongly, with the disadvantage of a lower average profitability.

On industry level these solutions, i.e. less revenue management, more profit pressure in pricing, and more cost orientation in pricing, are found to mitigate airlines' profitability problems effectively. However, this does not imply that an individual airline that choses to test these policies in its usual business environment is comparatively successful.[105] Large airline organisations' or regulators' action would be required to achieve the above simulated results.

To increase their long-run profitability airlines can introduce ancillary yields. However, the current use of revenue management will offset the vast majority of their efforts.

4.5.7 Cost adjustment

The slow adjustment of costs, especially fixed costs, is named as a reason for the airline profit cycle.[106] For example airlines' contract negotiations to alter labour costs can be difficult and lengthy. To mitigate the profit cycle, managers emphasise the importance of cost reductions via consolidation, restructuring, variable contracts, and outsourcing.[107] The impact of those measures and the importance of the speed of actions for airlines' profitability will be examined in the following scenarios. (Find experiments with variable cost adjustments in section 4.5.3 'Aircraft utilisation strategies'.)

Scenario 'cost adjustment speed'

This scenario will assess what difference it makes if cost adjustments are achieved quickly or rather slowly.

Set-up: To simulate different speeds of cost adjustment the *FIXED UNIT COST ADJUSTMENT TIME* is first doubled than halved. For a more realistic setting the usual business cycle is inserted.

Results, see Figure 4.104: Fast cost adjustment mitigates airlines' profit cyclicality, slow cost adjustment magnifies it. When airlines manage to adjust their fixed costs more quickly the resulting profit cycle has an amplitude of 6.3 %-points, which is 1 %-point less than the business cycle reference's 7.3 %-points. Slower cost adjustment lead to a profit cycle with 8.5 %-points amplitude.

Overall, the impact of the cost adjustment speed is moderate. If airlines managed to accelerate labour contract negotiations and additionally achieved contract durations that are only half as long (so fixed costs are better adjustable), airlines would only gain 1%-point profitability.

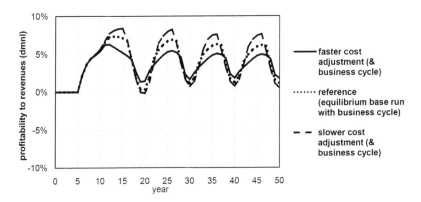

Figure 4.104 Cost adjustment speed

Scenario 'costs flexibility'

Managers often aim to gain a more flexible cost base.[108] Airlines' attempts to achieve this include for example aircraft 'wet leases',[109] which means to lease an aircraft and its corresponding crew on a very short-term basis. Ideally, all costs would be variable and could be adjusted with the level of output. On the other extreme, in the worst case, fixed cost adjustment would be entirely impossible. Both cases will be examined for their impact on airline profitability in the following scenario.

Set-up: In the first simulation all fixed costs are turned variable. The *FIXED UNIT COST ADJUSTMENT TIME* is set as short as the aircraft utilisation adjustment (= 0.125 years). In the second simulation fixed costs cannot be adjusted. The *FIXED UNIT COST ADJUSTMENT TIME* is set extremely long. The usual business cycle is inserted.

Results, see Figure 4.105: Having a fully flexible cost base dampens the profit cycle significantly. If fixed cost adjustment is entirely impossible, the cycle is magnified. Fully flexible costs result in a cycle with 4.5 %-points amplitude which is 38% lower then the business cycle reference's amplitude. Unchangeable fixed costs lead to a cycle with 10.1 %-points profitability amplitude, which is larger than the reference's 7.3 %-points. Both the unchangeable fixed costs simulation and the reference exhibit a cycle period of ten years. With fully flexible costs the cycle period is at first only seven years and then transitions to the ten-year period when the 'shock' of the sudden injection of a business cycle is processed in the industry.

The results confirm the previous scenario's finding that a more flexible cost base with shorter adjustment time mitigates the airline industry's profitability cycle. The potential impact of flexibilisation measures seems high. However, it is unrealistic to assume all costs could be made variable, especially without paying extra for full flexibility of fleet, crew, buildings, etc. So realistically, as in the previous scenario, airline management only has moderate potential to dampen profit cyclicality by flexibilising fixed costs.

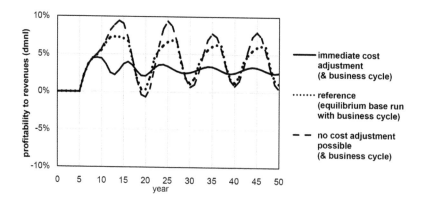

Figure 4.105 Cost flexibility

Scenario 'aggressiveness of cost adjustment'

How airlines seek to adjust their cost base depends on their profitability (see section 3.3.4). In profitable times labour unions may pressure airlines for higher wages and aircraft are more expensive. When airlines make losses, the pressure to reduce costs is high. For airline managers, cost reductions are a prime objective to mitigate the profit cycle (see section 2.4). This scenario will assess what impact it has on profitability if cost pressures, upwards and downwards, were more aggressive.

Set-up: In the model the relationship between airlines' expected profitability and the resulting fixed cost adjustment is captured in the table function *T effect of expected profitability on overheads*. In a first simulation this is set so adjustments are twice as aggressive, in a second simulation they are half as aggressive. The usual business cycle is inserted.

Results, see Figure 4.106: More aggressive cost adjustment mitigates the profit cycle. The cycle's amplitude is 6.3 %-points which is 1 %-point less than the reference's. Less aggressive cost adjustment results in a 1.1 %-points higher amplitude than the reference.

In conclusion, whether airlines are more or less aggressive in their fixed cost adjustment has only moderate impact on profitability. More aggressive behaviour mitigates the cycle because although in upcycle periods this policy allows more cost increases, the cost reductions airlines achieve in downturns predominate.

Scenario 'trade-off between speed and aggressiveness'

Previous scenarios revealed that airlines' profitability becomes more stable with fast and aggressive cost adjustments. In reality, airlines may have to choose whether they want their cost adjustments to be quick or large. For example in labour negotiations airlines may either take time to hold the pressure up and achieve a major cost reduction. Or airlines may want to end negotiations

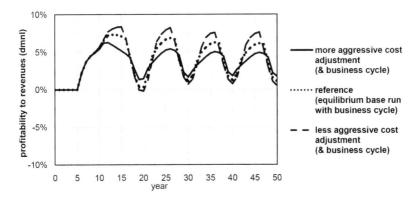

Figure 4.106 Aggressiveness of cost adjustment

quickly and compromise on a mild cost reduction. This scenario will examine the trade-off between speed and aggressiveness in cost adjustments.

Set-up: The usual business cycle is inserted. As in the previous scenario the table function *T effect of expected profitability on overheads* is set to make airlines' cost reductions twice as aggressive for any expected profitability level. Now, numerous simulations are conducted to find the speed, i.e. the *FIXED UNIT COST ADJUSTMENT TIME*, which offsets the more aggressive cost adjustment policy and produces a profitability close to the business cycle reference.

Result: The *FIXED UNIT COST ADJUSTMENT TIME* can be twice as long. This means airlines improve their profitability if they manage to achieve their twice more aggressive goals in less then twice the usual cost adjustment time. For example, assumed that airlines usually aim to reduce costs by 2% over the duration of one year, and they now aim for a 4% reduction. If they manage to complete the process in less than two years, their profitability will be more stable than before. Likewise, if airlines allow twice as much time for their cost adjustment, they need to be more than twice as aggressive to achieve the a better (less cyclic) profitability than before.

Given the non-linear nature of relationships in the airline industry, the result stated above cannot be applied to all constellations. It needs to be understood as a rule of thumb.

4.5.8 Summary for airline behaviour influence

In this section the results of model experiments with alternative airline behaviour will be summarised. Identified profit cycle causes, cycle eliminating policies, and airline decisions which significantly impact the profit cycle's shape are listed in Table 4.7–4.9.

Airlines' behaviour can cause a profit cycle. Airline decisions which cause cyclic profitability are to change the aircraft retirement age, to increase ancillary yields, as well as to choose an unsuitable aircraft delivery forecasting approach. However, these policies cause only mild profit cycles which are less pronounced than the reference (usually a demand shock with −10% real GDP for the duration of one year).

Airlines can theoretically eliminate their profit cyclicality. Yet, the policies necessary to achieve a completely stable profitability may not be feasible in reality. Nonetheless, airlines can take steps to mitigate their profitability cycle immensely.

The extensive use of revenue management is found to be a major cycle amplifier. If airlines refrained entirely from revenue management as a technique for short-term demand stimulation by price, they would eliminate the profit cycle after a demand shock. By making less use of revenue management airlines could dampen the cycle in terms of amplitude, period, and transition time. Since it may be unrealistic to assume that airlines completely redesign their revenue management practice, it was explored whether other price-setting aspects could be strengthened to compensate for revenue management's negative effects. Such a compensatory effect can be achieved, first, if airlines set their prices with closer orientation to costs and, second, if they stress the attainment of profitability targets and corresponding margins, especially in unprofitable times.

The profit cycle would be greatly mitigated if airlines could operate on a very flexible cost base. For example having a fleet which consists only of short-term leased aircraft with a lease duration of one year would eliminate the profit cycle after a demand shock, provided that no minimum usage requirements restrict the airlines' flexibility. If airlines managed to achieve quicker or more vigorous cost adjustments, their profit cyclicality would be dampened.

Constant or more gradual aircraft ordering can also eliminate the profit cycle after a demand shock. While the requirement that airlines keep order-ing a constant amount of aircraft regardless of any circumstances is certainly extreme, a routine with more gradual capacity enlargement appears more real-istic. The airline profit cycle will be magnified if airlines choose a responsive aircraft ordering policy.

In contrast, while responsive fleet enlargements magnify the profit cycle, responsive fleet utilisation adjustments dampen it. Experiments show that if air-craft utilisation adjustments after a demand shock were completely prevented for some reason, the profit cycle's amplitude would double compared to the reference and the industry would not manage to return to stability within the simulated 50 years.

Which forecasting approach airlines choose to inform their capacity planning business case determines the profit cycle's shape. In a steady envi-ronment with only singular anomalies (such as the demand shock) a more short-term trend extrapolation results in a small profit cycle. In contrast, in a volatile environment (with a business cycle in the economy) the short-term forecasting approach magnifies the cycle and a more long-term trend extrapolation mitigates it. Since the airline industry's environment is volatile, forecasting by long-term trend extrapolation is advised for the capacity plan-ning business cases.

With regard to aircraft delivery forecasts, airlines can mitigate their profit cycle by believing in manufacturers' delivery schedules or even preparing for early deliveries. The reason is that aircraft which arrive earlier than expected lead to overcapacity and thus magnify the profit cycle.

Aircraft retirement policies influence the profit cycle's shape. Choosing a shorter aircraft service lifetime makes airlines' capacity more flexible and thus dampens the profit cycle. The chosen retirement age should depend on long-term profitability expectations. If, in contrast, aircraft were retired at a fixed age, cyclicality would be magnified due to the entailed lack of flexibility in capacity adjustment.

With their behavioural choices airlines can determine their long-run profit-ability level. To augment it, airlines can introduce ancillary yields. However, extensive use of revenue management will offset much of their efforts. Policies which facilitate overcapacities in the market have even worse effects on the airlines' long-run profitability level. Implementing buffers in aircraft delivery planning or accidentally estimating the manufacturing delay too long deteriorates long-term profitability. In contrast, policies which imply a capacity enlargement constraint proof effective to increase airlines' long-run profitability level. If airlines expect new aircraft to be delivered earlier than they actually are, it enhances their future profitability level. Similarly, if they choose to constantly order a fixed small amount of aircraft, or enlarge their capacity only slowly and gradually, their long-run profitability augments. Policies which increase airlines' flexibility to adjust their existing cost base, for example short-term aircraft leases, can also improve the industry's future profitability level.

Table 4.7 Cycle causes in airlines' behaviour

Cycle causes
(These changes in airlines' behaviour cause a cycle.)

more cyclic than reference	/
less cyclic than reference	• aircraft retirement age older/younger
	• price setting: ancillary yield increase
	• capacity planning: inaccurate aircraft delivery forecasts: expected acquisition delay shorter/longer than actual
	hardly cyclic (max. amplitude < 2 %-point)
	• price setting: more profit pressure on price (and no aircraft utilisation adjustment)
	• price setting: full/no cost orientation in pricing (and no aircraft utilisation adjustment)
	• price setting: more long-term market developments in pricing (and no aircraft utilisation adjustment)
	• aircraft ordering: planning with time buffer: expected acquisition delay estimated 50% longer than actual CAD
	• aircraft ordering: planning with volume buffer

Table 4.8 Cycle eliminators in airlines' behaviour

Cycle eliminators
(These airline behaviour changes eliminate or extremely dampen cyclicality.)

without rebound	• aircraft ordering: steady aircraft ordering (constant, profit-independent ordering)
one rebound after the demand shock	• price setting: no revenue management (and no aircraft utilisation adjustment)
	• cost adjustment: full cost flexibility (incl. fixed costs)
	• aircraft leasing: short-term aircraft leasing (one-year contract)
	• aircraft ordering: long aircraft order adjustment time
	• perfect forecast for business case (elimination only in stable environment with singular anomalies such as the demand shock)

Table 4.9 Cycle shape definers in airlines' behaviour

Cycle shape definer
(These policies change the cycle's shape. Only the most influential ones are selected.)

	drivers	dampers
amplitude[1]	• no short-run aircraft utilisation adjustment (203%) • lease with strict minimum usage (75%)	• no revenue management (and no aircraft utilisation adjustment) (no cycle, −72%); little revenue management (and no aircraft utilisation adjustment) (−43%) • short-term lease contracts (duration 1-year) (no cycle, −66%) • shorter aircraft service lifetime (−46%) • more profit pressure on price (and no aircraft utilisation adjustment) (−42%)
period[2]	• cost flexibility: fixed costs adjustment change as fast as variable costs (−30%) • shorter aircraft order adjustment time (−29%) • forecasts for the business case (and demand shock): short-term approach (−14%)	• forecasts for the business case (and demand shock): long-term approach (43%) • little revenue management (and no aircraft utilisation adjustment) (14%) • no weight on supply line (14%) • aircraft delivery forecast: expected CAD shorter then actual (14%)
transition time[3]	• shorter aircraft order adjustment time (111%) • profit-independent aircraft retirement (constant age retirement) (74%) • no weight on the supply line (42%)	• no revenue management (and no aircraft utilisation adjustment) (no cycle, −68%); little revenue management (and no aircraft utilisation adjustment) (−43%) • full cost orientation in pricing (and no aircraft utilisation adjustment) (−42%)

(continued)

Table 4.9 Continued

Cycle shape definer
(These policies change the cycle's shape. Only the most influential ones are selected.)

	drivers	dampers
		• steady aircraft ordering (no cycle, −63%) • longer aircraft order adjustment time (no cycle, −53%) • perfect forecasts for the business case (no cycle, −79%)
	no transition after demand shock: • no aircraft utilisation adjustment • forecasts for the business case (and demand shock): long–term approach	
stability value[4]	negative profitability in steady state: • steady aircraft ordering (no cycle, −1.2%) (or positive if smaller order size chosen) • aircraft delivery forecasts: expected CAD longer than actual (−1.1%) • planning with time buffer: expected CAD 50% longer than actual (−1.1%) • planning with volume buffer (−0.5%) • lower average profitability: • full cost orientation in pricing (−69%)	positive profitability in steady state: • aircraft delivery forecast: expected CAD shorter than actual (1.8%) • ancillary yield increase (0.2%) • higher average profitability: • gradual ordering (and business cycle) (+50%) • short-term lease contracts (and business cycle) (+33%)

1 A *driver's* amplitude is more than 40% bigger than the reference's, a *damper's* more than 40% smaller.
2 A *damper's* period is more than 10% longer than the reference's, a *driver's* more than 10% shorter.
3 A *driver's* transition time is more than 40% longer than the reference's, a *damper's* is > 40% shorter.
4 These factors cause the profitability stability value to deviate from zero.

4.6 Main causes and dynamics constituting the airline profit cycle

Experiments with the airline profit cycle model have answered the research questions developed in Chapter 1:

1 Why are airline profits cyclical?
2 What are the causes and dynamics that determine the cycle's shape?
3 How can the situation be improved?

In the following sections the answers will be consolidated. The discussion will reference back to researchers' and industry practitioners' opinions about the profit cycle causes, drivers, and mitigation measures, which were gathered in Chapter 2. Some of these findings are confirmed in model experiments presented in Chapter 4, others are disproved. Airline profit cycle influences will be categorised as in section 2.5 (see Figure 4.107). Detailed explanations for each finding can be found in the corresponding section in previous sections.

1 Answer to 'Why are airline profits cyclical?'

The origin of the airline profit cycle is a mismatch between airlines' desired and actual capacity. Theoretically, the airline industry is able to sustain a steady state with stable profitability (see section 4.1.1). Two preconditions must exist to make profitability oscillate: (1) a cycle cause, and (2) an unsuitable reaction.

1 A profit cycle cause is a disturbance which moves the airline industry away from its steady state. The imbalance which generates cyclicality in profits is found to be the mismatch between desired and actual aircraft capacity (see Figure 4.108 and section 4.1).[110] The level of desired capacity reflects airlines' and investors' beliefs about future demand, supply, yield, and cost developments in the industry. The actual capacity determines airlines' supply and hence their cost base which translates directly into profit. A disturbance which directly or indirectly influences either airlines' desired or actual capacity and makes them diverge, is called a profit cycle cause.
2 In case actual and desired capacity diverge, airlines will introduce corrective actions. If these are exactly adequate to remove the imbalance, the industry returns directly to a steady state. However, if airlines' actions are unsuitable in size or nature or timing, the goal will be missed and eventually overshot. This again provokes corrective actions, and so on. A cycle is generated.[111] Factors which influence the suitability of airlines' actions are called profit cycle drivers or dampers (see research questions 2 and 3).

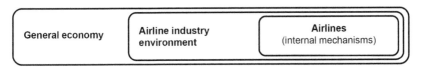

Figure 4.107 Categorisation of factors influencing the airline profit cycle

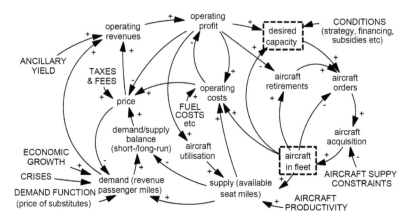

Figure 4.108 The mismatch between desired and actual capacity generates the profit cycle in the airline industry

The finding that the profit cycle's origin is a mismatch between the industry's desired and actual capacity (supply) differs from common opinions held by industry practitioners. Among aviation managers it is widely accepted that the airline profit cycle's origin is a mismatch between actual supply and demand, not actual supply and desired supply.[112] In contrast, and in line with this study's finding, previous airline profit cycle studies and classic industry cycle theories see the origin of cyclicality within the capacity (supply) sector.[113] The difference between this study's finding and the managers' common opinion is that according to this study a change in demand is not necessary to cause a profit cycle. Only the desired supply needs to diverge from the actual one. This divergence can, for example, be caused by a fuel price change which alters the business case that determines airlines' desired supply. Or it can be caused by airlines altering their aircraft retirement policy which also changes that business case. All factors that directly or indirectly influence airlines' desired supply level can cause a cycle. (Whether cyclicality emerges or not depends on the suitability of airlines' reactions; see 2. above).

As a consequence, the airline profit cycle is not necessarily caused externally. It can be generated within the industry, too. In the following, cycle causing factors in the general economy, in the airline industry environment, and in airlines' behaviour will be presented.

Factors in the **general economy** cause the largest profit cycles. These factors are:

- *GDP growth change*
- *fuel cost change*
- *shock* (positive or negative event)

As expected by airline managers and literature, a GDP increase has a positive effect on airline profitability, a fuel price increase has a negative effect.[114] It was found that a 30% fuel cost increase causes a similarly large cycle as a GDP growth drop by −10% during one year (see section 4.3.3). A positive event which entails additional demand initially causes a profitability upswing. But since a cycle is started, the positive event does not necessarily have only positive consequences. The initial upswing is followed by a downswing, all other things equal.

Each change in the general economy is a disturbance which requires action. Since the general economy is in reality never completely stable, airline profit cycles are frequently triggered. General economy factors thus have a major impact on the airline profit cycle's shape, which will be examined in the next section.

The **industry environment** factor which causes the most pronounced cycle is a

- *change in the price sensitivity of demand*: If customers become more price sensitive, airlines need to reduce prices less to stimulate the same amount of demand. Hence, airlines' profitability initially increases.

Other changes in the industry environment cause profit cycles with smaller amplitudes. The main factors are:

- *ticket-tax increase*: A tax increase initially decreases airlines' profitability. Yet, contrary to airline managers' and Pilarski's statements, the impact of a tax increase is found to be small.[115]
- *aircraft price (fixed costs) higher/lower*: Higher fixed costs lead to an initially lower profitability.
- *factors which cause excess/constraint capacity*: The emergence of overcapacity entails a higher cost base which initially deteriorates profitability; supply constraints allow higher yields and hence initially increase profitability. Factors causing an initial capacity surplus/shortfall are primarily:
  - technical aircraft service lifetime longer/shorter
  - innovation in aircraft productivity (new technology or planning systems) leads to a sudden capacity increase which deteriorates airlines' profitability. Hence, counter-intuitively, an innovation does not initially enhance airline industry profits[116]
  - normal aircraft utilisation higher/lower [117]
  - capacity acquisition delay (e.g. aircraft manufacturers' order fulfilment behaviour) shorter/longer

Airline behaviour can also cause a profit cycle. However, even big changes in airline behaviour do not cause as large a profit cycle as changes in the general economy or industry environment. Airline decisions which result in a divergence between desired and actual capacity are primarily:[118]

- *increase in ancillary yields*: Ancillary yields augment airlines' revenues and hence profits, so the initial cycle movement after an ancillary yield increase is positive.
- *change in aircraft retirement age* (decision for a generally longer or shorter aircraft service lifetime): A prolonged aircraft service lifetime generates additional capacity and thus has an initially negative effect on airlines' profitability.
- *inaccurate aircraft delivery forecasts*: If airlines receive ordered aircraft later than planned, the unexpected capacity constraint causes an initial profitability upswing.

Once a profit cycle is triggered, the question is how profitability will develop. Whether the triggered airline industry profit cycle is merely a hardly noticeable fluctuation or amounts to billions of dollars depends on factors described in the next sections.

2 Answer to 'What are the causes and dynamics that determine the cycle's shape?'

The airline profit cycle's shape is defined by its amplitude, its period, and the stability level which is the profitability level the industry returns to in the long run after a singular disturbance (find definitions illustrated in Figure 4.35 on p. 190). The transition time, i.e. the time until oscillating profitability becomes stable again after a singular disturbance, is found to depend mostly on the cycle's amplitude. Large swings need a long time to expire whereas small ones die out quickly.

General economic factors, such as GDP growth, fuel costs, and shocks, influence airlines' profits by triggering cyclicality. Every change in these factors causes a new profit cycle and hence impacts the overall shape of the airline profit development curve. Depending on the industry's state, changes in the general economy can aggravate or mitigate cycle swings.

Yet, model simulations reveal if general economic factors were completely stable, airline industry profits would still be substantially cyclical. Figure 4.109 shows how the profitability of US airlines would have developed if the general economy had been perfectly stable, that means if GDP growth and fuel costs had not changed at all and no shocks had occurred. The resulting simulation still exhibits significant cyclicality. Compared to the real historic profit development the cycle period would have become longer and only half of the cycle's amplitude would have disappeared. Consequently, against airline managers' frequent statements but in line with previous airline profit cycle research, changes in the general economy are by far not sufficient to explain the airline profit cycle's shape.[119] The airline industry's environment and the dynamics within the industry (airlines' behaviour) have a large impact on the industry's profitability development, i.e. on the profit cycle's shape.

The following discussion of cycle drivers will centre on factors in airlines' behaviour and within the airline industry's environment. This focus is chosen

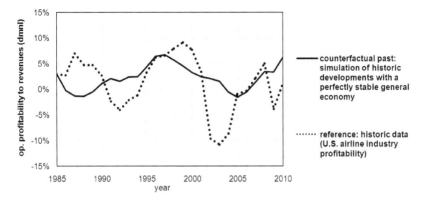

Figure 4.109 If the general economy had been stable (counterfactual simulation)

because it is assumed that among all stakeholders airlines have most interest to understand and improve their industry's financial performance. Besides, airlines cannot change the general economy but their own behaviour, and airlines also have some degree of influence on their environment.

The discussion will be presented in three sub-sections. First, airline behaviour and industry environment factors which drive the airline profit cycle's *amplitude* will be presented in section 2.1, then factors which drive the cycle's *period* will be outlined in section 2.2. Lastly, in section 2.3, factors which influence the cycle's *long-run profitability* value will be specified.

2.1 Profit cycle amplitude

Factors which amplify the airline profit cycle have been identified in model experiments in sections 4.1–4.5.

Model simulations have shown that **airlines' behaviour** can more than quadruple the profit cycle's amplitude. The following airline decisions mainly drive the cycle's amplitude:

- *revenue management (short-term price adjustments)*: The use of revenue management as a mechanism for short-term demand stimulation by price is found to be a great cycle amplifier. This settles a controversy among experts and in the literature as to whether highly responsive price setting, which revenue management systems are made for, has a positive or negative effect on profitability (see section 2.5).[120] In previous airline profit cycle research the role of revenue management is discussed only by two sources: this study's finding that the heavy use of revenue management hugely amplifies the airline industry's cyclicality confirms research by Sgouridis.[121] It disproves Pierson/Sterman's conclusion that revenue management is a cure to the profit cycle.[122]

- *measures that make the airlines' cost base inflexible*: Inflexibility can result from a high level of fixed costs. That confirms the many researchers and experts who see the airline industry's high fixed cost share as a problem.[123] Furthermore, inflexibility can be increased by restrictions on short-run cost adjustments.[124] Model simulation experiments with either source of inflexibility produce a magnified profit cycle. Airline decisions which make the cost base more rigid, and thus drive the cycle, are primarily:

  - no efforts to adjust fixed costs (highly theoretical)
  - aircraft service lifetime longer [125]
  - profit-independent (fixed age) aircraft retirement
  - no short-run aircraft utilisation adjustment (e.g. no opportunity to cancel flights after a shock): Simulations reveal that airlines already exploit the full benefit of short-run aircraft utilisation adjustment
  - minimum usage requirement for leased aircraft

- *measures that augment fixed costs/ build up overcapacities*: Overcapacities emerge if more capacity is added than the industry needs.[126] Airline behaviour which results in overcapacities is primarily found to be:

  - responsive capacity ordering: Frequently adding capacity responsive to current expectations about the profitability of new investments.[127]
  - buffer in capacity ordering (for time or volume): Though Meadows and Lyneis claim buffers lead to less cyclicality, buffers in the capacity ordering process are found to increase it.[128] With buffers aircraft are planned to arrive later than they are actually delivered. In case they are delivered on time, the unexpected capacity deteriorates airlines' profitability.[129]

In the airline **industry environment** the following main factors are found to magnify the airline profit cycle's amplitude:

- *lower barriers to market exit*: Facilitated market exit is a great cycle driver. Model simulations reveal that profit volatility would increase if capacity was free to exit the market because the level of desired capacity in the industry would change more drastically. In simulations the industry would recover more quickly from the demand shock and profits in the rebound phase are much higher due to the more severe shake out. This finding opposes Sgouridis, Pilarski, and the IATA who argue that the industry would benefit from low exit barriers.[130]
- *slow information flows*: Slow information flows within the industry and among supply chain partners as well as inaccurate forecasts magnify the profit cycle. This confirms widely accepted findings in supply chain research, e.g. by Lee et al., as well as previous airline profit cycle research by Lyneis and Weil.[131]

Airline industry environment factors which have a less significant impact but also amplify the profit cycle are:

- *easy access to capital*: Airlines' easy access to capital magnifies the profit cycle, as expected by Weil, Pilarski, and Wohjan.[132] Likewise Lyneis, Jiang/Hansman, and Sgouridis see aggressive investment behaviour in the race for market shares as a cycle driver.[133] However, the effect of aggressive investing, i.e. easy access to capital, is only moderate compared to, for example, low exit barriers or slow information processing.
- *shorter capacity acquisition delay* (time between aircraft ordering and delivery): If the time until aircraft are delivered was shorter, capacity could be built up more responsively to current conditions. Given airlines' easy access to capital, the resulting overcapacities deteriorate profitability. This finding contradicts previous airline profit cycle research by Lyneis, Skinner/Stock, Skinner et al., Liehr et al., and Jiang/Hansman who state a shorter capacity acquisition delay would be beneficial.[134]
- *lower price sensitivity of demand*: If customers become less sensitive to price changes, this not only triggers a cycle (see section above) but also increases its amplitude. The reason is that airlines need larger price adjustments to stimulate the same amount of demand. This confirms previous findings by Meadows.[135] It disproves claims by the IATA that the airline industry's very price sensitive demand would deteriorate the industry's profitability.[136]

2.2 Profit cycle period

Model experiments revealed factors which drive the airline profit cycle's period, i.e. which make it shorter so that it swings more often within the same timeframe.

The cycle period depends on the *airlines' speed of information processing, expectation formation, and the time airlines need to take actions*. If information flows take longer, the profit cycle period is longer, and vice versa. Model experiments revealed that these two time periods are especially critical:

- the time necessary to adjust fixed costs
- the time to plan and place aircraft orders (which determines how responsive airlines build up capacity)

The airline industry environment also determines how fast profitability oscillates. Yet, these factors are less influential than the airlines' speed of processing and action. Mainly two factors increase the frequency of cycle swings. As they also amplify the profit cycle, they have already been explained above:

- lower barriers to market exit
- easy access to capital

Since each change in the general economy gives the impulse for a new profit cycle, the economy's business cycle translates into airline profitability. A business cycle with a period of for example ten years causes a profit cycle which swings with a ten-year period (all other things equal). The length of the phase lag between business cycle and profitability, which was observable in simulation experiments (see section 4.3.1), depends on airlines' processing times, especially the time it takes to form yield expectations and the fixed cost adjustment time.

2.3 Stability level of profitability

Only few factors are found to impact the airlines' stability level of profitability. Usually several years after a cycle-causing singular disturbance airlines' profitability returns to the same level as before the disturbance. In a few cases the long-run profitability level was different from the one before the disturbance.

The airlines' long-run profitability level depends on airlines' abilities to adapt to new circumstances. In most simulated cases airlines learn to deal with changes in the general economy, the industry's environment, or the industry. In those few cases where airlines' learning processes are disturbed, their cost base may permanently become too large compared to revenues, so their long-run profitability deteriorates.

Hence, *airline behaviour which produces persistent overcapacities* results in a lower long-run profitability. (Apart from the aspect of persistence this airline behaviour has been presented in section 2.1 on amplification.)

- buffers or mistakes in capacity planning: In case aircraft are constantly delivered earlier than airlines expect, either because they choose to implement buffers in their planning process or because they fail to adapt their expectation to the new circumstance that aircraft arrive earlier, the constant unexpected capacity addition leads to a capacity surplus.
- profit-independent steady capacity enlargement (big fixed order): If, theoretically, airlines chose to constantly order a fixed large amount of aircraft, this would lead to persistent overcapacities and thus stable but negative airline industry profitability.

Likewise, forecasting or ordering behaviour which leads to a persistent capacity shortage augments the airline industry's long-run profitability.

A constant negative change in the airline industry environment or in the general economy deteriorates airlines' long-run profitability if airlines constantly fail to acknowledge the deteriorating trend it. Such changes are for example:

- declining GDP growth
- constantly rising fuel prices

Airlines' attempts to achieve a long-run profitability increase by augmenting their ancillary yields did not prove helpful in simulation experiments. Due to the enormous price pressure in the industry, airlines use the additional revenues to subsidise their ticket yields. As a result the long-run profitability gain from ancillary yield increase is almost completely extinguished.

3 Answer to 'How can the situation be improved?'

Model experiments have revealed several policies to mitigate the airline profit cycle successfully. These measures can be undertaken by airlines themselves or by their stakeholders, i.e. the airline industry environment.

The listed cycle mitigation measures dampen the airline profit cycle severely and can even prevent it after a singular cycle-causing shock. Mitigation policies are appropriate corrective actions in response to the cycle cause so profitability returns (almost) directly to stability, all other things equal (see 1. in section 1). The discovered cycle mitigation policies are extreme policies which may be unrealistic to implement. Yet, even implementing them to some degree diminishes airlines' profit cyclicality significantly.

Policies are tested on industry level which means that their industry-wide application is assumed. Whether an individual airline that choses to act as a first mover will succeed over competitors or suffer disadvantages from this decision is not part of this study. Here, areas for industry-wide improvements are identified. Corresponding action could be taken by large industry organisation or regulators.

Four airline profit cycle mitigation policies have been identified. Each will be presented in a sub-section:

- price setting with focus on long-term profitability (section 3.1)
- gradual and slow capacity enlargement (section 3.2)
- flexible adjustment of existing capacity (section 3.3)
- perfect information (section 3.4)

3.1 Price setting with focus on long-term profitability

The use of revenue management systems as a means of short-term demand stimulation by price makes airlines' profitability very unstable (see section 2.1). Experiments showed that without revenue management systems, airline profits would hardly or even not all be cyclical.[137] Yet, the abolishment of revenue management systems seems unrealistic because they are a widely appreciated tool. Assuming that revenue management stays as it is, model experiments revealed two price-setting approaches which can mitigate its negative effects:

- *A more cost-oriented price setting* can compensate much of the amplification produced by revenue management. If prices are anchored closely to total unit costs, they cannot change as fast because cost adjustments take time (i.e. significantly more time than revenue management systems need for alterations). Hence, the volatility in prices is dampened. This policy's disadvantage is, however, that while more stable the average profitability level will be lower.
- *Giving the overall profitability target more weight* in the price-setting process counteracts revenue management's profit cycle amplification. The increased profit pressure forces yields upwards whenever the airlines' target profitability is not met. Giving this profit pressure more weight can be understood as a stricter instruction to achieve the target margin on each ticket sale. This policy does not stabilise profitability as successfully as a cost oriented price-setting approach because it allows higher upswings. In consequence, the resulting average profitability level is higher than with increased cost orientation.

This finding may encourage airlines to reconsider the effectiveness of their price-setting policies. Besides, industry organisations and regulators may want to study measures that limit airlines' ability to adjust prices in the short run.

Figure 4.110 illustrates the impact on alternative price setting policies on the profit cycle. If airlines could not change prices as frequently as they do today, their profitability would be more stable. In the extreme, if prices were fixed by regulation and no adjustments possible, airlines' profitability would not oscillate even when facing the economy's business cycle.[138]

3.2 Gradual and slow capacity enlargement

Policies which slow down and moderate airlines' capacity enlargement can eliminate the airline industry's profit cycle and increase its profitability level. The suggested policies provide stabilisation and improvement by preventing

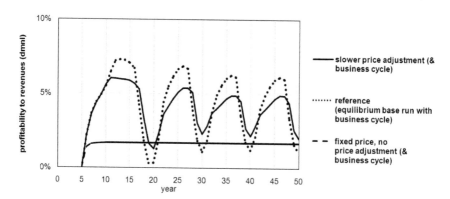

Figure 4.110 Slower price adjustment or no price adjustment (fixed price)

overcapacities and hence fixed costs. Cycle mitigating action which airlines and their stakeholders can take are listed below. Whether or not airline industry stakeholders choose to support the airline industry in the suggested fashion will depend on their expected benefits and motivation, which airlines can try to enhance.

- *For airlines: gradual capacity build-up.* Airlines should carefully consider aircraft orders, infrastructure investments, and workforce enlargements. This process may take time. Decisions are best based on a long-term trend. Furthermore, it is more beneficial to order small amounts than large bundles so the resulting build-up is gradual. A more extreme but also more successful policy would be to constantly order the same small amount of capacity.

  In the literature the stabilising effect of gradual capacity enlargements is stated by Forrester and Meadows.[139] The cycle mitigating effect of slow ordering was recognised by Sterman, Neidl, and Chin/Tay,[140] whereas Jiang/Hansman and Skinner et al. saw benefits in faster ordering.[141] Steady ordering was suggested in previous airline profit cycle research by Skinner and colleagues.[142] And supply chain researchers Lee et al. even postulate order limits.[143]

- *For aircraft manufacturers: limit the delivery or production of aircraft.* Limiting aircraft manufacturers' production (or allowing only slow adjustment) mitigates the airline profit cycle. This opposes airline managers' claims that late aircraft delivery deteriorates airlines' profitability.[144] However, it is in line with supply chain research by Lee et al. and previous airline profit cycle research by Sgouridis et al.[145] The latter finds that slow or limited production adjustment would not only mitigate cyclicality but also increase aircraft manufacturers' financial returns, which increases their probability of conducting this policy.

- *For investors: make access to capital more difficult* so new capacity cannot easily be financed. This implies that if investors wanted a stable airline industry profitability, they would get it. (Find a short literature discussion on access to capital in section 2.1 on amplification.)

- *For regulators: implement high barriers to market exit* (with for example bankruptcy protection or subsidies) to prevent sharp capacity reductions and boom bubbles. Model experiments have shown that given the industry's easy access to capital low exit barriers result in great instability. (Find a short literature discussion on exit barriers in section 2.1.)

3.3 Flexible adjustment of existing capacity

Measures which enable airlines to quickly adjust their existing capacity stabilise the airline industry's profitability. In unfavourable times flexibility in their short-run supply allows airlines to avoid costs and thus prevent price reductions. In boom periods airlines can exploit the revenues of additional supply.

Measures to achieve quick capacity adjustments are primarily:

- *reduce fixed cost share*: A lower fixed cost base effectively increases airlines' flexibility to lower costs in the short-run if necessary. Model simulations suggest that the amount of a cost reduction, for example in labour negotiations, is more important than its speed. The finding that a lower fixed cost share increases the airline industry's stability supports airline managers' endeavours to cut costs (see section 2.4). Furthermore, the finding confirms the majority of researchers who see the airline industry's high fixed costs as a central problem.[146]
- *adjust aircraft utilisation in the short run*: Airlines already exploit the full benefit of short-run aircraft utilisation adjustment by elaborate flight schedule modifications (see amplification above).
- *retire aircraft depending on profit*: This stabilising policy is already employed by many airlines. Its impact is comparatively moderate. Previous airline profit cycle research by Liehr et al. and Skinner/Stock also stated the mitigating effect of profit-dependent aircraft retirement.[147]
- *hold very short-term aircraft leases*: Model simulations show if airlines operated a fleet consisting of only leased aircraft with one-year contracts (including crew, maintenance, and insurance), there would hardly be a profit cycle in the long run. Yet, in in the medium term, in the transition phase during which the fleet is restructured to include more very short-term leases, their high costs would deteriorate airlines' profitability. Lease contracts with a period longer than one year have a much weaker profit cycle damping effect. With the common five-year operating leases it hardly matters whether the fleet is leased or owned. This opposes several aviation managers (see section 2.4.2) and Liehr et al. who call for more aircraft leases (in the common five-year contract form), and confirms Skinner/Stock's and Werner's advice to employ very short-term ('wet') leases in the fleet.[148]

The question arises if airlines and regulators should focus more on gradual capacity enlargement (see 3.2 above) or on flexible adjustment of the existing capacity (here 3.3). A model experiment provides the answer. In a first simulation airlines hold half of their fleet as one-year lease contracts. Then, in the second simulation, airlines test the alternative approach and enlarge their capacity only gradually, i.e. take twice as much time to process aircraft orders. Figure 4.111 shows that one-year leases dampen profit cyclicality even more than gradual aircraft ordering. However, keeping half of the airline industry's fleet as one-year leases would be an unrealistic change.[149] If this assumption is relaxed a little and only a quarter of the fleet is simulated to operate on one-year leases, the industry's profitability situation is hardly mitigated (see Figure 4.112). Meanwhile, when capacity enlargement is only slowed down half as much, the resulting profitability is still considerably damped (see Figure 4.112). Hence, airlines and regulators are advised to take steps which encourage more gradual aircraft capacity enlargement in the airline industry to stabilise airlines' profitability.

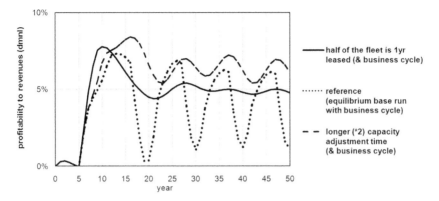

Figure 4.111 Big steps towards flexible compared to slow capacity adjustment

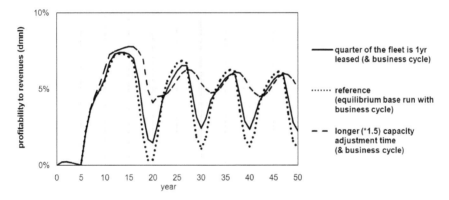

Figure 4.112 Smaller steps towards flexible compared to slow capacity adjustment

3.4 Perfect information

If information flows were perfect, all expectations were correct, and all forecasts were accurate, the profit cycle would be strongly dampened (see Figure 4.113). It is thus advised to *improve forecasting and information sharing* within alliances, the industry organisations, and along the supply chain.

As a forecasting method model experiments revealed that trend extrapolation is suitable in a volatile environment such as the airline industry's. This contradicts previous research by Lyneis who claims that trend extrapolation aggravates the airline profit cycle.[150]

The finding that airline profitability would benefit enormously from excellent information flows and accurate forecasts is supported in airline profit cycle studies, for example by Sgouridis or Lyneis or the IATA, in the aviation literature, as well as in supply chain research.[151]

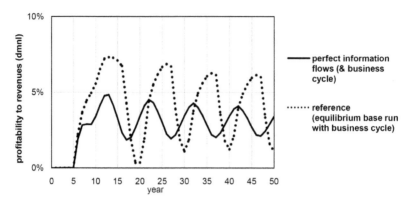

Figure 4.113 Perfect information flows in a business cycle setting

Notes

1 Mankiw, N. Gregory, *Principles of macroeconomics*, 6th edn. (Cengage Learning, 2012).
2 See Sterman, John D., *Business dynamics: Systems thinking and modeling for a complex world* (Boston: Irwin/McGraw-Hill, 2000), p. 512.
3 Ibid., p. 232.
4 See Pindyck, Robert S. and Daniel L. Rubinfeld, *Microeconomics*, Prentice-Hall series in economics, 5th edn. (Upper Saddle River, NJ: Prentice Hall, 2001) pp. 273–274.
5 Forrester, Jay W., *Industrial dynamics*, 6th printing 1969 edn. (Cambridge, MA: MIT Press, 1961), p. 51.
6 See for example: Doyle, James K. et al., 'Design of a Master of Science degree program in System Dynamics at WPI', *27th International Conference of the System Dynamics Society* (Albuquerque, New Mexico, 2009), p. 9.
7 As calculated within the System Dynamics software Vensim. The SDM-Doc Tool counts 843 feedback loops. See section 3.2.2 for more model statistics.
8 For example *operating profit* is involved in 32 feedback loops.
9 More precisely, the shock is inserted into the variable *desired capacity owned*. Thus, only the structure concerned with owned and not the one with leased aircraft is inspected. This is done to avoid possible compensations between owned and leased aircraft. The model structure of the two sections is identical except for the delay type (see section 3.3.3). The dynamically more challenging 3rd order delay structure is used in the owned aircraft section. Also, the larger share of aircraft in the industry are owed.
10 The demand shock used so far is a drop in demand growth lasting one year. Since ceteris paribus demand growth before and after the shock is 0%, the one-year shock implies a permanent demand reduction in absolute terms. To match the supply effect of the demand shock a STEP change is used: in year t = 5 supply changes and then stays at the new *desired capacity* level.
11 Note: The 19-year oscillation period of profitability corresponds with the one of aircraft in the fleet.
12 Calculation: 12,300 seats in the fleet cause a cost difference of roughly 12,300 seats * 40,000 dollar/(year*seat) = 492,000,000 dollar/year. Hence the profitability difference is roughly: 492,000,000 dollar/year / 31,110,000,000 dollar/year = 1.6 %-points

13 Despite the supply shock the number of aircraft increases because there is no mechanism active in this scenario to reduce the fleet. Due to the shock no orders are placed anymore, but orders already in process are fulfilled. Those aircraft augment the fleet.

14 The Beer Game is a classic supply chain experiment. For details see for example: Sterman, *Business dynamics*, pp. 684–694.

15 Forrester, *Industrial dynamics*, chapter 15.

16 Meadows, Dennis L., 'The dynamics of commodity production cycles: A dynamic cobweb theorem', Massachusetts Institute of Technology, 1969.

17 See section 2.2.1, and: See Forrester, Jay W., *Principles of systems*, 2nd edn. (Cambridge, MA: Wright-Allen Press, 1968), pp. 2–15 and 12–37.

18 See Liehr, Martin et al., 'Cycles in the sky: Understanding and managing business cycles in the airline market', *System Dynamics Review* 17.4 (2001): 316. And see Jiang, Helen and R. John Hansman, 'An analysis of profit cycles in the airline industry', *6th AIAA Aviation Technology, Integration and Operations Conference (ATIO)*, (Wichita, Kansas: 2006), pp. 13, 16. And see Skinner, Steve and Elane Stock, 'Masters of the cycle', *Airline Business* 14.4 (1998): section 2. And see Skinner, Steve et al., 'Managing growth and profitability across peaks and troughs of the airline industry cycle', in *Handbook of airline finance*, eds Butler, Gail F. and Martin R. Keller, 1st edn, An aviation week book (New York and others: McGraw-Hill, 1999). And see Lyneis, James M., 'System Dynamics for business strategy: A phased approach', *System Dynamics Review* 15.1 (1999): 63–64.

19 Calculation: The amplitude of 1st trough to 1st peak is 31,270 seats. They cause a cost difference of roughly 31,270 seats * 40,000 dollars/(year*seat) = 1,250,880,000 dollars/year. Hence the profitability difference is roughly: 1,250,880,000 dollars/year / 31,110,000,000 dollar/year = 4.0 %-points.

20 See section 2.2.1, and: See Sterman, *Business dynamics*, p. 684.

21 See Sterman, John D., 'Modeling managerial behavior: Misperceptions of feedback in a dynamic decision making experiment', *Management Science* 35.3 (1989): 334.

22 See section 3.3.3 for model equations and their explanation.

23 See Forrester, *Industrial dynamics* p. 186.

24 See Meadows, 'The dynamics of commodity production cycles', pp. 119–121.

25 Calculation: The amplitude of 1st trough to 1st peak is 12,810 seats. They cause a cost difference of roughly 12,810 seats * 40,000 dollars/(year*seat) = 512,400,000 dollars/year. Hence the profitability difference is roughly: 512,400,000 dollars/year / 31,110,000,000 dollar/year = 1.6 %-points.

26 In comparison, doubling the *CAD* yields an amplitude of 4.0 %-points profitability change while the full model's reaction has an amplitude of 9.8 %-points.

27 For more detail on revenue management, also called yield management, see section 3.3.2.

28 The model's steady state is described in section 4.1.1, its calibration parameters can be found in appendix C.

29 See Perelman, Lewis J., 'Time in System Dynamics', *TIMS Studies in the Management Science* 14 (1980): 82.

30 For example Forrester states: 'Model runs of several times the natural period of the system are of interest.' Forrester, *Industrial dynamics*, p. 199.

31 Sterman, *Business dynamics* p. 94.

32 Keating, Elizabeth K., 'Everything you ever wanted to know about how to develop a System Dynamics model but were afraid to ask', *16th International Conference of the System Dynamics Society*, (Quebec City, Canada: 1998), p. 10. Her statement is referenced to Forrester, *Industrial dynamics*.

33 See Forrester, Jay W. and Peter M. Senge, 'Tests for building confidence in System Dynamics models', *TIMS Studies in the Management Science* 14 (1980): 212.

34 See Sterman, *Business dynamics*, pp. 90–91.

35 Factors constituting the demand curve are for example national income, price elasticity, and price. See section 3.3.1 for details.

36 For layout reasons, such as the thickness of lines, the graph appears slightly smoother than the actual simulation. However, cycle measures are calculated based on the original model data.

37 Peak at 353 USD cents/gallon in 3rd quarter 2008 compared to 206 USD cents/gallon in 3rd quarter 2007 and 192 USD cents/gallon in 3rd quarter 2009. Data source: A4A Airlines for America (formerly ATA Air Transport Association), 'ATA Cost Index for US Passenger Airlines, 3rd quarter 2010', 2011, web page, accessed: 23 Feb 2011.

38 Precisely, a fuel cost per ASM increase by 0.005 USD. – Note: A fractional GDP growth decrease for one year results in a persisting GDP reduction. Thus, two persisting changes are compared.

39 See International Air Transport Association (IATA), *Vision 2050* (Singapore 2011), p. 22.

40 Button, Kenneth, 'Empty cores in airlines markets', *5th Hamburg Aviation Conference* (Hamburg: 2002), p. 7. – Indirect tests involve comparing different suppliers' cost structures, market shares, and demand variability. These analyses need to be conducted on individual market participant level, which is not within the airline industry model's scope.

41 See Wojahn, Oliver W., 'Why does the airline industry over-invest?', *Journal of Air Transport Management* 19 (2012): 1.

42 Easy access to capital is a cycle driver: See Pilarski, Adam M., *Why can't we make money in aviation?* (Aldershot, UK; Burlington, VT: Ashgate, 2007), pp. 119–124. And see Weil, Henry B., 'Commoditization of technology-based products and services: A generic model of market dynamics', *Massachusetts Institute of Technology: Sloan Working Paper* 144–96 (1996): 8–14.

43 See Pearce, Brian, 'The state of air transport markets and the airline industry after the great recession', *Journal of Air Transport Management* 21 (2012): 7.

44 Wojahn, 'Why does the airline industry over-invest?', p. 2.

45 Details about this part of the airline industry model can be found in section 3.3.3.

46 See Sgouridis, Sgouris et al., *Taming the business cycle in commercial aviation – Trade-space analysis of strategic alternatives using simulation modelling*, Massachusetts Institute of Technology: Working Paper Series, Cambridge, MA, pp. 5–6. And see Pilarski, *Why can't we make money in aviation?*, pp. 179–186. And see International Air Transport Association (IATA), *Vision 2050*, p. 45.

47 See Garvett, Donald S. and Kyle J. Hilton, 'What drives airline profits? A first look', in *Handbook of airline finance*, eds Butler, Gail F. and Martin R. Keller, 1st edn. (New York: Aviation Week, 1999), pp. 180, 184. And see International Air Transport Association (IATA), *Vision 2050*, pp. 53–54.

48 Details about this part of the airline industry model can be found in section 3.3.3.

49 The function *T effect of profits on desired capacity* is calibrated with the following tuples (*expected profitability of new investments; expected of expected profit on desired capacity*). Low exit barriers: (0;1), (−0.1;0.87), (−0.2;0.6), (−0.3;0). High exit barriers: (0;1), (−0.1, 0.98), (−0.2;0.9); (−0.4;0.5); (−0.5;0.4).

50 See airline managers' statements in section 2.4.1. And see Pilarski, *Why can't we make money in aviation?*, p. 187. And see classic and neo-classical business cycle theories in section 2.1.1.

51 See A4A Airlines for America, 'US aviation tax increases on airline tickets', web page, accessed: 7 Nov 2014.

52 Details about this part of the airline industry model can be found in section 3.3.2.

53 See Porter, Michael E., 'Five forces in the airline industry', in *Vision 2050*, ed. International Air Transport Association (IATA) (Report, 2011) p. 23. And see Meadows, 'The dynamics of commodity production cycles', pp. 119–121.

54 See International Air Transport Association (IATA), *Vision 2050*, p. 45. – Price sensitive demand stabilises: See Meadows, 'The dynamics of commodity production cycles', pp. 119–121.

55 See International Air Transport Association (IATA), *Profitability and the air transport value chain* (2013), p. 17. And see Weil, 'Commoditization of technology-based products and services', p. 9.

56 See Lyneis, James M., 'System Dynamics for market forecasting and structural analysis', *System Dynamics Review* 16.1 (2000): 9. – Herding behaviour is phrased as 'experience effect'.

57 The concept of elasticities is explained in section 3.3.1.

58 See International Air Transport Association (IATA), *Profitability and the air transport value chain*, pp. 17–18. And see Weil, 'Commoditization of technology-based products and services', pp. 2, 9.

59 See Lyneis, 'System Dynamics for market forecasting and structural analysis', p. 9. – Herding behaviour is phrased as 'experience effect'.

60 See Werner, Frank M., 'Leverage and airline financial management', in *Handbook of airline finance*, eds. Butler, Gail F. and Martin R. Keller, 1st edn. (New York: Aviation Week, 1999), p. 188. And see Borenstein, Severin and Nancy L. Rose, *How airline markets work . . . Or do they? Regulatory reform in the airline industry* (2007), p. 36. And see Button, Kenneth, 'Liberalising aviation: Is there an empty core problem?', *Journal of Transport Economics and Policy* 30.3 (1996): 288. And see Skinner et al., 'Managing growth and profitability across peaks and troughs of the airline industry cycle', p. 26. And see Sgouridis et al., *Taming the business cycle in commercial aviation*, p. 6. And see literature on industry cycles, for example Petersen, Bruce and Steven Strongin, 'Why are some industries more cyclical than others?', *Journal of Business and Economic Statistics* 14.2 (1996): 194–196. And see aviation experts' statements in section 2.4.2.

61 See Liehr et al., 'Cycles in the sky', p. 322. And see Chin, Anthony T.H. and John H. Tay, 'Developments in air transport: Implications on investment decisions, profitability and survival of Asian airlines', *Journal of Air Transport Management* 7.5 (2001): 329. And see Skinner and Stock, 'Masters of the cycle', section 5.

62 See Jiang and Hansman, 'An analysis of profit cycles in the airline industry', pp. 13, 16. And see Liehr et al., 'Cycles in the sky', p. 316. And see Segers, Rafael, 'An analysis of external and internal drivers of profit cycles in the airline industry – An industry dynamics approach', Masters thesis, Cranfield University, 2005, p. 15. And see Skinner et al., 'Managing growth and profitability across peaks and troughs of the airline industry cycle', pp. 26–28. And see Lyneis, 'System Dynamics for business strategy', pp. 63–64.

63 See Meadows, 'The dynamics of commodity production cycles', p. 127. And see Lyneis, 'System Dynamics for market forecasting and structural analysis', p. 23.

64 Airline managers criticise unreliable aircraft deliveries, see section 2.4.

65 See Sgouridis et al., *Taming the business cycle in commercial aviation*, pp. 17–19.

66 Lee et al. postulate order limits to avoid shortage gaming in supply chains. See Lee, Hau L., V. Padmanabhan and Seungjin Whang, 'Information distortion in a supply chain: The bullwhip effect', *Management Science* 50.12 (2004): 1883–1884.

67 This supply chain research is, for example: ibid., p. 1884. Also discussed in Steckel, Joel H., Sunil Gupta and Anirvan Banerji, 'Supply chain decision making: Will shorter cycle times and shared point-of-sale information necessarily help?', *Management Science* 50.4 (2004).

68 For example, see Lee et al., 'Information distortion in a supply chain.' And see Croson, Rachel and Karen Donohue, 'Behavioral causes of the bullwhip effect and the observed value of inventory information', *Management Science* 52.3 (2006): 333–334.

69 Pro information sharing: See Sgouridis, Sgouris P., 'Symbiotic strategies in enterprise ecology: Modeling commercial aviation as an Enterprise of Enterprises', PhD thesis, Massachusetts Institute of Technology, 2007, pp. 292–294. And see Skinner and Stock, 'Masters of the cycle', section 6. And see International Air Transport Association (IATA), *Profitability and the air transport value chain*, p. 41. And see Forrester, Jay W., 'Industrial dynamics: A major breakthrough for decision makers', *Harvard Business Review* 36.4 (1958): pp. 47–49. And see Croson and Donohue, 'Behavioral causes of the bullwhip effect and the observed value of inventory information', pp. 331–334. And see Lee et al., 'Information distortion in a supply chain', p. 1883. And see Chen, Frank et al., 'Quantifying the bullwhip effect in a simple supply chain: The impact of forecasting, lead times, and information', *Management Science* 46.3 (2000): 436–442. And see Smaros, Johanna et al., 'The impact of increasing demand visibility on production and inventory control efficiency', *International Journal of Physical Distribution and Logistics Management* 33.4 (2003): 336–354. Pro accurate forecasting: See Lyneis, 'System Dynamics for market forecasting and structural analysis', pp. 22–23. And see Chin and Tay, 'Developments in air transport', p. 329. And see Sterman, *Business dynamics*, p. 751.

70 See Schumpeter, Joseph A., 'The explanation of the business cycle', *Economica* 21 (1927): 295–298.

71 For example, see Lyneis, 'System Dynamics for market forecasting and structural analysis', pp. 7–9. And see Jiang and Hansman, 'An analysis of profit cycles in the airline industry', p. 9.– Find more references in corresponding scenarios.

72 See Weil, 'Commoditization of technology-based products and services', pp. 8–14. And see Lyneis, 'System Dynamics for market forecasting and structural analysis', pp. 22–23. And see Lee et al., 'Information distortion in a supply chain', p. 1883.

73 See Lyneis, 'System Dynamics for market forecasting and structural analysis', pp. 7–9.

74 See Sgouridis, ,Symbiotic strategies in enterprise ecology', pp. 288–290.

75 The trend extrapolation method applied in the model is adaptive expectations by exponential smoothing. See, for example, Sterman, *Business dynamics*, chapter 16.

76 Trend extrapolation is a popular forecasting method among airlines: see Lyneis, 'System Dynamics for market forecasting and structural analysis', p. 7. Trend extrapolation is generally a popular forecasting method: see Sterman, *Business dynamics*, pp. 431–432.

77 For better visibility the simulation with halved adjustment times is not depicted.

78 See Jiang and Hansman, 'An analysis of profit cycles in the airline industry', p. 9. And see Sgouridis et al., *Taming the business cycle in commercial aviation*, pp. 5–6. And see Lyneis, 'System Dynamics for market forecasting and structural analysis', p. 7.

79 A similar set-up was used to simulate investors' aggressive investment behaviour, i.e. easy access to capital, in section 4.4.1.

80 Find references in the following scenario sections.

81 See Liehr et al., 'Cycles in the sky', pp. 321–322. And see Skinner and Stock, 'Masters of the cycle', section 2. And see Tan, Hao and John A. Mathews, 'Cyclical

industrial dynamics: The case of the global semiconductor industry', *Technological Forecasting and Social Change* 77 (2010): 193–194. And see aviation expert statements in section 2.4.2.

82 See Skinner and Stock, 'Masters of the cycle', section 5. And see Skinner et al., 'Managing growth and profitability across peaks and troughs of the airline industry cycle', p. 26.

83 See Sterman, *Business dynamics* p. 681. And see Neidl, Raymond E., 'Can the aviation industry shield itself from business cycles?', in *Handbook of airline finance*, eds Butler, Gail F. and Martin R. Keller, 1st edn (New York: Aviation Week, 1999), p. 21. And see Chin and Tay, 'Developments in air transport', p. 329. – Responsive ordering is problematic: See Meadows, 'The dynamics of commodity production cycles', pp. 119–121. And see Tan and Mathews, 'Cyclical industrial dynamics', pp. 348–349. And see classic industry cycle theories in section 2.1.2. – Pro gradual capacity enlargement: See Meadows, 'The dynamics of commodity production cycles', pp. 119–120. And see Forrester, *Industrial dynamics*, p. 186.

84 See Jiang and Hansman, 'An analysis of profit cycles in the airline industry', p. 11. And see the 'Order Adjuster' strategy in Skinner et al., 'Managing growth and profitability across peaks and troughs of the airline industry cycle', p. 26.

85 Previous research by Jiang and Hansman, 'An analysis of profit cycles in the airline industry', p. 11. And by Skinner et al., 'Managing growth and profitability across peaks and troughs of the airline industry cycle', p. 26.

86 Lyneis and Meadows state buffers mitigate cyclicality. See Lyneis, 'System Dynamics for market forecasting and structural analysis', p. 23. And see Meadows, 'The dynamics of commodity production cycles', p. 127.

87 See Sterman, 'Modeling managerial behavior', p. 334.

88 See ibid.

89 Also see Lyneis, 'System Dynamics for market forecasting and structural analysis', p. 7.

90 See Liehr et al., 'Cycles in the sky', p. 322. And see Skinner and Stock, 'Masters of the cycle', section 5. And see Chin and Tay, 'Developments in air transport', p. 329. And see aviation experts' statements in section 2.4.2.

91 See Liehr et al., 'Cycles in the sky', p. 322. And see Skinner and Stock, 'Masters of the cycle', section 5. – Both state old aircraft should be used longer in upswings. In contrast Neidl suggests to retire old aircraft early to prevent overcapacities. See Neidl, 'Can the aviation industry shield itself from business cycles?', p. 21.

92 See industry practitioners' statements in section 2.4. And see Liehr et al., 'Cycles in the sky', p. 323. And see Skinner and Stock, 'Masters of the cycle', section 5. And see Werner, 'Leverage and airline financial management', p. 196.

93 See section 3.3.3: Operating leases are termed between one and seven years, usually for five years. See Morrell, Peter S., *Airline finance*, 3rd edn (Aldershot, England; Burlington, VT: Ashgate, 2007), p. 200.

94 See Skinner and Stock, 'Masters of the cycle', section 5. And see Werner, 'Leverage and airline financial management', p. 196.

95 Operating leases, which are the most common for of aircraft leases, usually last for at least two years. There is, however, an option of shorter lease contracts if a 'wet lease' is chosen. This includes crew, maintenance, and insurance in addition to the aircraft. Wet leases are termed between a few months and two years. See GlobalPlaneSearch.com, 'Aircraft leasing options', web page, accessed: 15 Feb 2015.

96 See Garvett and Hilton, 'What drives airline profits?', p. 181. Pro quick price adjustments see Deleersnyder, Barbara et al., *Weathering tight economic times: The sales evolution of consumer durables over the business cycle* (Erasmus Research Institute

of Management (ERIM), Rotterdam School of Management, 2003), p. 20. And see Keynesian business cycle theory in section 2.1.1. Flexible price setting is also the self-correcting mechanism in Classical business cycle theories, see section 2.1.1.

97 See Pierson, Kawika and John D. Sterman, 'Cyclical dynamics of airline industry earnings', *System Dynamics Review* 29.3 (2013): 145.

98 See Sgouridis, 'Symbiotic strategies in enterprise ecology', p. 330.

99 See interviews with airline managers in section 2.4.2. And see International Air Transport Association (IATA), *Vision 2050*, p. 46. And see Pilarski, *Why can't we make money in aviation?* p. 154.

100 Pro minimum price regulation see Tretheway, Michael W. and W. G. Waters, 'Reregulation of the airline industry: Could price cap regulation play a role?', *Journal of Air Transport Management* 4.1 (1998): 53. And pro fixed prices see Werner, 'Leverage and airline financial management', p. 196.

101 The price mechanism is very sensitive towards changes. Hence, to avoid a shock reaction in the moment the business cycle is inserted, the injected cycle has a lower base value than the usual one (1% instead of 3%).

102 The price mechanism is very sensitive towards changes. Hence, to avoid a shock reaction in the moment the business cycle is inserted, the injected cycle has a lower base value than the usual one (1% instead of 3%).

103 For the simulation shown in Figure 4.100 the *TIME TO PERCEIVE PROFITABILITY TREND* is two years.

104 See Sgouridis, 'Symbiotic strategies in enterprise ecology', p. 330. And see Pierson and Sterman, 'Cyclical dynamics of airline industry earnings', p. 145.

105 Studying the competitive dynamics of individual airlines amongst each other, and for example testing advantages and disadvantages of implementing a policy as a first mover or follower, requires a much more detailed version of the airline industry model. This is a project for further research (see Chapter 5). Here, the focus is on explaining why there is a profit cycle in the airline industry, to understand the dynamics driving its shape, and to identify areas for improvement.

106 See for example Jiang and Hansman, 'An analysis of profit cycles in the airline industry', p. 16. And see Borenstein and Rose, *How airline markets work*, p. 36. And see Skinner et al., 'Managing growth and profitability across peaks and troughs of the airline industry cycle', p. 26. And see Sgouridis et al., *Taming the business cycle in commercial aviation*, p. 6. And see Liehr et al., 'Cycles in the sky', pp. 322–323. And see Werner, 'Leverage and airline financial management', p. 188. And see Button, 'Liberalising aviation', p. 288. And see industry cycle research in section 2.1.2, for example Petersen and Strongin, 'Why are some industries more cyclical than others?', pp. 194–196. And see aviation experts' statements in section 2.4.

107 See interviews in section 2.4. And, for example, see Werner, 'Leverage and airline financial management', pp. 195–196. And see Adler, Nicole and Aaron Gellman, 'Strategies for managing risk in a changing aviation environment', *Journal of Air Transport Management* 21 (2012): 26. And see Neidl, 'Can the aviation industry shield itself from business cycles?', p. 21. Pro industry consolidation see International Air Transport Association (IATA), *Profitability and the air transport value chain*, p. 41.

108 See interviews with airline managers in section 2.4.

109 'A wet lease is the leasing of an aircraft complete with cockpit and cabin crew, and other technical support. [...] The aircraft retains the paint scheme and logo of the lessor, although a temporary sticker can be used to show the lessee's name.' Definition by Morrell, *Airline finance*, p. 204.

110 Airlines' capacity comprises their fleet, personnel, infrastructure, etc. Find details in sections 3.3.3 and 3.3.4.

111 Goal seeking behaviour with a delay is a structural prerequisite for system oscillations. See section 2.2.1.

112 See expert statements in section 2.4.

113 For example, see Liehr et al., 'Cycles in the sky', p. 320. See Skinner and Stock, 'Masters of the cycle', section 2. And see Sgouridis et al., *Taming the business cycle in commercial aviation*, pp. 5–6. – Find classical industry cycle theories such as the 'hog cycle', the 'cobweb theorem', or the 'shipbuilding cycle' in section 2.1.2.

114 See sections 2.4 and 4.3.

115 See aviation managers' statements in section 2.4. And see Pilarski, *Why can't we make money in aviation?* p. 187.

116 In line with Schumpeter's findings an innovation initiates cyclicality. However, in his view the innovation initiate prosperity not downcycles. See Schumpeter, 'The explanation of the business cycle', p. 295.

117 The normal utilisation is the number of days per year which an aircraft is ready for service. It depends on technology and maintenance regulations. See section 3.3.3.

118 There are other airline decisions which can cause a profit cycle, but the cycles they cause have an amplitude of less then 2 %-points profitability. They are listed in Table 4.8 on page 281.

119 See sections 2.4 and 2.3.1.

120 Pro revenue management: See Garvett and Hilton, 'What drives airline profits?', p. 181. And see Neidl, 'Can the aviation industry shield itself from business cycles?', p. 21. And see Deleersnyder et al., *Weathering tight economic times*, p. 20. And see Keynesian business cycle theory, e.g. in Maußner, Alfred, *Konjunkturtheorie [Business cycle theory]* (Berlin et al.: Springer, 1994). – Against revenue management: See Pilarski, *Why can't we make money in aviation?*, p. 154. And see Adler and Gellman, 'Strategies for managing risk in a changing aviation environment', p. 26. And see International Air Transport Association (IATA), *Vision 2050*, p. 46. And see airline managers' statement in section 2.4.2.

121 See Sgouridis, 'Symbiotic strategies in enterprise ecology', p. 330.

122 See Pierson and Sterman, 'Cyclical dynamics of airline industry earnings', p. 145.

123 For example see Borenstein and Rose, *How airline markets work*, p. 36. And see Skinner et al., 'Managing growth and profitability across peaks and troughs of the airline industry cycle', p. 26. And see Sgouridis et al., *Taming the business cycle in commercial aviation*, p. 6. And see Werner, 'Leverage and airline financial management', p. 188. And see Button, 'Liberalising aviation', p. 288. And see literature on industry cycles in section 2.1.2, for example, Petersen and Strongin, 'Why are some industries more cyclical than others?', pp. 194–196. And see aviation experts' statements in section 2.4.2.

124 Inflexible cost adjustment is problematic: See Borenstein and Rose, *How airline markets work*, p. 36. And see Jiang and Hansman, 'An analysis of profit cycles in the airline industry', p. 16. And see Liehr et al., 'Cycles in the sky', pp. 322–323. And see expert interviews in section 2.4.2.

125 A long aircraft service lifetime is identified as problematic: See Liehr et al., 'Cycles in the sky', p. 322. And see Skinner and Stock, 'Masters of the cycle', section 5.

126 This confirms Weil who regards overcapacities as the main reason for cyclicality in industries. See Weil, 'Commoditization of technology-based products and services', pp. 8–14. Also see Wojahn, 'Why does the airline industry over-invest?'.

127 Responsive capacity enlargements are problematic: see Meadows, 'The dynamics of commodity production cycles', pp. 119–121. And see Tan and Mathews, 'Cyclical industrial dynamics', pp. 348–349. And see classical industry cycle theories in section 2.1.2.

128 See Meadows, 'The dynamics of commodity production cycles', p. 127. And see Lyneis, 'System Dynamics for market forecasting and structural analysis', p. 23.

129 This confirms Sterman's finding that it aggravates cyclicality if the supply line is not correctly accounted for, as in the buffers' case. See Sterman, 'Modeling managerial behavior', p. 334.

130 They argue that high barriers to exit retain capacity in the market and hence facilitate overcapacity and in consequence cyclicality. See Sgouridis et al., *Taming the business cycle in commercial aviation*, pp. 5–6. And see Pilarski, *Why can't we make money in aviation?*, pp. 179–186. And see International Air Transport Association (IATA), *Vision 2050*, pp. 45, 53–54.

131 See Lee et al., 'Information distortion in a supply chain', p. 1883. And see Weil, 'Commoditization of technology-based products and services', pp. 8–14. And see Lyneis, 'System Dynamics for market forecasting and structural analysis', pp. 22–23.

132 See Weil, 'Commoditization of technology-based products and services', pp. 8–14. And see Pilarski, *Why can't we make money in aviation?*, pp. 119–124. And see Wojahn, 'Why does the airline industry over-invest?', p. 1.

133 Market share targets cause overcapacities: see Jiang and Hansman, 'An analysis of profit cycles in the airline industry', p. 9. And see Sgouridis et al., *Taming the business cycle in commercial aviation*, pp. 5–6. And see Lyneis, 'System Dynamics for market forecasting and structural analysis', p. 7.

134 See Lyneis, 'System Dynamics for business strategy', pp. 63–64. And see Lyneis, 'System Dynamics for market forecasting and structural analysis', p. 7. And see Skinner and Stock, 'Masters of the cycle', section 2. And see Skinner et al., 'Managing growth and profitability across peaks and troughs of the airline industry cycle', pp. 27–29. And see Liehr et al., 'Cycles in the sky', pp. 312, 316. And see Jiang and Hansman, 'An analysis of profit cycles in the airline industry', p. 11.

135 See Meadows, 'The dynamics of commodity production cycles', pp. 119–121.

136 See International Air Transport Association (IATA), *Vision 2050*, p. 23.

137 This opposes conclusions of Pierson/Sterman and Garvett/Hilton, but confirms statements of Sgouridis, Adler/Gellman and the IATA. Find more references in section 2.1. – See Pierson and Sterman, 'Cyclical dynamics of airline industry earnings', p. 145. And see Garvett and Hilton, 'What drives airline profits?', p. 181. And see Sgouridis, 'Modeling commercial aviation as an Enterprise of Enterprises', p. 330. And see Adler and Gellman, 'Strategies for managing risk in a changing aviation environment', p. 26. And see International Air Transport Association (IATA), *Vision 2050*, pp. 46, 55.

138 Fixed prices are suggested to stabilise profitability for example by Werner, 'Leverage and airline financial management', p. 196. – As a softer version Tretheway/Water suggest to consider a minimum price regulation, see Tretheway and Waters, 'Reregulation of the airline industry', p. 53.

139 See Forrester, *Industrial dynamics*, p. 186. And see Meadows, 'The dynamics of commodity production cycles', pp. 119–120.

140 See Sterman, *Business dynamics*, p. 681. And see Neidl, 'Can the aviation industry shield itself from business cycles?', p. 21. And see Chin and Tay, 'Developments in air transport', p. 329.

141 See Jiang and Hansman, 'An analysis of profit cycles in the airline industry', p. 11. And see Skinner et al., 'Managing growth and profitability across peaks and troughs of the airline industry cycle', p. 26.

142 See Skinner and Stock, 'Masters of the cycle', section 5. And see Skinner et al., 'Managing growth and profitability across peaks and troughs of the airline industry cycle', p. 26.

143 See Lee et al., 'Information distortion in a supply chain', pp. 1883–1884.

144 Airline managers criticise unreliable aircraft deliveries, see section 2.4.

145 See Lee et al., 'Information distortion in a supply chain', pp. 1883–1884. And see Sgouridis et al., *Taming the business cycle in commercial aviation*, pp. 17–19.

146 Find a short literature discussion of the inflexible cost base in section 2.1 on amplification.

147 See Liehr et al., 'Cycles in the sky', p. 322. And see Skinner and Stock, 'Masters of the cycle', section 5.

148 See experts' statements in section 2.4.2. And see Liehr et al., 'Cycles in the sky', p. 323. – And see Skinner and Stock, 'Masters of the cycle', section 5. And see Werner, 'Leverage and airline financial management', p. 196.

149 Lease periods are usually much longer: Operating aircraft leases with a contract duration of five years are common. See Morrell, *Airline finance*, p. 200.

150 See Lyneis, 'System Dynamics for market forecasting and structural analysis', pp. 7–9.

151 Pro information sharing: see Sgouridis, 'Symbiotic strategies in enterprise ecology', pp. 292–294. And see International Air Transport Association (IATA), *Profitability and the air transport value chain*, p. 41. And see Skinner and Stock, 'Masters of the cycle', section 6. And see Forrester, 'Industrial dynamics: A major breakthrough for decision makers', pp. 47–49. And see Lee et al., 'Information distortion in a supply chain', p. 1883. And see Croson and Donohue, 'Behavioral causes of the bullwhip effect and the observed value of inventory information', pp. 331–333. And see Chen et al., 'Quantifying the bullwhip effect in a simple supply chain', pp. 436–442. And see Smaros et al., 'The impact of increasing demand visibility on production and inventory control efficiency', pp. 336–354.– Pro accurate forecasts: see Lyneis, 'System Dynamics for market forecasting and structural analysis', pp. 22–23. And see Chin and Tay, 'Developments in air transport', p. 329. And see Sterman, *Business dynamics*, p. 751.

5 Conclusions for the airline industry

For decades financial results in the airline industry have been strongly cyclical. In aggregate, airlines earn high profits in upswings and lose large amounts of money in downturns (see Figure 5.1 and section 1.1).[1] As a result, the world airlines' net profit average is zero. The profit cycle's period was ten years but became shorter after 2007. Its amplitude has been rising and amounted to over 50 billion US dollars after 2000.

More stable returns could not only facilitate airline management decisions and improve investors' confidence but also preserve employment. To achieve the desired stability a better understanding of factors causing and driving airline profitability dynamics is needed. The required research was guided by three questions:

1 Why are airline profits cyclical?
2 What are the causes and dynamics that determine the cycle's shape?
3 How can the situation be improved?

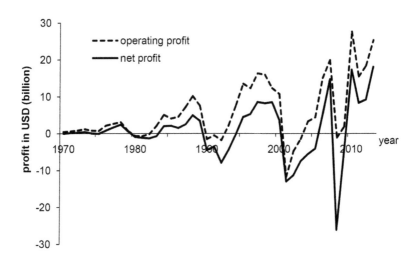

Figure 5.1 Worldwide aggregate airline profits (same as Figure 1.3)

To answer these questions the following approach was taken. Potential airline profit cycle causes, drivers, and possible cycle mitigation measures were derived from an interdisciplinary literature review and expert interviews. Airline managers often claim GDP changes, fuel price developments, or shocks[2] drive the cycle. Yet, a statistical analysis of world airline profits exposed, none of these factors can sufficiently explain the airline profit cycle. Hence, in order to incorporate more factors and dynamics in the investigation a system model of the airline industry was formulated. It allowed to test the impact of the derived potential cycle causes, drivers, and mitigation measures in quantitative scenario simulations. Results are summarised in the following sections.

Why are airline profits cyclical?

Model experiments revealed that the airline industry is an oscillating system that is inherently stable. This means the industry is theoretically able to achieve and sustain a state of stable profitability. Yet, when 'disturbed', the industry's profitability starts to oscillate with diminishing amplitude until it regains a stable profitability level.

What is meant by 'the industry is disturbed'? — A disturbance can be any influence that causes airlines' actual and desired air traffic supply to diverge. System analyses disclosed this divergence is the profit cycle's origin. Disturbances can be changes in the general economy, in the airline industry's environment, or in airlines' behaviour.[3] This means airlines can cause cyclicality themselves; changes in industry environment or general economy are not necessary. In reality, GDP or fuel prices, for example, are rarely completely stable so that the airline industry's profit stabilisation process is disturbed over and over again. Cycle causes with most impact in model experiments are:[4]

- variations in GDP growth or fuel prices, as well as shocks
- changes in the price sensitivity of air transport demand
- inaccurate aircraft delivery forecasts

Why does the disturbance lead to a cycle? — When a disturbance causes airlines' desired and actual capacity to diverge, airlines seek to correct this imbalance. Oscillations occur because airlines' corrective actions are not perfect in terms of size, nature, and/or timing and need to be readjusted. Reasons for inadequate decisions are that they are taken under a certain degree of uncertainty. Information may be incomplete, perceptions biased, reporting lags behind actual developments, and forecasts cannot incorporate all eventualities. As a consequence stabilisation is a set of iterative approximation processes, which over- and undershoot until actual and desired capacity match. Hence, if the process is not disturbed, the airline industry's profitability returns to stability after several years. (From a system research perspective this matching or goal-seeking process with delays is the generic structure of an oscillating system.

The fact that model experiments revealed that the airline industry returns to its initial profitability level makes it inherently stable.)

In conclusion, why are airline industry profits cyclical? — In reality the airline industry's profitability is cyclical, not stable. The reasons are that (1) the industry's profit stabilisation process takes time, and (2) the industry is frequently disturbed. So while the stabilisation process is still running, conditions change and necessitate restarting the stabilisation process, and hence a profit cycle. How intensely airline industry profits swing, whether there are minor fluctuations or large changes, is attended by research question 2.

What are the causes and dynamics that determine the airline profit cycle's shape?

The airline profit cycle's shape is determined by the general economy, the industry environment, as well as by airlines' behaviour. The latter can have at least as much effect on airline profitability as the general economy. Airlines' behaviour can, for example, more than quadruple the airline profit cycle's amplitude.

What influence does the general economy have? — Every change in general economic factors, such as GDP growth, fuel costs, and shocks, triggers a cycle and hence impacts the overall shape of the airline profit development curve. Depending on the industry's state, changes in the general economy can aggravate or mitigate cycle swings. The general economy's business cycle translates into airline profitability. Its period reappears in airline profits, its amplitude is magnified in airline industry profits. GDP growth is the most influential general economic factor because it directly impacts airline customers' ability or willingness to pay. Model experiments showed that the airline industry suffers much longer as a result of a drop in GDP growth than because of a sharp fuel price increase. Furthermore, model experiments revealed that positive GDP growth induces positive long-run profitability in the airline industry. Yet, although the economy grew progressively over the past decades, the airline profit cycle's average over time is zero. This shows how much the airline industry's environment and airlines' behaviour influence the airline industry's profit development.

Why did the profit cycle's amplitude rise? — The airline industry's growth increased aggregate airline profits. Adjusted for industry size, airlines' profitability to revenues exhibits a more constant amplitude over time (see Figure 1.4 on p. 4). Nonetheless, the amplitude of the airline profitability swings is much larger than in the economy's business cycle (GDP development). Model experiments exposed the following main airline profitability cycle magnifiers, which were at work in the airline industry's past:

- airlines increasingly use revenue management: Revenue management systems allocate seats to price categories and have become increasingly widespread and elaborate over time. In a downturn this short-run demand stimulation technique reduces yields to facilitate sales and gain more revenues. Yet, due to the resulting price war, the industry's revenues decrease overall and aggravate the downturn. In upswings, on the other hand, revenue management systems assist airlines to exploit the favourable situation. (With revenue management airline customers' increasing price sensitivity, which the IATA diagnoses, actually dampens cyclicality because the more sensitive demand needs less price adjustment to show the same response.)[5]

- airlines have an inflexible cost base: The high fixed cost share gives airlines high leverage, which again emphasises the importance of airlines' price decisions. (Model simulations revealed that airlines already exploit the potential of short-run cost adjustment, e.g. by rescheduling or cancelling flights.)
- the industry augments capacities: Between 1997 and 2013 worldwide passenger air traffic more than doubled (see section 1.1). Yet, declining yields indicate, and model experiments confirm, that the airline industry built up more capacity than can profitably be sold. Factors which encouraged this development are found to be:

  - airlines' ordering responsive to current profitability expectations (Accordingly, it dampens the profit cycle if capacity can less responsively be augmented. If aircraft arrive late, the airline industry benefits from this artificial capacity constraint.)
  - easy access to capital (Investors provide capital though the airline industry has a history of destroying shareholder value; see section 1.2.)

Why is the average net profit over time zero? — The airline profit cycle's long-run mean value depends primarily on the following factors which were at work in the airline industry's past:

- airlines build up too much capacity: Competitive pressures, strategic growth targets, or buffers in the planning process motivate airlines to invest more than they can profitably sell.
- developments in the general economy: Weak GDP growth, rising fuel prices, and shock deteriorate the airline industry's profitability.

What determines the length of cycle swings? — Model experiments revealed that the following factors drive the airline profit cycle's period, i.e. how often it swings within a certain timeframe, apart from the influence of the general economy's business cycle (see above). The cycle period depends mainly on the airlines' speed of information processing, expectation formation, and the time airlines need to take actions. If information flows take longer, the profit cycle period is longer, and vice versa. Especially the time necessary to adjust fixed costs, and the time to plan and place capacity orders (which determines how responsive airlines build up capacity) are found to be critical. Correspondingly, airlines' easy access to capital increases volatility whereas high barriers to exit dampen it.

How can the airline industry's profitability situation be improved?

To mitigate the airline profit cycle four policies are found to be most effective in model experiments. They lie within the airlines' and their stakeholders' area of influence:

- *focus on long-term profitability in price setting*
  Revenue management as a short-run price determination mechanism is a major cycle driver. Ideally, it should be discarded. Since this is hardly realistic, revenue management's negative effects can be compensated by setting prices with closer orientation to costs and/or by emphasising profitability targets that force yields upwards in unprofitable times.
- *enlarge capacity gradually and slowly*
  More gradual and slow capacity enlargement prevents overcapacity, and thus mitigates volatility while augmenting profitability. Cycle mitigation measures especially effective in model simulations are:

  - for airlines: more gradual capacity build-up (allow more time for more careful planning, based on long-term trend extrapolations, less dependent on profit)
  - for aircraft manufacturers: limited aircraft delivery or production
  - for investors: more difficult access to capital for airlines
  - for regulators: higher barriers to market exit (retain capacity in the industry and thus counteract volatility)

- *make existing capacity flexibly adjustable*
  Flexibly adjustable capacity implies, first, flexible short-run capacity adjustments by flight schedule modifications. Second, it comprises the reduction of airlines' high fixed cost share by productivity improvements, contract negotiations, and profit-dependent aircraft retirement. Furthermore, very short-term aircraft leases (one-year contracts) are found to dampen cyclicality strongly. Longer lease contacts have a much weaker effect, so with the common five-year operating leases it hardly matters whether the fleet is leased or owned.
- *aim for 'perfect information'*
  Improved forecasting and information sharing within the industry and along the value chain diminish the airline profit cycle because they help to minimise the divergence between actual and desired capacity in the airline industry.

The recommended policies aim to improve airline profitability at industry level. An individual airline that implements them may not attain the desired improvements (see section 'further research'). The proposed mitigation measures are designed as coordinated actions within airline alliances or an industry-wide organisation. Whether airlines' stakeholders choose to take recommended action will depend on their interests. Since they have to handle the airline profit cycle's negative consequences (see section 1.2), they may be persuaded to cooperate in fighting them. Not all recommended cycle mitigation measures may realistically be expected to find full implementation. Yet, even steps in the right direction will stabilise the airline industry's profitability.

The power of cycle mitigation measures: 'What would have happened if . . .'

To illustrate the impact of cycle mitigation policies, a counter-factual simulation of the airline industry's past is conducted. It shows how the US airline industry's operating profitability to revenues would have hypothetically developed since 1985 if the respective policies had been implemented (all other things equal).[6]

If in their price-setting processes airlines had focused more on long-term profitability, the airline profit cycle's amplitude would have been reduced considerably (see Figure 5.2). The applied mitigation measures are less revenue management and more weight on overall profit goals in the price determination process to compensate revenue management's negative effects. The simulated profitability cycle's amplitude (minimum to maximum) is only half as large as the 20 %-points amplitude the US airline industry experienced in the past.

If aircraft capacity had been built up more gradually, the airlines' profitability cycle would have been slightly dampened and more importantly it would have had a much higher mean value (see Figure 5.3). Making airlines' access to capital more difficult or investors more hesitant would have had a similar effect (Figure 5.3).

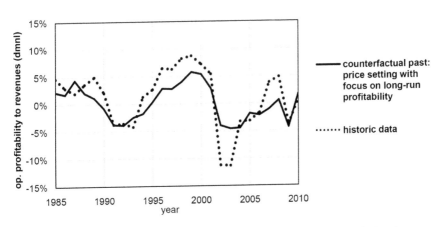

Figure 5.2 If airlines had given long-term profitability more impact on their price setting (counterfactual simulation)

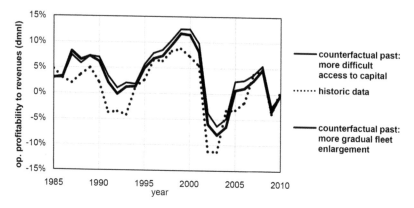

Figure 5.3 If airlines had built up their aircraft capacity more gradually or if access to capital had been more difficult (counterfactual simulations)

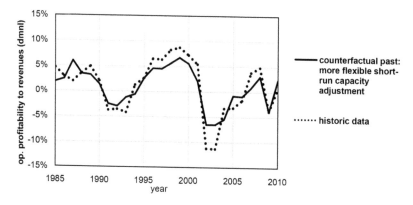

Figure 5.4 If airlines had been able to adjust their fleet even more flexibly in the short run (counterfactual simulation)

If airlines had been able to adjust their fleet more flexibly in the short run than they have in the past, their profit cycle could have been dampened, especially after the 2001 crisis (see Figure 5.4).

If the forecasts airlines base their aircraft capacity adjustment decisions on had been perfect, the airline profit cycle's amplitude would have been reduced as well (see Figure 5.5).

A combination of mitigation measures would have resulted in a completely different, excellent profit development in the airline industry, without any negative phases. From the aforementioned policies, only two which airlines can influence themselves are applied simultaneously: a more long-term focus in price setting, and a more gradual aircraft capacity enlargement. If airlines had

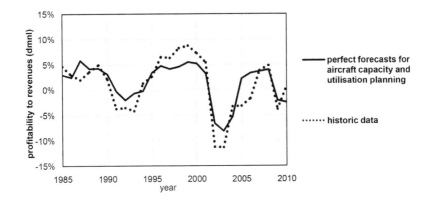

Figure 5.5 If forecasts around aircraft capacity and utilisation planning had been perfect (counterfactual simulation)

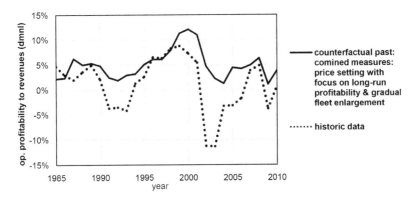

Figure 5.6 If airlines had focused more on long-term profitability in their price setting and had enlarged their fleet more gradually (counterfactual simulation)

followed those two rules, the airline industry's profitability would have been tremendously better (see Figure 5.6). It would still have been cyclic but with an amplitude only half as large. Moreover, the average profitability level would have been 5% instead of 0%, despite all crises, GDP growth fluctuations, and fuel price changes, which occurred in the past. None of those influences would have caused negative operating profitability. Furthermore, airlines would have benefited from profitability peaks which would have been even higher than they were in reality.

The counterfactual simulations illustrate the seminal impact mitigation measures proposed in this study can have on the airline industry's profitability. Taking steps in their direction could already improve the airline industry's profit situation.

Conclusion

This research has shown that the airline profit cycle is the product of changes in the general economy, factors in the industry environment, as well as airlines' behaviour. To dampen the profit cycle and achieve a higher long-run profitability level airlines, their stakeholders, or regulators could take action. Promising measures are: (1) focus on long-term profitability in price setting; (2) gradual and slow capacity enlargement; (3) flexible adjustment of existing capacity; and (4) improved forecasting and information sharing within the industry and along the value chain.

From a methodical point of view the contribution of this research lies, first, in capturing the airline industry's complex dynamics in a comparatively small, and thus more comprehensible, System Dynamics model. The model is able to reproduce historic developments in the airline industry exceedingly well, which invites confidence in its structure and behaviour. Second, the developed model is the first documented airline industry model with a completely endogenous price-setting process (i.e. which is not driven by external time series). Since price is the central connecting element between demand and supply, this modelling advancement strengthens the credibility of model simulation results. Third, the conducted simulation experiments analyse the airline profit cycle in more detail than previous studies, especially because drivers of amplitude, period, and average profit are distinguished. This allowed us to explain the airline profit cycle's shape, in addition to its existence. It also served to design measures which mitigate the airline profit cycle's amplitude successfully in model simulations while increasing average profitability.

Suggestions for further research

The presented study offers several opportunities for further research. Interviewed aviation managers and researchers encouraged pursuit of the following three objectives:

1   **Use the model to evaluate the impact of planned strategic or regulatory action**: The model can be used to further research suitable mitigation measures for the airline profit cycle. Planned regulatory changes can be tested for their impact on airlines' profitability, especially in the interaction with other policies. Airlines can simulate the effects of strategic decisions under different circumstances.
2   **Explain industry phenomena**: The airline industry model can be used to explain different phenomena in the industry. For example, while air traffic demand rose almost exponentially, yields have fallen drastically over the past decades. Intuitively, a service that is much wanted should sell for a high price. Yet, mechanisms in the industry and airlines' interaction with their environment lead to deteriorating prices. The airline industry model can enlighten the dynamics which drive this and other phenomena in the industry. Model experiments can then be used to test alternative policies.

3 **Add an individual airline's perspective**: To achieve a profound understanding of the airline industry's profitability dynamics, the airline industry model was built to simulate industry-wide airline profits. Correspondingly, the aggregation level for the model is at industry level. Individual decisions of all airlines are summarised into an industry perspective. Yet, in some cases it may be beneficial for airlines to make opportunistic moves and counteract the industry trend. The airline industry model could be extended to capture this individual perspective.

Model experiments with an individual airline's perspective could be used to derive an airline's success factors. Experiments would reveal what airline features or strategies result in the best financial performance under different circumstances.[7] Furthermore, the individual airline model could inform airline managers how employing a profit cycle damping policy impacts their competitive position. For example, in some cases first movers may be disadvantaged, in others there may be long-term benefits from pioneering. The competitive effects of each strategy could be tested in the modelling environment before implementation.

Notes

1 Data source: A4A Airlines for America, 'World airlines annual results: Financial results 1947–present', web page, accessed: 21 Nov 2014.
2 Shocks are for example the 9/11 terror attack or the oil crises. See sections 3.1.1, 3.3.1, and 4.3.
3 Find definitions for these categories in section 2.5.
4 Further airline industry environment factors, which can cause a profit cycle, are: tax increases, variations in aircraft manufacturers' lead times, aircraft price changes, and innovations which improve aircraft performance. – Further airline behaviour changes, which can cause a profit cycle, are: a change in aircraft retirement age, an increase in ancillary yield.
5 See International Air Transport Association (IATA), *Vision 2050* (Singapore 2011), p. 23.
6 Data source for US airlines' operating profitability: A4A Airlines for America, 'World airlines annual results: Financial results 1947–present', accessed: 21 Nov 2014.
7 For systemic success factor research see for example Piepenbrock, Theodore F., 'Toward a theory of evolution of business ecosystems: Enterprise architectures, competitive dynamics, firm performance and industrial co-evolution', Massachusetts Institute of Technology, 2009.

6   References

A4A Airlines for America. 'About A4A.' Accessed 5 June 2013: www.airlines.org/Pages/About A4A.aspx.

A4A Airlines for America. 'Annual financial results: World airlines.' Accessed 8 Oct 2013: www.airlines.org/Pages/Annual-Results-World-Airlines.aspx.

A4A Airlines for America. 'Chapter 4: Airline economics.' Accessed 13 Sept 2013: www.airlines.org/Pages/Airline-Handbook-Chapter-4-Airline-Economics.aspx.

A4A Airlines for America. 'U.S. aviation tax increases on airline tickets.' Accessed 7 Nov 2014: http://airlines.org/downstream-tableau-chart-3/.

A4A Airlines for America. 'World airlines annual results: Financial results 1947–present.' Note: Financial results reflect the systemwide activity of scheduled passenger and cargo airlines operating worldwide, as recorded by ICAO; domestic operations within the former USSR are excluded prior to 1998. Traffic and operations data reflects the systemwide scheduled activity of passenger and cargo airlines operating worldwide, as recorded by ICAO; domestic operations within the former USSR are excluded prior to 1970. Accessed 21 Nov 2014: http://airlines.org/data/annual-results-world-airlines/.

A4A Airlines for America. 'World airlines: Annual results. Financial results 1947-present.' Accessed 15 Nov 2013: www.airlines.org/Pages/Annual-Results-World-Airlines.aspx.

A4A Airlines for America. 'World airlines: Annual results. Traffic and operations 1929–present.' Note: Traffic and operations data reflects the systemwide scheduled activity of passenger and cargo airlines operating worldwide, as recorded by ICAO; domestic operations within the former USSR are excluded prior to 1970. Accessed 21 Nov 2014: http://airlines.org/data/annual-results-world-airlines.

A4A Airlines for America. 'Air Transport Association changes name to Airlines for America (A4A).' 2011. Accessed 5 June 2013: www.airlines.org/Pages/news_12-01-2011.aspx.

A4A Airlines for America. 'Government-Imposed Taxes on Air Transportation.' 2013. Accessed 9 Oct 2013: www.airlines.org/Pages/Government-Imposed-Taxes-on-Air-Transportation.aspx.

A4A Airlines for America (formerly ATA Air Transport Association). 'ATA quarterly cost index for U.S. passenger airlines: Methodology.' Accessed 13 Dec 2011: www.airlines.org/Pages/ATA-Quarterly-Cost-Index-U.S.-Passenger-Airlines.aspx.

A4A Airlines for America (formerly ATA Air Transport Association). 'ATA Cost Index for US Passenger Airlines, 3rd quarter 2010.' 2011. Accessed 23 Feb 2011: www.airlines.org/Economics/DataAnalysis/Pages/QuarterlyCostIndex.aspx.

Adler, Nicole and Aaron Gellman. 'Strategies for managing risk in a changing aviation environment.' *Journal of Air Transport Management* 21 (2012): 24–35.

Airbus. 'Historical orders and deliveries 1974–2009.' 2010. Accessed 8 Sept 2010: www. airbus.com/fileadmin/media_gallery/files/reports_results_reviews/Summary_ Historical_Orders_Deliveries_1974-2009.xls.

Airbus. 'Airbus summary results 1989–2012, updated Jan 2013.' 2013. Accessed 21 Nov 2013: www.airbus.com/presscentre/corporate-information/key-documents/? contentId=%5B_TABLE%3Att_content%3B_FIELD%3Auid%5D%2C&cHash= 22935adfac92fcbbd4ba4e1441d13383.

Airbus. Global market forecast 2013–2032. 2014.

Amadeus and IdeaWorks. Amadeus guide to ancillary revenue. 2010.

Azzam, Mark and Eva-Maria Cronrath. 'Airline network structures and development strategies.' *13th Annual World Conference of the Air Transport Research Society (ATRS).* 2009.

Barlas, Yaman. 'Formal aspects of model validity and validation in System Dynamics.' *System Dynamics Review* 12.3 (1996): 183–210.

BBC News. 'Alitalia seeks bankruptcy measure.' 2008, August 29. Accessed 15 Nov 2013: http://news.bbc.co.uk/2/hi/business/7588475.stm.

Belobaba, Peter. 'Application of a probabilistic decision model to airline seat inventory control.' *Operations Research* 32.2 (1989): 183–197.

Belobaba, Peter. 'Overview of airline economics, markets and demand.' In *The global airline industry*. Eds Belobaba, Peter, Amedeo R. Odoni and Cynthia Barnhart. Chichester, UK: Wiley, 2009, pp. 47–72.

Belobaba, Peter, Amedeo R. Odoni, and Cynthia Barnhart. *The global airline industry*. Aerospace series (PEP). Chichester, UK: Wiley, 2009.

Ben-Yosef, Eldad. *The evolution of the US airline industry: Theory, strategy and policy*. Studies in industrial organization. Dordrecht: Springer, 2005.

Bils, Mark. 'Testing for contracting effects on employment.' *The Quarterly Journal of Economics* 106.4 (1991): 1129–1156.

Bittlingmayer, George. 'Did antitrust policy cause the great merger wave?' *Journal of Boeing. 'Orders and deliveries.' 2010. Accessed 18 Aug 2010: http://active.boeing. com/commercial/orders/index.cfm?content=displaystandardreport.cfm&pageid=m 25065&RequestTimeout=20000.

Boeing. 'About us: Boeing employment numbers.' 2013. Accessed 21 Nov 2013: www.boeing.com/boeing/aboutus/employment/employment_table_2012.page.

Boeing. 'Orders and deliveries.' 2013. Accessed 20 Nov 2013: http://active.boeing.com/ commercial/orders/index.cfm?content=timeperiodselection.cfm&pageid=m15523.

Borenstein, Severin. On the persistent financial losses of US airlines: A preliminary exploration. 2011.

Borenstein, Severin, and Nancy L. Rose. 'Competition and price dispersion in the US airline industry.' *Journal of Political Economy* 102.4 (1994): 653–683.

Borenstein, Severin, and Nancy L. Rose. *How airline markets work. . . Or do they? Regulatory reform in the airline industry*. National Bureau of Economic Research Working Paper No. 13452. Issued in September 2007.

Brons, Martijn, Eric Pels, Peter Nijkamp, and Piet Rietveld. 'Price elasticities of demand for passenger air travel: A meta-analysis.' *Journal of Air Transport Management* 8.3 (2002): 165–175.

Button, Kenneth. 'Liberalising aviation: Is there an empty core problem?' *Journal of Transport Economics and Policy* 30.3 (1996): 275–291.

Button, Kenneth. 'Empty cores in airlines markets.' *5th Hamburg Aviation Conference.* 2002.

Cachon, Gérard P., Taylor Randall, and Glen M. Schmidt. 'In search of the bullwhip effect.' *Manufacturing & Service Operations Management* 9.4 (2007): 457–479.

CAPA Centre for Aviation. 'Gol's operating margin drops as Brazil's carriers refuse to raise fares.' 2011. Last updated: 13 May 2011. Accessed 18 Feb 2014: http://centreforaviation.com/analysis/gols-operating-margin-drops-as-brazils-carriers-refuse-to-raise-fares-51405.

CAPA Centre for Aviation. 'High fuel prices and weak load factors erode SIA's profits.' 2011. Last updated: 13 May 2011. Accessed 18 Feb 2014: http://centreforaviation.com/analysis/high-fuel-prices-and-weak-load-factors-start-to-eat-into-sias-profits-51406.

CAPA Centre for Aviation. 'Rising fuel costs dominate airline bottom lines.' 2011. Last updated: 13 May 2011 Accessed 18 Feb 2014: http://centreforaviation.com/analysis/rising-fuel-costs-dominate-airline-bottom-lines-51466.

CAPA Centre for Aviation. 'Thai's profits drop in 1Q2011 as oil prices and external factors affect demand.' 2011. Last updated: 13 May 2011. Accessed 18 Feb 2014: http://centreforaviation.com/analysis/thais-profits-drop-in-1q2011-as-oil-prices-rise-and-external-factors-impact-demand-51459.

CAPA Centre for Aviation. 'Bankruptcy of Denmark's Cimber Sterling will leave no long-lasting network gaps.' 2012. Last updated: 8 May 2012. Accessed 15 Nov 2013: http://centreforaviation.com/analysis/bankruptcy-of-denmarks-cimber-sterling-will-leave-no-long-lasting-network-gaps-73330.

CAPA Centre for Aviation. 'Unit cost analysis of Emirates, IAG & Virgin; about learning from a new model, not unpicking it.' 2014. Last updated: Jan 2014. Accessed 23 Feb 2015: http://centreforaviation.com/analysis/unit-cost-analysis-of-emirates-iag--virgin-about-learning-from-a-new-model-not-unpicking-it-147262.

Carlton, Dennis W. 'The rigidity of prices.' *American Economic Review* 76.637–658 (1986): 637.

Chen, Frank, Zvi Drezner, Jennifer K. Ryan, and David Simchi-Levi. 'Quantifying the bullwhip effect in a simple supply chain: The impact of forecasting, lead times, and information.' *Management Science* 46.3 (2000): 436–443.

Chin, Anthony T.H., and John H. Tay. 'Developments in air transport: Implications on investment decisions, profitability and survival of Asian airlines.' *Journal of Air Transport Management* 7.5 (2001): 319–330.

Clark, J. Maurice. 'Business acceleration and the law of demand: A technical factor in economic cycles.' *Journal of Political Economy* 25.3 (1917): 217–235.

Clark, Paul. *Buying the big jets: Fleet planning for airlines.* 2nd edn. Aldershot, UK; Burlington, VT: Ashgate, 2007.

Clark, Paul. *Stormy skies: Airlines in crisis.* Farnham, UK: Ashgate, 2010.

CNN Financial News. 'Airline 1Q losses mount.' 2001. Last updated: 18 April 2001. CNN Money Online. Accessed 18 Feb 2014: http://money.cnn.com/2001/04/18/news/airlines_earnings/.

Compustat. 'Fundamentals Annual Data.' Accessed 28 Jan 2015: http://wrds-web.wharton.upenn.edu/wrds/connect/.

Conklin & de Decker. 'Lease pros and cons – The things you should know.' Accessed 13 Sept 2013: www.conklindd.com/Page.aspx?hid=927.

Croson, Rachel and Karen Donohue. 'Behavioral causes of the bullwhip effect and the observed value of inventory information.' *Management Science* 52.3 (2006): 323–336.

Cuadrado-Roura, Juan R. and Alvaro Ortiz V.-Abarca. 'Business cycle and service industries: General trends and the Spanish case.' *Service Industries Journal* 21.1 (2001): 103–122.

Dejonckheere, J., S.M. Disney, M.R. Lambrecht, and D.R. Towill. 'Measuring and avoiding the bullwhip effect: A control theoretic approach.' *European Journal of Operational Research* 147.3 (2003): 567–590.

Deleersnyder, Barbara, Marnik G. Dekimpe, Miklos Sarvary, and Philip M. Parker. *Weathering tight economic times: The sales evolution of consumer durables over the business cycle*. Erasmus Research Institute of Management (ERIM), Rotterdam School of Management, 2003.

Delfmann, Werner. *Strategic management in the aviation industry*. Cologne; Aldershot, UK; Burlington, VT: Kölner Wissenschaftsverlag; Farnham, UK: Ashgate, 2005.

Dempsy, Paul Stephen. *Airline regulation: The US example*. McGill University, 2009.

Deseret News. 'Airline industry to present "perilous" financial picture.' 2004. Last updated: 3 June 2004. Accessed 14 Feb 2014: www.deseretnews.com/article/595067608/Airline-industry-to-present-perilous-financial-picture.html?pg=all.

Discussant. 'Why airlines fail – Too costly or bad management?'. 2004. Last updated: 26 July 2004. Airliners.net Forum. Accessed 18 Feb 2014: www.airliners.net/aviation-forums/general_aviation/read.main/1669072/.

Doganis, Rigas. *Flying off course – Airline economics and marketing*. 4th edn. London and New York: Routledge, 2010.

Douglas, Evan J. 'The pricing and competitive strategies of US airlines.' *Journal of Applied Business Research* 5.2 (1989): 23–29.

Doyle, James K., Bob Eberlein, Andy Ford, Jim Hines, James M. Lyneis, Ken Parsons, Oleg Pavlov, Michael J. Radzicki, Khalid Saeed, and Kim Warren. 'Design of a Master of Science degree program in System Dynamics at WPI.' *27th International Conference of the System Dynamics Society*. Albuquerque, New Mexico, 2009.

Edgeworth, Francis Y. Mathematical psychics – An essay on the application of mathematics to the moral science. London: C. Kegan Paul & Co., 1881.

Emirates. 'Financial statements 2004–2014.' Accessed 28 Jan 2015: www.emirates.com/de/german/about/investor_relations/investor_relations.aspx.

Emirates. Airlines and subsidy: Our position, 2012.

Ezekiel, Mordecai. 'The cobweb theorem.' *The Quarterly Journal of Economics* 52.2 (1938): 255–280.

Flouris, Triant G. and Ayse Kucuk Yilmaz. *Risk management and corporate sustainability in aviation*. Farnham, UK; Burlington, VT: Ashgate, 2011.

Flouris, Triant G. and Sharon L. Oswald. *Designing and executing strategy in aviation management*. Aldershot, UK; Burlington, VT: Ashgate, 2006.

Ford, Andrew. Modelling the environment: An introduction to System Dynamics modelling of environmental systems. Washington DC: Island Press, 1999.

Ford, David N. 'A behavioral approach to feedback loop dominance analysis.' *System Dynamics Review* 15.1 (1999): 3–36.

Forrester, Jay W. 'Industrial dynamics: A major breakthrough for decision makers.' *Harvard Business Review* 36.4 (1958): 37–66.

Forrester, Jay W. *Industrial dynamics*. 6th printing 1969 edn. Cambridge, MA: MIT Press, 1961.

Forrester, Jay W. 'Industrial dynamics – After the first decade.' *Management Science* 14.7 (1968): 398–415.

Forrester, Jay W. *Principles of systems*. 2nd edn. Cambridge, MA: Wright-Allen Press, 1968.

Forrester, Jay W. '"The" model versus a modeling "process".' *System Dynamics Review* 1.1 (1985): 133–134.

Forrester, Jay W. 'The beginning of System Dynamics.' *System Dynamics Society Meeting.* 1989.

Forrester, Jay W. 'System Dynamics and the lessons of 35 years.' In *A systems-based approach to policymaking.* Ed. Greene, Kenyon B. New York: Springer, 1993, pp. 199–240.

Forrester, Jay W. and Peter M. Senge. 'Tests for building confidence in System Dynamics models.' *TIMS Studies in the Management Science* 14 (1980): 209–228.

Franke, Markus. 'Innovation: The winning formula to regain profitability in aviation?' *Journal of Air Transport Management* 13.1 (2007): 23–30.

Freshfields, Bruckhaus, and Deringer. 'Olympic Airlines: Judgement clarifies definition of "establishment" in secondary insolvency proceedings.' 2013. Accessed 15 Nov 2013: www.freshfields.com/uploadedFiles/SiteWide/Knowledge/36293_Olympic_Airlines_Proof 1.pdf.

Friedman, Milton. *Studies in the quantity theory of money.* Phoenix books. Chicago: University of Chicago Press, 1956.

Friedman, Milton and Rose D. Friedman. *Capitalism and freedom.* Chicago/London: University of Chicago Press, 1982.

Frisch, Ragnar. 'Propagation problems and impulse problems in dynamics economics.' In *Reprinted from: Economic Essays in honour of Gustav Calles.* London: George Allen & Unwin Ltd., 1933, pp. 1–35.

Gabisch, Günter and Hans-Walter Lorenz. *Business cycle theory – A survey of methods and concepts.* 2nd ed. Berlin and others: Springer, 1989.

Garvett, Donald S. and Kyle J. Hilton. 'What drives airline profits? A first look.' In *Handbook of airline finance.* Eds. Butler, Gail F. and Martin R. Keller. 1st edn. New York: Aviation Week, 1999, pp. 173–185.

Gavazza, Alessandro. 'Asset liquidity and financial contracts: Evidence from aircraft leases.' *Journal of Financial Economics* 95.1 (2010): 62–84.

Gelhausen, Marc, Peter Berster, and Dieter Wilken. 'Do airport capacity constraints have a serious impact on the future development of air traffic?' *Journal of Air Transport Management* 28 (2013): 3–13.

Ghaffarzadegan, Navid, John Lyneis, and George P. Richardson. 'How small System Dynamics models can help the public policy process.' *System Dynamics Review* 27.1 (2011): 22–44.

Gibson, William. *Aircraft lessor prospects and lease valuation for airlines.* International Air Transport Association (IATA), October 2008.

GlobalPlaneSearch.com. 'Aircraft leasing options.' Accessed 15 Feb 2015: www.globalplanesearch.com/aviation_library/leasing_options.htm.

Grampp, William D. 'What did Smith mean by the invisible hand?' *Journal of Political Economy* 108.3 (2000): 441–465.

Gritta, Richard and Ellen Lippman. 'Aircraft leasing and its effect on air carriers debt burdens: A comparison over the past several decades.' *Journal of the Transportation Research Forum* 49.3 (2010): 101–110.

Größler, Andreas. 'Modelltests [Model tests].' *System Dynamics für die Finanzindustrie: Simulieren und Analysieren dynamisch-komplexer Probleme* Eds. Strohhecker, Jürgen and Jürgen Sehnert. Frankfurt: Frankfurt-School-Verlag, 2008. 253–267.

Größler, Andreas, Frank H. Maier, and Peter M. Milling. 'Enhancing learning capabilities by providing transparency in business simulators.' *Simulation Gaming* 31.2 (2000): 257–278.

Größler, Andreas, Jörn-Henrik Thun, and Peter M. Milling. 'System Dynamics as a structural theory in operations management.' *Production and Operations Management* 17.3 (2008): 373–384.

Haberler, Gottfried von. *Prosperity and depression*. 3rd edn. New York: United Nations, 1946 (originally published 1937).

Halsey, Ashley. 'Global airline profits expected to drop below 1% next year, industry official says.' 2011. Last updated: 10 Nov 2011. *The Washington Post*. Accessed 18 Feb 2014: www.washingtonpost.com/local/commuting/global-airline-profits-likely-to-drop-below-1percent-next-year-industry-official-says/2011/11/10/gIQ Abwsh8M_story.html.

Harlow, Arthur A. 'The hog cycle and the cobweb theorem.' *Journal of Farm Economics* 42.4 (1960): 842–853.

Harvey, Geraint. *Management in the airline industry*. London: Routledge, 2007.

Hines, James H. and Dewey W. Johnson. 'Launching System Dynamics.' Proceedings of the 12th International Conference of the System Dynamics Society. Stirling, Scotland. 1994.

Holloway, Stephen. *Straight and level: Practical airline economics*. 3rd edn. Farnham, UK: Ashgate, 2008.

IdeaWorks and Amadeus. 'Press release: Ancillary revenue reported by airlines grew to €18.23 billion in 2011 and jumped 66% in two years.' 23 July 2012. Accessed 8 Oct 2013: www.amadeus.com/amadeus/x224196.html.

IdeaWorks, and Amadeus. 'Press release: Airline ancillary revenue projected to reach $36.1 billion worldwide in 2012.' 29 Oct 2012. Accessed 8 Oct 2013: www.amadeus.com/amadeus/x225417.html.

International Air Transport Association (IATA). *Press Release No. 28*. 2004.

International Air Transport Association (IATA). *Cost structure – Irreconcilable differences?* 2010.

International Air Transport Association (IATA). *Fact sheet: Industry statistics, December 2010*. 2010.

International Air Transport Association (IATA). *Fact sheet: Industry statistics, March 2010*. 2010.

International Air Transport Association (IATA). *Special report: Opportunities in aircraft leasing*. 2010.

International Air Transport Association (IATA). *Vision 2050*. Singapore 2011.

International Air Transport Association (IATA). *Fact sheet: Economic and social benefits of air transport*. 2012.

International Air Transport Association (IATA). *Fact sheet: Industry statistics, September 2013*. 2013.

International Air Transport Association (IATA). *Profitability and the air transport value chain*. 2013.

International Air Transport Association (IATA). *Fact sheet: Economic and social benefits of air transport*. 2014.

International Air Transport Association (IATA). *Fact sheet: Industry statistics, December 2014*. 2014.

International Air Transport Association (IATA). 'Publications > Economics > Market & Industry Issues > Profitability.' 2014. Accessed 3 Feb 2014: www.iata.org/publications/economics/market-issues/Pages/profitability.aspx.

International Air Transport Association (IATA). *Cargo e-chartbook*. Q4 2010.

International Civil Aviation Organisation (ICAO). Air transport reporting form: Financial data – Commercial air carriers (FORM EF). 2013.

Intervistas. *Estimating air travel demand elasticities.* Prepared for IATA, 2007.

Isidore, Chris. 'US Air files Chapter 11 – again.' 2004. Last updated: 13 Sept 2004. CNN Money Online. Accessed 18 Feb 2014: http://money.cnn.com/2004/09/13/news/fortune500/usair_bankruptcy/.

Jacobs, Jan. *Econometric business cycle research.* Boston, London: Kluwer Academic, 1998.

Jayanti, Rama K. and S.V. Jayanti. 'Effects of airline bankruptcies: An event study.' *Journal of Service Marketing* 25.6 (2011): 399–409.

Jiang, Helen and R. John Hansman. 'An analysis of profit cycles in the airline industry.' Masters thesis. Massachusetts Institute of Technology, 2004.

Jiang, Helen and R. John Hansman. 'An analysis of profit cycles in the airline industry.' *6th AIAA Aviation Technology, Integration and Operations Conference (ATIO).* American Institute of Aeronautics and Astronautics, 2006.

Kahn, Alfred E. *Lessons from deregulation: Telecommunications and airlines after the crunch.* Washington, D.C.: AEI-Brookings Joint Center for Regulatory Studies: Distributed by Brookings Institution Press, 2004.

Keating, Elizabeth K. 'Everything you ever wanted to know about how to develop a System Dynamics model but were afraid to ask.' *16th International Conference of the System Dynamics Society.* Quebec City, Canada, 1998.

Keesman, Karel J. *System identification: An introduction.* Advanced Textbooks in Control and Signal Processing. London et al.: Springer, 2011.

Keynes, John Maynard. The General Theory of Employment, Interest and Money. London: Macmillan, 1936.

Kirkpatrick, Larry D., and Gregory E. Francis. *Physics: A conceptual world view.* 7th edn. Belmont, CA: Brooks/Cole, Cengage Learning, 2010.

Kydland, Finn E. and Edward C. Prescott. 'Time to build and aggregate fluctuations.' *Econometrica* 50.6 (1982): 1345–1370.

Lane, David C. 'Should System Dynamics be described as a "hard" or "deterministic" systems approach?'. *Systems Research and Behavioural Science* 17 (2000): 3–22.

Lederer, Phillip J., and Ramakrishnan S. Nambimadom. 'Airline network design.' *Operations Research* 46.6 (1998): 785–804.

Lee, Hau L., V. Padmanabhan, and Seungjin Whang. 'Information distortion in a supply chain: The bullwhip effect.' *Management Science* 50.12 (2004): 1875–1886.

Lee, Hau L., V. Padmanabhan, and Seungjin Whang. 'The bullwhip effect in supply chains.' *Sloan Management Review* 38.3 (1997): 93-102.

Liehr, Martin, Andreas Größler, Martin Klein, and Peter M. Milling. 'Cycles in the sky: Understanding and managing business cycles in the airline market.' *System Dynamics Review* 17.4 (2001): 311–332.

Ljung, Lennart. 'Perspectives on system identification.' *Annual Reviews in Control* 34.1 (2010): 1–12.

Longair, Malcolm S. Theoretical concepts in physics: An alternative view of theoretical reasoning in physics. Cambridge: Cambridge University Press, 2003.

Lucas, Jr, Robert E. 'Understanding business cycles.' *Carnegie-Rochester Conference Series on Public Policy* 5 (1977): 7–29.

Lucas, Jr, Robert E. *Models of business cycles.* Oxford: Basil Blackwell, 1987.

Lufthansa. 'Financial statements 1988–2013.' Accessed 28 Jan 2015: http://investor-relations.lufthansagroup.com/de/finanzberichte/geschaeftsbericht/2013.html.

Lyneis, James M. 'System Dynamics in business forecasting: A case study of the commercial jet aircraft industry.' *16th International Conference of the System Dynamics Society.* Québec City, Canada, 1998.

Lyneis, James M. 'System Dynamics for business strategy: A phased approach.' *System Dynamics Review* 15.1 (1999): 37–70.

Lyneis, James M. 'System Dynamics for market forecasting and structural analysis.' *System Dynamics Review* 16.1 (2000): 3–25.

Lyneis, James M. and Maurice A. Glucksman. 'Market analysis and forecasting as a strategic business tool.' *Computer-Based Management of Complex Systems*, eds Milling, Peter M. and Erich O.K. Zahn: Springer Berlin Heidelberg, 1989, pp. 136–143.

Maier, Matthew. 'A radical fix for airlines: Make flying free.' 2006. CNN Money. Accessed 10 Oct 2013: http://money.cnn.com/magazines/business2/business2_archive/2006/04/01/8372814/.

Mankiw, N. Gregory. *Principles of macroeconomics.* 6th edn. Andover, UK: Cengage Learning, 2012.

Martinez-Moyano, Ignacio J. 'Documentation for model transparency.' *System Dynamics Review* 28.2 (2012): 199–208.

Mass, Nathaniel J. *Economic cycles: An analysis of underlying causes.* Cambridge, MA: Wright-Allen Press, 1975.

Maußner, Alfred. *Konjunkturtheorie [Business cycle theory].* Berlin et al.: Springer, 1994.

Meadows, Dennis L. 'The dynamics of commodity production cycles: A dynamic cobweb theorem.' Massachusetts Institute of Technology, 1969.

Metters, Richard. 'Quantifying the bullwhip effect in supply chains.' *Journal of Operations Management* 15.2 (1997): 89–100.

Michl, Thomas. *Macroeconomic theory: A short course.* Armonk, New York: M.E. Sharpe, 2002.

Milling, Peter M. 'Der technische Fortschritt beim Produktionsprozeß: Ein dynamisches Modell für innovative Industrieunternehmen.' Wiesbaden: Gabler, 1974.

Milling, Peter M. 'Leitmotive des System-Dynamics-Ansatzes.' *Wirtschaftswissenschaftliches Studium (WiSt)* 13.10 (1984): 507–513.

Milling, Peter M. 'Systems research and corporate policy making.' In *Advances in information systems research.* Eds Lasker, George E., Tetsunori Koizumi, and Jens Pohl. Windsor, Ontario: The International Institute for Advanced Studies, 1991, pp. 44–49.

Milling, Peter M. 'Kybernetische Überlegungen beim Entscheiden in komplexen Systemen.' *Entscheiden in komplexen Systemen.* Ed. Milling, Peter M. Berlin: Duncker & Humblot, 2002, pp. 11–26.

Mitchell, Wesley C. *What happens during business cycles: A progress report.* Cambridge, MA: National Bureau of Economic Research, 1951.

Morecroft, John D.W. 'The feedback view of business policy and strategy.' *System Dynamics Review* 1.1 (1985): 4–19.

Morecroft, John D.W. 'System Dynamics and microworlds for policymakers.' *European Journal of Operational Research* 35 (1988): 301–320.

Morrell, Peter S. *Airline finance.* 3rd edn. Aldershot, UK; Burlington, VT: Ashgate, 2007.

Morrell, Peter S. 'Current challenges in a "distressed" industry.' *Journal of Air Transport Management* 17.1 (2011): 14–18.

Nash, Jr, John F., 'The bargaining problem.' *Econometrica* 18.2 (1950): 155–162.

Nash, Jr, John F., 'Two-person cooperative games.' *Econometrica* 21.1 (1953): 128–140.

Neidl, Raymond E. 'Can the aviation industry shield itself from business cycles?' *Handbook of airline finance.* Eds Butler, Gail F. and Martin R. Keller. 1st edn. New York: Aviation Week, 1999, pp. 13–23.

Neidl, Raymond E. 'Current financial and operational trends in the airline industry.' In *Handbook of airline finance*. Eds Butler, Gail F. and Martin R. Keller. 1st edn. New York: Aviation Week, 1999, pp. 611–625.

O'Connell, John F. 'Ancillary revenues: The new trend in strategic airline marketing.' *Air transport in the 21st century: Key strategic developments*. Eds O'Connell, John F. and George Williams. Farnham, UK; Burlington, VT: Ashgate, 2011, pp. 145–170.

O'Connell, John F., and George Williams. *Air transport in the 21st century: Key strategic developments*. Farnham, UK; Burlington, VT: Ashgate, 2011.

O'Connor, William E. *An introduction to airline economics*. 6th edn. Westport, CT: Praeger, 2001.

Oum, Tae Hoon, Anming Zhang, and Yimin Zhang. 'Optimal demand for operating lease of aircraft.' *Transportation Research Part B: Methodological* 34.1 (2000): 17–29.

Oxford Dictionaries. 'Definition of "commodity".' Accessed 31 July, 2013: http://oxforddictionaries.com/definition/english/commodity?q=commodity.

Oxford Economics in partnership with Amadeus. The travel gold rush 2020: Pioneering growth and profitability trends in the travel sector. November 2010.

Pearce, Brian. 'The state of air transport markets and the airline industry after the great recession.' *Journal of Air Transport Management* 21 (2012): 3–9.

Pearson, David. 'Air France-KLM Net Loss Widens.' 2013. Last updated: 22 Feb 2013. *The Wall Street Journal* Online. Accessed 18 Feb 2014: http://online.wsj.com/news/articles/SB10001424127887323549204578319440882179944.

Pels, Eric. 'Airline network competition: Full-service airlines, low-cost airlines and long-haul markets.' *Research in Transportation Economics* 24.1 (2008): 68–74.

Perelman, Lewis J. 'Time in System Dynamics.' *TIMS Studies in the Management Science* 14 (1980): 75–89.

Petersen, Bruce, and Steven Strongin. 'Why are some industries more cyclical than others?' *Journal of Business and Economic Statistics* 14.2 (1996): 189–198.

Peterson, Joel. 'American + U.S. Airways: A match made in heaven?.' 2013. Last updated: 5 Mar 2013. Forbes Online. Accessed 18 Feb 2014: www.forbes.com/sites/joelpeterson/2013/03/05/american-u-s-airways-a-match-made-in-heaven/.

Piepenbrock, Theodore F. 'Toward a theory of evolution of business ecosystems: Enterprise architectures, competitive dynamics, firm performance and industrial co-evolution.' Massachusetts Institute of Technology, 2009.

Pierson, Kawika. 'Modeling the cyclic nature of aggregate airline industry profits.' *27th International Conference of the System Dynamics Society*, 2009.

Pierson, Kawika. 'Profit cycle dynamics.' PhD thesis. Massachusetts Institute of Technology, 2011.

Pierson, Kawika and John D. Sterman. 'Cyclical dynamics of airline industry earnings.' *System Dynamics Review* 29.3 (2013): 129–156.

Pilarski, Adam M. *Why can't we make money in aviation?* Aldershot, UK; Burlington, VT: Ashgate, 2007.

Pindyck, Robert S., and Daniel L. Rubinfeld. *Microeconomics*. Prentice-Hall series in economics. 5th edn. Upper Saddle River, NJ: Prentice Hall, 2001.

Pirrong, Stephen Craig. 'An application of core theory to the analysis of ocean shipping markets.' *Journal of Law and Economics* 35.1 (1992): 89–131.

Porter, Michael E. 'Five forces in the airline industry.' *Vision 2050*. Ed. International Air Transport Association (IATA): Report, 2011. 22–42.

Powell, Michael J.D. 'An efficient method for finding the minimum of a function of several variables without calculating derivatives.' *Computer Journal* 7.2 (1964): 155–162.

Reed, Ted. 'Airlines, not yet where they want to be, make 21 cents per passenger.' 2013 Last updated: 25 Feb 2013. Forbes.com. Accessed 18 Feb 2014: www.forbes.com/sites/tedreed/2013/02/25/airlines-not-yet-where-they-want-to-be-make-21-cents-per-passenger/.

Reuters. 'American Airlines issues layoff notices, cuts flight schedule.' 2012. Last updated: 18 Sept 2012. Accessed 15 Nov 2013: www.reuters.com/article/2012/09/19/us-amr-flights-idUSBRE88H1CQ20120919.

Richardson, George P. 'System Dynamics.' In *Encyclopedia of operations research and management science*. Eds Gass, Saul and Carl Harris. Kluwer Academic Publishers, System Dynamics Society, www.systemdynamics.org/what-is-s/, accessed: 30 Jan 2014, 1999/2011.

Richardson, George P. and Alexander L. Pugh. *Introduction to System Dynamics modeling with DYNAMO*. MIT Press/Wright-Allen series in System Dynamics. Cambridge, MA: MIT Press, 1981.

Rose, Nancy L. 'After airline deregulation and Alfred E. Kahn.' 102.3 (2012): 376–380.

Sabena. 'A historic airline is gone.' 2013. Accessed 15 Nov 2013: www.sabena.com/EN/Historique_FR.htm.

Schumpeter, Joseph A. 'The explanation of the business cycle.' *Economica* 21 (1927): 286–311.

Schumpeter, Joseph A. The theory of economic development: An inquiry into profits, capital, credit, interest and the business cycle. Cambridge, MA: Harvard University Press, 1934 (German original 1911).

Schumpeter, Joseph A. 'The analysis of economic change.' *The Review of Economics and Statistics* 17.4 (1935): 2-10.

Schumpeter, Joseph A. Business cycles: A theoretical, historical and statistical analysis of the capitalist process. New York: McGraw-Hill, 1939.

Schwaninger, Markus and Stefan Grösser. 'System dynamics as model-based theory building.' *Systems Research and Behavioral Science* 25.4 (2008): 447–465.

Segers, Rafael. 'An analysis of external and internal drivers of profit cycles in the airline industry – An industry dynamics approach.' Masters thesis. Cranfield University, 2005.

Senge, Peter M. The fifth discipline: The art and practice of the learning organization. 1st edn. New York: Doubleday/Currency, 1990.

Senge, Peter M. *The fifth discipline: The art and practice of the learning organization*. Rev. and updated. edn. New York: Doubleday/Currency, 2006.

Sgouridis, Sgouris P. 'Symbiotic strategies in enterprise ecology: Modeling commercial aviation as an Enterprise of Enterprises.' PhD thesis. Massachusetts Institute of Technology, 2007.

Sgouridis, Sgouris, Joseph Sussman, Henry Weil, and Kirkor Bozdogan. *Taming the business cycle in commercial aviation – Trade-space analysis of strategic alternatives using simulation modelling*. Massachusetts Institute of Technology: Working Paper Series, Cambridge, MA, 2008.

Sheehan, John J. *Business and corporate aviation management*. 2nd edn. New York: McGraw-Hill Education, 2013.

Simon, Bernhard. 'Air Canada is granted bankruptcy court protection.' 02 April 2003. New York Times. Accessed 15 Nov 2013: www.nytimes.com/2003/04/02/business/air-canada-is-granted-bankruptcy-court-protection.html.

Sitkin, Sim B., Kelly E. See, C. Chet Miller, Michael W. Lawless, and Andrew M. Carton. 'The paradox of stretch goals: Organizations in pursuit of the seemingly impossible.' *Academy of Management Review* 36.3 (2011): 544–566.

Sjostrom, William. 'Antitrust immunity for shipping conferences: An empty core approach.' *The Antitrust Bulletin* 38. Summer (1993): 419–423.

Skinner, Steve, Alex Dichter, Paul Langley, and Hendrik Sabert. 'Managing growth and profitability across peaks and troughs of the airline industry cycle.' *Handbook of airline finance*. Eds Butler, Gail F. and Martin R. Keller. 1st edn. An aviation week book. New York and others: McGraw-Hill, 1999, pp. 25–39.

Skinner, Steve and Elane Stock. 'Masters of the cycle.' *Airline Business* 14.4 (1998): 54–59.

Smaros, Johanna, Juha-Matti Lehtonen, Patrik Appelqvist, and Jan Holmstrom. 'The impact of increasing demand visibility on production and inventory control efficiency.' *International Journal of Physical Distribution and Logistics Management* 33.4 (2003): 336–354.

Steckel, Joel H., Sunil Gupta, and Anirvan Banerji. 'Supply chain decision making: Will shorter cycle times and shared point-of-sale information necessarily help?' *Management Science* 50.4 (2004): 458–464.

Sterman, John D. 'Appropriate summary statistics for evaluating the historical fit of System Dynamics models.' *1st International Conference of the System Dynamics Society*. 1983.

Sterman, John D. 'A behavioral model of the economic long wave.' *Journal of Economic Behavior & Organization* 6.1 (1985): 17–53.

Sterman, John D. 'Modeling managerial behavior: Misperceptions of feedback in a dynamic decision making experiment.' *Management Science* 35.3 (1989): 321–339.

Sterman, John D. Business dynamics: Systems thinking and modeling for a complex world. Boston, MA: Irwin/McGraw-Hill, 2000.

Sterman, John D. and David C. Lane. 'Jay Wright Forrester.' *Profiles in operations research: Pioneers and innovators*. Eds Assad, Arjang A. and Saul I. Gass. International Series in Operations Research & Management Science. New York: Springer, 2011, pp. 363–386.

Strohhecker, Jürgen. 'System Dynamics als Managementinstrument [System Dynamics as a management instrument].' In *System Dynamics für die Finanzindustrie: Simulieren und Analysieren dynamisch-komplexer Probleme*. Eds Strohhecker, Jürgen and Jürgen Sehnert. Frankfurt: Frankfurt-School-Verlag, 2008, pp. 17–33.

SWISS. 'Swissair: Switzerland's former national airline ceased operations in 2002.' 2013. Accessed 15 Nov 2013: www.swissair.com/index_en.html.

System Dynamics Society. 'The SDM-Doc tool.' Accessed 15 Dec 2014: http://tools.systemdynamics.org/sdm-doc/.

System Dynamics Society. 'The beer game.' 2013. Accessed 15 Dec 2013: www.systemdynamics.org/products/the-beer-game/.

Tan, Hao and John A. Mathews. 'Cyclical industrial dynamics: The case of the global semiconductor industry.' *Technological Forecasting and Social Change* 77 (2010): 344–353.

Telser, Lester G. 'The usefulness of core theory in economics.' *The Journal of Economic Perspectives* 8.2 (1994): 151–164.

The Agence-France Presse. 'Olympic Airways changes name, strategy but keeps rings.' 2003. Last updated: 12 Dec 2003. USA Today. Accessed 15 Nov 2013: http://usatoday30.usatoday.com/travel/news/2003-12-12-oly-airways_x.htm.

The Airline Monitor. United States jet aircraft fleet – Status as of December 31, 2007 and selected earlier years. July 2008.

The Associated Press. 'American joins long list of airline bankruptcies.' 2011. Accessed 15 Nov 2013: www.boston.com/business/articles/2011/11/29/american_joins_long_list_of_airline_bankruptcies/.

Tinbergen, Jan. 'Ein Schiffbauzyklus? [A shipbuilding cycle?].' *Weltwirtschaftliches Archiv* 34 (1931): 152–164.

Tretheway, Michael W., and W.G. Waters. 'Reregulation of the airline industry: Could price cap regulation play a role?' *Journal of Air Transport Management* 4.1 (1998): 47–53.

Tucker, Irvin B. *Macroeconomics for today.* 7th edn. Australia; United Kingdom: South-Western/Cengage Learning, 2011.

US Bureau of Transportation Statistics. 'Air Carrier Financial: Schedule B-43 Inventory.' Accessed 10 Sept 2013.

US Bureau of Transportation Statistics. 'Table T1: U.S. air carrier traffic and capacity summary by service class.' Accessed 8 Aug 2011.

US Bureau of Transportation Statistics. 'No. 289 – Reporting ancillary revenues on Form 41.' 2009. Accessed 2 Oct 2013.

US Bureau of Transportation Statistics (BTS). 'Data profile: air carrier financial reports (Form 41 financial data).' Accessed 5 June 2013: www.transtats.bts.gov/DatabaseInfo.asp?DB_ID=135&Link=0.

US Bureau of Transportation Statistics (BTS). 'Schedule P-1.2 Air carrier financial.' Accessed 28 Jan 2014: www.transtats.bts.gov/TimeSeries.asp?Apply_Rate=No.

US Centennial of Flight Commission. 'Deregulation and its consequences.' Accessed 17 Nov 2014: www.centennialofflight.net/essay/Commercial_Aviation/Dereg/Tran8.htm.

US Code of Federal Regulations. '§ 121.311 (b) and § 121.317 (f).' Accessed 15 Oct 2013: www.ecfr.gov/cgi-bin/retrieveECFR?gp=&SID=c6b6faa8f6729c5d3e4d7d64097bcdf8&r=SECTION&n=14y3.0.1.1.7.11.2.9.

US Department of Transportation (US DOT), Bureau of Transportation Statistics. 'Schedule B-43 Inventory, number of seats by aircraft status (capital lease, operating lease, owned).' Accessed 10 Sept 2013: www.transtats.bts.gov/databases.asp?Mode_ID=1&Mode_Desc=Aviation&Subject_ID2=0.

UN Statistics. 'United States. GDP, at constant 2005 prices – US Dollars.' Last updated: December 2011. Accessed 27 Jan 2012: http://unstats.un.org/unsd/snaama/resQuery.asp.

UN Statistics. 'World. GDP, at constant 2005 prices – US Dollars.' Last updated: December 2012. Accessed 14 Nov 2013: http://unstats.un.org/unsd/snaama/resQuery.asp.

UN Statistics. 'World. GDP, at constant 2005 prices – US Dollars.' Last updated: December 2012. Accessed 14 Nov 2013: http://unstats.un.org/unsd/snaama/resQuery.asp.

UN Statistics. 'World. GDP, at current prices – US Dollars.' Last updated: December 2012. Accessed 14 Nov 2013: http://unstats.un.org/unsd/snaama/resQuery.asp.

UN Statistics. 'World. GDP, Implicit Price Deflators – US Dollars. Implicit Price Deflator (2005=100).' Last updated: December 2013. Accessed 21 Nov 2014: http://unstats.un.org/unsd/snaama/resQuery.asp.

UN Statistics. 'World. GDP, Implicit Price Deflators – US Dollars. Implicit Price Deflator (2005=100).' Last updated: December 2012. Accessed 14 Nov 2013: http://unstats.un.org/unsd/snaama/resQuery.asp.

Vasigh, Bijan, Ken Fleming, and Liam Mackay. *Foundations of airline finance: Methodology and practice.* Farham, Surrey; Burlington, VT: Ashgate, 2010.

Vasigh, Bijan, Reza Taleghani, and Darryl Jenkins. *Aircraft finance: Strategies for managing capital costs in a turbulent industry.* Ft. Lauderdale, FL: J. Ross Pub., 2012.

Veal, Sarah. 'How one airline cut costs and held onto profits.' 1994. Last updated: 5 Sept 1994. *New York Times*. Accessed 18 Feb 2014: www.nytimes.com/1994/09/05/news/05iht-britair.html.

Ventana Systems. 'Optimization options.' Accessed 20 May 2014: www.vensim.com/documentation/index.html?vendemo_help.htm.

Ventana Systems. *Documentation for Vensim*. 2013.

Ventana Systems. *Vensim*. System Dynamics modelling software.

Vigeant-Langlois, Laurence. 'Overview of the aircraft leasing industry.' CIT Aerospace, April 2011.

Vogt, Paul W., Dianne C. Gardner, and Lynne M. Haeffele. *When to use what research design*. New York: Guilford Press, 2012.

Weil, Henry B. 'Commoditization of technology-based products and services: A generic model of market dynamics.' *Massachusetts Institute of Technology: Sloan Working Paper* 144–196 (1996).

Werner, Frank M. 'Leverage and airline financial management.' *Handbook of airline finance*. Eds Butler, Gail F. and Martin R. Keller. 1st edn. New York: Aviation Week, 1999, pp. 187–197.

Wittmer, Andreas, Thomas Bieger, and Roland Müller. *Aviation systems management of the integrated aviation value chain*. Springer texts in business and economics. Berlin; New York: SpringerLink, 2011.

Wojahn, Oliver W. 'Why does the airline industry over-invest?' *Journal of Air Transport Management* 19 (2012): 1–8.

World Bank. 'United States. Inflation consumer prices, annual %.' Note: Inflation as measured by the consumer price index reflects the annual percentage change in the cost to the average consumer of acquiring a basket of goods and services that may be fixed or changed at specified intervals, such as yearly. The Laspeyres formula is generally used. Accessed 29 Nov 2012: http://data.worldbank.org/indicator/FP.CPI.TOTL.ZG.

Zarnowitz, Victor. *Business cycles: Theory, history, indicators, and forecasting*. NBER Studies in business cycles, Vol. 27. Chicago, London: University of Chicago Press, 1992.

Zimmermann, Nicole. *Dynamics of drivers of organizational change*. Wiesbaden: Gabler, 2011.

7 Appendix

7.1 Appendix A: cost classification

Application of Holloway's scheme to ATA Cost Index

Holloway's cost classification scheme (Holloway 2008, p. 274), which is presented in section 3.3.4, is applied to the ATA Cost Index, which is the financial data set used to calibrate the airline profit cycle model for the US airline industry (see sections 3.5.1–3.5.2).

Items of the ATA Cost Index are listed with their definitions in the following table. Its last column informs which item is attributed to which of Holloway's cost classes. Some items cannot clearly be assigned; their attribution is a compromise.

7.2 Appendix B: background information ATA Cost Index

ATA Cost Index website, accessed 24 Feb 2011:

> ATA produces the Airline Cost Index to monitor trends in the cost of inputs (e.g., labor, fuel, food, aircraft ownership, airport landing fees, insurance, utilities, interest) to the provision of air service over time. The various indices also facilitate comparisons among the components themselves and between airline costs and broader economic indicators. Long-term cost trends are important determinants of airfares. While the Airline Cost Index includes cost per available seat mile (CASM), the traditional measure of airline unit operating costs, the index values themselves are the superior bellwethers of the price of inputs to production. CASM can mask the true cost of an input because it also reflects changes in productivity over time.
>
> The vast majority of the Cost Index is derived from quarterly financial and operational information collected by DOT (principally Form 41 reports), and historical data may be restated as warranted. Neither the Cost Index nor its components are seasonally adjusted because 1) users may find seasonal fluctuations of great interest and 2) leaving the data unfettered allows users to impose adjustments of their own choosing. Consequently, quarter-to-quarter movements in certain indices may be driven in part by the seasonality of the variables used to compute them.

Table 7.1 Application of Holloway's scheme to ATA Cost Index

ATA cost item	base	explanation of cost item (as defined on ATA website)	cost category
fuel	per gallon	Cost of aviation fuel used in flight operations, excluding taxes, transportation, storage and into-plane expenses.	variable DOC
labour	per full-time equivalent employee	Wages, employee benefits (e.g. annuity payments, educational, medical, recreational and retirement programs) and payroll taxes (e.g. FICA, state and federal unemployment insurance). General management, flight personnel, maintenance labor, and aircraft and traffic handling personnel are all included in the calculation of labor costs.	fixed DOC
aircraft rents and ownership	per operating seat	The cost of aircraft rentals, depreciation and amortization of flight equipment, including airframes and parts, aircraft engine and parts, capital leases and other flight equipment.	fixed DOC
non-aircraft rents and ownership	per enplanement	Principally, the total cost of airport terminal rents. Non-aircraft rents and ownership also includes the cost of hangars, ground service/support equipment (GSE), storage and distribution equipment, and communication and meteorological equipment.	fixed IOC
professional services	per available seat mile	The cost of legal fees and expenses (e.g. attorney fees, retainer fees, witness expenses, legal forms, litigation costs), professional and technical fees and expenses (e.g. engineering and appraisal fees, consultants, market and traffic surveys, laboratory costs), as well as general services purchased outside (e.g. aircraft and general interchange service charges).	fixed IOC
food and beverage	per revenue passenger mile	The cost of purchasing beverages and food, commissary supplies and outside catering charges.	variable IOC
landing fees	per capacity ton landed	The cost of fees paid by the airlines to airports for runway and airport maintenance.	variable DOC
maintenance material	per aircraft block hour	The cost of maintaining and purchasing materials for airframes, aircraft engines, ground property and equipment (excluding labor costs). Also includes the costs of maintaining a shop and servicing supplies (e.g. automotive, electrical, plumbing, sheet metal, small tools, glass and glass products, cleaning compounds).	variable DOC
aircraft insurance	as % of hull net book value	The cost of flight equipment insurance, sometimes referred to as hull insurance.	fixed DOC

Category	Unit of measure	Description	Cost behavior	Cost type
non-aircraft insurance	per revenue passenger mile	The cost of insurance unrelated to the hull itself. This category is broken down by two categories: general insurance (i.e. buildings and contents, materials and supplies, third party liability, passenger baggage and personal property) and traffic liability insurance (i.e. passenger baggage and personal property, cargo liability and provisions for self-insurance).	fixed	IOC
passenger commissions	as % of passenger revenue	The costs paid to passenger travel agencies for services.	variable	IOC
communication	per enplanement	The total cost of equipment and intercommunication rental and installation charges, telephone and teletype equipment, telegraph and cable message charges and navigation facility charges.	variable	DOC
advertising and promotion		Includes the cost of producing tariffs, schedules, timetables and other promotional and publicity expenses (e.g. television, radio, entertainment, photography, graphics).	fixed	IOC
utilities and office supplies	per revenue passenger mile	The cost of light, heat, power and water, stationary, printing (e.g. labels, small signs, ticket stock, paper products, company manuals), shipping and mailing supplies and other office supplies as well as cleaning compounds, safety, electrical, engineering, drafting, blue prints and photographic supplies.	fixed	ICO
transport-related	per full-time equivalent employee	As defined by DOT, transport-related expenses are expenses incurred for providing air transportation facilities associated with the performance of service which emanate from and are incidental to air transportation services performed by the carrier. Following are some specific examples: • ABC Airlines issues tickets for flights operated by regional partner ABC Express. It pays ABC Express a fee to fly the code-share routes on its behalf. ABC Express reports the fee income as passenger revenue, to match the associated traffic, capacity and operating expenses. ABC Airlines reports the fare collected as transport-related revenue and reports the fee it paid to ABC Express as transport-related expense. • ABC Airlines performs maintenance for XYZ airlines. ABC Airlines reports the cost of labor, parts and materials for this in-sourced maintenance as transport-related expense. • ABC Airlines sells liquor and food on its flights. The amount that ABC Airlines paid for the liquor and food is reported as transport-related expense.	variable	DOC
	per available seat mile			
other operating expenses	per revenue ton mile	ABC Airlines operates a gift shop. The cost of running that gift shop is considered transport-related expense. Includes the cost of miscellaneous expenses such as personnel expense, outside flight equipment, excess of losses over insurance recoveries, interrupted trips expense, memberships, corporate and fiscal expenses, uncollectible accounts, clearance customs and duties.	fixed	

ATA publishes the Airline Cost Index and restates prior quarters as data becomes available from DOT. It reflects all US passenger airlines filing complete reports for the corresponding quarter. In addition to the summary below, you can view all of our Cost Index Tables (Excel, back to 1971), Charts and Methodology. [Note: We have recently retooled the dataset going back to 1977. To be included in the cost index, carriers must have met the following criteria on an annual basis: 1) must report both passenger revenue and RPMs and 2) passenger revenue must be greater than or equal to 25% of total operating revenue. Data prior to 1977 excludes airlines with annual revenues less than $100 million. Results for a given quarter are typically available within 120 days of its completion.]

Methodology to compose the *ATA Cost Index*

The following background information was downloaded from the ATA website on 24 Feb 2011:

U.S. PASSENGER AIRLINE COST INDEX: METHODOLOGY

			SOURCE: U.S. DOT FORM 41
	Components	*Schedule*	*Account*
LABOR*	Salaries + Employee Benefits + Payroll Taxes	P6	8 + 11 + 12
Average Full-Time Equivalents	Full-Time Employees + 0.5 * (Part-Time Employees)	P10	DOT Employment Report
FUEL	Aircraft Fuels	P5.2	5145.1
Gallons	Total Fuels Issued	T2	921
AIRCRAFT RENTS & OWNERSHIP*	Aircraft Rentals + Aircraft Depreciation (Airframes + Aircraft Engines + Airframe Parts + Aircraft Engine Parts + Other Flight Equipment) + Amortization Expense, Capital Leases	P5.2	5147 + 7075.1 + 7075.2 + 7075.3 + 7075.4 + 7075.5 + 7076.1
Seats	Total Daily Fixed Seat Count (Average AC Size x Average Daily Aircraft)	F41	(z320 / z410) x (z810 / days in quarter or year)
NON-AIRCRAFT RENTS & OWNERSHIP (Principally airport terminal rents)	Total Rentals + Depreciation + Amortization - Aircraft Ownership Costs (above)	P6, P5.2	(31 + 32 + 33) - Aircraft Ownership Costs
Enplanements	Revenue Passengers Enplaned	T1	Z110
PROFESSIONAL SERVICES	Professional Services	P6	28
Available Seat Miles	Available Seat Miles	T2	Z320
FOOD & BEVERAGE	Materials Purchased, Passenger Food	P6	18
Revenue Passenger Miles	Revenue Passenger Miles	T1	Z140
LANDING FEES	Landing Fees	P6	30
Capacity Tons Landed	(Available Ton Miles / Revenue Aircraft Miles Flown) * Revenue Aircraft Departures	T2	(Z280 / Z410) * Z510
MAINTENANCE MATERIAL	Materials Purchased, Maintenance Material	P6	17
Aircraft Block Hours	Aircraft Block Hours	T2	Z630
AIRCRAFT INSURANCE*	Airframe Insurance	P5.2	5155.1
Hull Net Book Value	Operating Property and Equipment, Net + Leased Operating Property under Capital Leases - Leased Operating Property under Capital Leases Amortization	B1	1675 + 1695 - 1696
NON-AIRCRAFT INSURANCE	Total Insurance - Airframe Insurance	P6, P5.2	24 - 5155.1
Revenue Passenger Miles	Revenue Passenger Miles	T2	Z140
PASSENGER COMMISSIONS	Services Purchased, Traffic Commissions	P6	26
COMMUNICATION	Services Purchased, Communication	P6	23
Enplanements	Revenue Passengers Enplaned	T1	Z110
ADVERTISING & PROMOTION	Services Purchased, Advertising and Other Promotions	P6	22
Revenue Passenger Miles	Revenue Passenger Miles	T1	Z140
UTILITIES & OFFICE SUPPLIES*	Utilities and Office Supplies	P6	19
Average Full-Time Equivalents	Full-Time Employees + 0.5 * (Part-Time Employees)	P10	DOT Employment Report
TRANSPORT RELATED EXPENSES	Expenses (transportation facilities, services, etc.) related to generation of transport related revenues	P1.2, P6	7100,35
OTHER OP. EXPENSES	Total Operating Expenses - Above Categories	P1.2	7199 - Above Categories
INTEREST*	Interest on Long-Term Debt and Capital + Other Interest Expenses	P12	8181 + 8182
Average Book Debt Outstanding	Current Maturities of Long-Term Debt + Notes Payable, Banks + Notes Payable, Others + Current Obligations Under Capital Lease + Long-Term Debt + Noncurrent Obligations Under Capital Lease	B1	2000 + 2005 + 2015 + 2080 + 2210 + 2280
Estimated Off-Balance Sheet Debt	Annualized Aircraft Rentals x 7	P5.2	5147
COMPOSITE	Weighted average of all components, including Interest		

*Cost annualized at 4 x quarterly value

Breakeven load factor: the load factor at which total operating revenues equal the sum of operating and nonoperating expenses.

Note: Carriers populating the dataset after 1977 must have met the following criteria on an annual basis: 1) must report both passenger revenue and RPMs and 2) passenger revenue must be greater than or equal to 25% of total operating revenue

Figure 7.1 Methodology to compose the ATA Cost Index

7.3 Appendix C: airline profit cycle model data and equations

The following information is given below:

1 Historic time series the model's base run simulation can be compared to (including data sources)
2 Initial values in the model and their data sources
3 Time series in the model and their data sources
4 Constants in the model and their data sources
5 Parameter values to calibrate the model in equilibrium

List of abbreviations — ACAS: A company offering aircraft data; ATA: ATA Cost Index; BTS: US Department of Transportation (DOT)'s Bureau of Transportation Statistics, estimate: discussion with experts; NBER: US National Bureau of Economic Research.

1 Historic time series the model's base run simulation can be compared to

Table 7.2 Historic time series for reference

Historic time series for reference			
module	*variable*	*units*	*source*
demand	revenue passenger miles	seat*miles/year	ATA
price	load factor	dmnl	ATA
	operating revenue real operating revenue	dollar/year	ATA, World Bank (infl.)
	price real price	dollar/(seat*mile)	ATA (yield), NBER (tax), World Bank (infl.)
	yield real yield	dollar/(seat*mile)	ATA, World Bank (infl.)
supply	available seat miles	seat*miles/year	ATA
costs	fixed unit cost per seat fixed unit cost real	dollar/(year*seat)	ATA, World Bank (infl.)
	fuel cost per ASM	dollar/(seat*mile)	ATA
	other variable cost per ASM	dollar/(seat*mile)	ATA
	sum fixed costs sum fixed costs real	dollar/year	ATA, World Bank (infl.)
	sum variable costs sum variable costs real	dollar/year	ATA, World Bank (infl.)
	total operating costs total operating costs real	dollar/year	ATA, World Bank (infl.)
	total unit cost per ASM total unit cost per ASM real	dollar/(seat*mile)	ATA, World Bank (infl.)
	variable unit cost per ASM	dollar/(seat*mile)	ATA

(continued)

Table 7.2 Continued

Historic time series for reference

module	variable	units	source
profit	operating margin	dmnl	ATA
	operating profit	dollar/year	ATA, World Bank (infl.)
	real operating profit		
	profitability to revenues	dmnl	ATA

2 Initial values calibrating the model for the US airline industry in 1985

Table 7.3 Initial values that calibrate the US airline industry model

Initials

module	variable	units	value	source
demand	–			
price	INI EXPECTED LF	dmnl	0.585	estimate, ATA
	INI PERCEIVED LF	dmnl	0.6	estimate, ATA
	INI PROFITABILITY	dmnl	0.05	estimate, ATA
	INI PROFITABILITY TREND	dmnl	0.05	estimate, ATA
	INI YIELD	dollars/ (seat*mile)	0.146	estimate, ATA
supply	INI BACKLOG	seats	35000	estimate, ATA, Boeing, Airbus
	INI EXPECTED DEMAND	seat*mile/ year	3.06E+11	estimate, ATA
	INI PERCEIVED REAL YIELD	dollars/ (seat*mile)	0.1371	estimate, ATA
	INI PERCEIVED TOTAL UNIT COST	dollars/ (seat*mile)	0.0777	estimate, ATA
	INI PRODUCTION CAPACITY	seat*mile/ year	6.16E+11	estimate, ATA
	INI TOTAL AIRCRAFT	seats	435000	estimate, ATA, BTS, Airline Monitor
cost	INI FIXED UNIT COST	dollars/ (seat*year)	54475	ATA

3 Time series calibrating the model for the US airline industry in 1985

Table 7.4 Time series that calibrate the US airline industry model

Time series

module	variable	units	source
demand	TS effect of financial crisis	dmnl	estimate
	TS terror attack effect on demand	dmnl	estimate
	TS inflation rate	dmnl	World Bank

	TS real GDP domestic	dollar/year	UN Statistics
	TS real GDP world	dollar/year	UN Statistics
	TS effect of financial crisis	dmnl	estimate
	TS terror attack effect on demand	dmnl	estimate
	TS inflation rate	dmnl	World Bank
	TS real GDP domestic	dollar/year	UN Statistics
	TS real GDP world	dollar/year	UN Statistics
price	TS real non ticket yield	dollar/ seat*mile	BTS, Amadeus, Oxford Economics, estimate
	TS tax per mile	dollar/ seat*mile	NBER, Borenstein
supply	TS leasing share	dmnl	BTS, Gritta/Lippman, estimate
	TS maximum aircraft productivity	miles/year	estimate, BTS, ATA
cost	TS other variable cost per ASM real	dollar/ seat*mile	ATA
	TS real fuel cost per ASM	dollar/ seat*mile	ATA

4 Constants calibrating the model for the US airline industry in 1985

Table 7.5 Constants that calibrate the US airline industry model

Constants				
module	variable	units	value	source
demand	DEMAND ADJUSTMENT DELAY	year	0.25	estimate
	INTERNATIONAL TRAFFIC SHARE	dmnl	0.25	BTS
	MAXIMUM AVG LOAD FACTOR	dmnl	1	estimate
	REFERENCE DEMAND ELASTICITY	dmnl	−1	Intervistas
	REFERENCE GDP DOMESTIC	dollars/ year	6.53E+12	UN Statistics
	REFERENCE GDP WORLD	dollars/ year	2.44E+13	UN Statistics
	REFERENCE INDUSTRY DEMAND	seat*miles/ year	3.06E+11	ATA
	REFERENCE PRICE	dollars/ (seat*mile)	0.1489761	ATA (yield), NBER (tax)
	REPORTING PERIOD	year	1	World Bank
	WEIGHT OF INCOME EFFECT	dmnl	0.73	estimate
	DEMAND ADJUSTMENT DELAY	year	0.25	estimate

(continued)

Table 7.5 Continued

	Constants			
module	*variable*	*units*	*value*	*source*
	INTERNATIONAL TRAFFIC SHARE	dmnl	0.25	BTS
	MAXIMUM AVG LOAD FACTOR	dmnl	1	estimate
	REFERENCE DEMAND ELASTICITY	dmnl	−1	Intervistas
price	SENSITIVITY OF PRICE TO COSTS	dmnl	0.2	estimate
	SENSITIVITY OF PRICE TO DEMAND SUPPLY BALANCE	dmnl	0.2	estimate
	SENSITIVITY OF PRICE TO PROFIT PRESSURE	dmnl	0.4	estimate
	SENSITIVITY OF YIELD TO REVENUE MANAGEMENT	dmnl	3.2	estimate
	STRETCH GOAL	dmnl	0.01	estimate
	TIME TO ADJUST EXPECTED YIELD	year	1	estimate
	TIME TO ADJUST LOAD FACTOR EXPECTATION	year	3	estimate
	TIME TO ADJUST VARIABLE COST EXPECTATION	year	2	estimate
	TIME TO PERCEIVE LOAD FACTOR CHANGE	year	0.125	estimate
	TIME TO PERCEIVE PROFITABILITY	year	0.25	estimate
	TIME TO PERCEIVE PROFITABILITY TREND	year	1	estimate
supply	AVERAGE LEASE PERIOD	year	5	Morrell
	AVERAGE LIFE OF CAPACITY	year	25	estimate, ACAS
	CAPACITY ACQUISITION DELAY	year	2	Boeing, Airbus, estimate
	CAPACITY ADJUSTMENT TIME	year	1	estimate
	CAPACITY ADJUSTMENT TIME LEASING	year	1	estimate
	LEASE ACQUISITION DELAY	year	1	estimate
	NORMAL UTILISATION	dmnl	0.83	estimate
	TIME TO ADJUST COST EXPECTATION	year	2	estimate

	TIME TO ADJUST DEMAND AND SUPPLY EXPECTATION	year	2	estimate
(supply)	TIME TO ADJUST YIELD EXPECTATION	year	2	estimate
	TIME TO PERCEIVE UNIT COST CHANGE	year	0.5	estimate
	TIME TO PERCEIVE YIELD CHANGE	year	0.25	estimate
	UTILISATION ADJUSTMENT TIME	year	0.125	estimate
	WEIGHT ON SUPPLY LINE LEASING	dmnl	0.5	estimate
	WEIGHT ON THE SUPPLY LINE	dmnl	0.5	estimate
cost	FIXED UNIT COST ADJUSTMENT TIME	year	1	estimate
	MINIMUM FIXED UNIT COST REAL	dollars/ (seat*year)	40000	estimate
	TIME TO ADJUST PROFITABILITY EXPECTATION	year	2	estimate
system	FINAL TIME	year	25	= Jan 2010
	INITIAL TIME	year	0	= Jan 1985
	TIME STEP	year	0.015625	later: 0.0078125

5 Equilibrium model calibration

The model is calibrated for the US airline industry and initialised for 1985 (see section 3.5). In simulation experiments an equilibrium calibration is used. It deviates from the US airline industry calibration as follows: external time series are set constant at their 1985 values and initials listed in the table below are modified.

Table 7.6 Initial values that place the model in equilibrium

Parameter alterations for equilibrium initialisation

variable	units	base run value	equilibrium value
INI BACKLOG	seats	35000	10717.7
INI EXPECTED DEMAND	seat*mile/year	3.06E+11	4.6239E+11
INI EXPECTED LF	dimensionless	0.584999979	0.99
INI FIXED UNIT COST	dollars/(seat*year)	54475	40000

(continued)

Table 7.6 Continued

Parameter alterations for equilibrium initialisation

variable	units	base run value	equilibrium value
INI PERCEIVED LF	dimensionless	0.600000024	0.99
INI PERCEIVED REAL YIELD	dollars/(seat*mile)	0.137099996	0.0673
INI PERCEIVED TOTAL UNIT COST	dollars/(seat*mile)	0.077699997	0.0666
INI PRODUCTION CAPACITY	seat*miles/year	6.16E+11	5.6273E+11
INI PROFITABILITY	dimensionless	0.050000001	0
INI PROFITABILITY TREND	dimensionless	0.050000001	0
INI TOTAL AIRCRAFT	seats	435000	401951
INI YIELD	dollars/(seat*mile)	0.145999998	0.0673

Index

For Product Safety Concerns and Information please contact our EU
representative GPSR@taylorandfrancis.com
Taylor & Francis Verlag GmbH, Kaufingerstraße 24, 80331 München, Germany

www.ingramcontent.com/pod-product-compliance
Ingram Content Group UK Ltd.
Pitfield, Milton Keynes, MK11 3LW, UK
UKHW021018180425
457613UK00020B/985